How Repentance Became Biblical

How Repentance Became Biblical

Judaism, Christianity, and the Interpretation of Scripture

David A. Lambert

OXFORD

UNIVERSITY PRESS

OXFORD

UNIVERSITY PRESS

Oxford University Press is a department of the University of
Oxford. It furthers the University's objective of excellence in research,
scholarship, and education by publishing worldwide.
Oxford is a registered trademark of Oxford University Press
in the UK and in certain other countries

Published in the United States of America by Oxford University Press
198 Madison Avenue, New York, NY 10016, United States of America

Library of Congress Cataloging-in-Publication Data
Lambert, David A., 1976- author.
How repentance became biblical : Judaism, Christianity, and the interpretation of scripture /
David A. Lambert.
pages cm
Includes bibliographical references and index.
Summary: "How Repentance Became Biblical explores the rise of repentance as a concept
within early forms of Judaism and Christianity and how it has informed the interpretation of
the Hebrew Bible, or Old Testament. It develops alternative accounts for many of the ancient
phenomena identified as penitential."— Provided by publisher.
ISBN 978-0-19-021224-7 (alk. paper) — ISBN 978-0-19-021225-4 (ebook) —
ISBN 978-0-19-021226-1 (electronic resource) 1. Repentance—Biblical
teaching. 2. Bible. Old Testament—Influence. 3. Bible—Criticism, interpretation,
etc. I. Title.
BS680.R36L36 2015
234'.509--dc23
2015010845

1 3 5 7 9 8 6 4 2
Printed in the United States of America
on acid-free paper

For A., at long last.

Concepts are not waiting for us ready-made, like heavenly bodies. There is no heaven for concepts. They must be invented, fabricated, or rather created and would be nothing without their creator's signature.
—Gilles Deleuze and Félix Guattari, *What Is Philosophy?*

Great is repentance for it preceded the creation of the world.
What was repentance? It was a heavenly voice that cried out and said:
"Repent you mortals!"
—Midrash Tehillim, 90:12

CONTENTS

PREFACE

The book that follows is an attempt to demonstrate the advantages that accrue for the student of biblical literature who not only attends to "the text itself" and aspects of its historical context but also turns critically to the interpretive frameworks in which it has been placed, identifying the presuppositions that readers have brought to bear and examining their history. The advantages are twofold: study of the past becomes an avenue for understanding the present, while critical awareness of the present ensures a more carefully differentiated account of the past. It is this sensibility, the persistent analysis of ourselves as interpreters, that I also try to instill in my students. How such an approach, aspects of which are new to biblical studies, might unfold is explored in the opening chapter and developed throughout.

The book itself is a product of a series of large-scale intellectual turns. Early on, it was the sense that, beneath the surface of everyday concerns and petty aspirations, there lay the potential for a view of individual life as meaningful when seen as a narrative, a story of growth. Later, it was the conviction that such stories are often best anchored in the particularities of religious traditions and the communal affiliations they afford. Finally, it was the realization that the very notion of such narratives as universal, basic to life at all times and places, is a powerful cultural construction susceptible to critique, a process in which the study of ancient texts have a special role to play. Perhaps we may continue to live our lives according to such dominant forms of self-understanding, but we must be aware of the nature of the claims such a choice entails and what they exclude.

The current project began, then, as a history of repentance, one of the earliest, most pervasive narrative conceptions of life within Judaism, Christianity, and, later on, Islam. One could say that it was a celebration of the concept as an early grounding for personal narrative. What pressed itself upon me, however, as I surveyed the literatures of ancient Greece, Rome, Israel, early Judaism, and Christianity, was not the continuity the concept affords but its unexpected absences. The real story of interest seemed to rest with its invention as a concept in the first place, its own story of becoming, how it secured its place as a naturalized component of our lives, and what alternatives might have been and could still be articulated. These realizations and the possibilities they opened up marked me indelibly as a scholar and as a person. The resulting book goes beyond a concern for repentance. It is a broad argument about the nature of the self and how it produces itself through interpretation, specifically, how it reads itself into that foundational religious and literary text, the Bible.

Many people contributed to my formation as a scholar and, hence, to this book. I find it a fitting moment to express my gratitude. At the Collegiate School in New York, I learned about historical argument, literary interpretation, and the importance to scholarship of political and social engagement from a remarkable group of individuals: Ryland Clarke, Adam Bresnick, Ivan Hageman, and Bruce Breimer. Stephanie Russell introduced me to the study of antiquity. As an undergraduate at Harvard University, the late Isadore Twersky elicited within me a passion for the study of Torah and Maimonides. The late Stephen Jay Gould taught me about the significance of how we structure history. My debt to one mentor, Bernard Septimus, cannot be readily expressed. It is only with a modest amount of hyperbole when I say that he taught me everything I know; he certainly taught me how to read texts. Shamma Friedman, as a visiting scholar, introduced me to the critical study of the Talmud and, later on, spent many hours personally instructing me.

I was fortunate to be at Harvard University as a doctoral student at a significant moment, when Gary Anderson, James Kugel, and Jon Levenson, with their thoroughgoing interests not only in the Hebrew Bible but also its history of interpretation, were all teaching. I learned a tremendous amount and received encouragement from each one, but it was James Kugel who first tapped me on the shoulder and told me to proceed with the present project, which I produced for him in embryonic form as a dissertation, giving me the imprimatur I needed to embark on what, in terms of its content, scope, and methodology, was a new sort of study. As a visiting scholar, Baruch Schwartz aided me decisively in comprehending ancient Israelite prophecy. Helmut Koester and the late François Bovon took time to instruct me personally in New Testament studies and graciously included me in the circle of scholars involved in the study of early Christianity at the Divinity School. Other scholars there had a formative influence on me and have continued to be supportive in a variety of ways: Shaye Cohen, Michael Coogan, John Huehnergard, Peter Machinist, Lawrence Stager, and Michael Stone (as a visiting professor).

I was able to embark on this ambitious book project with the support of the Jacob and Hilda Blaustein Fellowship and the scholars at Yale University who made my postdoctorate years there so productive: John Collins, Stephen Fraade, William Hallo, Christine Hayes, Ivan Marcus, Dale Martin, and Robert Wilson. Ultimately, it has been in the Department of Religious Studies at the University of North Carolina at Chapel Hill where I have found my intellectual home. I cannot list all the members of the department, past and present, who have contributed to making it such a wonderful place to work. All I can say is that it is with great satisfaction and, in retrospect, little surprise that it was here that I have been able ultimately to bring forth what has been a complex but highly inspiring project. A number of additional scholars, aside from those mentioned above, many of whom deeply engaged my work, have read portions of the manuscript and offered comments: John Barton, Marc Brettler, Andrew Bush, Shalom Holtz, Naphtali Meshel, Françoise Mirguet, Hindy Najman, Carol Newsom, Kevin Uhalde, and Jacqueline Vayntrub. I am grateful. The editor, Steve Wiggins, and anonymous reviewers from Oxford University Press were very helpful. I would also like to acknowledge two students who were able to absorb the main points of this work and further them in their own work: Matt Lynch and Adam Strich. Travis Proctor and Luke Drake provided me with great assistance in the preparation of the manuscript. Several of my early explorations of the topic appeared as: "Fasting as a Penitential Rite: A Biblical Phenomenon?" *Harvard Theological Review* 96, no. 4 (2003): 477–512; "Did Israel Believe That Redemption Awaited Its Repentance? The Case of Jubilees 1," *Catholic Biblical Quarterly* 68, no. 4 (2006): 631–50; and "Was the Dead Sea Sect a Penitential Movement?" in *Oxford Handbook of the Dead Sea Scrolls*, ed. Timothy H. Lim and John J. Collins (Oxford: Oxford University Press, 2010), 501–13. I appreciate their permission to reincorporate some of this material in the chapters that follow.

Finally, I would like to thank my loving family. There is no doubt in my mind that it was, above all, my father and mother, may her memory be for a blessing, who instilled in me the critical-mindedness and passion that propelled this project forward. My children, Isaac, Kobi, and Robin, are a constant source of satisfaction and delight. It is to my wife and partner, Avital, that I ultimately dedicate this volume. Her incessant love and perspicacity of mind run throughout these pages. More than any other, she pushed me to push my thinking on the subject as far as it has gone. I bring forth this book as a gift to her.

Chapel Hill, North Carolina
September 2015

Introduction

The Penitential Lens

AFTER REPENTANCE

"Repentance," for some, may still have resonance today, but for many twenty-first-century Americans, its very mention smacks of that "'ole time religion." They might not even be sure what, exactly, it means. Nevertheless, in recent years, a string of sports stars, politicians, and entertainment personalities, their misdeeds exposed by the media, have paraded before the public to acknowledge personal wrongdoing, express regret, ask for forgiveness, and commit to reforming their ways. Not previously known for their piety, these figures thereby participate in and model a penitential discipline usually strongly associated with the West's religious heritage.[1]

Actually, an ideal of repentance informs many contemporary secular practices.[2] We teach children to apologize when they hurt each other's feelings. In the principal's office, or even in front of the parole board, exhibiting regret and committing to or presenting evidence of improvement can reduce one's sentence. The narratives people tell about themselves often revolve around moments in which they recognize the emptiness of their current lives and make a positive change. Therapists encourage their patients to take responsibility for their actions and heal broken relationships through apology and forgiveness. Nations, too, that have committed atrocities are expected to express contrition to their victims and make amends.[3]

These practices strike us as both necessary and obvious, as natural. With sustained reflection, however, some problems do arise.[4] Are we comfortable with the media's intrusion into the private, indeed, inner lives of public figures, the spectacle of the apology? How can we ensure that apologies are "sincere"? Can we even speak of sincerity if the practice of apology ensues from threats of social opprobrium? Does repentance "work"? Does it effectively prevent relapse or make a difference to the offended party? Some might argue that feelings of guilt are not healthy. For these reasons and others, penitential discourse has been subject to some equivocation and has not always been explicitly taken up in our society.[5] Nevertheless, in many cases it continues to govern how we deal with wrongdoing. Indeed, if anything, repentance ends up being empowered by its absence from our common language and the lack of consciousness with which it is silently incorporated in our daily lives.

PROBLEMATIZATIONS OF REPENTANCE

The study that follows addresses three series of questions pertinent to the place of repentance in society today:

1. How does "repentance" shape the way we see ourselves and what we do? What behaviors do we associate with it, and what ontology of ourselves lies behind their deployment in its name? In other words, what sort of *interpretation* of our being—our nature, abilities, and purpose—and the practices in which we engage does a discourse of repentance presuppose and impose?
2. Are alternatives possible? In a restricted sense, are there other practices that can function in like circumstances and take the place of repentance? More broadly, are there competing frameworks available for the range of phenomena generally subsumed within it? Finally, are there alternative forms of self-understanding that do not allow for or even recognize such discourse?
3. How is it that repentance has come to be seen as natural and inevitable, an obvious aspect of human nature and component of religion and the moral life? What are the mechanisms by which a discourse around repentance is articulated and promoted, and what do they, in effect, impose? On a more basic level, when historically did such productions first take place, in what environment, and for what purposes?

Though these problematizations of repentance and its associated practices address matters of concern to the present, I would like to suggest that they stand to be developed most deeply by a study of what we commonly see as an essential component of our past. I refer specifically to the composition that is frequently celebrated as repentance's source,[6] what is known today as the Hebrew Bible, or, to Christians, the Old Testament.[7] As such, this historical study consists of several mutually illuminating but methodologically distinct endeavors. Each corresponds to one of the lines of inquiry raised above: (1) an analysis of the interpretive strategies whereby readers, from ancient to modern times, have located "repentance" in the Hebrew Bible (and, in select instances, the New Testament)—how they have shaped Scripture according to their own ontology of the self; (2) a critique of this dominant view of the identified phenomena that raises alternative forms of understanding through a fresh reading of relevant texts; and (3) a genealogy of repentance as a concept, an account of its prehistory, formulation, and formative effect on early Judaism and Christianity.

HERMENEUTICS OF REPENTANCE

In line with other areas of literary criticism, biblical studies has begun to move beyond an exclusive interest in authors and texts to bring the Bible's readers within its purview.[8] Major recent developments in the study of the Hebrew Bible—inner-biblical exegesis, analysis of the biblical text in its canonical form, and the striking expansion of the field to include postbiblical, late Second Temple Judaism[9]—all constitute attempts to address this collection of ancient texts' ongoing life as Scripture, rather than just the origins of its component parts. This broadened interest has received especially clear expression in studies of those early interpreters (from before or around the turn of the Common Era) who generated a multitude of traditions that governed for centuries how the Bible was read.[10] Such studies have underscored the basic indeterminacy of the biblical text, while denying its readers the presumptive ability to interpret freely, demonstrating that prior to the individual's interpretive judgment there lies the determinative, given reality of interpretive traditions. Readers define Scripture, as a continually redefined Scripture does its readers.

One aim of the present work is to develop further our understanding of the composition and its readers by examining what overall interpretive tendencies lie behind their renderings. Specifically, the present study identifies, among ancients and moderns, a practice of reading "repentance" into the Bible, which I propose to label the "penitential lens." Studying the history of tendentiousness historicizes the reader by foregrounding the culturally bound perspectives that inform interpretation. But it also redefines our understanding of Scripture and its effective temporal range; for, if readers produce what we know of the Bible, then the phenomenon known as "Scripture," for all intents and purposes, contains forms of thought and experience from a full array of historical periods. In a post-Enlightenment age, readers less frequently base their interpretive decisions upon specific, ancient *traditions*, but extensive evidence for the continuity of certain interpretive *tendencies* remains. To perceive the Bible, for all intents and purposes, *as it is*, biblical studies must turn what is generally dismissed as bias, that is, the prejudgments of readers, into its own legitimate object of inquiry.[11]

Interpretive tendencies survive because readers share elements of a common cultural background but also, more specifically, certain strategies, protocols for generating meaning.[12] These strategies appear natural to the communities who use them. They simply seem to be a component of what it means to read, though in fact they too are contingent—the product of historically bound assumptions. This book examines a group of highly successful strategies responsible for locating repentance in biblical texts that together constitute the "penitential lens." This lens affects a surprisingly broad community: not only most of us who have read or now read the Bible but also those who have never read the Bible and those readers of other "texts"—that is, everyday life situations. In short, they are part of how we today understand. How we make sense of the world around us, or the text in front of us, can shed light on aspects of our being that an analysis of consciously defined belief or purposeful constructions of identity cannot. The final aim of studying tendentiousness is to come to know ourselves in this intimate way. In this account, the Bible makes its contribution to humanistic inquiry as the West's most definitive interpretive object,[13] a chaotic mass, whose current form stands to reveal much about those who, by taking it in their hands, have given it shape.

Where is repentance understood, then, to be at play in the Hebrew Bible? At first glance, it is most conspicuous by its absence. Sacrifice would seem to be the main form of expiation. The prophets speak mostly of Israel's doom. Biblical Hebrew has no actual word, "repentance," and biblical texts few examples of anything quite like it. Why do Adam and Eve not repent to avoid expulsion from the Garden of Eden? Or why does Noah not warn his generation of the coming Flood? Feeling this lack, ancient biblical interpreters introduced repentance into their renderings of these narratives and many others.[14] Scholars today regard as "penitents" those in the Bible who engage in "penitential rites": fasting, prayer, or confession. The prophetic refrain that Israel must "return" to their God is commonly taken to be the very origins of repentance, and most view the prophets as having concerned themselves with Israel's reformation, in other words, as preaching repentance. Finally, the nation's redemptive expectations are thought to revolve around some notion of repentance. Indeed, as we shall see, historians portray repentance as a defining concern of postexilic Judaism, in particular, the apocalyptic-minded Dead Sea sect and the early Jesus movement.[15]

It is not hard to recognize why these biblical phenomena, and not others, would be identified by modern interpreters as penitential. From late antiquity to the present, analogous practices have been the channels with which a rich discourse of "repentance" has been sustained. By singling out and designating fasting, prayer, and confession as *rites*, penitential discipline and its institutions[16] created a performative space in which individuals could experience "repentance," and "repentance" achieve public demonstration. The development of penitential terminology, that is to say, the articulation of "repentance" as a concept or reified process—an actual existent and component of a lexicon of psychological events—provided *language* around which individuals could shape their experiences, communities their expectations, and theologians their treatises. Preaching and the practice of reading Scripture itself served as modes of moral instruction, *pedagogy*, that ensured the constant reiteration of a demand for repentance and assertion of its efficacy. Finally, redemptive expectations interlaced with concerns for repentance came to define the objective that religious movements were thought to pursue, what, in a sense, *religion* is: redemption through the conversion of those outside or the ongoing conversion of those inside the group. "Rites," "language," "pedagogy," and "religion" will serve as this book's main divisions, for these have been the frames within which most readers have comprehended and utilized the biblical phenomena we will be examining.

Any discourse that depends upon a literary canon for its authorization also must have a detailed and compelling hermeneutic component, hence the interpretive strategies of which we have spoken. In the case of repentance, the main ones, which we will encounter in various forms throughout the book, are the following:

(1) *Expressivity*: a certain physical act or representation of a material state is said to be merely an outward expression of an inner act or mental state that is, otherwise, off the text's plane of representation.[17]

(2) *Intentionality*: a particular aspect of a given context is used to discern the supposed intention or attitude of a subject that is otherwise not represented, and thus comes to define the nature and purpose of the act or speech in which the subject engages.

(3) *Teleology*: a certain act or state represented in the text is deemed to be significant only insofar as it purportedly constitutes the result or cause of a more privileged act or state that is not represented in the text but whose existence it is said to imply.

(4) *Nominalization*: a certain act or phrase in the text is thought to correspond to a known practice or psychological state, a hypostatization of its performative or semantic sense.[18]

These interpretive strategies, it will be recognized, are based on certain implicit ontological principles: *human subjectivity*, that we, as conscious beings, are the main matter of cosmic concern; *interiority*, that we have "outsides" and "insides" with our essence located in the latter; *virtue*, that moral and/or religious status is the fundamental measure of human value; *didacticism*, that much of our traffic with one another aims at improving each other; and *autonomy*, that we, to some measure, choose how to constitute our lives and can transform them. The strategies of "expressivity," "intentionality," and "nominalization" entail viewing material realities as, really, manifestations of interior acts and states. They point to something beyond or within that is primary. "Teleology" shapes complex and disparate phenomena into purposeful and principled intent, all tending toward the promotion of our moral and religious condition. Together, these strategies, all psychological forms of understanding,[19] place the human subject at the center. Observing their workings, as we will do in the coming chapters, gives us direct insight into some of the ways in which the modern self reads and asserts itself. One might speak of a certain evangelism of interiority, not unrelated, as we shall see, to the politics of repentance, that defines our hermeneutics.[20] We will have the opportunity to witness ourselves reading a variety of texts and, in so doing, gain insight into the interpretive forms cultural hegemony assumes, what happens when the collected works of a small, ancient Near Eastern people enter the study halls of the West.

CRITIQUE OF REPENTANCE

The Bible is generally engaged out of a sense of its immediacy, its significance for understanding our origins or for application to our present lives. But, this very closeness actually makes it an excellent place from which to, as one theorist of canon put it, "turn critically on immediate interests and enter the dialectical process of differing from ourselves."[21] Reassessing accepted readings can help "achieve new possibilities for representing and directing our actions."[22] In short, we might turn to the Bible out of an interest in its otherness and potential contribution to critique. Approaching the biblical canon contrastively holds out the promise not just of appreciating cultural difference, to "take the giant step away from the uniformitarian view of human nature,"[23] through, in this case, understanding how an ancient society differs from our own, but also of entering into dialogue with our own marginalized past—alternative biblical readings that our ontological principles and corresponding interpretive stances, hitherto, have disallowed.

The indifference facing historical criticism of the Hebrew Bible in certain circles today could be symptomatic of a certain failure to engage in its own critique, to consider all areas of presumption at work in the task of understanding.[24] Questions regarding its exclusivity, positivism, and value of its fragmentary reconstructions have become prominent, just as its conclusions have been challenged, enveloped in seemingly endless debate, and its main topics of inquiry purportedly exhausted.[25] This book aims at another area of continued presumption: the uncritical use of a common theological vocabulary to translate other cultures. Specifically, it questions whether the language of "repentance" proves useful in describing certain ancient Israelite phenomena and proposes redescriptions. The continued hegemony of Western religious terminology within biblical studies, such as the use of terms like "repentance," may help explain why its advances have occurred primarily outside of those areas for which the field's textual remains actually provide the richest database, namely, religion and culture. Adopting a maximalist sense of the possibilities for cultural-linguistic differentiation[26] would help refresh historical-critical study by allowing it to address anew matters currently dominated by "immediate interests."

How are alternatives to be produced? The program of critique pursued as the second form of inquiry in this book has three main bases:

(1) The work of discerning difference must unfold within the range of possibilities available in the interpreter's *present*. This allows for greater clarity around the nature of the alternatives at which we arrive. Such alternatives are not actual retrievals of an ancient past, but new encounters with its material remains, cracks in present presumption left by shifting forms of contemporary culture.

(2) *Language*, in a number of different registers of meaning, is the difference to be articulated. Concrete, material readings drawn from the actual material *language*—words and phrases—used to depict phenomena are considered before more mediated, psychological ones.[27] The ethnographic concern to give voice to others' conceptions, their distinct *language*, forms the primary occupation of interpretation, which, therefore, eschews immediate judgment to enter into the world of ancient Israel.[28] Engaging a wide array of texts within the Hebrew Bible and, as needed and available, from other ancient Near Eastern literatures, allows us to test how given phenomena relate to others—with what they are associated and to what opposed—and to discern, to the extent possible, the structural logic or *language* of the shared cultural worlds to which they belong. Finally, critical terminology is not applied a priori to the material as method, but developed along the way for rendering ancient phenomena in the *language* of contemporary discourse.

(3) To differ requires *comparison*. Alternatives are developed through juxtaposition, as the perceptible gap between dominant renderings and what now appears before us. The aim is not to address individual agendas, that is, each text's difference, but to use large-scale comparisons to perceive broad, previously unobserved divergences with contemporary practices.[29]

As a rubric applied to the Hebrew Bible, "repentance" brings together a collection of practices—fasting, prayer, confession, the language of *shuv* ("return"), and prophecy with its oracles of doom and redemption—whose grouping and definition, though anachronistic, are not arbitrary. In one way or another, they all articulate diminution, a real or threatened reduction of being, at a time prior to what has been called the "interiorization of abjection."[30] Individual chapters on each will explore the identified phenomenon in its ancient contexts. Together, they offer a reappraisal of major facets of what we know of Israelite religion and, in so doing, arrive at a number of recurring sites of difference around the themes of pain, power, and the ontology of the self. These themes run throughout the book and form its overarching concerns. It is in addressing such issues, basic to our understanding of ourselves, that we encounter the texts that comprise the Bible as a resource for articulating significantly different notions of the human, notions not truly compatible with our idea of repentance. Also receiving treatment will be questions of agency, the nature of speech, and the uses of culpability. What emerges are what we might label as more "materialist" forms of articulating the world that push beyond the dualism of body and spirit with which the Bible has been approached for much of its interpretive life.

THE GENEALOGY OF REPENTANCE

Historical studies of concepts, especially those that treat early Judaism and Christianity, face a number of inherent challenges: (1) Such studies may presume, indeed, they seem to imply, that the concept being studied has some essential unity, elements of a continuous identity through time, whether as a transcendent ideal, subjective-experiential reality, or inherent component of tradition. (2) They can treat the concept, our mental idea of something, in isolation as the definitive unit of meaning and, thereby, neglect its performative dimensions, along with the overall social, political, and ideological formations in which it participates. (3) They often focus, whether out of necessity or conviction, on finding what is unique in a single thinker, literary work, historical period, or movement's conception of a concept, thereby reifying their framework of study and falsely imagining its incommensurability, missing its continuities with other fields and inaccurately presuming discontinuities.[31] (4) Such studies too readily serve unacknowledged supersessionist or reactionary agendas, shaping history into tales of progress, the present's abrogation of the past, or devolution, an attempted escape from the present through idealization of the past.

How are we, then, to approach a history of "repentance?" Recently, within biblical studies, a number of scholars have managed to overcome some of these difficulties by surveying a broadly comparative and diachronic range of texts, mapping out alterations in their language and context as they go. They have written histories of concepts, such as "impurity" and "sin," that consider materials well beyond just the biblical period.[32] Focusing on the *longue durée* places changing conceptual topography in greater relief and allows lines of continuity and discontinuity between various fields of study to be redrawn on more immanent grounds. The current study draws from this approach in tracing anew when and where repentance is to be located.

This book also forwards a form of historical analysis that directs attention to questions of concepts' genealogy, their *becoming*. Specifically, it maintains that repentance did not always exist as such but arose in a particular time and place, for particular reasons, and it asks by what mechanisms and to what effect it took on the appearance of that which is natural, obvious, and necessary.[33] Even if aspects of the feelings associated with what we call "repentance" are, in some sense, universal, or what we might call "biological," not all societies necessarily idealize them, assign them a privileged place in religious and communal practices, or even bother to discuss them much at all. It is now possible to spell out that by "repentance" in this study, I do not intend a discrete, stable entity, a specific word with a single meaning, but rather a dynamic series of historical processes that are seen to have a certain unity, to be continuous with one another, for bringing into being a shared notion of the human. Together, these processes form what might be called a "discourse," a mode of organizing thought and experience that is rooted in the development of linguistic terms—a new penitential terminology—but that also involves performative, nonlinguistic elements as well.[34] The study concludes that discourse around repentance was a product of the Hellenistic period; it began within moral philosophy, as a technique for the progress of the sage, and was taken up around the turn of the Common Era, within emerging forms of Judaism and Christianity, as a practice of subjective control for shaping communal discipline and defining communal boundaries.[35]

Within this framework, the Bible makes its contribution to humanistic inquiry not as the source of our naturalized concepts, but as a resource for an "untimely meditation" upon them and upon the historical periodizations that support them.[36] It provides a special set of early data-points for the comparativist endeavor to develop new typologies of conceptual difference and change—in this case, by relocating repentance to the postbiblical period. Furthermore, a critical study of the Bible's use stands to reveal the mechanisms by which emerging practices of religion and the self, such as repentance, constituted themselves within early forms of Judaism and Christianity through reworkings of Scripture, imputing to Scripture the peculiar power to render natural, obvious, and necessary all that is associated with it.

Thus, as its third task, this study sets out to locate and explore repentance as a discourse with special attention to the Scriptural formations by which it was propagated. Ultimately, the aim of such a study is not to develop a full history of the concept, but to reveal the historical contingencies behind constructions that continue to inform, even today, how we "think our own nature."[37] Genealogy aspires to "free thought from what it silently thinks and so enable it to think differently,"[38] not necessarily to undermine contemporary notions but, by denaturalizing them, to allow us to mediate in a more conscious manner between present commitments, whether actual or potential. As a paradigm for the broader formation of subjectivity in the West,[39] a genealogy of repentance stands to shed considerable light on how we "think our own nature" as ethical, autonomous, introspective, and transformable beings and on its connection to the emergence of what we call "religion" as well.

BEFORE REPENTANCE

To sum up, this book sets for itself three tasks: (1) to identify dominant penitential modes of reading the Bible and understand their ontological underpin-
nings, (2) to explore the possibilities for articulating alternative readings of
so-called penitential phenomena, and (3) to examine the formations whereby
a discourse around repentance was brought into effect. Some of the contours
of the first task, the nature of the "penitential lens," have been spelled out in
this introductory chapter and will be returned to throughout. The first five
chapters dwell upon the task of generating and explicating alternatives, on
the basis of their biblical contexts, for each of the phenomena enumerated
earlier: fasting ("Fasting and the Artistry of Distress"), prayer ("The Logic
of Appeal"), confession ("Articulating Sin"), *shuv* phraseology ("A Material
'(Re)turn to YHWH'"), and prophecy ("Power and the Prophetic Utterance").
A chapter on redemptive expectations ("Agency and Redemption") will move
us from the biblical to the late Second Temple period and focus on Jewish sectarianism in that period, in which I include the early Jesus movement. Finally,
a concluding chapter ("The Genealogy of Repentance") brings us into the first
few centuries of the Common Era and addresses the emergence of repentance
as a concept alongside the rise of rabbinic Judaism and early Christianity as
religious movements.

Thus far, such scholarship that has made critical observations pertinent to
this project (some of them quite important!) has operated exclusively within
one of the three modes laid out above and with a confined set of textual data.
As a consequence, it has treated only isolated manifestations of a larger complex: the formation of a discourse out of an ancient collection of texts. What
motivates me to bring all three modes together is not only how the findings
of each provides support for the others or the interest in addressing diverse
scholarly interests, though it does do all that. Instead, the hope is that, by
accounting for the opposition between dominant readings and their alternatives, it will become possible to generate a basis for discussion that is broad
enough to comprehend, rather than merely play out, difference. A multivocal
analysis that embraces rather than contests existing understanding should
provide a more capacious space in which to further novel interpretation. It
allows us to step back from the need to locate our ideals at any given level of
the text. In that sense, this book should not just be understood as a historical claim, that there was a time *before* repentance.[40] It is first and foremost an
invitation to recognize the full force repentance exerts on our thinking and
to explore what its momentary displacement—what the experiment of setting other alternatives before *repentance*—might look like for present forms
of understanding.

PART I

Rites

CHAPTER 1

cɅɔ

Fasting and the Artistry of Distress

Surely I have seen my people's affliction.
Exodus 3:7

RITES AND THE STUDY OF FASTING

Studying fasting, prayer, and confession as "rites"—ritual practices—accords with the formal incorporation and definition they have come to receive within Western religious traditions, especially as components of a pervasive penitential discipline. It also lays the groundwork for vibrant, scholarly discussion of the nature, purpose, or symbolism, but it does so in a manner that goes a long way toward already making determinations about their meaning and, indeed, what an explanation of meaning should even constitute, determinations that, not surprisingly, end up securing their place in penitential discipline.[1] The next three chapters are framed as studies of ancient Israelite "rites" by way of recalling the control that the idea of ritual exerts over our interpretation, even as we attempt to move beyond it, toward other methods of organizing and analyzing the behaviors it now delineates.[2]

With respect to fasting in the Hebrew Bible, the central interpretive problem has been to explain how a single practice can figure in so many different contexts. Texts tell of fasting in times of mourning the dead, in times of drought, and on occasions of sin. The field of biblical studies has addressed such apparent diversity by mapping onto an ethnography of fasting, developed at the beginning of the last century, that sought to classify the various reasons for which people around the world fast. In the words of one influential account, fasting "may be an act of penitence or of propitiation; a preparatory rite before some act of sacramental eating or an initiation; a mourning ceremony; one of a series of purification rites; a means of inducing dreams and visions; a method of adding force to magical rites."[3] Among biblical texts, evidence has been found for several of these types: mourning, petition, penitence, and visionary preparation.[4]

We should pause, perhaps, to ask: What view of the human subject is bound up in this particular kind of account, which posits, on one hand, the stable identity of a ritual performance—"fasting"—throughout the world and, on the other hand, its diversity of types? It is a rendering that is also marked by a strong emphasis on liminality, the sense in which rites serve to transition the human subject toward another, more essential state. In view of the multiplicity of the act's possible meanings, it is the performer's intention that comes to define its nature. By objectifying fasting as a universal *practice*, such scholarly representations thus position the individual human as *actor*, one endowed with agency and consciousness.[5] While this classificatory scheme appears to place a limitation on the standard association of fasting with repentance, it ends up establishing an overall platform that is quite conducive to the constructions of interiority, autonomy, and transformation bound up in the idea of repentance.[6]

On an interpretive level, this reading of the rite eschews any substantive attempt to translate the communicative, material conditions of the behavior in question. It focuses, instead, on intention, on determining the nature of the act by attending to the most privileged aspect of the context in which it figures, at which the actor is presumed to take aim. Accordingly, fasting tends to be interpreted as penitential whenever and insofar as it appears in a context of sin. In such instances, in the words of one formulation, it is understood as being a way "to indicate repentance for transgressions committed."[7] Fasting, thereby, is rendered an external sign, an expression of an internal feeling whose generation and experience are the primary matters of importance.[8] Other penitential accounts suggest a view of fasting as an efficacious rite that provides satisfaction for sin by paying off, through preemptive self-deprivation, the debt that is its due.[9] And, it is, of course, especially in this latter sense, as a form of satisfaction for sin—that is, along with prayer and almsgiving, as part of the sacrament of penance—that fasting came to be so indelibly associated with repentance in the practice of the church.

An alternative starting point for interpretation would be to step back from the analysis of fasting as a specialized rite and allow it to merge with the broader behavioral manifestations with which it frequently occurs in the Hebrew Bible, the weeping, donning of sackcloth, application of ashes, and other forms of self-affliction that accompany deprivation from nourishment. Various texts reflect upon and develop aspects of the structures in which this complex of behaviors participates, but elements of a unified meaning, broadly attested in ancient Israelite and other ancient Near Eastern literatures, can be noted, at least when set against later understandings. This suggestion of commonality itself undercuts the autonomy usually attributed to both practitioners and authors in determining the meaning of fasting and favors, instead, a broad cultural account of the practice.

Instead of the accepted typology, this chapter and the ones that follow organize their discussions of texts around the different entities found therein: (1) individuals, (2) leaders (kings and/or prophets), and (3) communities. This division is not meant to suggest essential differences along these lines but, on the contrary, to exploit differences in the types of contexts in which these entities appear, to realize the full range, the pervasiveness and versatility, of shared cultural practices. This ordering should place us in a better position to appreciate variation while, at the same time, recognizing unacknowledged unities. What follows immediately is an attempt to formulate an alternative, nonpenitential, overall account of fasting, which will be followed then by a detailed exploration of the most relevant biblical passages.

FASTING AS AN ACT OF MOURNING

The image of fasting and its concomitant rites that I would like to suggest is of a dramatic physical-emotional response to disaster, a manifestation and communication of grief whereby the afflicted comes to be defined by a perceived object of dread.[10] Such practices, which fit into patterns of mourning found throughout the ancient Near East,[11] do not respond to adversity by attempting to deflect its claim over the sufferer, as Stoic exercises might aim to do, but rather by encoding that suffering upon the body:

> Then El the Kind, the Compassionate, came down from his throne, sat on his stool, came down from his stool, sat on the ground. He poured dirt on his head in mourning, dust on his skull in lamentation; he covered his loins with sackcloth. He cut his skin with a stone, made incisions with a razor; he cut his cheeks and chin, raked the length of his arms; he plowed his chest like a garden, he raked his back like a valley.[12]

In this paradigmatic example of mourning found in Ugaritic mythology, the great god El's response to the death of Baal, it is more than abundantly clear how the mourning individual manifests publicly the diminishment that has befallen him or her. At times, this decision appears particularly odd to modern sensibilities. Tamar pleads with her brother Amnon not to rape her on account of the "shame" (ḥerpa) she would bear. Yet after being raped and driven from his home, Tamar herself publicly reveals this ḥerpa by placing dust upon her head, rending her garments, and screaming loudly (2 Sam. 13:12–19). Loss is perceived along objective lines, as an actual lessening of the person, rather than merely as shame, a subjective account of how one is viewed by others. Because status and possession, not to mention health, are seen as basic to the ontology of the self, not extraneous to it, the sufferer has no choice but to reflect his or her circumscribed status. Above all, fasting and its associated practices suggest a way around the supposedly inherent problem of pain's inarticulacy.[13] It uses the body as a canvas upon which to represent that suffering, to externalize a state that, in another cultural milieu, might remain private.

When suffering is of apparent divine authorship, mourning serves as a visible manifestation of the deity's power, part of the destruction left in the wake of its exercise. Indeed grief ultimately indicates the subjection of the human will to the superior power that has overwhelmed it, evidence of an inability to retrieve what has been lost. That is why weeping or tearing a garment is deemed the pious response to prophetic oracles of doom attached to the name of Israel's god, YHWH.[14] Such performances do not indicate contrition, but show that the threatened divine punishment has registered with its victims. It marks the bodies of its victims and thereby goes part of the way toward a restitution of the deity's power, as measured by his ability to impose justice.[15]

The mourning dynamic functions whether a loss is already actualized or still only imagined. The assuredness with which future disaster may be contemplated through prophetic channels and the evocative quality of the prophets' verbal art means that a threatened fate is experienced as a fait accompli. In the Deir ʿAllā Plaster texts, found in the eastern Jordan Valley and generally dated to the eighth century B.C.E.—and which show, incidentally, that fasting was not the province of Israelites alone—we encounter fasting as an act of mourning a still-looming loss as though it were already accomplished. The prophet Balaam, known also from the Hebrew Bible, is made privy one night to the plans of the divine council. The next day, the people find him in mourning. "Why do you fast [and w]hy do you weep?" they demand. He explains his behavior by vividly conjuring the vision of destruction he has had.[16] He mourns now, for there is no significant distinction in this strongly imaginative system between actual disaster and the specter of disaster. In fact, fasting and other rites of self-affliction tend to operate in situations in which loss remains oblique, in which it effects a diminishment of the self that is real but, otherwise, would not be or is not yet evident upon the body. Thus, the timing of the disaster matters but little. That is why fasting can occur in mourning the dead, and yet also in the vicinity of petition. That the loss is still only threatened, and therefore potentially reversible, does not change the meaning of the fast. For ancient Israelites, there appears to have been only one occasion for fasting, that of loss.

Fasting exhibits a paradoxical combination of preoccupation with personal loss and theatrical visibility; it is at once solipsistic and performative. "See," the one fasting declares, "how awful is my state!" Beginning as *expressive*, any articulation of pain can quickly become *effective*, when the loss is not irreversible and the observer is empowered and disposed to give succor. Practitioners may express a consciousness of this efficacy and fast to secure its benefits. Or fasting can be presented as a spontaneous response to disaster. There is, indeed, a continuum of representation, but we are not dealing with different kinds of fasts. In the manifestation of distress, passion and function can mix and one or the other come to the fore depending upon the demands of context.

Once penitential assumptions are held at bay, it is not hard to grasp the nature of the mechanism at work. In many biblical texts, fasting appears closely related to prayer.[17] The visual manifestation of distress leads into and attends the verbal articulation of that same distress. Seeing and heeding go together,[18] and one may speak of the peculiar contribution of the visual toward eliciting divine pity.[19] Indeed, throughout the literary corpora of ancient Israel, it is the poor and afflicted whose prayers are heard.[20] As we find in the Covenant Code: "You shall not afflict any widow or orphan. If you do afflict them and they cry out to me, I will heed their outcry" (Exod. 22:21–22).[21] There is, potentially, little difference between persistent deprivation and induced affliction—between the poor, widows, and orphans and those who, subject to some oblique distress, can assume the persona of the afflicted, altering their ontological status through rites of self-diminishment.[22] For suffering only moves the deity when writ large upon the body itself, an impossible demand (without fasting) for those who occupy an otherwise respectable societal position.[23] This situation suits the anthropopathic qualities of the deity, his pathos, as frequently portrayed in the Bible:[24] human impotence and dependence are physically demonstrated just prior to the sudden and total reversal that divine intervention brings. Indeed throughout biblical literature—Job's is a dramatic example—the path to success always lies through Sheol. Unlike the modern gradualist model of progress, redemption follows from extreme states of deprivation.[25] One may also speak of the power of mourning rites to elicit empathy as a sort of irritant to the deity. Like the lament literature with which it is frequently associated, physically manifesting distress protests that distress and challenges God to remove it from his sight.[26] Through its extreme, stark[27] expression, it creates an untenable situation that demands divine response. In that sense, fasting is not desired by the deity but is rather a human prerogative, a recourse that can be taken in a time of need.

This general account, which we will now fill in and test through an examination of specific texts, leaves little room for repentance: distress is over disaster not sin; fasting is an integrated physical-emotional response to suffering, not an outward signifier of repentance; and fasting appeals directly to divine mercy, itself possessing no atoning power. Actually, fasting, as it is generally represented in the Bible, may have been closer in aim to the modern-day hunger strike than to current religious versions.[28] The refusal to eat, like the lamenter's refusal to fall silent, is in many ways the last recourse of protest for one otherwise powerless to change the course of events.

THE POWER OF THE POOR

One highly successful "hunger striker" was the biblical figure Hannah. The Hannah narrative (1 Sam. 1:1–28) furnishes our discussion with an in-depth example of the relationship between affliction, prayer, and the refusal to eat. Great anguish over her barrenness and the cumulative taunts of her rival wife leads Hannah to pray. Her state of affliction (in Hebrew, *'oni*) is fundamental to her ultimate success, and she directly alludes to it in her votive prayer: "O LORD of Hosts, if you will look upon the affliction [*'oni*] of your maidservant and will remember me..." (1:11). That Hannah is a woman is significant; it highlights her powerless, marginal position in light of her barrenness and, yet, paradoxically provides her with the nearly unstoppable power of the pathetic plea.[29] And indeed Hannah's anguish is regarded, and she is remembered by the deity, who bestows upon her not just any child but the great leader, Samuel.

The psalm of thanksgiving that she subsequently is said to recite fittingly picks up on the theme of the afflicted being exalted through the agency of God: "He raises the *poor* from the dust, lifts up the *needy* from the dunghill, setting them with nobles, granting them seats of honor" (2:8; my italics). Indeed, the book of Psalms consistently emphasizes the oppressed position of the petitioner. There, the petitioner frequently refers to himself as an *'ani*, a term related to the above for "affliction," one who is poor or, perhaps better, afflicted: "Good and faithful as you are, save me. For I am afflicted [*'ani*] and needy" (Ps. 109:22). Affliction is directly linked to prayer being heard: "Here was an afflicted man [*'ani*] who called, and the LORD listened, and delivered him from all his troubles" (Ps. 34:7).[30] Hannah's plea can be regarded as an enactment of such verses.

Hannah also "wept and would not eat" (1 Sam. 1:6). Her refusal to eat, not depicted here as a formal fast, represents a spontaneous outpouring of her grief. One cannot very well weep and eat at the same time. But it also entails a rejection of her elevated status as preferred wife—a status represented precisely by the honored portion of the sacrifice she now forgoes—and an embrace, instead, of the persona of the *'ani*, her status as an isolated, barren, taunted woman. She thereby manifests an absence or loss, the significance of which might not be otherwise noted, and is contested, in fact, by her husband. These stark choices lead to and compound the pathos of the narrative's central dramatic moment, Hannah's outpouring of her grief to YHWH (1:11). She eats as soon as her prayer is completed (1:18).

Like Hannah, David fasts on behalf of a child, the condemned fruit of his illicit union with Bathsheba (2 Sam. 12:16–23). Unlike Hannah, David is portrayed as purposely refraining from food and aware of the potential efficacy of such fasting. "I fasted and wept because I thought: 'Who knows? The LORD may have pity on me, and the child may live'" (12:22). This unusually clear programmatic statement of a religious phenomenon's function provides essential clarity to our current discussion. Against the common penitential reading of David's fast, a function of its appearance in a context of sin and its proximity to David's confession,[31] to be discussed in chapter 3, its manifest purpose is to serve as a form of entreaty. Fasting and "lying on the ground" (12:16) enable the king to assume the lowered persona that is necessary to successful appeal. The degree of intentionality behind David's act contributes to the narrative—it presents the king's religious behavior as innovative, in that he mourns before rather than after the death of his son—but it hardly changes the basic meaning of the act. In both cases, fasting is a response to anguish that highlights the afflicted state of the supplicant and has the potential to move the deity to overturn the present state of things.

THE UNSEEMLINESS OF AFFLICTION

There is one apparently minor detail in the above account that, when subjected to careful analysis, actually offers us further insight into the social dynamics of fasting: "The senior servants of his household tried to induce him to get up from the ground; but he refused, nor would he partake of food with them" (2 Sam. 12:17). In his assumption of the persona of an afflicted person, David has cut himself off from normal society, and his servants are disquieted. They attempt to persuade him to join them in their customary repast, to shed his mourner's garb and relinquish the extreme stance that he has adopted. They withhold from him word of his son's death lest he extend this position in unimaginable new ways. Later on, they even question the king's behavior (12:18). Why do they exhibit so little understanding of David's comportment?

In this regard, it may be useful to return to an odd moment in the Hannah narrative. Elkanah, Hannah's husband, challenges her: "Hannah, why are you crying and why aren't you eating? Why are you so sad? Am I not more devoted to you than ten sons?" (1 Sam. 1:8). He protests because Hannah, through her extreme expression of affliction, has effectively removed herself from participation in the feast and therefore from his society. By assuming the persona of the *'ani*, she has chosen to descend into a position of isolated grief that bestows upon her a potency with regard to the merciful God. But to those who remain in the world of joyous festivities, like Elkanah, or of everyday affairs, like David's servants, there is an unseemliness in the affliction manifested by these individuals with their private griefs. Indeed fasting with its accompanying rites produce results that are grotesque: dirty, bedraggled bodies—the abject.[32] The natural human impulse is either to withdraw from them or to force them to clean themselves up.[33] Society, to maintain its own integrity, has a stake in preventing individuals from slipping into the stark and horrid.

The unseemliness of affliction also figures in the Psalms. As in the narrative passages examined, fasting in the Psalms serves as a manifestation of affliction that flows naturally and quickly into petition: "My knees give way from fasting; my flesh is lean, has lost its fat. I am an object of scorn [ḥerpa] for them; when they see me, they shake their head. Help me, O LORD, my God; save me in accord with your faithfulness" (Ps. 109:24–26).[34] The psalmist uses the image of his fasting-induced emaciation to produce an evocative visual image of need; then he sets forth his verbal petition. Two of the three explicit references to fasting in the Psalms connect fasting to *ḥerpa*, a word that we saw applied to Tamar as well. It signifies the diminishment of the victim vis-à-vis others through misfortune and his or her own ritual enactment of loss. In these passages, those around the psalmist taunt him as a result of his fast. In addition to the passage just quoted, consider the following: "When I wept and fasted, I was reviled for it. I made sackcloth my garment; I became a byword among them" (Ps. 69:11–12). Why should the psalmist be so reviled (*la-ḥarapôt*) for fasting?[35] Extreme fasting, and its concomitant rites, have so altered the psalmist's appearance as to produce disgust in others at the sight of him.

In part, the portrayal of societal disgust sharpens the individual's fasting-induced affliction by adding an element of isolation. More fundamentally though, it provides a mirror through which the horror and starkness of the individual's assumed stance can be viewed.[36] What is wretched to humanity, and hence subject to suppression, irritates the deity as well. However, he is in a position to remove the source of irritation rather than merely mask its effect. The portrayal of a negative societal response serves as a powerful tool in the hands of both narrator and psalmist by which to emphasize the depth of affliction experienced and underscore the need for divine intervention. Use of this tool helps point to the nature of fasting and its efficacy: a manifestation of affliction that has an immediate, concrete effect on those who perceive it.

Until now, we have only considered passages that explicitly mention fasting. However, throughout the psalms and other lament literature, there is a strong emphasis on the dissolution of the mourner's body.[37] Consider the following passage: "I am poured out like water; all my bones are disjointed; my heart is like wax, melting within me; my vigor dries up like a shard; my tongue cleaves to my palate; you commit me to the dust of earth" (Ps. 22:15). Scholars believe that verses such as this would have been recited by those who were ill and seeking healing.[38] There is undoubtedly some truth to this view. However, in the poetics of lament, there is a fine line between the undesired dissolution wrought by illness and the purposeful dissolution of body wrought by fasting. Affliction is very much a *stance*, a state adopted and articulated by the supplicant. When distress did not directly impinge upon the body, fasting and its concomitant rites could be used to induce such a state.

The Fasting King

When Elijah prophesies the doom of Ahab on account of the murder of Naboth, the otherwise impious king responds with surprising alacrity: descending from the throne and rending his royal garb, Ahab lies on the ground in sackcloth and fasts (1 Kings 21). These measures seem to pacify the deity: "Have you seen how Ahab has submitted [*nikhna*] to me?" he inquires of Elijah. "Because he has submitted to me, I will not bring the disaster in his lifetime" (21:29). Most interpret the act of which God approves, submission (*nikhna*), to be a quasi-technical term for an internal penitential state intimated by Ahab's rent clothes and fasting.[39] I would like to suggest that "submission" refers to the concrete rituals of mourning themselves, that is to say, what is actually represented in the text. Why would God desire this display? It is important to recognize that the verb *nikhna* is taken from the realm of military terminology and signifies the subjugation of a defeated party to the victor: "Thus Midian submitted to the Israelites and did not raise its head again" (Judg. 8:28). By mourning in response to the divine decree, removing himself from the throne, Ahab gestures at the dreaded fate that awaits him, acknowledging the ability of his enemy to act on his threat, to impose his will freely. He accepts defeat and thereby avoids the intransigence, often designated by the biblical locution "hardness of heart," that leads to the utter destruction of other kings. In short, it is the rituals of humiliation themselves, not Ahab's emotions, that enable him to duck God's threatened blow and avoid an actual loss of his throne.[40]

In this case, submission is an end unto itself; it provides a way for the God of Israel to demonstrate his power over even the greatest of the nation, the kings of Israel. The example of kings proves particularly instructive, not only because the king's affliction offers a unusually stark display when set against his customary glory, but also because he is the specimen of humanity who exercises the greatest "radius of the will"[41] and therefore most readily crosses God. The thwarting of his will, that he cannot freely murder Naboth and take his vineyard, is accomplished through ritually enacted defeat and mourning. Along with David's descent from the throne, it offers a poignant example of the power dynamic behind fasting.

"GREAT AND SMALL ALIKE" (JON. 3:5)

Understandably, in the book of Kings, attention is focused on the kingly body as the locus of manifested distress. In the other biblical texts to be examined now, the scope of self-affliction can be seen to widen to envelop the whole body politic. Time and time again, depictions of fast days emphasize the participation of the entire community, while continuing to stress the presence of society's elite members.[42] Though scholars have tended to view the rites of the communal fast day as penitential and its purpose as resto-ration of the moral order,[43] many depictions fail to even mention anything about sin. What comes to the fore, instead, is prayer, which frequently con-stitutes the climactic culmination of the day's mourning rites.[44] Here is an example of a fast proclaimed by Jehoshaphat, king of Judah, in response to an imminent invasion: "Jehoshaphat was afraid; he decided to beseech the LORD and proclaimed a fast for all Judah .... They came from all the towns of Judah to beseech the LORD." The king prays at considerable length, and the passage concludes: "All Judah stood before the LORD with their little ones, their womenfolk, and their children" (2 Chron. 20:3–13). We can understand Jehoshaphat's comportment well enough through the model of kingly sub-mission just explored. The fast day's dual foci of leadership *and* community tell us something about the text's corporate construal of Israel, but it also underscores a few more central aspects of fasting. Fasting encodes impend-ing doom on the body of the damned. In the event of invasion, plague, or other such disaster, the whole community is condemned and must reflect this reduced status. Along with the lowering of the elite, manifesting the dis-tress of society in its totality, especially with regard to its most vulnerable members, may be expected to more readily elicit divine pity.[45] And so the assembly of *all* Judah forms the necessary backdrop to what constitutes the central drama, Jehoshaphat's appeal.

The account of a communal fast in the book of Joel is particularly illumi-nating. It begins with the dramatic proclamation of a fast day:

> Lament—like a maiden girt with sackcloth for the husband of her youth! ...
> The country is ravaged, the ground must mourn; for the new grain is ravaged,
> the new wine is dried up, the new oil has failed. ... Gird yourselves and lament,
> O priests, wail, O ministers of the altar; come, spend the night in sackcloth, O
> ministers of my God. For offering and libation are withheld from the House of
> your God. Solemnize a fast, proclaim an assembly; gather the elders—all the
> inhabitants of the land—in the House of the LORD your God, and cry out to the
> LORD. (1:8–14)[46]

Several important points emerge from this passage. The call to fast appears after the call to mourn and before the call to prayer; one flows naturally into the other.[47] This suggests a fluidity between fasting as an act of mourning and fasting as an act of petition that belies facile efforts at classification. Furthermore, one notes how the author exploits the power of visualized dis-tress to elicit pity. He sets the evocative natural image of the reduced state of the land—the environmental plight—next to the induced ritual state of its inhabitants, thus adding to the pathos that ultimately spills forth in prayer.

With this passage in view, we are also able to say something more precise about how the body fasting reflects the reality of affliction. The proclamation in Joel gathers diverse instances of suffering that together suggest an account of affliction as a state of cessation and absence: the loss of procreative potential ("like a maiden . . ."), the lack of food (grain, wine, and oil), and the interruption of the temple service. In many texts from the Hebrew Bible, these themes, ultimately the conditions of death, are juxtaposed with their opposites: fertility, abundance, and praise—the province of the living.[48] The presence of this heightened polarity generates a destabilizing tension that allows individuals or groups to flip suddenly from one extreme state to another. This process of transformation is usually seen as conditioned on divine intervention and is exemplified above by the case of Hannah. By forswearing sustenance and other acts of self-abnegation, the practitioner keys into this chain of associations; the cessation of normal bodily functions provides a way to ape the ultimate cessation that is the object of dread, as when fasting is used to help the living achieve ritual identification with the deceased. As for Joel, fasting allows those assembled to mirror the emaciated condition of the land upon their bodies and to hope for the reversal of the deathlike state into which they have entered.

When Fasting Fails

Sometimes, fasting fails. "Why, when we fasted, did you not see? When we starved our bodies, did you pay no heed?" (Isa. 58:3). We might be inclined to suggest that fasting fails when this "external" rite lacks the necessary sincerity, the proper intention, or, perhaps, because the God of Israel truly does not care for such ritualistic performance in the first place. Both explanations would see in the stated failure of fasting a displacement of its significance in favor of a more privileged inner space. What God wants is repentance, real moral transformation. Are there other structures of thought available for comprehending the occasional failure of fasting?

To elucidate the problem of inefficacy, it would be helpful to look at a little incident from the book of Jonah (1:4–16). As is well known, Jonah boards a ship for Tarshish to escape his prophetic office. YHWH brews a mighty storm at sea that menaces all aboard his vessel. The sailors pray fervently to their gods and jettison the cargo that weighs them down. When their appeals fail to calm the power of the storm, they conclude that there must be some unknown sin in their midst, the weight of which their ship cannot bear. The casting of lots identifies the cause of their distress, the Hebrew who has secreted himself in the hold of the ship. With profuse apologies, they throw their hazardous cargo overboard, and the fury of the sea abates. What the sailors know instinctively, when they make the decision to cast lots, is that their appeals have failed not because of insincerity—they could have prayed harder—nor, again, because prayer is impotent, but rather because it is infelicitous in the current circumstance. Sin renders prayer ineffective and requires instead a procedure that ensures its identification and removal.

The pattern exemplified within Jonah—a process of appeal transitioning to the removal of sin—highlights the existence of a deep structure in the thought patterns of ancient Israel that can be found to be at work in a vast number of biblical texts. For lack of better terms, I would suggest that what these texts reflect is a sense of there being two spheres of religious activity, different avenues to the deity, what we might label the "mercy" track and the "justice" track. Each has its own logic and obtains in distinct circumstances. The mercy track, which encompasses various forms of appeal and (often) sacrifice, the normal functioning of the cult, posits a god who saves because he is powerful and kind to his people, quite apart from their merits. Its activities aim at securing the deity's blessing, the continuation of life, not the disposal of sin. Since such practices do not take on sin directly, they are ineffectual in the presence of serious transgression. The justice track attempts to defuse the wrath of a deity confronted by sin. The presence of sin infuriates God, impairing his sensitivity to the communicative channels of mercy and driving him to the expedient of total annihilation. What humans can hope to accomplish is to preëmptively identify and excise the object inciting the deity and thereby avert indiscriminate suffering. This may be accomplished through the execution or banishment of an individual, the destruction or burial of idols and proscribed spoils, or the cessation of sinful activity.[49] What we see with great clarity in Jonah is the transition from one track to the other in the face of the failure of the first. This structure has not been adequately identified because of the force of the penitential lens, which would have us see elements of the mercy track as expressions of moral reformation, what belongs properly to the justice track.[50] As we shall see below, fasting fits squarely into the rubric of "mercy" and exhibits concerns distinct from those of "justice."

Defeated in battle by the men of Ai, Joshua and the elders of Israel rend their clothes, lie prostrate before God, apply dirt to their heads, and Joshua inquires of YHWH.[51] God rebuffs the plea for military succor. Sure enough, Israel has sinned: one of its number has taken proscribed plunder for himself. As in Jonah, Joshua must now pursue an alternate avenue to the deity, since the appeal for mercy has failed. He identifies the culprit by casting lots and removes both the condemned sinner and the accursed objects from Israel's midst, thus averting collective punishment (Josh. 7). What this passage makes particularly clear is that mourning and its attendant rites are not only insufficient in a situation of transgression, they are irrelevant and even undesirable: "Arise!" God commands Joshua. "Why do you lie prostrate? Israel has sinned!" (7:10–11). The posture of mourning cannot be collapsed into the removal of sin. In fact, in terms of the explanatory model we have adopted, we might speak of a certain opposition between the two.

More can be said about the actual dynamics behind mourning's rejection. Mourning by its very nature elicits either sympathy or antipathy, depending upon whether or not the interests of the sufferers are coextensive with those of their associates. Indeed, mourning for the dead itself may be seen as participation in the diminishment undergone by those deceased whose interests the mourners share. This is precisely what is at stake when Joab accuses David of "loving his enemies and hating his friends" and demands that he cease mourning the rebel, his son, Absalom (2 Sam. 19:7).[52] When interests do not align, participation in loss and mourning proves impossible, so sin poses a particular problem for divine sympathy. Israel, by transgressing, has set aside the interests of their deity, turning him into an adversary. When wrongdoing drives a wedge between parties, mourning and other rites of the mercy sphere may not only fail to compel; they can actually annoy.

It is not always recognized that the celebrated prophetic critique of the sacrificial cult extends beyond sacrifice to other forms of ritual behavior, in particular to those practices that together constitute the realm of religious activity that we have labeled the "mercy" track: "Do not pray for the benefit of this people. When they fast, I will not listen to their outcry; and when they present burnt offering and meal offering, I will not accept them" (Jer. 14:10–12). Prophetic intercession, fast-day gatherings—closely associated with communal prayer, "when they *fast*, I will not listen to their *outcry*"—and sacrifice are a part of the people's normal relationship with their god. When trouble arises, they appeal to YHWH. But sin, a severe disturbance in the sphere of justice, disrupts this relationship and creates a barrier between God and his people that prevents these theurgical acts from reaching him. Israel now enters into a highly volatile situation that can only be defused by physically removing (destroying) the irritant from before the deity, if need be by his own hand: "Even if Moses and Samuel were to intercede with me, I would not be won over to that people. *Dismiss them from my presence*, and let them go forth! . . . Those destined for the plague, to the plague; those destined for the sword, to the sword; those destined for famine, to famine; those destined to captivity, to captivity" (Jer. 15:1–2).

To call such passages prophetic *critiques* of prayer, fasting, and the sacrificial cult may miss the point.[53] There is not a theological rejection here of these rituals. Nor do the prophets criticize the sincerity with which they are performed. Rather, they would appear to present an argument about where Israel currently stands vis-à-vis YHWH. The time for rituals of appeal has passed and now only the more dreaded exercise of "justice" will do. Such prophetic passages clearly destabilize the role of the mercy track, but they do so without raising the banner of revolution. Ultimately, they follow the pattern of responding to affliction first with appeal and then, in light of its failure, with removal of sin, one seen as well in Jonah and Joshua, that would seem to confirm the utility of the heuristic model with which we have been working.

In the section that follows, we will see that these two spheres of activity could operate in tandem, not just sequence, without losing their distinctive logic.

"And Let Everyone Turn Back from His Evil Ways" (JON 3:8)

For now, I would like to return to a passage that we examined earlier in the context of kingly submission, the murder of Naboth and theft of his vineyard (1 Kings 21). Here Jezebel, the evil wife of the king, declares a fast day,[54] gathers the townspeople, accuses Naboth falsely of "cursing God and king," provokes them to stone him to death, and then seizes his prized vineyards. What has puzzled commentators is why she chooses a fast day as the context in which to launch her plot against Naboth. Some have suggested that fasting would have predisposed the inhabitants to introspection and penitence.[55] Others point out that the court proceedings against Naboth might have required a public gathering.[56] Neither explanation fits the circumstances Jezebel creates quite as readily as a simple application of the mercy-justice paradigm established above. It is not to penitence that the people are predisposed but to the idea that some sin hidden in their midst must be responsible for the proclaimed crisis and that they will not be safe until it is weeded out.[57] Rites of "mercy" readily give way to those of "justice." What is new here, for us, is how executing justice is presented as an unexceptional, even expected, component of fast day proceedings. The meaning of *fasting* does not change, but, clearly, the range of common *fast day* proceedings can be enlarged to incorporate not just components of "mercy" but of "justice "as well.[58] If fasting fails in the face of sin, and mourning therefore must transition frequently to a procedure for removing sin, perhaps beleaguered communities should regularly seek to eradicate evil from their midst alongside their appeals, pursuing the tracks of mercy and justice simultaneously?

Both the logic of fasting and the nature of its limitations are exploited in what must be the most powerful reflection on fasting—or, more accurately, fast days—found in the Hebrew Bible:

> They seek me daily . . . like a nation that has acted justly. . .: "Why have we fasted, and you haven't seen? We have afflicted ourselves, and you haven't attended?" Because on your fast day [*yom ṣomkhem*] you pursue your business and oppress all your laborers! . . . Your fasting today is not such as to make your voice heard on high. Is such the fast [*ṣom*] I desire, a day [*yom*] for men to afflict themselves?...Like that, do you proclaim a fast [*ṣom*], a day [*yom*] favorable to the LORD? No, this is the fast [*ṣom*] I desire: to unlock fetters of wickedness, and untie the cords of the yoke to let the oppressed go free; to break off every yoke. It is to share your bread with the hungry, and to take the wretched poor into your home; when you see the naked, to clothe him, and not to ignore your own kin. . . .

Then, when you call, the LORD will answer; when you cry, he will say: Here I am. (Isa. 58:2–9)

Israel fails to understand why God has not "seen" the distress they have manifested. But, he will not alleviate their suffering because a much more horrific scene has seized his attention: the oppression of the downtrodden. Only with the relative (if temporary) elevation of those who are truly downcast can the otherwise well-off supplicants compellingly present themselves among the ranks of the afflicted. Only then will the deity attend to *their* cries.

The common interpretation of this passage proceeds from a nominalization of the object in this passage; the word, *ṣom*, which appears throughout the passage, is said to refer to the practice of fasting. For some, the passage thereby becomes a repudiation of fasting, and even ritual in general, as *inherently* lacking. For others, it is a critique of the failure for an inner accounting to attend external rite.[59] But what this passage seems to argue with its constant reference to fast *days* (the word for "day," *yom*, appears throughout) is that the parameters of the proceedings as a whole must be enlarged beyond rites of appeal to include what we might call, for lack of a better term, social justice. The definition and continuity of fasting as a practice are not at stake. Indeed, the logical flow of this passage fits the pattern of the mercy-justice paradigm precisely: allowing economic oppression within one's midst is akin to harboring any other object unsightly to God and causes appeal to fail.

The fast of the Ninevites is also commonly held up as an example of the "penitential" fast.[60] Indeed, the passage has deep structural similarities to that of Isaiah. Here too methods of appeal appear side-by-side with the removal of sin, even as the latter receives special emphasis:

When the news [of impending doom] reached the king of Nineveh, he rose from his throne, took off his robe, put on sackcloth, and sat in ashes. And he had the word cried through Nineveh: "By decree of the king and his nobles: No man or beast—of herd or flock—shall taste anything! They shall not graze, and they shall not drink water! And they shall be covered with sackcloth—man and beast—and shall cry mightily to God. And let everyone turn back from his evil ways and from the injustice of which he is guilty . . . ." God saw their deeds, that they had turned back from their evil ways, and God renounced the punishment He had planned to bring upon them, and did not carry it out. (Jon. 3:6–10)

After himself performing rites of kingly humiliation (effectively relinquishing the throne), the king of Nineveh enjoins three acts as part of a communal fast: (1) refraining from food, (2) crying out to God, and (3) turning back from evil ways. Those who would interpret fasting (#1) in light of the command to turn away from evil (#3) skip over the intervening requirement for verbal petition (#2). The actual sequence of the proclamation—fasting, then prayer, then turning away from evil—suggests that here, as in other passages we have examined, it is with appeal that rites of self-affliction are most closely associated. This impression is confirmed by the participation of both herd and flock in the fast. They too are subject to Jonah's decree.[61] There is no reason to distinguish between their lowing from hunger—surely not an act of penitence—and the pleas of their more articulate human masters.

What is new here is the requirement to "turn back from evil ways" (#3). We will discuss this phrase and its development further in chapter 4. For now, what matters is to recognize how "turning back from evil ways" fits the visual sense of evil's presence that informs the activities encompassed by the "justice" sphere: "God *saw* their [present] deeds (for they had turned away from their evil ways), and God renounced the punishment." God only persists in anger when actively provoked by seeing evil done.[62] Leaving off sinful activities effectively removes sin from his sight and frees a now mollified God to experience pity: "should not I care about Nineveh, that great city, in which there are more than a hundred and twenty thousand persons who do not yet know their right hand from their left [i.e., children], and many beasts as well!" (Jon. 4:11).

These texts share the concern to distinguish between and ultimately privilege one type of religious concern over another.[63] The common way to define the split has been to maintain that one category, generally associated with repentance, constitutes the inner experience that must accompany the other, the outer ritual display. Actually, what we seem to have before us are two distinct ritual modes. One mode, that of "justice," is emphasized over the other not because it is the "real" theological concern at the "heart" of ritual practice, but rather because it must be pursued simultaneously, despite its difficulties, if the standard forms of appeal are to be successful. Space needs to be created for both within fast day proceedings. Fasting, for its part, continues to serve as a mode of reflecting doom and soliciting divine pity.

THE DAY OF ATONEMENT

The most famous of all fasts, that of *yom ha-kippurim* (known as the "Day of Atonement"), is highly atypical in that it is a regular, annual occurrence, not an ad hoc fast. The enumeration of the day's proceedings, as they appear in Leviticus, may be divided into two parts: (1) a description of the purifications to be performed by the high priest (Lev. 16:1–28); and (2) commandments to the community to afflict themselves and desist from all productive labor (Lev. 16:29–31). Like other representations of fast days, this priestly text presents us with a fast that revolves around two foci: the activities of the leadership and the participation of the community as a whole. In reading this chapter, one notices a rather abrupt transition between these two sections; the nonpriestly community, totally absent from the first section, suddenly comes into view in the second. The result is that the latter section reads rather like an appendix, an impression confirmed by the transmission in Leviticus 23:26–32 and Numbers 29:7 of equivalent material unaccompanied by priestly instruction. This has led scholars to question whether fasting originally attended the purification rites.[64] The literary disjunction between purification rites and communal fasting, however explained, undermines the common penitential reading of the day, which would view the people's fast as mirroring the actions of the priest, as reflecting the proper inner disposition for outer purifications.[65] But, in fact, it underscores the paradigm we have presented whereby the removal of sin (in this case through purification) and fasting appear as parallel, but distinct, ritual tracks that can appear separately or together.

One of the keys to decoding the meaning of fasting in Leviticus is to determine its relationship to the other command that devolves upon the people: "you shall afflict yourselves, *and* you shall do no manner of work" (Lev. 16:29). With the idea of *yom ha-kippurim* as a "day of utter cessation [*shabbat shabbaton*]," this passage underscores an element latent in all fast days, the temporary cessation of productive labor. For actually, every fast involves a setting aside of self, a negation of personal ontology, that goes beyond mere physical deprivation; the gathering of the entire society, essential to the manifestation of communal-wide distress on the fast day, takes its members away from their individual work and pleasures. Indeed, it is this "setting aside" that figures strongly in proclamations of fast days: "Wake up, you drunkards, and weep, wail, all you swillers of wine—for the new wine that is denied you" (Joel 1:5). Those still enjoying the fruits of last year's harvest must cast them aside and assume a state appropriate to the absence that awaits them next year.

The view of fast days as occasions of interrupted work also clearly informs the passage from Isaiah examined earlier. In the prophet's view, normal economic activity—the pursuit of selfish concerns—entails an element of oppression, "you pursue your business and oppress all your laborers!" (Isa. 58:3). The cessation of labor inherent in fast days thereby furnishes an opportunity to release the poor from the fetters that bind them (Isa. 58:6). While most fasts aim at securing the nation's ultimate weal through temporary limitations on its pursuit, Isaiah goes a step further by maintaining that God desires a fast that is altruistic, avowedly not self-interested. In the next passage in Isaiah, the prophet further explores how the interruption of labor constitutes a restriction on the pursuit of personal interests in favor of an other-directed concern, here the honoring of YHWH's sabbath (*shabbat*), a weekly day of cessation: "If you refrain from trampling the sabbath, from pursuing your affairs on my holy day; if you declare the sabbath a delight, the LORD's holy day honored; and if you honor it and go not your ways, nor look to your affairs, nor strike bargains—then you will receive delight from the LORD. I will set you astride the heights of the earth" (Isa. 58:13–14). Again, partial cessation of the self ensures its ultimate triumph.

The relationship between work stoppage and fasting is much more intricately developed in Isaiah than in Leviticus. But the example of Isaiah shows us that the confluence in Leviticus of these two forms of cessation is not incidental, but rather points to a common basis in the suppression of the self's immediate concerns. Some of what seems atypical in Leviticus—the new explicitness of the demand for the cessation of labor—may be attributed to the effect of taking a day once initiated by ad hoc proclamation and turning it into an annual institution enshrined by law. But as a fixed component within the priestly festival calendar, the meaning of fasting does not necessarily undergo a radical change. On the contrary, fasting and the cessation of labor may very well continue as a reflection of the extreme need and danger faced by the people on the Day of Atonement—the degraded state of the sanctuary and the ultimate cessation that will ensue if it is not cleansed.

At its heart, *yom ha-kippurim* is a series of rituals for the purification of the sanctuary and, according to the "appendix" that mandates fasting, the purification of the people as well. As noted, the incorporation of a communal fast reflects the day's gravity, but it also accomplishes an additional task. It provides the people with a way to signify their vested interest and even participation in the otherwise removed activities of the high priest. Mourning can function as a mechanism of participation because, as we saw earlier, it tests and reveals lines of societal interconnectedness. Affliction of the body and the broader suppression of the self involved in the interruption of labor provide Israel with concrete acts by which to constitute themselves as a community in need and thereby benefit from the purificatory process that unfolds (quite independently) within the sanctuary—a far cry from the expression of individual subjectivities bound up in the idea of fasting as penitential. And, it is for this reason that anyone who fails to fast, who does not subject themselves to the communal-wide affliction, "will be cut off from his kin" (Lev. 23:29).

SUMMARY

A wide range of instances of fasting in the Hebrew Bible have been examined, starting with cases of individuals and then moving to kings and communities. Along the way, it has been noted that themes commonly associated with repentance are usually absent altogether. This overall absence has led to a proposal for an alternative understanding of various modes of self-deprivation, that they are a form of embodiment, a way of inscribing upon the body cessation, a disaster that would otherwise remain remote. Even when, as noted, supposed penitential themes, several of which will be addressed in subsequent chapters, figure in the passages under consideration, the continued vitality of fasting as a manifestation of distress, rather than as merely an outward expression of internal feelings, did not seem to be much in doubt. Here, in particular, the paradigm of the "mercy" and "justice" spheres proved useful in delineating the relationship between rites of appeal, such as fasting, and those of removal of sin as parallel tracks rather than existing in an outer/inner dynamic. On the whole, the chapter revealed a powerful tendency among readers of the Bible to favor interiorizing interpretations of ritual behavior.

CHAPTER 2

⚜

The Logic of Appeal

And I have heard their cry.
Exodus 3:7

PRAYER AND PENITENCE

Much is bound up in the term "prayer." Among other things, it suggests a religious act, coextensive with the individual—in other words, an autonomous product of the human will. While the meaning of fasting comes to be determined, as we have seen, through a projection of its agent's intention, prayer's place as a specialized form of religious speech seems to render its words a pure extension of conscience, a mirror onto subjectivity itself. It is as this privileged sort of entity that prayer becomes an object of study in modern biblical scholarship. Form criticism sets out to discern, through various groupings of its literary representations, the basic modes of human experience that are said to receive expression in prayer.[1] The form-critical designation that concerns us, "penitential prayer" and its equivalents, has enjoyed particularly widespread usage, especially in recent years.[2] It is used to establish a certain identity among those prayer texts that happen to dwell on sin.[3] The effect of such a designation is to nominalize repentance as a category of human experience. Behind such prayers, it is assumed, is the contrite heart.

The reading strategies behind this identification consist of an amalgamation of various thoughts about expression, causation, and intention as they pertain to the individual subject, all against their apparent absence from the text. Mentioning sin perhaps suggests that a prayer serves as an expression of repentance, that it reflects a petitioner's inner conviction of guilt.[4] Alternatively, alluding to sin could produce contrition, and such prayers may be said to be penitential insofar as they "assisted in the process of repentance."[5] Another approach would be to focus on the propriety of the intention with which prayer is uttered.[6] If sin is present, a penitent attitude must be a prerequisite for petition to be effective. These strategies all craft an interior space for the penitent conscience—whether behind, after, or before the text at hand—and privilege it above overt formulations.

Contemporary use of the phrase "penitential prayer" helps reveal the contingency behind the long-standing association between prayer and repentance. It seems to be derived from the Western Christian tradition of the "penitential psalms," dating back to the sixth century, whereby certain psalms (Ps. 6, 32, 38, 51, 102, 130, and 143) are designated, not necessarily as "penitential," but for *use* as part of a broader series of rituals that play a role in penance.[7] In the earliest form of this tradition, prayer has not yet been claimed necessarily as the proper domain of interiority. It is in the modern critical category, with its turn toward conscience, that such prayers come to be seen as *about* repentance or, even, *to be* repentance.

In what follows, I would like to move past the differentiation of secular and religious speech inherent in those definitions that would see prayer as a privileged form of spiritual introspection, frequently bound up in repentance.[8] This redescription will focus on identifying some of the models from everyday speech and relations out of which what we call "prayer" is constructed in biblical texts, systems of communication that seem to reside in the realm of the material.[9] The alternatives at which we arrive will give us further insight into the social construction of pain, or what we might call "diminishment," as well as relations of power in ancient Israel. In what follows immediately, I will put forward in general terms how "appeal," rather than "repentance," could be seen as the main paradigm in ancient Israel for responding to suffering.

THE LOGIC OF APPEAL

With surprising consistency, a large range of biblical texts portray turning points in the fortunes of both individuals and the nation as hinging on processes of appeal.[10] While divine intervention may appear to dominate, it is often human plea that subtly sets it in motion. Thus, the catalyst for Moses' appointment as leader, for Israel's redemption from Egypt, according to one passage, is the cry of desperation arising from the people's servitude (Exod. 2:23–25). On the level of the individual, too, we see the critical importance of appeal. The punishment that God originally metes out to Cain would have destroyed that sinner had his appeal not forced the deity to arrive at a bearable sentence (Gen. 4:13–14). Diffuse, overwhelming wrath is honed to pinpointed, manageable justice. To do what's right, the God of Israel, as portrayed in these texts, seems to require appeal. Without human modulation of divine activity, he will act too much, too zealously—returning the world to chaos.[11]

Or too little: he will not take the necessary action toward redemption without the galvanizing cry of suffering.

From the human perspective, it is only natural to cry out at the violation wrought by suffering. Appeal has its basis in the involuntary expression of anguish. From the deity's perspective, as an agent empowered to relieve distress, he needs this outcry to direct his attention to its source. He does not act unilaterally. After all, this deity is not generally portrayed as omniscient in the contemporary sense; he is not all-knowing all of the time.[12] His mind is conceived as rather like a normal human one, albeit one with certain unusual abilities: something akin to a potent emperor. He has great powers of reconnaissance—through messengers and the expression of the needy themselves—but he needs to be told where to look and, even, reminded of his promises. This system of management ends up according great efficacy to human speech even as it confines human agency in general to reaction. Prayer, in this view, is hardly a privileged act of human righteousness; instead, it is an instinctual response to the negation of the human will that also happens to provide God with the information he needs to do his work as ruler.

Appeal does not just inform the sovereign of the facts; it evokes the situation vividly and elicits his pity. For while we tend to think of God as a "supernatural" being whose mercy is a constant state or attribute of his very existence, the anthropopathic deity represented in the literature of ancient Israel is actually far more human in this respect as well. Like a human ruler, he is susceptible to emotional inertia, holding on to anger or failing to act with alacrity on his people's behalf. To overcome this inertia and draw out divine altruism, prayer must present a trenchant description of suffering, potential or actual. Therefore, like fasting, it can become a sophisticated orchestration of distress. But such conscious intent does not fundamentally alter its significance as an articulation of pain. Indeed, the primal and inchoate cry of anguish exists in a continuum with the suasive rhetoric of more formal prayer.

This god also desires appeal because it affirms his power. Prayer articulates a dynamic whereby Israel is the dependent, and God the redeemer. The very act of request confers potent, salvific status on its addressee, especially when buttressed by the mention of salvations past. Furthermore, by directing its supplications to YHWH by name, Israel marks the ensuing deliverance as his work. Prayer serves ex post facto as a form of explanation, tying events to the heroics of an otherwise unseen savior. Because prayer is a reflection on the deity's power, failing to appeal to him—or worse yet, appealing to other gods or nations—is a grave affront and provokes his jealousy. The failure to call upon YHWH, like any other deity, suggests his impotence and therefore incites his wrath. The efficacy of appeal draws its logic not necessarily from the altruism of the deity but from his self-interest. The cycle of outcry begetting redemption is thus part of a symbiosis, a mutually beneficial relationship, between the powerful and the powerless.[13] Each party acts according to the dictates of its nature (expressing pain and relieving pain, respectively). Quite apart from any discourse around morality, from these natural, social elements, a moral system emerges.

In the examples that follow, I will seek to affirm the essentially nonpenitential logic of the stage in the relationship with the deity when appeal still proves effective. Later in this chapter and in other chapters, we will examine situations of rupture deemed to be occasioned by serious sin. For our purposes, it will be enough to focus on the quite ample biblical material, but it is important to note that an argument for the primacy of appeal to the deity within ancient Israel underscores its connections to its ancient Near Eastern neighbors as well.[14]

DESPERATE, NOT REPENTANT

We turn first to cases of individuals praying. Today, when we read prayer texts from the Bible, many of us imagine an individual conscience expressing its purest thoughts and innermost feelings. For instance, what has been described as the "open and metaphorical" language of the Psalms allows for certain spiritualizing interpretations.[15] "Enemies" may be seen as referring to sins, and "illness" to emotional suffering. That the Psalms give no explicit indication of their original contexts abets the multiplication of such readings and their penitential applications.

When considering narrative material, however, a more materialist view of prayer, one that is bound up in a robust sense of the afflicted's self-interest, emerges with ample clarity. The many depictions of appeal in connection to infertility form one compelling example. In ancient Israel, the expanse and continuity of the self was bound up, ultimately, in the possession of children. Thus, in the midst of God's promising him great reward—"land and prosperity"—Abraham interrupts to complain about his lack of offspring: "Oh LORD GOD, what can you (really) give me, if I am to go childless?" (Gen. 15:2). Isaac, having inherited his father's vast holdings, must appeal to YHWH as he still finds himself materially lacking with Rebecca's womb shut (Gen. 25:21). Once men have children by one woman, they do not take up the cause of another's barrenness. With Ishmael born and his own permanence secured, Abraham assures God that further progeny are unnecessary, though his wife, Sarah, remains without children (Gen. 17:18). Jacob rebuffs Rachel, and Elkanah, Hannah. Each woman must pray on her own behalf. This is not just a question of men being obtuse but cuts to the very nature of prayer: it is neither altruistic nor idealistic, but arises from the threatened diminishment of the self, impingement upon what one personally needs for survival. Throughout biblical narrative, appeal consistently figures in situations in which prosperity and continuity are at stake, occasions that require a straightforward plea for help.[16] We might presume that the same sorts of contexts would have been behind recitations of psalms as well.[17]

In the above cases, the act of appeal ties the birth of a child to the name of YHWH, affirming his role as the agent bestowing life. God's self-interest, his reputation, is also at stake. However, in considering prayer, we tend to project a vision of a god who is purely altruistic, a pedagogue who afflicts the petitioner in order to improve his or her moral or religious caliber. The entire theater of appeal thus assumes the form of an operation on the consciousness of the afflicted in which the propriety of attendant mental attitudes assumes primary importance. In other words, we tend to emphasize the necessity of what might be called the "sincerity" of petition. Certain biblical terms and their common translations open the door to this emphasis. Thus, for instance, the common root *bṭh* is usually taken as denoting a concern for the feeling of trust or faith that is appropriate for a petitioner: "Preserve my life, for I am steadfast; you, my God, deliver your servant who trusts [*boṭeaḥ*] in you" (Ps. 86:2).

In fact, *bṭh* probably suggests something more like "rely," denoting the fact of the petitioner's turning to YHWH—active dependence—rather than his or her state of mind, as the passage continues: "for I call to you all day long" (Ps. 86:3). I might retranslate the verse in question: "Protect me! I am loyal [as a worshipper]. Save your servant—*you* are my god!—who relies on you." The petitioner has turned exclusively to YHWH for help, and his god must come through for him. Indeed, one finds in the Psalms, in particular, a preponderance of terms used to refer to YHWH as a "stronghold," an objectification of this notion of reliance: "I seek refuge in you, YHWH . . . rescue me . . . be a rock, a stronghold for me, a citadel, in order to save me. You are my rock and my fortress. For the sake of your name, you lead me and guide me" (Ps. 31:2–4). The theme of YHWH as a "stronghold" is one of the basic images that informs the very possibility of appeal and may reflect its basis in cultic sites, which would have been seen as a space whose protection and life-giving qualities were ensured by the presence of the deity.[18] Among these terms, we find one, *miḇṭaḥ*, which, in fact, derives from *bṭh*: "Successful is the one who makes YHWH his stronghold [*miḇṭaḥô*] and does not turn to the arrogant or to followers of falsehood" (Ps. 40:5). To return to our initial passage, the psalmist identifies himself as one "who relies on you," in order to remind the deity of what's at stake: YHWH's potential loss of an ally, his reliability as a patron, and the acknowledgment he stands to get if his dependent survives—all matters of a quasi-political nature. Is YHWH a reliable "stronghold"? How this question is answered depends on the constancy of his followers' appeals, which alone attest to his dependability. It is this constancy, not sincerity or the subjective quality of faith, which seems to be the main demand placed on petitioners.[19]

This is true even when supplicants allude in prayer to their sinfulness, an aspect of petition to which we now turn. As we saw in the preceding chapter, sin could be a basis for rejecting all sorts of appeals—for shutting a fugitive out of the city of refuge, in a manner of speaking. For that very reason, prayers uttered in a context of sin must anticipate and forestall potential rejection by admitting guilt upfront and asking God to overlook it: "O LORD, listen to my cry; let your ears be attentive to my plea for mercy. If you keep account of sins, O LORD, LORD who will survive? Yours is the power to forgive so that you may be dutifully worshipped" (Ps. 130:2–4). It is as if the psalmist says to God: "Please help me, YHWH! Oh, and don't tell me that my sins stand in the way, because in that event no one would be left to worship you." Allusion to sinfulness can constitute a rhetorical strategy aimed at defusing likely criticism. Sin need not be neatly and precisely disposed of but can be roughly bundled and shunted aside. In short, the psalmist assumes that a normal relationship with the deity must be sufficiently expansive to encompass sin. By virtue of their very supplications, worshipers remain among an in-group whom God values for their persistent reliance upon him. As the Psalm continues, "I look to the LORD; I look to him; I await his word" (Ps. 130:5). This is the constancy of worship YHWH desires.

Because sin has an objective, residual effect on the sinner, in the poetics of prayer, sin can also become a metonym for the suffering it engenders.[20] It is therefore frequently woven into the very fabric of lament and used to indicate the need for divine intervention. Its removal spells relief from affliction and demonstrates the deity's salvific powers. Accordingly, to ask for forgiveness is a plea for help like any other. There is no need to superimpose an unmentioned penitential event onto these prayers in order to understand their efficacy. What we encounter is a spectrum whereby sin figures more or less explicitly. On one side of the spectrum, we have the vast majority of psalms, which do not allude to sinfulness. On the other side, we have those psalms and narrative cases that are marked by pleas for forgiveness of sin. Where we are along the spectrum, however, does not impact appeal's basic function, the securing of physical well-being.

It is striking that most psalms do not allude to sinfulness since so many narrative representations of suffering place sin at its root. This would seem to suggest that for some who could have conceived of themselves as culpable, it was possible to recite a psalm that included no mention of sin at all. This is certainly true of the psalm embedded in the book of Jonah. Though the narrative makes it clear that wrongdoing is the underlying cause of his unusual confinement, the psalm-like prayer that he utters lacks any mention of sinfulness, contrition, or a change of mind regarding his refusal to act as YHWH's prophet: "In my trouble I called to the LORD, and he answered me; From the belly of Sheol I cried out, and you heard my voice" (2:3–10). It seems likely that this psalm preexisted the narrative—their only connection being the association between the belly of Sheol and the belly of the whale—but the willingness of the author of Jonah to use it to represent Jonah's situation indicates that a straightforward plea for help was deemed an appropriate response even to distress induced by sin.

Moving along the spectrum of sin's representation, we find instances in which personal responsibility is vaguely and briefly alluded to as part of a larger attempt to elicit divine compassion. Consider, for instance, Psalm 6: "O LORD, do not punish me in anger, do not chastise me in fury. Have mercy on me, O LORD, for I languish; heal me, O LORD, for my bones shake with terror" (Ps. 6:2–3). The language of anger and chastisement suggests guilt, but the psalmist swiftly moves on to other matters, the vivid description of his burden of which this language is ultimately a part. In Psalm 38, the imagery of sin and its effects proves more elaborate but still melds with that of the depiction of physical suffering to heighten the pathos of plea: "O LORD, do not punish me in wrath; do not chastise me in fury. For your arrows have struck me; your blows have fallen upon me. There is no soundness in my flesh because of your rage, no wholeness in my bones because of my sin" (Ps. 38:2–4).

Psalm 51 is unusual among the Psalms in its exclusive focus on the removal of sin: "Wash me thoroughly of my iniquity, and purify me of my sin" (Ps. 51:4). Its pervasive concern with sin clearly gives rise to a psychological reading based on a notion of the guilty conscience.[21] However, even as the psalm is steeped in the rhetoric of sin and forgiveness, this text may be viewed not as a penitential gesture but as a plea for help just like other prayers; at least that would seem to be the assumption of whoever added its superscription: "A psalm of David when Nathan the prophet came to him after he had gone in to Bathsheba" (Ps. 51:2). It is important to understand why this psalm came to be associated with this moment in David's life. The author of the superscription seems to have noticed and read as biographical the following: "Indeed I was born through iniquity; with sin my mother conceived me" (Ps. 51:7). Here David could be seen as speaking in the voice of his doomed son, the offspring of his illicit union with Bathsheba. And indeed, in what forms the historiographic basis of the superscription (2 Sam. 12:13), David does confess before Nathan and shortly thereafter fasts and prays, a prayer that the narrative does not record. Could Psalm 51 not constitute David's lost prayer? Perhaps, but only if one makes a noteworthy interpretive move. The prayer that his sin be forgiven must be seen as truly a plea for the life of his son; "sin" serves as the all-encompassing representation of the distress from which the king requires relief.[22]

THE CRIES OF THE PEOPLE

The focus on appeal over repentance is yet more pronounced when we turn to national instances of response to disaster. There are various models, common intersections of language and practice that are taken up within various biblical texts as the bases with which to conceive of the possibilities for appeal. In the previous chapter, we touched upon the lament tradition and its relationship to appeal, and considered briefly, in this chapter, the imagery of asylum. In chapter 4, we will look at oracular inquiry as a further occasion of appeal and nexus of prayer language. For now, I would like to single out for special consideration one recurring paradigm that figures at central moments in the representation of the nation's history, namely "crying out" (ṣ/z ʿq).[23] Only when Israel, suffering, *cries out* to God, does he take up their cause in Egypt: "Surely I have seen my people's abjection, and I have heard their outcry" (Exod. 3:7). God acts to protect the Israelites from the approaching Egyptians at the Red Sea *after* they "cry out" to him (Exod. 14:10). The miraculous provision of victuals in the wilderness ensues from the people's forceful articulation of need, their complaints.[24] These moments in the nation's historical memory become defining episodes, etiologies of appeal that justify current expectations that prayer will be heard and, therefore, come in for special reflection in petitionary texts: "On you *our fathers* relied [*baṭḥû*]. . .. To you they cried out [*zaʿaqu*] and they escaped" (Ps. 22:2–6). And again: "Some lost their way in the wilderness . . . in their adversity they cried to the LORD, and he rescued them from their troubles" (Ps. 107:4–6).

The case of "crying out" proves so informative for our purposes because it is an instance of appeal whose nuances we are able to unpack with surprising specificity. "Outcry" arises from a *violation* of personal welfare. Abel's blood, whose vitality remains even as Cain has done away with the rest of him, "cries out" (Gen. 4:10). Mephibosheth "cries out" to David over the theft of his ancestral land (2 Sam. 19:29). Most strikingly, the Deuteronomic Law uses the actual or merely potential presence of "outcry" as a way of establishing lack of consent in cases of rape (Deut. 22:23–27). The latter instance highlights another aspect of "outcry:" its *reflexive immediacy* and usual *lack of intentionality*. "Crying out" need not be a cry for help (none may be available) and certainly not formal prayer. In one representation, the Israelites in Egypt do not cry out *to God*; they simply cry out as a direct result of their burdens (Exod. 2:23; compare Deut. 26:7). It is commonly applied to stirring utterances of limited articulacy, from Esau's "Bless me too, Father!" (Gen. 27:34), after Jacob's theft of his blessing, to David's "My son Absalom! Absalom my son, my son!" (2 Sam. 19:5).

"Crying out" bears within it an implicit charge against a violator. In certain passages, "outcry" appears as a metonymy for violence, as its audible dimension. Such is the case with the "outcry" that ascends from Sodom and Gomorrah to YHWH (Gen. 18:21) or in Isaiah's damning play on words: "He [God] expected justice, but saw bloodshed; righteousness, but heard outcry [*ṣadaqa*]" (Isa. 5:7). Indeed, a few texts suggest that "Violence!" (*ḥamas*) might have been a standard single-word articulation of the "outcry" (Jer. 20:8, Hab. 1:2, Job 19:7). Its effect on the violator could be devastating. It identifies oppression and singles out an individual or nation as oppressor, exposing them to retribution. Does Tamar intend to incite Absalom to kill Amnon when she "cries out" after he rapes her (2 Sam. 13:19)? Probably not. But, even without the victim's calculation, the fact of the crime, the outcry, is portrayed as having a natural, barbed efficacy.

As the audible dimension of victimization, the "outcry" is meant to be heard by *someone*, specifically someone empowered to save (or revenge) the oppressed. For instance, to return to the Deuteronomic Law, there is a presumption that, in populated areas, there will be a champion, literally "savior" (*môshia*), that *hears* and responds to the cry of the victim of rape (Deut. 22:27). While sight can be obstructed, sound travels freely. But sound proves only moderately informative; the prospective champion drawn by cries seeks out their source and then beholds the actual site of violence, thereby obtaining a complete picture of the situation. Thus, upon hearing the "outcry" arising from Sodom and Gomorrah, God (in the form of his angelic appointees) descends to earth and approaches Sodom to "see" the atrocities for himself (Gen. 18:20–21). Ultimately, sight furnishes the motivation, and proximity provides the means for justice to be dispensed immediately.

Outcry precedes and, in a sense, produces the champion, who figures consistently in biblical narrative as an institution of salvation: "The Israelites cried out to the LORD, and the LORD raised a champion [*môshia*]" (Judg. 3:15). The appointment of Moses is God's response to the Israelites' cry, and when someday the Egyptians cry out to YHWH for help, it will come in the form of a *môshia* (Isa. 19:20). The people's dependence upon these individuals is truly extraordinary; they are the ones, not the people, who are portrayed as securing military victory. The martial cast of this terminology is underscored by the use of the same terms for the mustering of troops from another tribe and the military reinforcement that they provide: "I [Jephthah] and my people were in a bitter conflict with the Ammonites, and I cried out [*va-'ez'aq*] to you [the Ephraimites], but you did not save [*hôsha'tem*] me from them" (Judg. 12:2). Individual heroes, too, in a sense, come from afar; they have been overlooked due to their marginal position (Ehud, Deborah, Gideon, Saul, David) or else were banished from their people (Moses, Jephthah, Samson, David). Their emergence sparks a sudden reversal in the fortunes of Israel. An element of altruism is usually present, but protection comes at a price; the people must invest their saviors with political power. As the elders of Gilead promise Jephthah, "If you come with us and fight the Ammonites, you shall be our commander over all the inhabitants of Gilead" (Judg. 11:8).[25] Correspondingly, failure to enlist the aid of a potential champion degrades him and occasions a rift. The Ephraimites attack Jephthah and the Gileadites over precisely such a purported failure (Judg. 12:1–6). The king is the champion whose appointment and invested power have become permanent through a promise of loyalty not only to him but to his descendants as well. The people now cannot cry out against him (1 Sam. 8:18).[26]

In the poetic discourse of the Psalms, YHWH himself is presented as champion: "I lift up my eyes to the hills; from where will my help come? My help comes from the LORD, maker of heaven and earth" (Ps. 121:1–2). The mythic language of the Song at the Sea presents YHWH rather literally as champion, as a "man of war" (Exod. 15:3), and functions as the sort of praise we might expect a returning war hero to receive.[27] Finally, God, in response to the cry of the violated, can inhabit fully the role of a different kind of champion, that of avenger.[28] God is to Cain and Abel (Gen. 4:10) as Absalom is to Amnon and Tamar. However, God as champion represents what might be labeled a strongly supernatural form of the institution. Biblical narrative often presents a subtler, more recondite picture of redemptive activities as embodied in a human champion associated with YHWH. The arrival of the successful human warrior gives flesh to the renewal of the deity's presence in Israel's midst. The supposed move away from idols in ancient Israel need not constitute a step back from practices of embodiment. To take the case of the Israelites' first leader, Moses promises victory, enacts most of the plagues against Pharaoh, and orchestrates the people's escape; in his absence, they stray and erect another object to manifest God (Exod. 32:1–6). Israel presents their plaints directly to him, the champion, who has become their leader.

In these ways, the image of the champion appointed by outcry proves to be a richly suggestive way of framing the relationship between Israel and its deity. Crying out offers a model of plaint that avoids presenting God as its object and instead positions him as a third party responding to circumstances of victimization. Imagining the deity as champion helps account for the ongoing national cycle of suffering and relief, by establishing a framework for his initial remoteness and subsequent emergence. This on-again, off-again quality suggests that the institution of the champion cannot be encompassed entirely within a covenantal framework of steady commitment. Rather, the relationship is in some ways reinitiated with the advent of each moment of redemption. This renewal highlights the altruism of the deity but also provides grounding for attainment of the more permanent power that ultimately serves as the basis for the very different political model of kingship.

In the depictions of YHWH as champion, the operative metaphor appears to have retained its vitality. Violation produces outcry, which attracts the champion, who eventually secures power in exchange for the aid he provides. Nevertheless, astute exegetes, both medieval and modern, have heard a penitential note in the people's outcry. The medieval Spanish exegete, Abraham ibn Ezra, asserts in his commentary to Exodus 2:23 that the people's "outcry" in Egypt was not a cry of pain but an expression of repentance. What lies behind this, in part, is an assumption that our discussion of the institution of the champion belies, that only the spiritual transformation of the subject, not mere speech, could occasion redemption. Slightly more plausible but still problematic is the attempt of modern scholarship to present the cycle of sin-oppression-*outcry*-champion that recurs throughout the first half of the book of Judges (e.g., Judg. 3:7–11) as being in accord with a so-called deuteronomistic paradigm of sin-affliction-*repentance*-deliverance.[29] The appointment of a champion entails a change in both the people's fortunes and their loyalties. A penitential account of these events would propose that it is the change in loyalty that triggers the improvement in national fortunes, that inner states produce material welfare. The actual language of the text, however, seems to move in the opposite direction. The suffering people cry out, a champion redeems them, and, subsequently, they duly transfer their loyalty to that champion and his declared patron, YHWH. Loyalty figures as a by-product, not a precondition, to redemption. When the individual champion dies, the people again abandon YHWH (e.g., Judg. 3:11–12).

The cycle of sin-oppression-outcry-champion provides a compelling framework for the pre-monarchic period of the judges. Its very last iteration, however, represents the people's outcry in a significantly different light and has been used to provide support for those who would advocate a penitential reading of the framework as a whole. The passage begins typically enough: "The Israelites again did what was offensive to the LORD. They served the Baalim and the Ashtaroth ... they forsook the LORD and did not serve him. And the LORD, incensed with Israel, surrendered them to the Philistines and the Ammonites. ... Then the Israelites cried out to the LORD" (Judg. 10:6–10). But now it continues with a verbal formulation of what purports to be their actual cry: "We stand guilty before you, for we have forsaken our god and served the baalim" (Judg. 10:10). Generally, it seems to be assumed that the same confessional utterance and process of removing idols that follows (Judg. 10:16) must be implicit in the earlier framework passages. Actually, this final passage in the framework presents itself as exceptional: *only now* does God reach the point in which he declares, "I will not deliver you again" (Judg. 10:13).

Overall, the passage's explicit concern with the removal of idols suggests the work of a later editor, influenced by deuteronomistic language and reforms, who has augmented an earlier editorial framework with a new, expanded set of concerns.[30] It accords with other relatively late passages that move away from relying exclusively on appeal by predicating redemption upon the cessation of sin. Even so, to put matters in terms of a discussion in chapter 1, the move introduces a rectification in the realm of "justice" that, ultimately, serves to restore the efficacy of "mercy." That is to say, once the irritant of the idols is removed, appeal can operate in normal fashion. Indeed, after the rejection of their first cry, the Israelites appeal again: "Just save us this day!" (Judg. 10:15). It is clear that compassion for suffering, "He could not bear the miseries of Israel" (Judg 10:16), not the cessation of sin, proves to be the immediate catalyst, the efficient cause of redemption.

Most importantly, we note the new formulation of outcry as a form of confession, a practice also attested in other late texts, including Lamentations and parts of Solomon's prayer in 1 Kings 8. Confession as a practice and as a component of petition will be considered in the following chapter, but some discussion of a few texts paradigmatic for the history of appeal in ancient Israel is warranted now. Throughout the book of Lamentations, Israel clearly blames itself for the disaster it has undergone: "Jerusalem has greatly sinned, therefore she is become a mockery" (Lam. 1:8). However, in context, allusion to sin seems to serve to deepen the sense of the people's diminishment, rather than communicate contrition: the people are in desperate straits and, what's more, it is because of something *they did*. Sin has a place in lament because it provides another angle from which to behold the people's degradation. What we do find, if not repentance, is appeal, encapsulated in the recurring refrain of the book's first two acrostics, which gathers up the laments' portraits of affliction and demands that God look upon this horrid picture: "See, O LORD, the distress I am in!" (Lam. 1:20).[31]

It is in the third acrostic that we find the instance of prayer as confession: "Let us lift up our hearts with our hands to God in heaven. We have transgressed and rebelled, and you have not forgiven" (Lam. 3:41–42). One may be inclined to see this passage as the climax of the chapter. However, this chapter, as a whole, is rife with the imagery of appeal, and interestingly enough, like the confession-based prayer found in Judges, confession here figures in the context of a continued rejection that it reflects and ultimately justifies. It is accorded no special status. By way of contrast, the section at the end of the lament concludes on a relatively hopeful note: "I have called on your name, O LORD, from the depths of the Pit. . . . You have ever drawn nigh when I called you. You have said, 'Do not fear!' . . . You have seen, O LORD, the wrong done me; Oh, vindicate my right!" (Lam. 3:59). No sign of repentance here, only appeal![32] This text holds out the hope that God's anger will eventually abate, and he will finally see the people's affliction. In fact, the lamenter insists that he will not cease from crying until that eventuality is achieved: "My eyes shall flow without cease, without respite, until the LORD looks down and beholds from heaven" (Lam. 3:49–50).

While Psalm 107, as mentioned earlier, builds an etiology of prayer around Israel's historic "crying out" in Egypt and the wilderness with the refrain, "In their adversity they cried out to the LORD, and he rescued them from their troubles" (Ps. 107:6; compare 107:13, 19, 28), 1 Kings 8 does so, instead, around the supposed prayer of Solomon upon the inauguration of the new temple site. Solomon is said to offer seven petitions, asking that the temple's god respond to his people in various situations of adversity, of the sorts found in Psalm 107. Here, too, we find a refrain running throughout: "[when] they offer prayer and supplication to you in this house, oh, hear in heaven and pardon the sin of your people Israel." As in Psalm 107, despite the fact that it is understood to be sin that generates suffering, a straightforward appeal is put forward as the form petition should assume in six out of the seven cases; it is Solomon alone, with his meta-awareness of the people's responsibility, that shapes his petition as a request for their forgiveness. Indeed, the term that is used here, "make supplication" (*hithannen*), suggests, within the realm of human relations, not repentance but an attempt to secure pity from one who has the petitioner fully within his or her power. Joseph pleads with his brothers from the pit (Gen. 42:21), an army captain pleads with Elijah not to destroy his company as the prophet has done to two others (2 Kings 1:13), and the angel pleads with Jacob to release him (Hosea 12:5). Its use in Solomon's prayer not only speaks to God's ability and right to destroy Israel on account of sin, but the altruism that he shows in refraining from doing so. He "hears" and "pardons."

There are some divergences among the petitions. In chapter 4, we will discuss the language of "turning back to YHWH," which appears in two of the petitions; but for now, we will focus on the last instance of appeal, which concerns military conquest and exile. Here, we find an unusual elaboration of the wording of the people's prayer as including confession: "they will make supplication to you in the land of their captors, saying: 'We have sinned, we have acted perversely, we have acted wickedly'" (1 Kings 8:47). As was the case with Judges, on the basis of this final instance, scholars have concluded that Solomon presents a cycle of sin-affliction-repentance-deliverance throughout as the paradigmatic resolution to Israel's future crises. It is quite possible that here, too, we are dealing with a later interpolation or, perhaps, a sense that a cognizance of sin is appropriate to and taken up specifically as a form of practice in exile.[33] Either way, what we find is another instance of the introduction of confession in a clearly exilic text. Is this "penitential" prayer?

One factor, at least, should hold us back from drawing such a conclusion: these prayers never cease to be seen as forms of appeal, as operating on a sense of divine mercy, in the case of Solomon, with an element of *quid pro quo*. Solomon has built a house for God, and God now must honor his request to take care of his people. An alternative account of this confessional language might see in these communal prayers the same sort of concerns that animated the prayers of individuals. As we suggested with regard to Lamentations, allusion to sin deepens the profundity of the people's diminishment and places it before the deity for removal, but it also takes its place as part of a certain etiquette of prayer. Introducing confession into prayer justifies the neglect, especially evident in exile, from which the people have been suffering. It displaces blame from the addressee to the petitioner, so request can be made anew: "We stand guilty. Do to us as you see fit; just save us this day!" (Judg. 10:15).

THE RELENTLESS FEW

The people's cry was one response to affliction. Yet the peculiar economy of appeal in ancient Israel may have made another form of petition, namely prophetic intercession, even more common.[34] Such appeal figures prominently in narrative depictions of prophetic activity. Either the people (sometimes individuals) approach the prophets with something like the following: "Please pray on our behalf to the LORD our God" (Jer. 37:3); or, the prophet intercedes on his own cognizance. Indeed, figures such as Moses, Samuel, and Jeremiah occupy a quasi-official role as intercessors. In narrative, we can see how prophetic prayer provokes an oracular response, and it may be that it is this sort of petitionary inquiry, like elsewhere in the ancient Near East,[35] that occasioned at least some of the many oracles that appear, without a narrative framework, in prophetic literature.

The institution of prophecy will be examined more fully in chapter 5, but it is necessary to inquire as part of our analysis of appeal: Why is intercessory prayer privileged? The phenomenon of intercession highlights the extent to which appeal in many biblical texts operates in accord with the demands of communication, as opposed to concerns for human virtue or interiority. There is no hesitation in imagining a theater of action that displaces the people—their agency and experience. Instead, all eyes turn to the lone intercessor, who functionally seems to occupy a liminal place between God and people; he retains a concern for their welfare, yet enjoys special access to the supernal realm both in terms of being privy to what transpires there and his ability to deliver messages. In a sense, in the more monotheistic system of ancient Israel, human prophets assume the role that would have been played otherwise by lesser deities in other Levantine religions. In the ancient Canaanite myth of Aqhat, for instance, it is the god Baal who takes up the cause of the childless Danel in the divine assembly: "Danel . . . laments, the Hero . . . moans: for he has no son as his brothers do. . . . So, my father, El the Bull, bless him . . . . Let him have a son in his house."[36] That effective communication requires status and proximity to the source of ultimate power is the starting assumption behind the institution of the intercessor.[37]

Exceptional communicative power also ensues from the prophet's being for the people, but not quite of the people. From his vantage point, the prophet is able to keep in view the metanarrative of sin that accounts for the people's suffering, even if they themselves are ignorant of it. He takes undirected anguish—recall the "reflexive immediacy" of the people's outcry—and packages it for the appropriate party in appropriate terms: "Judah is in mourning, her settlements languish. Men are bowed to the ground, and the outcry of Jerusalem rises. . . . Though our iniquities testify against us, act, O LORD, for the sake of your name" (Jer. 14:2, 7). By a quirk in human perception, the representation of another's suffering can prove more evocative and compelling than the victim's own depiction. We have already seen how the unseemliness of affliction can quickly alienate a potential helper. This is particularly true in situations in which the victim does not or, in the case of sin, no longer enjoys close bonds with the one empowered to help. The intercessor can skirt past these obstacles and set about removing them. What is perhaps Moses' greatest moment comes when God has set out to destroy the children of Israel and make of Moses a new nation. It is only the relentlessness with which Moses uses his continued access to the deity that brings the nation back into the realm of the living (Exod. 32:11–14). Prophetic intercession remains an option long after other avenues of appealing to the deity have closed. The prophet's dissociation from the people contains within it a darker side as well. He may switch loyalties and fully absorb the perspective of the enraged deity: "Remember how I [Jeremiah] stood before you to plead in their behalf, to turn your anger away from them! Oh, give their children over to famine, mow them down by the sword. Let their wives be bereaved of children and husbands" (Jer. 18:20–21). Here, the effect of the intercessory function is reversed.

Rhetorical strategies ranging from harshness to outright manipulation mark the speech of the prophetic intercessor. On a better day (at least from a certain perspective), we find Jeremiah taunting God with suggestions of impotence: "Why are you like a man who is stunned, like a warrior who cannot give victory?" (Jer. 14:9). The prophet's peculiar vantage point allows him to move beyond the people's pain, at a point when God has become inured to it, and formulate arguments entirely in terms of God's own self-interest. With one stunning line, Moses effectively immobilizes the enraged deity: "Let not the Egyptians say, 'It was with evil intent that he delivered them, only to kill them off in the mountains and annihilate them from the face of the earth'" (Exod. 32:12).

The power of well-chosen words over the deity (by no means assured of success) highlights the humanlike affective qualities frequently attributed to Israel's god. Anthropopathism underlies the institution of prophetic intercession in another fashion as well. We find in one of Amos' oracles: "My LORD GOD does nothing without having revealed his purpose to his servants the prophets. A lion has roared, who can but fear? My LORD GOD has spoken, who can but prophesy?" (Amos 3:7–8). It is this inability to withhold his intentions from his intimates that exposes God to the peppering intercession of Abraham: "Shall I hide from Abraham what I am about to do?" (Gen. 18:17). God needs to express himself. As such, the prophets can operate as an early warning system that detects and attempts to intercept impending disaster before it is even felt by the people: "This is what my LORD GOD showed me: He was creating [a plague of] locusts at the time when the late-sown crops were beginning to sprout . . . I said, 'O LORD GOD, pray forgive. How will Jacob survive? He is so small.' The LORD relented concerning this. 'It shall not come to pass,' said the LORD" (Amos 7:1–3). Appeal, in all its various forms, can prove efficacious even when the people lack any consciousness of sin.

While prophets are sometimes able to forestall disaster altogether, most often they only succeed in mitigating impending doom. This may very well be true, for instance, in the case of Abraham. If Abraham had not contended with God regarding the destruction of Sodom and Gomorrah, would the deity have taken it upon himself to save the righteous Lot from their midst? It is certainly true with regard to Moses. After the sin of the spies, God sets out to destroy the nation. Moses intercedes, and YHWH declares: "I have forgiven, as you asked" (Num. 14:20). Immediately thereafter, he condemns the present generation to death (Num. 14:21–23). How does that constitute forgiveness? Wrath unchecked devours the whole, but with the limitation the prophetic intercessor imposes by exercising the "mercy" track, it envelops *only the guilty party* and not their innocent descendants. We may thus add to the picture already suggested above: An enraged deity vents before his intimates. They point out the injustice of a plan conceived in wrath and talk him down from his extreme anger; they advise him, as it were. What emerges is restrained response, pinpointed "justice," and a very different construction of anger, not as an emotion that must be controlled by the individual subject but as an event, the effects of which must be socially mediated.

That the prophet, with his special access to the deity, could become thoroughly associated with YHWH as his representative in the earthly world points to one last facet of intercessory prayer. Elijah's triumphant intercession at Mount Carmel and the subsequent return of the rains clearly marks YHWH as the true source of sustenance and denigrates that rival storm god, Baal, as Elijah says: "Let it be known today that you are God in Israel and that I am your servant . . . . Answer me, LORD, answer me, that this people may know that you, LORD, are God" (1 Kings 18:36–37). For the YHWH prophet to succeed impresses the power of YHWH upon the people. This element of association proves so central that the phrase "those who call out his name" becomes a way of referring to the prophets in their intercessory capacity: "Moses and Aaron among his priests, Samuel, among those who call out his name—when they called to the LORD, he answered them" (Ps. 99:6). The role of intercessory prayer in the manifestation of divine power comes into full force, in particular, in one account of YHWH's victory over Pharaoh. Pharaoh must beseech Moses: "Plead with the LORD to remove the frogs from me and my people" (Exod. 8:4). So much is bound up in that simple request! YHWH is responsible for the plague; Pharaoh cannot save himself. This articulation of dependence actualizes the deity's mastery over the all-powerful emperor and presages the utter destruction and subjugation that await him. Not only a powerful method of communicating, intercession served to communicate power.

SUMMARY

We have examined instances of individuals and communities praying and also of intercessors. Throughout, it has been noted that appeal does not appear to derive its logic as a verbal expression of internal states. It is rather a series of strategies for encapsulating material realities, for communicating distress to a deity who is deemed empowered to help. Even allusions to sin appear to be a way of packaging suffering, merging cause and symptom in a plea for relief. Such processes will be taken up further in the chapter on confessional utterances that follows. Indeed, appeal is often most noteworthy for its immediacy, its sense of being an instinctual "crying out" in the face of violation, lacking the intentionality often associated with "prayer." It is a response to suffering that seeks to mitigate its pain not through control over the self but through social engagement—verbal articulation.

Most importantly, procedures for moral transformation, for pedagogy, need not be imputed where the texts themselves allude to none. What the deity gets out of it, out of responding to such appeal in the imagined world of these texts, is a name, an identity. He is the one who responds to prayer, who meets the needs of his people. That prayer, like fasting, can fail, ("Someday they shall cry out to the LORD, but he will not answer them; at that time he will hide his face from them, in accordance with the wrongs they have done")[38] (Mic. 3:4), even when offered by his intimates, "As for you [Jeremiah], do not pray for this people, do not raise a cry of prayer on their behalf, do not plead with me; for I will not listen to you" (Jer. 7:16) does not suggest that some necessary internal state is lacking. Rather, the very logic of appeal erodes in the face of severe sin. Or, to put it differently, sustained adversity despite the continued operation of appeal can be explained only by the existence of some source of interference. "And when you lift up your hands, I will turn my eyes away from you; though you pray at length, I will not listen. Your hands are full of blood" (Isa. 1:15). Perhaps, it can be framed as a form of distraction—the failure of the "justice" track draws attention away from the "mercy" track—or an actual punitive blockage: "You have clothed yourself in anger and pursued us, you have slain without pity. You have screened yourself off with a cloud, that no prayer may pass through" (Lam. 3:43–44). Either way, the failure of appeal leads the world to slip into a state of chaos, as unfettered divine wrath undoes the nation God had formed and other modes of engagement become necessary for its restoration. This is the register and stage of the relationship (or lack thereof) in which prophecy usually dwells, as will be taken up in chapter 5.[39] Still, appeal retains its logic as the basis for the functioning relationship between YHWH and his people, and, in the prophetic imagination, once again: "He will grant you his favor at the sound of your cry; he will respond as soon as he hears it" (Isa. 30:19).[40]

CHAPTER 3

֎

Articulating Sin

We have sinned against you.
Judges 10:10

CONFESSION AND REPENTANCE

For modern biblical scholarship, to study fasting and prayer has meant to differentiate their types through, respectively, the practices of ethnography and form criticism. We have seen how such critical activity ends up helping to establish repentance's claims by positioning it as one among different universal categories of human experience, all of which are given definition by the inner thoughts of author and actor. In the case of confession, however, we find that scholarship has not turned the phenomenon into a similar object of study and classification, inquiring into the varied contexts and potentially different purposes of declaring, "I have sinned." It would seem that confession and repentance have become so closely associated that such a line of questioning is rarely pursued.[1]

If we are to overcome present inarticulacy around the relationship between confession and repentance, we may need to turn to earlier proponents of repentance for whom the relationship between the two still appeared, in some fashion, to be problematic, that is to say, in need of elucidation and establishment. A particularly illuminating example is found in the Mishneh Torah, the legal compendium of the medieval Jewish philosopher Moses Maimonides.[2] Here is my translation of the beginning of his discussion, the "Laws of Repentance":

The laws of repentance [contain] one positive commandment, namely, that a sinner repent of his sin before the LORD and confess.

> . . . When he does repentance and repents of his sin, he is obligated to confess before God, may he be blessed, for it is written: "When a man or woman commits any wrong . . . incurs guilt, they must confess the wrong that they have done" [Num. 5:6–7]. This refers to verbal confession, and this confession is a positive commandment.
>
> How does one confess? One says: "O LORD! I have sinned, erred, rebelled against you, doing such and such. And, behold, I am regretful and ashamed of what I have done, and I will never revert to this practice!" (Mishneh Torah, "Laws of Repentance," 1:1)

From Maimonides' account, it is possible to develop three complementary models for understanding the association of confession with repentance: (1) Repentance precedes confession as its *prerequisite*. An actual correspondence between the mental disposition and the rite itself need not be posited. We simply do not imagine that certain physical performances—and Maimonides expands this model to apply to the atoning power of sacrifice, corporal punishment, death, and the Day of Atonement (1:1–1:3)—would be efficacious in the absence of this privileged inner state.[3] (2) Confession is an *expression* of repentance. Repentance precedes confession, because confession is nothing other than the mental disposition's external manifestation, that is, its material, verbal form. As Maimonides writes later on: "One must confess *with his lips* and state all those matters that he has already determined *in his heart*" (2:2). Most strikingly, he reformulates the confessional formula to ensure its identification with repentance, adding to the standard, "I have sinned . . . against you," an additional phrase, ". . . and, behold, *I am regretful*" (1:1). (3) Confession also *causes* repentance. Thus, Maimonides positions repentance, in his revised confessional formula, as the logical consequence of confession: "I have sinned . . . *and, behold*, I am regretful" (1:1). Discourse around sin generates feelings of remorse. He develops this model further in his discussion of other "penitential practices" (2:4), and, especially, the blowing of the shofar on New Year's Day, the purpose of which, he says, is to rouse the sinner from his slumber to repentance (3:4). In short, the physical rite exists to prompt the mental disposition; a correspondence, not total identification, is therefore posited between the two.

For our purposes, what needs to be recognized is that these models are also tacit reading strategies, vital to our production of interiority,[4] whether as interpretations of ritual or as interpretations of those biblical passages, like Numbers 5:6–7, that are used to authorize ritual. They share a view that the represented phenomenon (i.e., confession) is a material manifestation indicating the presence of that which is not (i.e., repentance). Thus, Maimonides begins his "Laws of Repentance" with a discussion of confession by way of grounding repentance in the only manifestly mandated, "biblical" act that was available. Elements of each model may be at work when we read confession as repentance, but I believe that it is the second model, confession as an expression of repentance, that generally dominates,[5] as it does in Maimonides' own account. It accords with a common view of speech as the mind's register[6] and explains why confession and repentance elide in contemporary scholarship. If language voices thought, then repentance's speech act must be that long-standing Scriptural practice of confession, even if, as Maimonides realized and struggled with, confessional utterances make no allusion to repentance.[7] In the end, such reading strategies operate with a dualism of mind and body, thought and speech, that continues to define interpretation.

To restate the problem to which Maimonides' comments point: are we to understand confession as expressing repentance if the verbal utterance by which it is constituted, "I have sinned against you," fails to do so in its own terms?[8] In what follows, I will ask what alternatives ensue if we attach significance to the actual, material form of the confessional formula, if we attend to the fact that, when ancient Israelites and, for that matter, other ancient Near Eastern peoples talk about sin, they opt for linguistic constructions that develop the drama of sin around the very fact of sin's articulation, not its subjective residue. I come to the conclusion that confession concentrates within a single utterance many of the themes we explored with regard to fasting and prayer. It objectifies a subject's diminishment but does so in a manner that specifically locates its cause in the harm one has done to another, thereby placing the erstwhile agent at the disposal of a now-empowered victim. While moving broadly from cases of individuals to kings to communities, I will highlight in the readings that follow three different aspects of the phenomenon: confession as the realization of an entity's status,[9] as initiation of a particular social, relational state, and as participation in a broader restitutive process.

REALIZING SIN

Upon being accused of spying, and facing imminent incarceration, Joseph's brothers turn to each other and declare: "Alas, we are in a state of guilt [*'ašemim*][10] on account of our brother; we saw the distress he was in as he beseeched us, but we did not respond. Therefore, this distress has come upon us" (Gen. 42:21). The brothers make this confession-like utterance in private, or so they imagine, which may be what, for many readers, lends it a sense of being a window onto the brothers' inner worlds, a manifestation of what transpires when "events finally force to the surface their ever-present but hitherto unarticulated sense of guilt."[11] Such a penitential reading also depends upon the notion that pain, itself subjectively experienced, produces or "forces to the surface" a feeling of guilt, which, it is posited, was already latently present. For, how else are we to explain the immediacy with which the brothers, realizing the precariousness of their situation, move to declare their guilt?

If we view the brothers' utterance as reflecting events *around* them rather than *in* them, another way of contending with this immediacy presents itself. Recent studies have emphasized the ways in which "sin" in various biblical texts seems to have a quasi-objective existence; unless removed, it drags its agent down into a state of utter deprivation.[12] Accordingly, the brothers' statement may be seen as the verbal reflex of events, an announcement of the horrific trap that has come into evidence. It articulates what is oblique, what might have otherwise remained an amorphous string of bad luck as a purposeful, determined arraying of events against them brought on by the sin they identify. In so doing, they help realize their own punishment: estab-lishing their responsibility for events, attributing them to their own agency, firmly attaches their being to their newly emergent material conditions.[13] Quite apart from any particular ritual or religious end, the afflicted declare and, thereby, materialize their diminishment because that is their state. Like mourning and appeal, confessional speech can be seen as a behavioral pattern that, with a certain automaticity, follows upon and underlines the desperation of events.

Another association informing readings of the Joseph cycle as a drama of the brothers' repentance may be that of narrative with character develop-ment. Scholars inclined to look at the Hebrew Bible through the lens of litera-ture often see in Judah an arc of personal growth, beginning with the lessons he learns from his missteps with Tamar (Gen. 38).[14] Against this backdrop, it is not surprising to find that Judah's "powerful" utterance at the end of that narrative continues to be construed as "confession" or, at least, as repre-senting an initial moment in "his painful moral education,"[15] even as ancient readers' close association of confession with repentance helped establish a tra-dition of reading in this fashion long ago.[16] A less mediated reading of Judah's declaration, "she is in the right, as against me,"[17] for I did not give her to my son Shelah" (Gen. 38:26), which he utters upon being presented with evidence that exonerates Tamar, might be that this statement is not the opening of a psychological drama within Judah but the closing of a case against Tamar. After all, this utterance possesses a rather significant sort of legal efficacy: it stops Tamar's execution. In terms of both syntax and plot, such speech is the binary opposite of confession; it constitutes Judah's dismissal of his claim against Tamar. But, like confession, it realizes an entity's state of being, which, though discovered through events—the presentation of Tamar's totems (Gen. 38:25–26)—must be drawn out and activated in words.

Achan and his theft of proscribed property (Josh. 7) provides us with one last example of confessional speech's declarative power. It is hard, indeed, to arrive at an account of Achan's confession that revolves around a positive account of his subjectivity, for it is clear that his confession does nothing *for him*. After he fulfills Joshua's command to confess, he and his family are promptly stoned. What purpose, then, does his confession serve? Actually,

Joshua explicitly spells out the terms by which to understand its necessity: "My son, pay honor to YHWH, the God of Israel, give him acknowledgment, and tell me what you have done" (Josh. 7:19). Here, we even have the displacement of Achan as a matter of concern. Achan's "acknowledgment" constitutes a form of material exchange with YHWH—it *gives* him "honor"; he has stolen from YHWH, but now furnishes him with the acknowledgment he needs to justify his retributive actions and, thereby, restore his loss.[18] Achan is needed only to verify the overall proceedings in the midst of which he finds himself. He is asked to reflect and, ultimately, bring into effect, the condemnation and punishment that await him.

"WHEN ONE SINS AGAINST ANOTHER" (1 SAM. 2:25)

In each of the cases examined, we may detect a component to the force of confessional speech that goes beyond the announcement of individual states of being: the speech-act also initiates a certain relational state between wrongdoer and victim, placing oppressor into the hands of the oppressed, victimizer under the power of victim. It is for this reason that confession in biblical texts tends to occur in dialogue, assuming the form: "I have sinned *against you*," and not as the private murmurings of an overwhelmed conscience. Thus, Achan's confession allows Joshua, as representative of the aggrieved deity, to destroy him. Conversely, protestations of innocence place would-be victims, who press their claims, in the position of oppressors. Thus, in justifying war against Ammon, Jephthah carefully counters the claim that Israel has stolen Ammonite land, concluding: "I have done you no wrong; yet you are doing me harm by making war against me. May the LORD, who judges, judge today between the children of Israel and those of Ammon" (Judg. 11:27). Guilt or wrongdoing, it would seem, is the relational state whereby judgment invests one party with power over another. As such, while appreciating the "thingness," the quasi-objective reality commonly attributed to sin in biblical texts, it may be necessary to locate that material actuality, at least in certain cases, not in sin as a separate, nominalized existent, the private burden of individuals, but in sin relationships, the restructuring of social realities that ensues from the improper appropriation of another's property.

I would like to consider this dynamic further by examining literary evidence for what may have been an early Israelite practice around confession. Elements of this practice seem to be reflected in a poorly understood biblical proverb, which I reproduce here according to the Septuagint: "If one person sins against another, they may appeal on his behalf to the LORD. But, if he sins against the LORD, who will appeal on his behalf?" (1 Sam. 2:25). Whatever the original version of the verse (and the Septuagint version does most clearly develop the contrast that seems to be at work here between sinning against another and sinning against God),[19] what it recognizes is a practice whereby victim appeals on behalf of victimizer. Behind this practice may be a human institution involving the appropriation of property and its mediated return, but it is with YHWH as mediator that we encounter it in the otherwise unmediated terrain, one nation against another nation, that usually forms the context of biblical narrative. In two instances (Gen. 20 and Exod. 9:13–33), YHWH holds a foreign people and their leader in a deathlike state until they agree to release the Israelites of whom they have illegally taken possession *and* until a representative of Israel prays on their behalf. In the book of Numbers, Aaron and Miriam and, in another instance, the people challenge Moses and are made to suffer until they declare their act an error and beseech Moses to appeal for them (Num. 12:10–13, 21:4–9).

In each case, confession announces a judicial truth that is, by itself, contestable. That is to say, there is no attempt to establish the validity of certain claims through the production of evidence, nor is there some truth to which the wrongdoer must be forced to admit. Rather, the dynamic seems to be one of the ordeal, whereby truth is imposed through the exercise of power, through the successful production of pain.[20] Thus, YHWH contends with Pharaoh for his people, and, when Pharaoh declares, "I am guilty this time; the LORD is in the right, and I and my people are in the wrong" (Exod. 9:27), he is carrying out something closer to an act of submission, surrender, than to what we think of as confession, in the sense of an expression of conscience. Likewise, it is the fact of Miriam's leprosy that demonstrates the very force of the power structure, YHWH-backed Mosaic authority, to which she and Aaron accede by declaring their guilt. In these narratives, the theme of culpability is used to develop a desired hierarchy, whether of Israel over other nations or Moses over Israel. This concern is further evinced by their focus on prayer, which renders victimizer subject to victim, in the words of Aaron to Moses: "Oh *lord*, please do not place upon us [the burden of] sin" (Num. 12:11). In short, this interpersonal practice of affliction and appeal effectuates a certain power structure, with confession marking the decisive shift in relations between the two parties. Within this dynamic, the subjective state of the accused would appear to be of little consequence.

Earlier, we considered the brothers' confession as an effective utterance, as bringing into being their state of guilt, but does it have broader implications for the state of their relationship with Joseph? Throughout the narratives,[21] Joseph hides his true identity from his brothers and uses the fact of his control over their food source to subject them to various tortures, false accusations, entrapment, and even imprisonment. Why? In considering this question, which has come to be construed as an interpretive crux,[22] we might attend first to what the narrative itself immediately mentions upon Joseph's recognition of his brothers: "Joseph recalled the dreams that he had dreamed about them, and said to them: 'you are spies . . .'" (Gen. 42:9). Is the notion not that Joseph, brothers in hand, intends to pick up where the famine itself has left off, fulfilling the dreams he had of "reigning" over his brothers (Gen. 37:8), of their "prostrating themselves" before him (Gen. 37:10)? Perhaps, but readers of the Joseph narrative have betrayed a fairly consistent anxiety around any suggestion that Joseph shares nature's intention for him—that he aims at power. Accordingly, his actions have been understood as retributive, probative (testing his half-brothers' potential attitude toward him by seeing how they treat his full brother, Benjamin), and, above all, pedagogic—aiming at the transformation of his brothers through suffering.[23] In particular, Judah's willingness to make himself Joseph's slave in lieu of Benjamin has been read as an indication of the brothers' repentance, a culmination of Joseph's efforts.[24]

Still, the alternative presses itself upon us. Joseph has been engaged in a struggle with his brothers for the social and economic benefits, the expansion of the material self, that ensue from possessing the status of favored son. In getting rid of Joseph, his brothers are making sure Joseph never enjoys the fruits of his position, but covenantal promise, with all its arbitrariness, has been bestowed upon Joseph through his dreams, as it had been upon his father, Jacob, through an oracle to Rebecca. As Jacob had done, Joseph participates in its execution and obtains an unambiguous position of superiority as paterfamilias by the end of the narrative. And of course, in its traditional telling, this story of competition within the social unit of an ancestral family serves as a cipher for the later struggles of Jacob/Israel's tribes. It accounts for the eventual political and economic superiority of Ephraim and Manasseh, the tribes who trace their lineage to Joseph, over the others.

Against this backdrop of power struggle, we may see confession, again, as participating in a narrative of ordeal; culpability serves as an instrument that transforms and defines hierarchical relations among the brothers and, by extension, among the tribes. The brothers threw Joseph into the pit, and now he toys with them through incarceration on the basis of a pointedly trumped-up charge that only masks the real one to which they have confessed. Judah hardly comes before Joseph out of his own volition. Rather, Joseph and the force of events *compel* Judah to offer himself as slave in Benjamin's stead. As he says, "your servant has pledged himself for the boy to my father, saying, 'If I do not bring him back to you, I shall stand guilty before my father forever'" (Gen. 44:32). Judah must submit to Joseph if he is to preserve his standing in the house of his father, Jacob. And indeed, upon his deathbed, Jacob accords to Judah the status of a firstborn, precisely because his older brothers—Reuben, Simeon, and Levi—sinned against their father, while he never did (Gen. 49:3–10). In the idiom of Israelite politics, Judah and his descendants, the "House of David," may have their kingdom but only if they bow to Joseph, the tribal kingdom of the north, and show a willingness to protect their weaker neighbor, Joseph's brother, Benjamin. What we have then, when viewed through the prism of an ontology that would consider the self not as a spiritual being with a variable moral status but as a material expanse of power and possession, albeit one subject to the demands of justice, is a practice of confession as an act of surrender, as a way of effectuating the shift in power dynamics mandated by culpability. Sin places the oppressor into the hands of the oppressed, and so it is that Joseph's brothers, upon the death of their father and the loss of the protection he might have afforded, again acknowledge their guilt and ask for mercy, placing themselves before Joseph and announcing: "we are your slaves" (Gen. 50:18).

SIN'S TRANSLATION

Strikingly, "Joseph wept as they spoke to him" (Gen. 50:17). Likewise, the brother's earlier confession brought Joseph to the point of tears (Gen. 42:24). Joseph's recurring tears present us with a dramatic representation of confession's efficacy. If the story of Joseph is one of familial reintegration, albeit along new hierarchical lines, then confession plays a primary role in that restoration. Indeed, the other times Joseph weeps are all moments of reunion that stir him (Gen. 43:30, 45:16). But, how does confession produce pity? Why does Joseph cry?

In other contexts, it is not hard to see how confession might contribute to the successful denouement of the sin-based relationship. With wrongdoing defined, restitution can ensue. For instance, in the generalized scenario found in Numbers 5:5–7, a sequence is followed in which the wrongdoer first confesses and then makes whatever payment is due. Likewise, after an unsuccessful rebellion, Hezekiah declares to his Assyrian overlord: "I have erred; withdraw from me; and I shall bear whatever you impose upon me" (2 Kings 18:14). The declaration of sin slides immediately into the payment of tribute, all against the backdrop of Sennacherib's continued military hold over his wayward vassal. In the narratives we have already considered and a host of prayer texts, however, confession appears to accomplish something more. It does not just serve to establish legal status and hierarchy: it contains within it an element of appeal.

To understand confession's peculiar efficacy, we might do well to return to the point with which this discussion began, that confession is a form of practice whereby a subject realizes diminishment. Like fasting and prayer, it articulates and materializes what would otherwise remain oblique—amorphous and unmanageable—by locating suffering within the agency and, therefore, as adhering to the body of the sufferer. Even as it thereby brings matters to a head, confession tames and localizes affliction, empowering another to remove its burden from you. Its application of sin as a theory of explanation opens up possibilities for disposal or translation, whether through the means of restitution mentioned above or, directly, through confession's ability to formulate and manifest suffering and dependence. Indeed, in the preceding chapter, we discussed how evocations of affliction and sin often merge in petition, both serving as markers of need, but now we are in a better position to comprehend why that might be the case. Declaring guilt disrupts ordinary relations to bring on an extreme state that requires the victim's tending. Culpability and its attendant practice of confession must be seen as another mode of shaping pain.

In shedding tears upon his brothers' confessions, Joseph confronts their reduced state, weeps at their distress. In so doing, he can be seen as illustrating the proverb: "One who [attempts to] cover up his wrongdoings will not succeed, but one who acknowledges and abandons [them] will receive mercy" (Prov. 28:13),[25] with "mercy" here understood in its sense of a kin-based, pity-induced reintegration into the familial unit.[26] It is Joseph, not his brothers, who ends up in tears. He is moved to tears but also responds to their plight because he has been granted what he wants, because, in caring for them, he is fulfilling his new role as benevolent ruler. And so, he willingly translates the destruction they deserve into a state of vassalage.

SACRIFICE AND REPENTANCE

In order to get at confession's judicial and relational dimensions, this discussion began with instances drawn largely from the world of human affairs with a focus on the rich narratives of Joseph and his brothers. To continue exploring the dimensions of confession's efficacy, we may wish to consider whether the same structures of meaning and relation hold in the realm of divine–human affairs. Let us begin then with the ways in which repentance, through confession, is commonly mapped onto the sacrificial system and then continue with instances of prayer.

Repentance has been seen as a central "doctrine" of the cult, with direct correspondences in the priestly lexicon.[27] The chief interpretive instrument may be said then to be the identification of confession and repentance in the Bible as efficacious rites, their nominalization as practices. Thus, one term, 'ashem, is taken as denoting a psychological state of inner remorse, while another, hit-vadda, is seen as constituting an external rite of repentance, involving verbal acknowledgment of sin, that is reserved for cases of intentional transgression. The net result of these contrition-based construals is to push sacrifice toward being rendered as a system for the expression of individual "conscience"[28] or a disciplinary regime that develops "character" by demanding repentance as a prerequisite to participation.[29]

I would like to consider what alternatives might emerge if we were to encounter Leviticus 4–5, the key passages to employ these terms, without the hypostatization of repentance and confession as practices in mind. To be sure, my point is not whether temple worshipers ever experienced something like repentance. It would have been foolish indeed to not regret an error for which one incurred the cost of an animal sacrifice and not ensure that it did not recur. Rather, the question is whether the actual words and articulated practices surrounding offerings are aimed at cultivating such forms of subjectivity—was repentance identified and deployed as a relevant category of experience?—or whether they address other discursive concerns.

Rather than taking the individual subject and the unfolding of his or her mental processes as our point of departure, an approach perhaps encouraged by the casuistic form assumed by these passages of sacrificial law, I would like to focus attention on the overall system of sin- and guilt-offerings brought into effect. While other forms of sacrifice provide for a system of exchange between cult and patrons that is based on an expectation of future or acknowledgment of past divine succor, sin- and guilt-offerings operate according to a principle of compensation. As we have seen, practices of culpability can be used to establish power relations, states of liability and dependence, that require translation. In this case, such a practice grounds an entire system of financial support for the cult, and such translation has come to be referred to as "atonement." An entity sins against the deity, incurs liability, and must provide some form of compensation.

What sort of discourse would support such a system? Clearly, highlighting liability as a state of being, and addressing its mode of initiation and removal, would form primary concerns. The term 'ashem, which also happens to be that used by the brothers in their confessional declaration, most likely indicates not an interiorizing sense of guilt but precisely such a state of liability. It constitutes the necessary condition for the sacrificial proceedings laid out in these passages[30] and seems to bear with it the connotation that one is liable, specifically, to make a sin- or guilt- offering ('asham): "it is a guilt offering ['asham]; he is liable ['ashom 'asham] to the LORD" (Lev. 5:19). The presence of guilt can become clear on its own (e.g., Lev. 4:14), be made known by another (e.g., Lev. 4:23), or discovered by its agent (e.g., Lev. 5:2–4). In any event it needs to be made manifest. It is in the last scenario alone that the term hitvadda, "acknowledge" or "confess," operates, in which the subject is the one to ascertain and declare his or her state of guilt (Lev. 5:5). There is little reason to identify hitvadda as a specialized rite, that is, confession, pulling it away from the modes of identification found in the other cases and, thereby, attributing to it a special subjective weight or efficacy. Instead, like the others, it announces and brings into effect the culpability that forms the very basis of the sacrificial system these passages authorize, to which alone efficacy is attributed.

Confession not only establishes a general fact of culpability; it articulates the exact sin (or sins) responsible for that state, preparing each to be removed through the operation of the cult. Indeed, on the Day of Atonement, the effective disposal of sin requires the high priest's uttering Israel's sins while resting his hands upon the scapegoat. His confession is not brought on by some specific consciousness of sin but out of a sense of the danger that sin regularly poses for the sanctuary. This adds a new dimension to a theme explored earlier, namely, confession's ability to forestall disaster by giving it a name, identifying it, and packaging it as sin that, now properly contained, can be borne away safely.[31] In the case of the sin- and guilt-offerings brought upon discrete occasions, we may speak of a certain rationalization of the sin-suffering complex. To be *'ashem* is to be condemned; sacrifices are brought in anticipation of the affliction that is thought to follow from a state of guilt. In this reading of confession, we encounter in the practice of enumerating sins not the unburdening of a guilt-ridden conscience but the preemptive production of sin in order to translate the affliction that is thought to ensue from a state of guilt.

THE CHOICE OF CONFESSION

In the preceding chapter, we considered how the logic of appeal, as opposed to one of repentance, seems to dominate even when sin is mentioned in prayer. Now, we are in a position to see whether our further insights into the nature of confession can deepen our understanding of such prayers.

What is bound up in the choice to confess, in the decision to declare as "sin" one's affliction? We have seen what a state of affliction might look like that is not packaged by such a pronouncement. Mourning embraces helplessness and inexplicability and, ultimately, ends up in protest, as it embeds disaster upon the body and moves its practitioner toward the state of the abject and, even, the dead. This is the choice of Job. It sets God back, placing him in the position of Jephthah's Ammonites, of one who assails another without due cause. That can leave few avenues open for relief. Against this option, Job's friends urge him to declare sin, for they know that its announcement allows for a readier translation of suffering. Elihu's speech even identifies a precise method, a practice of confessional prayer, for affliction's removal: the sufferer "prays to God and is accepted by him . . . . He declares to men: 'I have sinned; I have perverted what was right; but I was not paid back for it'" (Job 33:26–27).

As we have seen, confession can be seen as one more mode of constituting pain, of packaging affliction, one that attempts to translate its effects by delineating its cause (i.e., the sin), and identifying a being who might have power over it (i.e., the victim). It renders affliction interpersonal and, therefore, subject to mediation and some form of control. It is thus peculiarly well suited to prayer. And so, we find in Psalm 32:

When I said nothing, my limbs wasted away, from my anguished roaring all day long.

> For night and day your hand lay heavy on me, my vigor waned as in the sum-
> mer drought.
>
> My sin I made known to you, my guilt I did not cover up.
>
> I declared, "I will confess my transgressions to the LORD," and you bore away
> the guilt of my sin. *Selah*. (Ps. 32:3–5)

It is God's hand that rests heavily upon the psalmist and his unnamed transgressions that are responsible for his affliction, but that reality is only determined as the psalmist's narrative unfolds. Is confession giving expression to
the guilty feelings of an increasingly overwhelmed conscience? I would suggest, otherwise, that what is at stake here is quite similar to what we saw with
regard to the sacrificial system, the necessity of a process of "making known,"
whether initiated by others or by oneself, whereby affliction is identified as
"sin" thus paving the way for its successful removal. Articulating sin makes
suffering disposable at the hands of a deity empowered to remove the burden
of guilt. What we have here is a form of appeal, a rather successful one according to the testimony of the psalmist, based not on a strategy of expression
but on one of identification. That is precisely the process at work, albeit in a
heightened form, in the so-called penitential psalm, Psalm 51: "Wash me thoroughly of my iniquity, and purify me of my sin; for I recognized my transgressions, my sin is before me always" (Ps. 51:4–5). What lies now clearly before
the psalmist is an entity, "sin," an objectification of his difficulties, that exists
in a form that he believes can be washed away. Again, defining sin has draw-
backs because of the liability it generates, but, ultimately, it allows for a not
uncomplicated removal of affliction.

The same sequence from suffering to sin as found in Psalm 32 can be
found in other psalms: "I said, 'YHWH, have mercy on me/heal me, for I have
sinned against you'" (Ps. 41:5).[32] What is the pertinence of sin in this psalm
and, specifically, in this verse, which otherwise focus on relief from affliction? I would suggest that its mention does more than simply spell out the
reason why divine intervention is needed; it spells out the power structure
whereby such intervention becomes plausible. The psalmist is in the power
of YHWH because of sin against him, and it is for that reason that he can
turn to *him* with hope for a resolution of his or her suffering. As such, the
sin relationship becomes just one of the many metaphorical bases, several
of which were discussed in the preceding chapter, in which the possibility
of divine intervention, help from some external power, is constructed and
comprehended.

Finally, confessional prayer should not be seen as a special case of subjectivity, as an evolution in ancient Israelite mentality, as is commonly assumed.[33]
In fact, such prayers are already found in much earlier Mesopotamian sources,
as they are based on the intertwined linguistic registers and social practices of
the ancient Near East, well attested in the following:

Today let me take my trespasses to you, snatch me from my foes,

and when you have seen where I fell, take pity on me,

When you have turned my dark stretches [of road] into daylight

let me pass through your gate, which releases from sin and wrongdoings, let me sing your praises,

let me confess, [roaring] like a bull, my trespasses to you, and let me tell of your greatness.[34]

Here, too, the process of "making known" sin, like that of praise "making known" the deity's greatness, revolves around a certain objectification, an articulation, one that allows for the ready translation of the petitioner's state.

THE KING'S SPEECH

Confession as a constructive practice, determining legal status and defining power relations, emerges particularly clearly in the context of kingship. Looking at the stories of David gives us the opportunity to examine one of the most elaborate narratives involving the articulation of sin, the account of the prophet Nathan's dramatic confrontation with David after his sin with Bathsheba through the so-called parable of the poor man and his beloved lamb (2 Sam. 12:1–6).[35] At stake in many interpretations of this passage has been the question of why Nathan confronts David with a parable rather than directly with an accusation. In one way or another, most readers view this choice as bound up in an appeal to David's conscience: "The direct appeal to the conscience of the offender intends to provoke a confession of wrongdoing."[36] What actually amounts to indirection is comprehended within this dualistic theory of rhetoric as persuasion, as a special way of directly accessing interiority; it is meant to amplify the murmurings of David's guilty conscience and overcome his psychological resistance to its expression. The narrative is thought to be structured around the unfolding of David's emotions: in hearing the parable, the king's pity for the poor man flows into anger against the rich one, which gives way to remorse for his own sin. The stirring of inner feelings is supposed to generate the pathos necessary for contrition and to lead the way to his confessional utterance, "I have sinned against the LORD" (2 Sam. 12:13), whose very brevity, rather than suggesting the tenuousness of this interpretation, is taken as indicating the intensity and sincerity of the remorse it is said to express.[37]

An alternative to the penitential reading, one that ensues from a hermeneutical refusal to move away from the materiality of both the prophet's and the king's speech in this narrative, would begin by attending to the transactional, effective quality of its various speech-acts. David responds to Nathan's speech, which is, after all, a plea for judicial intervention, with a declaration: "As the

LORD lives, condemned to death [*ben mavet*] is the man who did this!" (2 Sam. 12:5). In the mouth of the king, this utterance is not a representation of legal truth but a determination of the rich man's judicial state.[38] When Nathan turns to him and declares, "you're that man!" and proclaims the punishment that will befall David (2 Sam. 12:7–12), David effectuates the transfer of that state to himself through the declaration, "I have sinned against the LORD." It is this state, that of the *ben mavet*, "one who is condemned to death," which drives the narrative and forms the focal point of the remission that Nathan then declares: "The LORD has remitted your sin; *you shall not die*" (2 Sam. 12:13). Whereas the standard reading might see a progression of interior states within the narrative, I would suggest something more like a parallelism of speech-acts. David's judicial declaration and his confessional utterance both, in the end, realize his status as condemned. This principle receives explicit formulation elsewhere in the David narratives, "in making this pronouncement [against another], the king [himself] becomes like one who is condemned [*ke-'ashem*]" (2 Sam. 14:13). Formally and functionally, confession figures as the equivalent to judgment—as condemnation of the self.

Indeed, the necessity of Nathan's displacement of blame, his use of the parable, may proceed precisely from the impossibility in ancient Israel of self-judgment (as we see it today) as a product of didactic engagement and interior realization. Judgment, ultimately, is not a propositional statement of truth but an act of power.[39] As such, self-judgment, in the sense of confession, is only possible as a response to the prospective power arrayed against one, as we saw in the case of Joseph's brothers. Confession immediately follows upon Nathan's announcement of judgment against him. David used his power inappropriately against another weaker than he, and now matters have turned against him. In articulating sin, David acknowledges this diminishment, that he is now susceptible to divine punishment. His confession leads directly to the remission of his sin for, like Ahab's fasting in response to Elijah's pronouncement of his doom, it acknowledges YHWH's ultimate superiority, that there is a realm of justice beyond the king. It, therefore, goes a long way toward restoring and, indeed, generating the deity's power. What Nathan exploits through his indirection is David's position as king and, thus, as judge. The king's speech is the king's judgment, which now can be handily turned against the king to carve out a place—power—for YHWH in a world in which the king, otherwise, might be the only manifest form of justice.[40]

JUSTIFYING GOD

We have been speaking of a practice of "confession" in the Hebrew Bible. In fact, we have seen so-called confession operating in a variety of contexts, defying any attempts to identify it as a singular phenomenon. Nevertheless, when set against its contemporary instantiations and current understandings, common threads of difference emerge from within the ancient Israelite sources. It is possible to speak of a certain linguistic mode of expression, the declaration of sin, that has shared interchangeable characteristics, at least when viewed from our vantage point, which runs throughout the corpus. I would like to conclude by highlighting one last aspect of this practice of confession in the context of a rather distinctive genre of literature, a series of long, communally situated prayers that are represented in a number of postexilic texts. Here we encounter the practice of confession as a form of justification.

In several of the texts already examined, we can see how declaring sin is, ultimately, a way of accepting and validating an exercise of violence against oneself, of incursion into the otherwise-inviolable boundaries of one's being and its possessions. In the realm of human affairs, this could be used to justify, for instance, a transfer of wealth. But in the realm of divine affairs, it could be used to justify other forms of violation, those initiated by human communities in the name of the deity or other forms of suffering deemed to be brought on directly by God. Thus, as we have seen, Joshua commands Achan prior to his death: "My son, pay honor to YHWH, the God of Israel, give him acknowledgment, and tell me what you have done" (Josh. 7:19). God's honor, the repute of his power and authority, requires Achan to acknowledge his sin and, thereby, while also validating his excision from Israel, invalidate the complaint of abandonment Joshua had previously lodged against YHWH. Returning to Psalm 51, we find a very clear juxtaposition between declaring sin and the assertion of divine righteousness: "Against you, you alone, I have sinned; I have done what is evil in your sight. [I have announced it] so that you might be justified in your sentence, correct in your judgment" (Ps. 51:6). Drawing on the judicial backdrop of such language, declaring sin justifies the divine powers arrayed against one by identifying them as a legitimate product of the sin-based relationship. The confessional prayers to be examined below elevate this theme into a principle for comprehending exile.

Before looking at these texts, however, I would like to consider another that would appear to situate the sort of practice they represent as a single historical moment rather than an ongoing form of prayer. At the end of the book of Leviticus, we find a series of blessings and curses that, among other matters, describe the conditions of the nation's exile and return: "Those of you who survive will rot away because of their sin in their enemies' lands, and also because of their fathers' sins that are with them, they will rot. They shall acknowledge their sin and their fathers' sin" (Lev. 26:39–40).[41] Most commentators would see confession, here, as an expression of repentance and as an efficacious religious performance that is responsible for the redemption that ensues.[42] But, in this passage, confession does not appear to follow from contrition, but from the fact of their "rotting away,"[43] and redemption does not follow as a consequence of confession. Only after Israel is brought to its knees and pays its dues does God recall his covenant with their forefathers and redeem them from exile, out of his own faithfulness (26:41–44). What comes into clearest focus is not Israel's repentance but the remarkable contrast between Israel's behavior and that of their god; despite the evidence of the exile or, actually, in light of it, it is YHWH who remains faithful throughout.[44] In this context, I would suggest that acknowledging sin functions as a historical marker, a realization of exile's cause. It is said to be produced by Israel in the depths of exile, driven by the evident dissolution of their very beings, their "rotting away," captive in a foreign land. Rather like Joseph's brothers, they are forced to reflect and pronounce their state of deprivation as one that has its derivation in having sinned against another. In so doing, they justify action against them and highlight the beneficence of their ruler as seen in any continued intervention on their behalf.

In the confessional prayers found in Psalm 106, in the books of Ezra (9:5–15), Nehemiah (1:4–11, 9:6–37), and Daniel (9:3–19) as well as in a number of extrabiblical sources (e.g., Baruch 1:15–3:8), we encounter very much the same theme: a rehearsal of historical events that is replete with confessional utterances and that consistently juxtaposes God's faithfulness with Israel's iniquity. The prayers invariably come to something like the following conclusion: "You are in the right with respect to all that has come upon us, for you have acted faithfully, while we have acted wickedly" (Neh. 9:33). These texts, which have been subjected, as a group, to exhaustive study in recent years,[45] have been understood as "penitential prayers," as expressions of the people's repentance or, alternatively, as provoking them to repentance by reminding them of their sins, models that we explored earlier through the writings of Maimonides. Unlike in the case of Maimonides, where some awareness of the equivocal quality of confession still seems to reign—of the necessity, at the very least, for an exposition of these models—contemporary scholarship, to return to the point with which we began, simply seems to take them for granted and, thereby, to further the totalizing hermeneutics of repentance.

Rather than view confession in these prayers as an expression of a privileged inner act that is off the texts' plane of representation, I would suggest that we take the texts' own material representations most seriously, in this case the constant juxtaposition of divine righteousness with Israel's confession of sin. Indeed, it is possible to see them as two sides of the same coin: exile is Israel's responsibility, not God's. Establishing this fact is central to these prayers on a number of levels. There is, to be sure, a certain matter of etiquette, discussed in the previous chapter. It is hardly possible to turn to God for relief from your present difficulty, if it is one of your own making, without acknowledging that fact. To do otherwise would be to condemn one's request to failure.

And, indeed, in the case of exile and Israel's continued difficulties after the exile, there could be good cause to place the blame upon YHWH. But this leads us to a more fundamental observation regarding confession's place in these prayers. In these texts, confession is used to ground the very conditions that make prayer possible in a world after exile. It is a way of constructing divinity and a relationship to it when material realities would suggest, instead, the severing of ties. In this situation, the social practice of acknowledging sin with its implications for the formation of a relationship, albeit fraught, between victimizer and victim offered a pathway for continuing to conceptualize the possibilities of divine presence: "O YHWH, God of Israel, you are in the right. We were left a remnant, as is the case today. We are in a state of guilt before you; because of this, we cannot stand before you" (Ezra 9:15). And, yet, in so saying, of course, they managed to do precisely that.

SUMMARY

Despite a general lack of explicit scholarly treatment, the notion of confession as a penitential act seems to be based largely on a psychological interpretation of the phenomenon as the expression of a guilty conscience. Using the story of Joseph and his brothers' "confession" to develop alternative, less-mediated possibilities, we noted that saying "I have sinned" realizes sin, in that it declares its practitioner to exist in a state of liability and, ultimately, diminishment. That proves significant in establishing certain social realities, the subjection of the erstwhile victimizer to victim, and, at the same time, allowing for their successful translation. Beginning with cases drawn largely from the realm of human relations, we then moved on to consider the place of confession in the sacrificial system as well as in individual prayer. From there we treated the rather involved instance of a king's confession, David's guilt, and then the quite significant phenomenon of postexilic confessional prayers, where confession plays a role in justifying divine absence. As with practices of mourning and appeal, we sought to comprehend articulating sin as effecting material states, enmeshed in social relations, and shaped according to the needs of communication, rather than as the private murmurings of any core, inner being.

PART II

Language and Pedagogy

CHAPTER 4

✧

A Material "(Re)turn to YHWH"

When you are in distress . . . and return to the LORD your God.
Deuteronomy 4:30

THE NOMINALIZATION OF *SHUV*

The possibility of identifying concepts such as repentance as real existents—indeed, of any sort of theological discourse—and of arranging a structure of performances—rites—around them is dependent on their formulation as components of a technical, in this case, religious terminology. This process invariably entails taking available, local, and, ideally, already prestigious (and, hence, often "biblical") terms and positing them as universals. In prior chapters, we have already encountered a tendency to fold the penitential self into common renderings of specific terms. "Submission" (*nikhna*) has been understood as a lowering of the inner self, a sort of humility that is commonly identified with repentance.[1] Use of "sin" language too has been seen as indicative of a speaker's contrite consciousness, rather than as a reference to an objective existent to be contended with and disposed of. We even saw, among several interpreters, *'ashem* being put forward as a technical priestly term for "remorse." But none of these, apparently, have the number of attestations or the suggestiveness to stand as the appointed articulation of "repentance" in the Hebrew Bible. That honor has been reserved for a peculiar phrase, "return [*shuv*] to YHWH," whose range proves far more impressive, from the early, eighth-century prophets, to Jeremiah, to the deuteronomistic writings, and on to a variety of postexilic texts.[2] Here, we have an ancient Hebrew lexical item—what's more, an utterance of prophets—that could be seen as voicing, indeed, as giving birth to, the idea of "repentance."[3] In fact, we shall see in a concluding chapter that it is from the biblical root, *shuv*, that the term for repentance in rabbinic literature, *teshuva*, is formed. The Greek term for repentance, *metanoia*, comes to be associated with it as well, though not yet, as is sometimes presumed, in the Septuagint, which prefers to render it more literally with variations of the verb -*strepho*, "turn." We thus find a traditional identification of the phrase, "return to YHWH," with the very idea of repentance, an association that has been upheld, more or less, by modern scholarship.

But what precisely does it mean to "return to YHWH"? In the standard scholarly rendering, "return," *shuv*, indicates that "the mover arrives again at an original point of departure,"[4] that the subject was once with God, left him, and then came back to him again. Obviously, this is not intended in anything like a literal or physical sense. Accordingly, the idea of "returning to God" is seen as metaphorical, as expressing something other than its material meaning. Indeed, the most definitive study of the phrase has concluded that it ultimately communicates an abstract concept: a return to obedience, a renewed fulfillment of the covenantal obligations to YHWH.[5] Bound up in this notion of covenantal obedience we find the familiar prioritization of subjective, moral, and religious states.[6]

Against the common identification of *shuv* with repentance stands the evidence of its apparent diachronic diversity. Thus, for instance, in the writings of the eighth-century prophets, among whom this usage is said to have begun, we are missing the components necessary for a complete narrative of return. In direct connection to the phrase, "return to YHWH," we do not find a sense of a prior state of closeness, a current state of distance, or a possibility of renewed closeness to YHWH. In fact, the so-called "covenantal usage" only receives clear expression in later biblical passages, as in the following: "You admonished them in order to turn them back to your teaching" (Neh. 9:29). Here the anthropomorphism of "return to YHWH" fades into the background and is replaced by an explicitly nomistic concern for obedience. According to the accepted theory, this is a difference in form but not a significant difference in meaning. But, is that really all?

What lies behind this disinterest in differentiation is the attempt, already evidenced in early Judaism and Christianity, to provide a "supraclass, eternal character to the ideological sign" of, in this case, biblical *shuv*, "to make the sign uniaccentual."[7] The dominance of "repentance" as a concept is partly assured through the common scholarly nominalization of *shuv* as a singular process concerned with "obedience," a conscious decision to follow the will of God. Even those scholars who would speak of different authors and works having different *conceptions* of repentance, depending on time and place, end up positing repentance as a universal, eternal type, just one that is refracted through ever-changing individual subjectivities.[8] An alternative would be to recognize that the phrase and its elements are variously constituted by fundamentally *distinct* ideological superstructures within ancient Israelite literature and beyond, that language is, in other words, conventional and interpersonal, a matter shaped by society and its needs, not an essence or expression of individual consciousness.[9] In what follows, I will attempt to sift through and account for variation in the linguistic material found in the Hebrew Bible that has come to be univocally associated with repentance and to explore alternative material concerns not marked by interiority and moral states, the abstractions that metaphorical renderings of *shuv* have generated. To do so, we will need to estrange ourselves from our current associations with the phrase, especially as they appear in prophetic literature, which will be discussed more broadly in next chapter, for the language of "return to the LORD" has become a commonplace and attained a falsely natural hue.

THE PHILOLOGY OF *SHUV*

To begin, we must clarify something about the meaning of the verb *shuv* itself, generally (and, often, mistakenly) translated as "return."[10] I would suggest that *shuv* instead describes a dramatic change in direction, motion that is opposite in some fashion, a turning away/aside/around/back/off.[11] The difference between *shuv* and "return" is located in their respective points of reference. The Hebrew term *shuv* apprehends a situation from the perspective of the one in motion, indicating a reversal in his or her trajectory. The English term "return" perceives movement in relation to an original point of departure and, therefore, denotes arrival back at that location.[12] To state the matter in slightly different terms, *shuv* depicts the actual process of motion, the turning, while "return" focuses on its result, the arrival back.[13] Let us throw this subtle distinction into bolder relief by exploring a few uses of *shuv* in the biblical material.

One of the main problems addressed by scholarship on the root *shuv* has been that it seems to possess two very different, even opposite, meanings.[14] It can mean both turning back toward a place (often translated as "return") and turning away from a place. Consider the following two examples: "You shall hallow the fiftieth year and proclaim release throughout the land for all its inhabitants. It shall be a jubilee for you: each of you shall return to [*ve-shavtem 'el*] his holding and each of you shall return to [*tashuvu 'el*] his family" (Lev. 25:10). "Then Joab sounded the horn, and the troops turned off from [*vayyashov min*] their pursuit of Israel, for Joab held them back" (2 Sam. 18:16). I would argue that the need to translate *shuv* differently in these two verses tells us more about the English language and its perspectival emphasis than about the Hebrew verb. Both passages use *shuv*, because both speak of a complete alteration in course. Whereas *shuv* lends the sense of a particular kind of turn, it is the prepositions with which *shuv* is paired that determine whether the emphasis in the verse is placed on what the agent turns toward or what he or she turns away from. Turning "away" (*min*) and turning "toward" (*'el*) can be, ultimately, the same physical motion of reversal. For that reason, we might do better to translate the Leviticus verse as, "head back to his hold-ing", "head back to his family," for an important element of the emphasis here lies not with the attainment of former place by the disenfranchised ("return") but with their release, the freedom to go back home. The fact that *shuv* may be joined with both "positive" and "negative" prepositions—most commonly "to" (*'el*) and "from" (*min*)—hardly indicates anything like two separate mean-ings.[15] On the contrary, as a verb of motion, the sense of *shuv* emerges relative to the points from which and toward which an individual moves.

In cases where prepositions are absent altogether, the inadequacies of "return" as a translation are particularly clear: "Return, return, O Shulammite! Return, return, that we may look upon you"[16] (Songs 7:1). Is the speaker really asking the Shulammite to "return" to him so that he can see her? (If she's so dis-tant, how can she hear his plea?) We might do better to translate as something like: "Turn back/around. Let's have a look at you!" Here is another example, taken from a different kind of human interaction: "[Wisdom] will save you from the alien woman . . . . All who go to her cannot return and find again the paths of life" (Prov. 2:16–19).[17] In order to understand *shuv* as "return," the translators introduce the word "again," not attested in the Hebrew. I would translate: "all who go into her won't get away; they won't survive" (i.e., attain the paths of life). The real drama of the verse is the impossibility of escape, of getting away, for "her house sinks down to Death, and her course leads to the shades" (Prov. 2:18).

Shuv is frequently employed in contexts of return, but even then it high-lights a different moment in the process. Consider the following: "he [the king] must not . . . return the people to Egypt . . . since the LORD has said to you, 'You must never return *that way* again'" (Deut. 17:16). The use of *shuv* in conjunction with the language of paths suggests that it actually depicts direc-tion and movement: "you must never head back that way again" (i.e., in the direction of Egypt). A similar point emerges from an exchange between Naomi and Ruth in the book of Ruth. One might translate: "And she [Naomi] said, 'See, your sister-in-law has returned[18] to her people and to her gods; return after your sister-in-law.' But Ruth said, 'Do not press me to leave you or to turn back from following you!'" (Ruth 1:15–16). But the use of "return" to describe the action of Ruth's sister-in-law, Orpah, is misleading, as the primary point is not the return of Orpah to Moab but her abandonment of Naomi. It main-tains both aspects. Furthermore, we find side-by-side the purportedly dif-ferent meanings of *shuv*. Naomi's imperative that Ruth "return after her sister-in-law" and Ruth's refusal to "turn back from following Naomi" each use the same verb to depict the same proposed act, Ruth's altering her course to follow Orpah rather than Naomi.

Biblical Hebrew (especially in narrative) frequently atomizes movement by using a chain of motion verbs.[19] This stylistic tendency provides us with a further opportunity to isolate the range of *shuv*. The following translation tries to preserve the feel of the Hebrew in a verse from the book of Numbers: "Then Balaam got up, left, and went back [*vayyashov*] to his place, and Balak also went his way" (Num. 24:25). But in its attempt to avoid redundancy in English, the translation extends the action depicted in the verse beyond what the Hebrew probably denotes to include Balaam's actual travel back home. Coming on the heels of the more elaborate clause about Balaam, the parallel clause about Balak probably encapsulates in fewer words what its actual sense is: Balaam and Balak departed from one another. This displacement of *shuv* in the second clause involving Balak leaves us with a rather clear picture of *shuv*'s role in the first. "Getting up" indicates the initial breaking-up of a meeting, "leaving" motion away, and *shuv* the direction of that motion.

To depict arrival, an attainment of place, biblical Hebrew often uses the verb *bo'*. It is therefore significant to find that *shuv* can appear before *bo'* in a chain of motion verbs: "Then the LORD said to him [Elijah], 'Go, return [*shuv*] on your way to the wilderness of Damascus; when you arrive [*u-ḇa'ta*], you shall anoint Hazael as king over Aram'" (1 Kings 19:15). Once again, we should translate "head back on the (same) path (you took before)," rather than "return." *Shuv* clarifies the direction of the departure already indicated with the first verb in the sequence, "go," and *bo'* indicates actual arrival at the intended destination. *Shuv* alone does not do the work of indicating attainment of place.[20]

This alteration in the definition of *shuv* very much contravenes the narrative assumed in the standard account of "return to YHWH," which relies heavily on the metaphor of attaining a prior point of departure for depicting a return to covenantal obedience. Its focus on relative motion, on performance, rather than on the habitation of a defined space does not permit the sort of nominalization of an inner state, "repentance," that *shuv* commonly undergoes in its metaphorical understanding. It suggests, instead, something closer to an act of appeal, an active turning to or seeking out the person of God, a more material, less mediated understanding. This possibility, of course, fits in well with the primacy of appeal in ancient Israel, as explored in earlier chapters. As we shall see, early attestations of the phrase place its operative image outside the realm of covenant, in another area of human activity altogether, a special instance of appeal, namely that of oracular inquiry.

THE *SHUV* OF APPEAL

Oracular Inquiry as Institution

The interpretation of ancient Israelite religion on the basis of a concept of covenant—forged, in part, through the drawing of parallels between ancient Near Eastern political treaties and biblical literature—has become a hallmark of modern biblical scholarship.[21] It suggests a certain structuring in the power dynamics of the relationship between YHWH and Israel as based on moral and religious imperatives. Israel has entered into a relationship with its deity and, now, must obey a series of established laws. "Covenant" is an abstraction that is thought to undergird all,[22] which is, perhaps, why it is assumed to operate in our case, even if *shuv* phraseology is completely absent from political treaties, where irrevocable curses are the promised fate of the rebellious.

While covenantal practices are attested in ancient Israelite literature and may be responsible, even, for elements of its literary shaping, such ceremonies would have been, at best, periodic, not a quotidian part of life in ancient Israel. Though perhaps less visible to modern readers, oracular inquiry, by contrast, is ubiquitous there and would have figured prominently and regularly in a variety of social settings. Rebecca, when she perceives a struggle within her womb, "went to inquire of the LORD" (Gen. 25:22). Jacob stops at the sanctuary in Beersheba to determine whether to depart from the land (Gen. 46:1–4). Israelite kings consult prophets on everything from illness (e.g., 1 Kings 14:1–18) to warfare (e.g., 1 Kings 22:6–28). Indeed, as is apparent in the narrative literature, oracles are the basic unit of prophetic speech and therefore form the building blocks of prophetic literature. Various terms for oracular inquiry, *bqš* and *drš* ("seeking"), appear prominently in the Psalms, where the pious, for instance, are referred to as YHWH's "seekers."[23] Aside from revealing the worshipper's fate, such "seeking" functions as petition: "I sought out the LORD, and he answered me; he saved me from all my terrors" (Ps. 34:5). In short, oracle seeking would have been a basic means of interfacing with the deity.

Assorted instances suggest that inquiry transpired either at established cultic sites, through a prophetic intermediary, or both together. Either way, inquiry would have necessitated and is represented as a form of movement. Saul travels to "seek" his lost asses and ends up going to Samuel to "seek" their whereabouts from God (1 Sam. 9:3–14). Seeking an oracle shares the spatial component that is basic to sacrifice but also associated with praise: "*Come,* let us sing joyously to the LORD" (Ps. 95:1). An interiorizing view of worship may lead us to dismiss such references to motion as figures of speech, but they are central to ancient Israelite representations of the encounter with the divine as localized in physical space: "O heeder of prayer, all *go* to you!" (Ps. 65:3). And the same holds true for the worship of foreign gods: "they *went* and worshipped other gods, bowing down to them" (Deut. 29:25).

Shuv too, in early biblical narratives, figures as a verb of motion that serves as a prelude to encounter with the deity. After Samuel indicates that YHWH has rejected Saul as king, Saul begs that Samuel "bear my sin and *return* with me, so that I might prostrate myself before the LORD." And Samuel responds: "I will not *return* with you; for you have rejected the LORD's command" (1 Sam. 15:26). What is intended here? Saul is proposing that Samuel "turn aside" with him at Gilgal to help him appeal to YHWH, that he utilize his prophetic power of intercession on his behalf. Likewise, after his first confrontation with Pharaoh ends unsuccessfully, Moses seeks another audience with the deity: "Then Moses *returned* to the LORD and said, 'O LORD, why did you bring harm upon this people? Why did you send me?'" (Exod. 5:22). Where does this conversation take place? According to one medieval commentator, Rabbi Samuel ben Meir, the use of *shuv* must mean that Moses returned to the place he first spoke with God. This seems highly unlikely. Moses communicates with and receives instruction from YHWH multiple times throughout the Pharaoh saga, apparently without extensive travel. More specifically, when Moses appeals to the deity on behalf of Pharaoh, he consistently "goes out from Pharaoh's presence" and then prays to YHWH (e.g., Exod. 8:8). Motion away from the normal, social company of others, "turning aside," conjoined with an element of a positive turn generate a sense of the deity as occupying a distinct space and provide the basic imagery used to mark out the dimensions of encounter.[24]

With outcry, considered in chapter 2, as a model of appeal, God or his representative, a divine hero, goes to the victim. The imagery of oracular inquiry functions differently, suggesting a purposeful attempt to seek help from the deity, movement toward him. By inquiring of God in his place or through his human representative, the supplicant pays homage and demonstrates dependence: whatever ensues, whether for good or for bad, is marked as the work of the deity. Failure to consult YHWH could suggest his impotence or irrelevance and force the deity to find another way to assert supremacy. When the wicked king Ahaziah suffers an injury, he sends forth messengers: "Go inquire of Baal-zebub, the god of Ekron, whether I shall recover from this injury" (2 Kings 1:2). YHWH sends his messenger, Elijah, to intercept them: "Go and confront the messengers of the king of Samaria and say to them, 'Is there no God in Israel that you go to inquire of Baal-zebub, the god of Ekron?'" (1:3). It is the insult of consulting Baal-zebub, not the violation of a covenantal norm, for which Elijah takes Ahaziah to task. The question is a quasi-political one: to whom does one turn when in trouble?[25]

We have altered our semantic sense of this "turn to YHWH," and now we have found in oracular inquiry, in terms of both its physical dimension and theopolitical significance as a way of marking dependence, a potential basis upon which to develop a nonmetaphorical understanding of the phrase, of the material processes that inform its sense. Let us turn then to the eighth-century prophets and test this alternative model in those works where we find the earliest evidence of the phrase's concerted use.

Amos and the Location of YHWH

While we cannot be certain that the passages therein are the authentic words of the named prophets, a certain common approach to *shuv* as a form of appeal does emerge in the scrolls associated with the early prophetic figures, Amos, Hosea, and Isaiah, that stands out against later usages found in those of Jeremiah and Ezekiel as well as other late nonprophetic texts.

As a confined test case, I begin with Amos. Our phrase figures prominently there in only one passage, albeit one that is extensive and central to the book. The passage begins on a sardonic note: "Go to Bethel and transgress; to Gilgal, and transgress even more: present your sacrifices the next morning and your tithes on the third day" (4:4). In this opening section, YHWH indicates his absence from these cultic sites; he is nowhere to be found at Bethel or Gilgal. He soon asserts his presence, however, in the people's suffering: "As for me, I have given you cleanness of teeth in all your towns, and lack of food in all your settlements" (4:6). Following this summary statement of Israel's condition, there appears a sequence of plagues detailing the means by which such famine has been effectuated, including drought, pestilence, and warfare. Like the plagues against Pharaoh in Egypt, these events partake of a gratuitously miraculous nature: "three months before harvest time: I would make it rain on one town and not on another" (4:7). In this fashion and by repeatedly adopting the first-person singular, the deity underscores that he is the author of Israel's affliction. It is in this context that we find, after mention of each plague or series of plagues, the refrain: "Yet you did not *shuv* to me."[26] The phrase does not figure as part of exhortation or as a present possibility. The people have failed to undertake a movement to YHWH, one that, in keeping with the theme of personal responsibility raised throughout the passage, presumably would entail some acknowledgment of YHWH's role. What is the nature of this movement?

In the standard reading, the plagues and the movement toward YHWH, which seem to be so closely bound together, must be assigned completely separate identities.[27] That is to say, affliction, an enforced, external physical state, is supposed to lead to, to produce, an event that is different in kind, that is freely-willed, personal and subjective—namely, repentance. This reading proceeds with a theory of mental processes that presumes a mind–body dualism. Furthermore, the repentance it proposes is bound up in a consciousness of sin, but none of the five sections describing plagues ever suggest that their sinfulness is even brought to the attention of the people. An alternative would be to posit an intrinsic connection between divine act and what was supposed to be the appropriate human response. The most obvious and immediate reaction to disaster would be petition; if you want for food, you ask for it. The question is: from where? The rhetorical power of these passages would seem to aim at providing an answer to this question. Israel's afflictions, as we have seen, are the personal responsibility of YHWH. To receive relief, Israel must turn to him. This passage therefore constitutes a variation on what we might see as a genre of enumerated affliction (several examples were seen in chapter 2), which establishes YHWH's power over the full range of natural and human-made crises (drought, pestilence, warfare, etc.) by presenting appeal to him, often in the form of a refrain, as the necessary mode of resolution for each affliction.

Instead of appealing directly to the deity, the people offer sacrifices at Bethel and Gilgal. Recall the pseudo-call to worship at these cultic sites with which the passage begins. Attendance there is juxtaposed to the sort of "turning" to him that YHWH desires. We find the same contrast in a related passage, here with the parallel term, "seek": "Thus said YHWH: Seek me, and you will live. Do not seek Bethel, nor go to Gilgal . . . for Gilgal shall go into exile, and Bethel shall become a delusion" (Amos 5:5). God has abandoned these sanctuaries, and it is futile to seek him there, but the two options presented in this verse are similar in kind. That is to say, the opposition between "seeking" YHWH, on one hand, and "seeking" Bethel or Gilgal, on the other, derives from the fact that they are rival destinations, alternative places from which to seek help and blessing. What exactly "turning aside to YHWH" would look like cannot be said with absolute certainty, but it is possible to recognize the structures of appeal in which it participates. It appears to have been envisioned as a form of inquiry that existed apart from the central cults, quite possibly in conjunction with the more peripheral figure of the prophet.[28] Amos himself is sent away and prevented from prophesying at Beth El (7:13). Along with his prophet, God has abandoned these sites and must be sought elsewhere, perhaps in the person of the prophet himself.

Hosea and the Source of Sustenance

Undoubtedly the richest collection of early *shuv* material is found in the scroll attributed to the eighth-century prophet, Hosea. We have already seen in Amos evidence of an association between *shuv* and the language of seeking. Hosea rather consistently uses this combination of terms: "Though Israel's glory was crushed before their very eyes, they did not *shuv* to YHWH, their God; they did not seek him in spite of everything" (Hosea 7:10).[29] The parallelism with "seek" strongly suggests that *shuv* should be seen as bound up in processes of appeal. And so does the context. As in Amos, the disciplinary discourse in which pain improves us does not appear to be what is at work here. If we untie the traditional association between *shuv* and "repentance," a less mediated reading would be that affliction should lead a nation to consult their deity and seek help from him. The failure to do so is an act of snubbing that itself becomes the central difficulty at hand. The above verse continues: "But Ephraim was like a silly dove with no mind; they cried out to Egypt and traveled to Assyria!" (Hosea 7:11). For Elijah, as we saw above, the problem was consulting other gods; for Amos, reliance on rejected cultic sites. For Hosea, it is dependence upon foreign nations—appealing to them, going to them—that constitutes a rejection of the fact that "I am the one who redeems them" (Hosea 7:13).[30] Since movement toward other sites of power is the crux of the problem, just as Elijah overtook the messengers of Ahaziah on their way to Baal-zebub and Amos, with his sarcasm, discouraged attendance at Bethel and Gilgal, according to Hosea, YHWH will overtake Israel *on their way* to the foreign nations: "As they go, I will spread my net over them; I will bring them down like birds in the sky" (Hosea 7:12).

The following may be the most prominent *shuv* passage in the book:

> Yet when Ephraim became aware of his sickness, Judah of his sores, Ephraim went to Assyria—he sent envoys to a king to act as champion! He will never be able to cure you, will not heal you of your sores. No, I will be like a lion to Ephraim, like a great beast to the House of Judah; I, I will attack and stride away, carrying the prey that no one can rescue; and I will return to my abode—till they are utterly destitute on account of their guilt.[31] In their distress, they will seek me and beg for my favor: "Come, let us turn aside to the LORD: he attacked, and he can heal us: he wounded, and he can bind us up." What can I do for you, Ephraim? What can I do for you, Judah? Your affection is like morning clouds, like dew so early gone. (5:13–6:4)

The dimensions of "turning aside" in this passage resemble what we have seen thus far: the close association between seeking and appeal, and the contrast between seeking YHWH and resorting to other nations for aid. The passage also happens to reveal the basis in physical reality for "going" to the nations, namely the sending of messengers. Like Amos, Hosea also depicts the deity as concerned to establish his identity as Israel's afflicter ("I, I will attack and stride away") and presents "turning aside to YHWH" as the natural response to suffering induced by the deity ("he attacked, and he can heal us").

Relief, however, is not forthcoming. Why? Scholars have been quick to suggest that *shuv* fails because it was not performed correctly.[32] This reading follows from the assumption that what God undoubtedly wants more than anything else is the religious or moral transformation of his subjects, that he is, in the end, a pedagogue, albeit a rather unsuccessful one who remains deeply disappointed in his pupils. But this passage provides little that suggests improper performance, a lack of the requisite sincerity. Rather, it focuses on the temporal inadequacies of Israel's "turn"; it comes too late, after they have already insulted their deity by appealing to Assyria.[33] The temporal limitations on *shuv* are more suggestive of the self-interested anthropopathic realities behind appeal than the self-control and teleological presumptions that are bound up in a notion that God desires the people's true repentance. The people can turn to their deity when in need—indeed, such petition is one of the basic ways of defining divine power and delineating God's relationship with the people—but he will turn on them if they come too late. Indeed, after having sought the help of others, there is a lot riding on their utterly failing not just by way of spite, but in order to clarify their true source of sustenance.

The well-known story in Hosea of the prophet and his prostitute wife further reinforces this concern for the identification of sustenance's source. Hosea marries a woman who, by dint of her trade, is accustomed to being provided for by multiple men, and the drama begins when Hosea's wife acts on the basis of a misperception: "She said to herself: 'I will go after my lovers, who supply my bread and my water, my wool and my linen, my oil and my drink'" (Hosea 2:7). In seeking her welfare through the others, "she did not realize this: 'It was I [Hosea] who bestowed on her the new grain and wine and oil; I who lavished silver on her and gold'" (Hosea 2:10). And Hosea, embodying YHWH, interferes with her misplaced pursuit, just as the deity interrupts Israel's attempt to seek sustenance from alien sources: "Assuredly, I will hedge up her roads with thorns and raise walls against her, and she shall not find her paths. Pursue her lovers as she will, she shall not overtake them; and seek them as she may, she shall never find them" (Hosea 2:8–9). Having learned now where to seek her support, "she will say to herself: 'I will go and turn back to my first husband, for then I fared better than now'" (Hosea 2:9).[34] But now, he refuses to support her: "Assuredly, I will take back my new grain in its time and my new wine in its season, and I will snatch away my wool and my linen that serve to cover her nakedness" (Hosea 2:11). Hierarchy is conceptualized not along the steady lines of obedience but in the more dynamic form of pursuing sustenance, material exchange, and acknowledgment, hence the necessity of the woman's properly identifying her source of well-being, "my bread and my water, my wool and my linen, my oil and my drink" (Hosea 2:7).[35] In the end, emphasizing yet more her dependence, restoration is said to ensue as a gift from the husband, who, having secured full recognition, resumes providing for his wife: "I will give her her vineyards" (Hosea 2:17). Then, she will call out only his name (Hosea 2:17–18), with the parallel in the life of Israel, of course, being that they commit their sacrifices to YHWH and seek blessing at sites dedicated to his name alone: "the Israelites will *turn* and seek the LORD their God and David their king—and they will thrill over the LORD and over his bounty in the days to come" (Hosea 3:4–5). *Shuv* enters into the political—it has implications beyond mere sustenance—but it does so along the model of exchange.[36] As we saw with "crying out," appeal generates hierarchical relations. As Hosea complains elsewhere, "they *turn* to the land of Egypt and Assyria is their king" (11:5).

Isaiah, Reliance, and the Agent of Pain

The book of Isaiah (and now I speak largely of those portions of the work likely to date from the pre-exilic period, i.e., "First Isaiah") continues in the same vein with regard to *shuv*. In certain respects, Isaiah develops themes already discussed with yet greater clarity: "For the people has not turned [*shav*] to him who struck it and has not sought the LORD of Hosts" (Isa. 9:12). Clearly, in the operative metaphor, the point is not to "return" to one who beats you but to "turn" to him and plead for the beating to stop, to have its effect removed. Once again conjoined with the language of seeking, *shuv* speaks to the necessity of identifying YHWH as Israel's assailant and, subsequently, as the one empowered to heal: "he heals the wound inflicted by his blow" (Isa. 30:26). To the extent that human action interacts with this divine exercise in pain and mastery, it is in the capacity of appeal to mark YHWH's agency and serve as a catalyst for his healing.[37]

Isaiah associates another instructive range of terms with the *shuv* tradition: "Ha! Those who go down to Egypt for help, who *lean* [i.e., rely] on horses! They have *put their trust*[38] in abundance of chariots, in vast numbers of riders, and they have not *looked* [*sha'u*] to the Holy One of Israel, they have not *sought* the LORD" (Isa. 31:1). The word for "look" in this verse is an unusual verb that has some suggestive orthographic resemblance to *shuv*.[39] In any event, another one of the terms in this verse, "lean" (*š'n*), also figures in another passage from Isaiah, this time with *shuv*: "the remnant of Israel and the escaped of the House of Jacob shall lean no more upon him that beats it [probably: Assyria],[40] but shall lean consistently on the LORD, the Holy One of Israel. Only a remnant, a remnant of Jacob, shall *turn* [*yashuv*] to the mighty God" (Isa. 10:20–21). The theme of competition between YHWH and the nations for Israel's reliance is already familiar from Hosea. What concerns the prophet is the question of dependence, that they should turn to their God rather than relying on other locales of power.

With regard to the present failure of *shuv*, we also find a striking innovation in Isaiah. YHWH commands the prophet: "Dull that people's mind, stop its ears, and seal its eyes—lest, seeing with its eyes and hearing with its ears, it also grasp with its mind and turn [*shav*] and be healed" (Isa. 6:10). Whereas Hosea maintains that YHWH rejects a late-breaking appeal, Isaiah suggests that YHWH seeks to prevent it in the first place. The people must remain ignorant of their doom and its source, otherwise they might "turn" and "be healed." Again, understanding this "turn" as appeal allows us to see it as existing in a natural sequence with what precedes, affliction, and what follows, healing. What we find in penitential readings of this passage is a well-attested but rather arbitrary tradition of translating *shuv* as "repent" whenever it is not followed by a prepositional phrase, exposing further the nominalization of *shuv* as repentance.[41] It usually asserts itself as a metaphorical reading of *shuv*, but is revealed overtly when that reading cannot be sustained due to the lack of a prepositional phrase.

One may note a final novelty with regard to *shuv* in the book of Isaiah, namely the expansion of its scope to include the nations: "The LORD will afflict and then heal the Egyptians; when they *turn* to the LORD, he will respond to their entreaties and heal them" (Isa. 19:22). The use of *shuv* with regard to the nations clearly argues against its metaphorical reading as "return." When were they with God, such that they must now return to him? Here, we find the same themes that we have highlighted in the rest of Isaiah: the attribution to YHWH of the power to wound and heal, the immediacy of *shuv* as a response to suffering, its close association with healing, and its appearance alongside other terms of appeal (Isa. 19:20). Undoubtedly, there are a number of reasons why these rich themes are applied beyond the nation of Israel to Egypt as well, but one is immediately pertinent. Egypt—and Assyria is taken up in the following oracle as well—is one of the chief difficulties in Israel's relationship with YHWH for they "lean" on that nation instead of their god. Here, the suggestion is that Egypt itself will come to need YHWH and will turn to him. What imagined event could better signify upon whom reliance must rest?[42]

THE *SHUV* OF RAPPROCHEMENT

The book of Jeremiah clearly marks a significant shift in the usage of *shuv*. From the time of Jeremiah on, that is to say the late seventh and early sixth centuries, with the exception of a few equivocal attestations, *shuv* as a form of appeal all but disappears.[43]

Any effort to understand its role in Jeremiah is complicated by evidence of variations within the book's different literary registers. There is a distinction to be drawn between the way *shuv* operates within the poetic oracles, on one hand, and the prose sermons and biographical notices, on the other. Whether or not this distinction, as well as others, is to be attributed to the existence of originally distinct sources[44] does not materially affect the central argument put forth here: the work employs two different constructions of *shuv*, both of which move away from the earlier understanding. The oracles reflect what I will call a "*shuv* of rapprochement," which will be discussed first, and the sermons and biography a *shuv* of cessation of sin, which matches up with its usage among later exilic and postexilic texts and will be discussed in the next section. Indeed, a haphazard blending of the oracles' poetic use of *shuv* as part of images of familial reunion with the sin orientation of the sermons and biography is partially responsible for the standard canon-wide approach to the term's meaning as a "return to covenantal obedience."[45]

Unlike the earlier prophets, Jeremiah does not represent *shuv* as a form of petition for relief; it is not juxtaposed with the language of "seeking" and does not immediately follow mention of affliction as its expected, reflexive response. Furthermore, Jeremiah does not deploy the language of *shuv* in contrast with an act of Israel's seeking out, consulting rival powers, but rather as part of a more sustained relationship with them. In short, *shuv* no longer appears to be imagined around a discrete petitionary act, "turning" as a form of oracle-seeking. It functions instead as part of an overall restoration of a relationship, that is, reunion with a loved one. It develops through an analogy with the social realities of familial relations—the natural inclination to reinitiate former relationships, whether between a husband and wife or father and son—to suggest that reconciliation can occur or could have occurred with relative ease, that God, for his part, would be ready to take Israel back freely: "Have you seen what wayward Israel did, going to every high mountain and under every leafy tree, and whoring there? And I thought: after she has done all these things, she will come back to me, but she did not come back" (Jer. 3:6–7).[46] Or, again, "Come back, wayward Israel—declares YHWH. I will not look on you in anger, for I am compassionate—declares YHWH; I do not bear a grudge for all time" (Jer. 3:12). Relations do sometimes stray, but they come back in the end.

In keeping with this focus on relationship, *shuv* evinces a degree of reciprocity in Jeremiah's oracles that is not developed extensively in the works of the earlier prophets: "Come back, wayward children, I will undo [the effects of] your backsliding!" (Jer. 3:22).The children must return but also be welcomed in. This dynamic is seen particularly clearly in an incident that transpires between YHWH and Jeremiah himself: "Thus said the LORD: If you come back, I will take you back, and you shall stand before me" (Jer. 15:19). The deity here is asking his prophet to bring a period of estrangement to an end. And again in Ephraim's call: "Receive me back, and I will come back, for you, the LORD, are my God" (Jer. 31:18). It is a question of Israel, like the prophet, assuming its rightful position within the family.

Does this constitute a "return to covenantal obedience"? The discourse that Jeremiah formulates seems to take up the theme of relationship not as a framework for obedience and commitment but rather as a way of substantiating supposedly preexisting affections, for establishing a preference for social ties that can be said to be *old* or *original*. Even as error is acknowledged, its aim is to emphasize the priority of the former relationship: "Here we are, we come to you, for you, the LORD, are our God! Surely, futility comes from the hills, confusion from the mountains. Only through the LORD our God is there deliverance for Israel" (Jer. 3:22–23). To construe this movement toward YHWH as an expression of an inner sentiment, regret for former ways, or, even, as a declaration of intent to follow certain religious imperatives is to shift the focus of these words away from their natural object in the realm of social ties and to impose our own more obvious set of concerns around interiority and obedience. In short, the analogy Jeremiah draws with various familial relationships—marriage and parenthood—seems to be designed to prioritize the notion of relationship itself, to envelop within it a sense of its inescapability and the ease, not the inner experience or behavioral requirements, of its restoration. Rather than serving as a metaphor for renewed obedience, it does the more fundamental work of staking out the very basis, the possibilities, for Israel's continued connection with their deity. As in the earlier prophets, this "turn" seems to be carried out largely in the realm of the cult—whom does Israel worship, to whom do they turn for help?—but *shuv* no longer denotes a specific act of appeal in Jeremiah. Instead, it has come to refer to a broader change, an abstraction of its relational dynamics, which sets up the possibility for further shifts in the understanding of *shuv*.

THE *SHUV* OF CESSATION OF SIN

The meaning of *shuv* attributed above to Jeremiah is not well attested elsewhere,[47] not even in the sermons found within the scroll that bears his name. In several later texts, we find the phrase, "turn back to YHWH," but now it bears a new meaning: "From the very days of your fathers you have turned away from my laws and have not observed them. Turn back [*shuvu*] to me, and I will turn back to you—said the LORD of Hosts. But you ask, 'How shall we turn back?' Ought man to defraud God? Yet you are defrauding me. And you ask, 'How have we been defrauding you?' In tithe and contribution" (Mal. 3:7–8). Formally, we have here the reciprocal component found in Jeremiah's *shuv* of rapprochement, but relationship itself is no longer the focal point; the notion has been translated, specified, in this postexilic prophetic passage as improvement in the fulfillment of certain cultic, behavioral injunctions. We are, to be sure, in an entirely new world of *shuv* now, albeit one that can be traced from its early representation as a specific act of cultic "turning" and from Jeremiah's reformulation of that "turn" in broader relational terms as renewed cultic exchange and fidelity.[48]

Most frequently, late biblical texts entirely reformulate the traditional prophetic phrase in negative terms as a "turn away": "If the wicked one turns away *from* all the sins that he has committed and keeps all my laws and does what is just and right, he shall live; he shall not die" (Ezek. 18:21). Similarly, in the so-called Deuteronomistic History, we find: "The LORD warned Israel and Judah by every prophet [and] every seer, saying: 'Turn away *from* your wicked ways and observe my commandments and my laws, according to the entire teaching that I commanded your fathers and that I transmitted to you through my servants the prophets'" (2 Kings 17:13). And, it is in this form that the language of *shuv* is ascribed to Jeremiah in his prose sermons: "Turn back, each of you, *from* your wicked ways, and mend your ways and your actions!" (Jer. 18:11), as well as in his biography: "Perhaps when the House of Judah hear of all the disasters I intend to bring upon them, they will turn back *from* their wicked ways" (Jer. 36:3).[49]

There appears to be an identity in the sense of *shuv* found in those late passages that preserve the archaic positive formulation and those that introduce the negative reformulation—indeed, both formulations are commonly found in the same passage or work[50]—but the latter shifts to fit what would appear to be the actual contemporary usage much more closely. We began this chapter with the problem of how the phrase "turning to YHWH" could be rendered, more or less, as a rectification of behavior, leading us to suggest alternatives. "Turning away from" what is bad obviates that difficulty, making manifest in form the underlying change in meaning. The existence of yet a third formulation reinforces this sense that the standard formulation was no longer felt to be adequate: "You admonished them in order to turn them back to your teaching" (Neh 9:29). This passage preserves the positive formulation of *shuv* but clarifies its meaning and removes its anthropomorphism by replacing YHWH with his Torah, a strategy attested in a number of postbiblical texts as well.[51]

These regular changes in *shuv*'s form in the later strata of the Hebrew Bible are exceedingly hard to understand according to the view of those who would see little diachronic development in its sense. Indeed, a relatively clear chronological picture would appear to emerge. It is impossible to find the *shuv* of cessation of sin before Jeremiah, and nearly impossible to find anything but it after him. Have we arrived at a notion of "repentance?" In a concluding chapter, I will argue that repentance, bound up in a particular time and place and exhibiting a particular series of concerns, has a rather particular sense that differs from the *shuv* of late biblical Hebrew in its formation of the human subject around the twin concerns of interiority and agency, in short, in its nominalization of *shuv* as a mental act. The *shuv* that we have here addresses a cessation of sin that is not exactly an act. Intention matters not at all, and it is not efficacious or meritorious as such. It is a state, a state in which sin, once present, is now absent, and disaster, therefore, can be averted. Thus, as we saw in an earlier chapter, Jonah declares the Ninevites' doom, but God renounces his plans upon reexamining the people and "seeing" their present "deeds," that they have now "turned away from their evil ways" (3:10). Or, as Ezekiel states it, "only the person who [currently] is sinning dies" (18:20). And so, the wicked son of a righteous man will die, while the righteous son of a wicked man will live (18:5–19). Likewise, the wicked man who becomes righteous, "who has turned away from the sins which he used to do," will not die, but the righteous man who "has turned away from his righteousness" will. What unites these cases is not any particular account of how transformation transpires, but the primacy accorded to current states; God only punishes in the visible, physical presence of evil, as punishment itself is construed in large measure not as a form of retributive justice, but as a removal of sin, the eradication of a hated object necessitated by and borne of immediate incitement.

How does this "turn away from sin" relate to other phenomena in ancient Israel? There is a certain reading of the Ezekiel passage mentioned above that would see it as radically discontinuous, as marking a legal revolution in ancient Israel the discovery of a new principle: whereas the God of Old punished descendants for the sins of their forefathers, not forgiving past indiscretions even in the face of improved behavior, he now gives second chances.[52] Whatever the rhetoric of this passage, I am not inclined to see in it an evolution in mindset. For our part, it is important that we not presume that discontinuities within a specific series of considerations, the philology of *shuv*, necessarily indicate fundamental discontinuities in broader structures of practice. In fact, this new *shuv* seems to operate with a logic that is really quite similar to those phenomena that we identified in earlier chapters as components of the justice track. Like *shuv*, they participate in a pinpointing of justice, the protection of the whole through the material removal or, in this case, cessation of a problematic part, a principle that is well attested throughout early narrative, law, and prophecy.

Furthermore, like the other phenomena that together constitute the justice track, the *shuv* of cessation of sin often appears in conjunction with practices of appeal, the mercy track: "You will search there for the LORD your God, and you will find him, for you will seek him out with all your heart and soul. When you are in distress and all these things have finally befallen you, you will turn back to the LORD and heed his voice" (Deut. 4:29–30).[53] These two elements, the language of "seeking" and the "turn back to YHWH," the appeal to mercy and the rectification of behavior ("heeding his voice"), roughly coexist side by side; they do not seem to inform the meaning of one another. Indeed "seeking" of the sort found in Deuteronomy acts independently in the book of Jeremiah as a catalyst for redemption: "For thus said the LORD: 'When Babylon's seventy years are over, I will take note of you . . . . When you call me, and come and pray to me, I will give heed to you. You will search for me and find me, if only you seek with all your heart" (Jer. 29:10–12). And, here is another example of the twin emphases: "Seek the LORD while he can be found, call to him while he is near. Let the wicked give up his ways, the sinful man his plans; let him turn back to the LORD, and he will pardon him; to our God, for he freely forgives" (Isa. 55:6–7). The same juxtaposition is observed even outside of the prophets: "If you turn back to Shaddai you will be restored, if you banish iniquity from your tent . . . . When you seek the favor of Shaddai, and lift up your face to God, you will pray to him, and he will listen to you" (Job 22:23–27).[54] As such, the introduction of the *shuv* of cessation hardly constitutes a radical break; the rectification of behavior becomes a prerequisite or, perhaps better, corequisite of the old concern for appeal on the model of the traditional coexistence of these realms. It results in a sort of double rendering of the original prophetic *shuv* of appeal; concerns for appeal remain, even as *shuv* itself shifts to address matters of "justice."

Still, the frequency and persistence of such *shuv* formulations suggest that something has changed. In earlier chapters and again now, we have seen a tendency among late biblical authors to insert a role for cessation of sin into contexts that traditionally incorporated only appeal. A most striking example of this development can be found in representations of the divine attributes of mercy. Whereas, early texts, such as Exodus 34:6–7, do not premise God's mercy on a rectification of behavior, there is a clear shift in postexilic attestations: "The LORD your God is gracious and merciful; he will not turn his face from you *if you turn back to him*" (2 Chron. 30:9).[55] What I think we have here, especially evidenced by the programmatic quality of the statements about the conjoining of appeal and cessation of sin quoted above, is not a fundamentally new practice of "repentance" but a specification and regularization of the appeal process itself. It is a systematization that is born of the exigencies of exile and the problematization of appeal that it generates, as well as an emerging process of scripturalization,[56] a looking back and reflection upon biblical material and terms, that is itself a product of exile.[57] What was previously left inchoate in the intermingling of practices from the mercy and justice tracks now achieves systematic expression. Prayer will only be answered "if you turn back to him," because the extreme rupture occasioned by exile can only be rendered comprehensible and, potentially, become traversable, as we saw in the preceding chapter in the practice of confession, through a thoroughgoing account of affliction as the people's responsibility. The response to the seemed impotence of Israel's rites of appeal is to articulate them with yet greater clarity, to tighten up the requirements. It is, therefore, in postexilic passages, where Jeremiah's *shuv* of rapprochement—the restoration of the broad covenantal relationship—is delineated into its specific forms—the performance of commandments and the cessation of sin—that this rubric receives its clearest formulation.

SUMMARY

We began this chapter by noting the dominant reading of *shuv* expressions in the Hebrew Bible as essentially "repentance." This univocal approach to language, the nominalization of *shuv*, is in keeping with the general need of ideology to establish as universals the linguistic signs upon which it depends. Evidence for diachronic diversity tells a different story, however. Rather than a "return to covenantal obedience," early attestations of the phrase, "(re)turn to YHWH," seem to be associated with the institution of oracular inquiry and to operate with a logic of appeal, of the sort explored in chapter 2. The issue at stake is not morality and personal transformation but concerns for how power is generated through systems of material exchange, how turning to another for support produces hierarchy. In the oracles of Jeremiah, there does appear to be a change. Now, the turn to the deity for support is seen along abstract lines as an overall change in state, a resumption of a prior relationship. Most striking is the change of formulation in exilic and postexilic texts, from the positive "turn to YHWH" to the negative "turn away from sin." This alteration moves *shuv* away from its anthropomorphic basis in appeal to a focus on cessation of sin, properly part of the justice track. In so doing, however, it should not be seen as effecting a revolution in thought, but as part of a systematization of an existing paradigm. This notion of "cessation of sin" still differs significantly from the later notion of "repentance," as spelled out in a concluding chapter, particularly for its lack of interiority and its denotation of an overall change in state rather than the act of an agent.

CHAPTER 5

⟡

Power and the Prophetic Utterance

The LORD warned Israel and Judah by every prophet [and] every seer,
saying: "Turn back from your wicked ways."
2 Kings 17:13

THE PEDAGOGICAL IMAGE OF SCRIPTURE

We have seen how the penitential interpretation of Scripture proceeds from a definition and organization of various biblical practices as rites, as well as from the identification of certain biblical words with known psychological concepts. But there is a much broader construction at work as well, one that pertains to the very notion of Scripture itself. One of the ways in which the anthology of ancient texts known as the Hebrew Bible assumes its place as canon has been as part of a "spiritual exercise" or "technology of the self,"[1] which sees in the relationship between text and readers an opportunity to reflect on the self for the sake of its betterment. Bible is thought to *instruct*,[2] to be a guide that engages a variety of rhetorical methods, from straightforward instruction to historical argument, warning, and encouragement, in order to teach the right path and persuade an audience, that is, to induce their minds, to follow it. Behind the biblical text, it is presumed, rests another mind, that of an author, whether divine or human, who is defined by benevolent intent and is free from material motivations, a pure pedagogue with a coherent message.[3] Some of this may strike us as obvious and natural, basic to how we think about "literature," but it is surely not the only way of configuring textual objects or our relationship to them.[4]

One manifestation of this pedagogical image of Scripture, one that, historically, contributed directly to a penitential reading of the Bible, has been a certain view of narrative wherein the lives of biblical figures are seen as *exempla*, models for readers' present-day lives.[5] The exploits of Israel's ancestors may not always strike us as worthy of emulation, but readers of Genesis and other biblical books around the turn of the Common Era cultivated interpretive traditions that attributed virtues to them and eliminated any semblance of error on their part.[6] Figures such as Adam and Eve, who sin but survive to tell the tale, came to be seen as penitents.[7] In turn, for centuries, communities of readers engaged Scripture in accordance with these traditions, encountering exemplars therein and receiving instruction from them in repentance's power to redeem from sin.[8] Despite its historical significance, this approach to biblical narrative need not detain us further at the moment because, in contrast to the other phenomena we have examined, modern forms of reading have limited its hold, delegitimizing the very bases of such interpretive traditions: assumptions about the cryptic nature and fundamental consistency of Scripture, and the place of tradition itself within the practice of interpretation. Thus, for instance, few today would infer, as ancient readers once did, from the apparent absence of Reuben at his brothers' feast upon the sale of Joseph (Gen. 37:30) that Reuben was fasting and repenting for his sin with Bilhah.[9]

While the existing critique of interpretive traditions obviates the need to counter such readings with alternatives, it has not been altogether felicitous. Indeed, their outright dismissal forestalls the attempt to properly comprehend the nature of the gap between such ancient readings and the readings we today perceive as acceptable, allowing an element of indifference to remain in the critique itself. Thus, while specific interpretive traditions have been abandoned, essential elements of the presuppositions that first produced them, in this case a common image of Scripture, often remain unexamined. And so, at times, scholars, especially those with self-proclaimed "literary" interests, still seem to read biblical narratives with the expectation of finding moral lessons.[10] In recent years, for instance, the practice of reading biblical stories as a form of negative exemplarity has not been uncommon; the Bible teaches, but it teaches through the defects of its characters.[11] Indeed, one might say that readers of Scripture are less concerned to derive any particular lesson from the Bible—"repentance" may be an exception—than with upholding the general principle that there are lessons there to be learned.

PREACHERS OF REPENTANCE

However the pedagogical image of Scripture continues to influence the interpretation of narrative literature, the interpretation of prophetic literature very much remains within its horizons. With respect to prophecy, it operates with a different technology of improvement, one that has proven to be even more dominant than exemplarity, namely that of exhortation. Thus, exhortation too was present as a practice for early interpreters of the Bible. They conceived of some figures as models of repentance and others, like Noah, as preachers of repentance.[12] But, over the course of Western history, preaching has become perhaps the most central institutional organ of popular religion, often as a component of a broader penitential discipline and always with reference to Scripture.[13] Indeed, sermons have been such a prominent part of religious culture, to judge from the sheer volume of their literary record alone, that they have come to inform our basic sense of what the Bible does, what it means for an individual voice, whether that of an author or a speaker, to address an audience. A figure of authority, endowed with specialized knowledge or moral perceptivity, identifies what he or she perceives to be others' shortcomings and uses threats or promises—words that provoke thought—to persuade them to choose the right path. All of this, of course, presumes certain ontologies of the person and, above all, speech, that we are autonomous beings with virtue as our aim and that, consequently, our truest form of discourse is didactic. Most importantly, it suggests to us the frame, the imagined theater of activity, within which the phenomenon of ancient Israelite prophecy has been situated and comprehended for millennia by readers of the Bible.[14] Indeed, scholars still speak of the prophets' "preaching" or "teaching," instances of their speech as a "sermon" or "diatribe,"[15] and their aim as "persuasion,"[16] as if these were basic human conditions, applicable in all times and places, and not rather particularistic expressions of institutional power in the West.

While the centrality of preaching as a practice, along with the dominant image of Scripture as literary instruction, may provide the background against which the prophets have been persistently understood to be preachers of repentance, taken alone it would not constitute a compelling reading of prophetic literature, which does not necessarily submit readily to such a framework. After all, prophetic texts contain much by way of accusation and judgment, but little explicit exhortation. In fact, prophetic speech employs the short utterance, not the long sermon; its basic unit would appear to be the oracle.[17] The penitential reading of prophecy, therefore, depends upon a variety of sophisticated strategies for finding in prophetic texts cues for a fundamental, pedagogic purpose that is otherwise off the text's plane of representation.

One model focuses on *accusation*, the prophets' insistence that Israel has sinned. Mention of sin can be construed as "reproach," implicitly informing the people of the need to repent or inducing them to do so by evoking feelings of guilt.[18] Another focuses on *judgment*, the prophets' declaration that Israel is doomed. The pronouncement of doom has been seen as "in itself an exhortation to repentance,"[19] because it is, potentially, at least, conditional and therefore closer to a "threat."[20] Oracles of *redemption*, which will be addressed briefly in the following chapter, have also been read as implicitly conditioned on repentance. If human virtue is the divine aim, why would God save the people unless they repent first? These models all proceed with certain assumptions about intentionality or expressivity: that prophetic utterances contain indications or are themselves mere verbal expressions of the prophets' real inner concerns, and teleology that prophetic utterances truly aim at an object—the consciousness of the people—that is beyond the utterance itself. These theories of how meaning is made each, in their own way, move us beyond the local, unmediated prophetic word to extract from it a deeper sense.

Another strategy has been to privilege instances of *exhortation*, such as those involving *shuv*, discussed in the preceding chapter, that are to be found in a limited number of prophetic passages,[21] certain components of the corpus, or particular periods in the history of prophecy and its editing, and to take them as summative and basic to its purposes or, at the very least, to its early reception. Even while the others remain subtly present, this strategy has come to dominate in the form of a common claim that prophets, such as Jeremiah, originally may not have been preachers of repentance but that they came to be portrayed as such by later editors, the so-called Deuteronomists.[22] Exilic and postexilic scribal groups, so the theory goes, introduced exhortative material and, thereby, configured existing prophetic texts as contemporary sources for exhortation to the people, warnings that they must change if they are to be redeemed.[23] The significance of this claim as an extension and reassertion of the pedagogic image, and not as a genuine limitation of it, cannot be underestimated. It supposes that redactors have successfully imbued diverse collected oracles with radically new theological intent, that their work—interpolations and other (often slight) modifications—is coherent and powerful enough to have left an authoritative layer in the text that constitutes the most accessible and, hence, determinitive reading of the prophetic corpus.[24] In short, the claim is that in the *received* canonical form of Scripture, prophets *are* preachers of repentance.

Behind this literary assessment of redaction's power—its novelty and thoroughness—can lie an evaluative sense that the evolution of repentance as a possibility is primarily a good and natural development, a positive innovation.[25] But, at times, it also can be in service of an opposing evaluation that would compare these preachers of repentance negatively to the prophets of old, who, rather than merely urging adherence to *torah*, some legalistic standard, were themselves the great revolutionaries, who laid out and *taught* the foundations of Israelite faith and ethics.[26] Indeed, the field of biblical studies has long been suspended between these polarities of evolution and devolution, narratives that are deeply ingrained in Western notions of history and the history of religious polemics. Be that as it may, what I would like to suggest is that, ironically, the view of the early prophets as brilliant theologians and insightful social reformers, aside from being influenced, quite obviously, by such modern movements as Romanticism with its notion of the inspired individual, may actually be an offshoot of the earlier, established view of the prophets as preachers. Despite the disconnect posited between them, both construals of prophecy ultimately participate in and further a pedagogical image of prophecy. They differ only in how to construct pedagogy's object, whether as a radical teaching against corrupt societal norms or as a reinforcement of established communal standards.

REFRAMING PROPHECY

What follows immediately is a series of introductions, an attempt to reframe prophecy in alternative terms. It will be followed, in turn, by a more detailed analysis of select bodies of prophetic texts. In particular, the suggestion will be made that the pedagogic model of prophecy, with its privileging of human agency, interiority, and virtue as concerns, fails to contend with, indeed denies and overwrites, those interpretive possibilities that would highlight instead what amounts to matters of *power* in and around the prophetic utterance.[27]

Liminality and the Power of the Utterance

The prophets are seen as occupying the liminal space between the divine and the human realms, between YHWH and his people. Indeed, ancient Israelite texts usually portray this sense of being in-between more richly for the prophet than for any figure—king, priest, or otherwise. To begin with, there is some ambiguity surrounding the ontological status of this "man of God/divine man." Though a normal human being, the prophet enters into the divine. The Hebrew term, *mal'akh,* is one way to signify either prophet or angel, and there can be confusion for characters within a biblical narrative (or for the reader) as to which type of intermediary is present (e.g., Judg. 13). Like an angel, Moses remains in the presence of YHWH without food for forty days and forty nights (Exod. 34:28). Elijah destroys a band of soldiers without any apparent recourse to an intervention of YHWH (2 Kings 1:9–14). Later, he is taken directly up into the heavenly realm (2 Kings 2:1–12). Samuel summons thunder and rain (1 Sam. 12:17). That the prophets, at times, must pray to the deity to carry out their shows of force surely limits any sense of their possessing independent divine power, but it still does not change the fact that such performances ensure that the miraculous is indelibly associated with their name. Indeed, the centrality of intercessory prayer to the mission of these early prophets, as discussed in an earlier chapter, places them in a functionally equivalent position to the minor deity in the ancient Near Eastern pantheon. They too enjoy a special proximity to the supreme god.

The nearly mythic accounts of the prophets of old stand in contrast to the oracular collections attributed to the later literary prophets, who seem

removed from the kinds of miraculous interventions enacted by their prede-
cessors and are portrayed generally as ineffective intercessors. Still there is
a kind of efficacy that attaches, not to their actions, but to these prophets'
words.[28] Our tendency is to view such speech as depictions of a divine plan or
expressions of prophetic conscience,[29] as directed at the inner workings, the
soul, of their listeners, but this account fails to recognize what words can be
seen as doing to the material world of an audience, what they establish about
it.[30] The prophets are not mere clairvoyants. Speaking in YHWH's name, their
speech describes the future but also makes it so. The prophets' articulation
of the divine plan may be seen as the effective instrument, the oral conduit,
by which it is brought down and unleashed in the world. It is for this reason
that they can be treated seriously as enemies by Israel's kings and made to
suffer from attempts to suppress their words. This destructive force also helps
explain the phenomenon of oracles against the nations.[31] The Balaam cycle
(Num. 22–24), in particular, presents the dismantling of the enemy as the
dominant aim of prophecy. As the opening chapters of Amos, which begin
with oracles against the nations and end with oracles against Israel and Judah,
make clear (Amos 1–2), prophecies to Israel are merely an extension, albeit
a rather horrific one, of this phenomenon. The prophetic voice provides an
earthly means of substantiating God's own and hence constitutes another
instance of a certain anxiety to embody, a concern to find a material basis
for YHWH in a cult without idols. To say that prophets are messengers conveying information does not render fully the implications of their ambiguous
ontological status, their position between human and divine. Prophets could
be seen, rather, as part and parcel of the destructive (or occasionally salvific)
forces that the deity saw fit at times to array against (or on behalf of) his
people, an aspect of hostility, of warfare, not pedagogy. And, indeed, the question of prophetic loyalty, the way the prophet can be caught between the deity
and the people, as discussed in chapter 2 with regard to the phenomenon of
intercession, reveals yet one more aspect of the prophet's liminal position and
how they should be seen as engaged, deeply invested in pursuing the material
interests of the parties they represent, at times, shifting their loyalty.

To understand, further, variation in the phenomenon of prophecy, I would
propose, as a heuristic model, that there are "three stages" in the relationship between God and Israel. In discussing fasting and other rites of appeal,
we explored the pattern and logic of "stage one." Disaster strikes, perhaps
because of sin, but a reasonably functional relationship with YHWH ensures
that appeal will move the deity to pity. Some of the prophets' defining features
pertain to this stage in the relationship. Through their oracles, they direct
the people or the king aright in military decisions and matters of law. When
suffering befalls Israel, the prophets intervene on the people's behalf with
a direct appeal to the deity. At times, the prophets even protect the nation
as a whole by eradicating a specific unwanted element in their midst, as in

Samuel's killing of Agag (1 Sam. 15). The prophets may be said to extend the reach of stage one; they prolong the period of appeal's efficacy by continuing to contend effectively with divine wrath long past the point that God has shut himself off from his people.

In previous chapters, we also saw how appeal fails in the face of serious, persistent sin. It is as if an iron curtain descends between the people and God; even prophetic intercession proves useless. The inefficacy of appeal is the salient feature of "stage two." Effective communication between the people and their God ceases. As an agent of YHWH, the prophet parts ways with the people and/or their leadership and turns his oracles, uttered against the other nations in more functional times, into oracles against Israel itself. God is now at war with his own people. Much of prophetic literature, I would suggest, is framed within this dysfunctional stage of the relationship.

The working out of this fate and its resolution occurs within the less common oracles of redemption. They describe an anticipated return to a normal relationship, "stage three," whose conception will be discussed in the following chapter. But, it is important to point out at this juncture that most attempts to formulate how redemption transpires envision the deity, not human beings and their reflective capabilities, as the agent of the necessary transition, a process that usually entails the violent removal of whatever cuts Israel off from him, the "stage two" reality, often through the elimination of a portion of the people.[32]

This account of prophets—their liminal status, the force of their utterances, the variability of their loyalties, and, ultimately, their position in the state of war between God and his people—all point to their role as effective agents, not pedagogues, as a unifying feature of the ancient Israelite phenomenon of prophecy. As God says to Jeremiah upon his appointment to the prophetic office: "See, I have appointed you today over nations and kingdoms: to uproot and to pull down, to destroy and to overthrow, to build and to plant" (Jer. 1:10).

Anthropopathism and the Divine Pursuit of Power

In taking up the question of prophecy, we continue our consideration of how an ancient collective of humans gave shape to suffering by examining their construal of the divine force that they took to be its agent. To understand prophetic speech is ultimately to engage what claim to be articulations of YHWH's own aims, that is, the nature of God. A certain strand of biblical scholarship has already brought to the fore of our attention the portrayal of divine pathos in prophetic literature and the prophets as sympathetic, in touch with, God's feelings.[33] In the phenomenon of prophecy, an ideal opportunity has been seen to address the "phenomenology of God as person" in ancient Israel and ultimately, through representations of him, the "psychology of the ancient Israelite."[34] In short, the prophets present an anthropopathic god, a god who possesses human-like passions.

The theory of divine anthropopathy does much for our analysis of prophetic speech. Above all, it emphasizes that personality, as opposed to the selflessness and purposefulness often assumed in the pedagogical model, might provide an important backdrop against which to assess the nature of prophecy. Thus, for instance, the notion that the deity has feelings can be used to dampen the problem of the inconsistency that reigns among a given prophet's different oracles. How is it that the same prophet can alternate between invitations to reinitiate a relationship with YHWH and pronouncements of certain doom? Form criticism has already taught us to attend to the particular unit of prophetic speech, the individual oracle. Now we are in a position to appreciate why individual oracles could express diverse sentiments. Each oracle must be read on its own terms, and not as part of an overall systematic project, because the very passions to which they give expression, that inform the envisioned divine need to speak, are inconstant.

Undoubtedly, however, the greatest contribution made through an appreciation of YHWH's anthropopathy involves the most common register of divine pathos, namely that of anger. In this regard, I would like to draw on a recent study of the emotions and their history, Philip Fisher's *The Vehement Passions*, that makes a vital distinction between an ancient theory of the passions and the modern notion of feelings.[35] In modern usage, "emotions" are meant to be moderate; when extreme, they are deemed to be out of control.[36] The passions, however, are always extreme or, as Fisher prefers to label them, "thorough." They "drive out every other form of attention or state of being."[37] This notion of the possessed self stands in contrast to the "standard modern idea of the prudential self, which weighs the near and long-term future, balances the full range of desires and obligations, and integrates the many inclinations into the actions of any one moment."[38]

Fisher develops a particularly deep account of anger as a passion. At the root of anger, Fisher sees infringement upon the radius of an individual's will, what he or she desires and expects to attain. The more effective and powerful the will—consider the case of a king or God himself—the larger its radius, the more numerous the circumstances in which an insult (i.e., disobedience) will be felt, and the more dramatic its expression. Anger does not arise from a single event (unless it is of the most horrendous sort), but from a series of actions and an anticipated future series—a relationship. It builds up over time and eventually spills forth; the injury is announced, and the injured moves into impassioned action.[39] In terms of the stages in the relationship between Israel and YHWH, this moment corresponds to the shift from stage one to stage two. Characterizing this insult, Fisher speaks of a "diminution" of the self endured by the offended party. The enraged engages the one who would intrude into his domain in a contest of wills, which aims at the "erasure of the source of offense."[40] Only such erasure can rectify the insult endured by the will. Thus, for instance, we find in Isaiah's "song of my lover about his vineyard" (5:1–7) that the beloved (YHWH) prepares a fine vineyard and *expects* superior grapes (Israel). He finds to his horror that wild grapes have grown instead. How does he react to this intrusion upon his will? He sets out to utterly destroy the vineyard, to remove its hedge and break down its walls, allowing it to be trampled and overgrown. The aim is not the rectification of souls but annihilation, and his response bespeaks the thoroughness that Fisher attributes to anger as a passion.

With the idea of the passions, Fisher unites an account of the assertion of power, a reaction to the diminution suffered through insult, with an account of justice, that is, rectification of wrongs done to the injured will. Coming from an analysis of state power and its punitive measures, Michel Foucault produces in *Discipline and Punish* a related account of premodern notions of justice. It too bears implications for understanding the portrayal in biblical texts of the actions taken by the (divine) king and their motivations. Indeed, Foucault assiduously maintains that the enactment of justice did not aim at the improvement of the punished but rather at their defeat. Punishment was an open spectacle with an emphasis on excess. The victim's body was branded, scarred, and displayed. Punishment was measured out as meticulous control was exerted over the body of the offender. Many prophetic pronouncements reveal a similar obsession with detail, control, and public display. Consider Ezekiel's oracle against Egypt: "You are like the dragon in the seas . . . I will cast my net over you in an assembly of many peoples, and you shall be hauled up in my toils. And I will fling you to the ground, hurl you upon the open field. I will cause all the birds of the sky to settle upon you. I will cause the beasts of all the earth to batten on you " (32:2–4). What is YHWH seen to accomplish through this demonstration of mastery?

"A successful public execution justified justice," as Foucault puts it.[41] Rather like medieval practices of tests or ordeals,[42] the dismantling of a victim and his or her body in public establishes a certain kind of truth and conviction. Agony, branding, and display of the broken body reify the victim's corruption. The process is not intuitive to us, but that is because our judicial system situates punishment as following upon a dispassionate analysis of truth. But here, the very success of punishment, the ability of the torturer to torture, comes to be taken as an indication of its rightness. Divine punishment need not be different. God's ability to have his way with his victims affirms the basic righteousness of his cause. The people must be guilty, of something.

Foucault's account also points out that such torture is not just a judicial ritual but a political one. Crime attacks the sovereign: "by breaking the law, the offender has touched the very person of the prince; and it is the prince [i.e., the state apparatus] . . . who seizes upon the body of the condemned man and displays it marked, beaten, broken."[43] Punishment is "a ceremonial by which a momentarily injured sovereignty is reconstituted."[44] Therefore, there must be excess in the state's response to the criminal, because it is only through such dissymmetry that a clear divide is redrawn between the subject and the all-powerful sovereign. In such a system, excessive punishment does not provide what Foucault calls an "economy of example" but rather the "reactivation of power."[45] Similarly, we might say that YHWH, as divine king, must exert control over his subjects. Punishment is not educative, but an exercise in sovereignty.

Prophecy as a Discourse on Power

Prophetic utterances can be seen as the speech acts that accompany this drama of anger and the will, of power and justice. Fisher's account makes it clear that the vehement passions are not susceptible to remaining within the inner mind of those in their throes. Anger possesses, in a demonic sense, and takes as its own the individual's thoughts, actions, and speech. Divine speech does not remain bottled up in the heavens but bursts forth onto the human scene with the prophets as its conduit. God needs to speak (to judge from the sheer volume of oracles, he cannot stop talking),[46] quite apart from any considered effect his words might have upon the people. In addition to this expressive dimension, this account also allows for an effective one. Articulating passion can have direct consequences for the object of vehemence. Fisher explores the question through the rubric of cursing: "A curse takes what is a momentary peak of vehemence and, instead of spilling it out at once in an equally momentary act like a blow, even a murderous blow, freezes it like a law into an abstract punishment."[47] Likewise, with the oracle of doom, God does not simply punish; he reifies his anger in an articulated sentiment that causes doom to hang over the people indefinitely.

Foucault's account of state power and its discursive formations invites us to take a more sustained look at prophetic speech as a form of discourse. An unseen monarch, as opposed to an actual state apparatus, requires, most obviously, publication through an extensive verbal component. By decreeing horrific events before they transpire, the prophets establish YHWH as the author of destruction, thereby branding victims with his name. In fact, through the imagery of dismantled bodies that their oracles produce, the prophets themselves create and communicate divine power; their evocative speech carves out a position and an identity for their god among a range of competitors. It projects a dreadful force that itself can only be met with mourning, a complete abnegation of its recipients' own power and status.[48]

What prophecy asserts is an account of what is happening as an effect of God's power and justice. It proceeds from a certain basis in reality: Israel occupies a relatively weak position, susceptible to natural disasters, without a hope of standing up to the imperial powers of Babylon or Assyria. If one posits a belief in a powerful national deity, this set of circumstances poses a serious dilemma. Does the deity lack sufficient power to turn back the invading armies? Why has he failed (or does it seem like he will fail) to protect them? In contending with these issues, prophetic speech possesses an extraordinary explanatory power. The prophets act as an ancient form of the media, the propaganda arm of the deity, adept at and responsible for interpreting events, drawing forth a compelling image of what is only partially seen and known. Far from an indication of impotence, they argue, suffering has been brought upon Israel by their own deity. It is YHWH, not the imperial powers, who has raised his arm against the nation.

If pronouncements of *judgment* establish the role of divine power in ensuing destruction, the role of *accusation* in prophetic speech reinforces the central preoccupation with reading events in light of God's sovereignty by asserting their central justice. In the ancient Near East, the very foundation of leadership depends upon an exercise of justice. There is no sense that power lasts without it.[49] Therefore, the prophets must simultaneously assert divine authorship of events and their justification. Notwithstanding centuries of religious polemics, the suggestion should not come as a surprise that Israel may not have been a particularly stubborn people with an acute propensity to sin but rather that prophetic preoccupation with their sin—however profound its sentiments are at times—emerges from the very need to establish them as opponents of a deity whose projected displeasure can explain their diminishment as a nation.[50] Therefore, as form criticism has shown, prophetic oracles often take on the form of a verdict.[51] Rather like confession, they pave the way for destruction by effectively placing the people in a state of condemnation, as it says in Jeremiah, "I am summoning all the peoples, the kingdoms of the north . . . and I will speak my case against [Jerusalem and Judah]" (1:16), a procedure to be conducted, as the passage makes clear, by the prophet himself.

In light of the above, the reasons for the collection and preservation of prophetic oracles and their eventual formation into books seems rather straightforward and need not require developmental explanations, that they became, for instance, sources of exhortation for later generations. As long as the notion of YHWH as a god who is powerful and just is taken as prediscursive, as an assured and natural component of Israelite faith, then there is room for such speculations as to the utility of old pre-exilic oracles in later exilic and postexilic times. But, on the most elementary level, it is the oracles themselves that stake out the power of Israel's god and the contours of his reign, his very identity, as well as the reasons for the people's current state. They are what establish the basis for any continued identification with YHWH in exile and beyond through the claim that he is the agent responsible for their condition.

A LETTER FROM MARI

In what follows, we will flesh out these dynamics through an examination of texts that, on one hand, enable a deep account of prophecy and that, on the other, allow us to develop further paradigms for understanding the place of injunction among prophetic pronouncements of doom. To begin, I would like to turn to an instance of extrabiblical prophecy found in the Mari letters, which date to the eighteenth century B.C.E. and have become an important comparative source for the study of the Israelite phenomenon.[52] In this letter, it is reported that a prophet has consumed a living (or, perhaps: raw) lamb in front of the city gate. Speech accompanied the act: "A devouring will take place! Give orders to the cities to return the taboo material. Whoever commits an act of violence shall be expelled from the city."[53] What is the relationship between the devouring and the orders to rectify the state of the city? We could see the initial utterance as devoid of its own intrinsic significance, as, in fact, productive of another, that the city ought to rectify itself. It is, in other words, a threat, a statement about the future whose *real* purpose is the improvement of the people's moral-religious state.

But is the actual devouring of a living lamb in this prophetic performance merely designed to add drama; is it for its psychological effect? The centrality of the devouring might induce us to arrive at an alternative explanation that frames the act of consumption as the fruition of the prophecy and not merely as propaedeutic. I would suggest that the prophet here acts as an earthly instantiation of the deity; he embodies the god who has set out to devour the people, with lion-like ferocity, establishing divine power and its finality with this horrific, public act. (Ancient Israelite prophets also made use of such "signs" or, better, enactments, as discussed later.) This act must be explained, placed within a comprehensible framework, and so it is accompanied by an utterance. At this stage, the consumption of the city should be seen as a foregone conclusion, no less than that of the lamb. In fact, the prophet's predatory act could be seen as possessing a magical-effective element; it helps in bringing about the very devastation aimed at the city.

Against this backdrop of impending violence, the prophet utters a series of generic demands, removal of taboo material and evildoers, that do not treat his bloody act directly. There seems to be a sense that, if sin is removed from the city, the deity *might not* destroy the place. Destruction, perhaps in this case in the form of a plague, comes as a slow and tarrying thing, not a sudden blinding flash; and, even after destruction has been unleashed, changing circumstances might lead to its mitigation. What is in evidence may be a certain prophetic capacity to issue cultic demands, as well as something that we might see as part of their intercessory function,[54] the responsibility to eradicate sin from the people's midst in order to ensure their survival, a process of *removal*, discussed in preceding chapters. Thus, Moses destroys the Golden Calf and slaughters a portion of the people, easing the way for the return of divine favor (Exod. 32:20–29),[55] just as Samuel personally destroys Agag, the taboo material that Saul had allowed to persist (1 Sam. 15:33). In ordering the rectification of the city, return of the taboo material, and expulsion of the wicked, the prophet in question acts in a capacity that is also common to other leaders. In the book of Jonah, the prophet announces Nineveh's doom, but there it is the king that responds with a call for a turn away from evildoing (Jon. 3:8). The splitting up of functions in Jonah spells out what I have already hinted at above: the delivering of oracles and exhortative utterances should be seen as two separate tasks, both of which are appropriate to divine intermediaries but each of which preserves its own integrity. This is true from a formal, literary perspective but also in terms of prophetic function. The prophet can announce doom but also have a certain hand in attempting to remove the irritant that has necessitated it. We should allow for this movement back and forth between devouring and injunction without necessarily allowing the logic of one to inform that of the other, a practice that has developed out of a persistent interiorizing hermeneutic that would locate the significance of all speech in the inner lives of its listeners.

MOSES THE WARRIOR

Moses' engagement with Pharaoh provides us with an extended narrative with which to continue exploring the dynamics laid out earlier—the prophet as part of YHWH's military machine—and the relationship between prophetic injunction and pronouncements of doom. For centuries, readers of the Bible have wondered why YHWH hardens the heart of Pharaoh, actually preventing him from releasing the people. Should not the primary concern of a merciful God be the repentance of the wicked?[56] To take the Mosaic narratives seriously as a potential model for prophecy is to recognize that YHWH turns on Israel and its kings in much the same manner, and for many of the same motivations, as he assails Egypt and its exalted leader, Pharaoh.[57]

In one account, Moses' prophecy to Pharaoh is framed by a request, not to release the people, but to allow them to worship in the desert (Exod. 5:1). By asking for access to his labor supply, YHWH is essentially demanding from Pharaoh tribute, a material contribution to his cult. The key difference between the present case and those found, for instance, in Mari, where the prophet also indicates to the king the demands of the cult, is that Moses represents a deity that can only be seen as peripheral to the world of Pharaoh. The demand itself, therefore, must be seen as more like a holdup than a call to repentance. It sets the stage, indeed could only result in the showdown that ensues: "Who is the Lord that I should heed him and let Israel go?" (Exod. 5:2). What is at stake, as it is in cultic worship in general, is not so much

Pharaoh's subjective recognition of YHWH as much as the deity's very assertion of his identity and power, which, at present, lacks demonstration.

Each time Moses conveys YHWH's demand, he states that a certain plague
will strike if the demand goes unheeded, for example: "if you refuse to let
them go, then I will afflict your whole country with frogs" (Exod. 7:27). At
first glance, such pronouncements might seem to aim to produce the rhetorical force necessary to ensure compliance. But the narrative never pauses to
consider Pharaoh's response, moving directly from utterance to action: "Say
to Aaron: 'hold out your arm with the rod over the rivers" (8:1). The focus,
instead, is decidedly on Pharaoh's reaction to the demonstration of YHWH's
power: "Plead with YHWH to remove the frogs" (8:4). In short, Moses' utterances do not seem to function as separate threats designed to induce Pharaoh
to acquiesce, on the model of exhortation, but to be conjoined with prophetic
action, to participate in the delivery of the plagues as a mode of identification, labeling the plagues that are to follow as the handiwork of YHWH. The
YHWH-centered interpretation of events is assured by the verbal prophetic
framework that surrounds them, from the prophet's initial prediction of the
plague to the prophet's subsequent removal of it through intercession. At the
same time, and, here, we arrive at an important point regarding the place of
prophetic command that will be developed later, Moses' demand also functions as a technical, quasi-legal pronouncement. It sets up the possibilities for
an assault on Pharaoh by justifying its grounds.

The priestly writer would have us focus our attention more on the wizardry
of Moses, usually executed through the agency of Aaron, and his competition
with Pharaoh's magicians, than on his prophecy.[58] Still, by publicly performing each plague, the dynamic team, thoroughly identified with the name of
YHWH, marks the events that ensue as the working of their deity. The prophet
does not merely explain events; he helps enact them. In chapter 2, we briefly
explored how Moses is portrayed as a champion, a human representative of
divine power. This warrior of YHWH and the plagues that serve as his weap-
ons do not aim at Pharaoh's repentance. When YHWH asks Pharaoh through
his prophet, "How long will you refuse to be humbled before me?" (10:3), the
question is not addressed to Pharaoh's individual consciousness but at his
political body. How much of a beating is it going to take before Pharaoh sub-
mits and publicly demonstrates YHWH's superior power by letting go of his
people? The prophet plays an integral role in administering this beating and
thereby, as the earthly representative of YHWH, connects the dismantling of
Pharaoh to his power.[59]

Pharaoh refuses to heed the command of the deity sometimes because "his
heart stiffened," that is, Pharaoh was sufficiently resilient (e.g., Exod. 8:11),
and sometimes because YHWH made him so (e.g., Exod. 9:12). The exact cause
of Pharaoh's intransigence may be immaterial. Either way, he is in a "stage
two" relationship with YHWH, one in which only the complete undoing of the

other can return or bestow requisite power to the offended. In this case, the injury to the will of the deity arises from two directions: the injustice against his people; but also, and, perhaps, most pressingly, from his own apparent limitations, the very denial of his identity. His dormancy, his geopolitical irrelevance, can only be undone with a dramatic exercise of the will. In the mythic imagination of a disempowered Levantine people, their deity must make himself and acquire his nation (compare Exod. 15:16) through a total triumph over the greatest emperor and power of the ancient Near East. It is upon beholding the drowned, broken bodies of their enemies, "Egypt dead on the shore" (Exod. 14:30), that the people affirm YHWH and his servant Moses (Exod. 14:31), that they declare YHWH to be king (Exod. 15:18). Pharaoh's premature capitulation would have diminished the ultimate glory YHWH achieves in open battle.[60] Furthermore, in the process, plague by plague, YHWH has the opportunity to demonstrate his mastery over the particularities of the natural world as well, revealing a control over all matters of creation, from water to darkness. Interpreters therefore miss the point when they attempt to justify YHWH's hardening of Pharaoh's heart. In the end, YHWH's actions in Egypt can only be explained through an account of justice that recognizes its intrinsic relationship to power.

FROM MIRACLE-WORKING TO REGIME CHANGE: THE DEUTERONOMISTIC HISTORY

As a compilation of earlier accounts, the history running from the book of Joshua through Kings, what scholars often refer to as the Deuteronomistic History,[61] contains narrative renderings of prophecy that will be important to us as they provide possible contextualizations for prophetic activity in general, something that is largely missing from the prophetic scrolls themselves. It is immediately striking that, as a whole, the collection puts forward a representation of prophecy that is nearly devoid of exhortation and in which not a single oracle of doom is reversed. I will suggest that, rather than preaching repentance, prophets serve as one of the Deuteronomistic History's main instruments in furthering its justification of YHWH, in articulating the claim that Israel's fall is the result of their abandonment of the deity[62] and that it has transpired through his agency.[63] They do so by offering interpretations of events that derive their authority from the fact that they precede them and by becoming active agents themselves, as representatives of YHWH, especially in cases of regime change. Indeed, by anticipating events, the prophets' words subvert their significance, creating the impression that they are nothing but a fulfillment of divine speech.

We will start with an example that isolates prophecy's explanatory function. In chapter 2, we examined how the people's crying out in Egypt provoked a response, as champion, on the part of YHWH. However, now in the Promised Land, portions of the redeemed nation still find themselves in a position of servitude vis-à-vis other nations and again "cry out" (Judg. 6:7). How could YHWH have allowed Israel to slip back into bondage? This requires explanation, a task assigned, in what is clearly an editorial passage, to the prophet, who states in the name of the deity: "I brought you up out of Egypt and freed you from the house of bondage . . . . And I said to you, 'I, the LORD, am your God. You must not worship the gods of the Amorites in whose land you dwell.' But you did not obey me" (Judg. 6:9–10). A failure to obey, not divine impotence, is to blame for their predicament, and justification, not preaching, appears to be the point of the prophetic utterance.

For us, there may be a gratuitous feel to the prophecy discussed above: God only needs to speak because he needs to explain. A similar sense attaches to a different kind of example, a series of prophecies that are all prediction and no condemnation. In the narrative of Ahab's (successful) battles with Aram, the king sets out to do battle against Ben-hadad. Throughout, unnamed prophets approach him, predicting victory and sometimes even offering specific counsel (1 Kings 20:13–14, 22, 28.) As "YHWH guys," his consummate representatives, their involvement ensures that—at least, in the narrative representation found in the Deuteronomistic History—the defeat of Ben-hadad is attributed not to Ahab, but to the God of Israel.

These two impulses, to justify YHWH's actions (or lack thereof) and to assert his agency, usually come together in a single prophecy. To return to the confrontation of Ahab and Ben-hadad, Ahab's decision to preserve the life of his enemy, in contradiction to the command of YHWH, leads to the prophetic pronouncement of his downfall: "Thus said the LORD: 'Because you have set free the man whom I doomed, your life shall be forfeit for his life and your people for his people'" (1 Kings 20:42). Proceeding from the well-known historical fact of Ahab's downfall, this narrative deploys prophecy as a way of positioning YHWH as the agent of that fall. Human commentary on events past possesses no status; the job of processing events, what we would call analysis, transpires, in the Deuteronomistic History, through the mouths of the prophets.

Still, the prophets are not only observers, who lay claim to an authoritative interpretation of Israel's history. They themselves are actual agents in that history and shape its most significant twists and turns. Any proper definition of the prophetic function must therefore emphasize its strong performative basis. Indeed, the History's narratives revolve around the rise and fall of Israel and Judah's kings. It is the prophet who is directly responsible for the overthrow of kings[64] and their appointment, a task that is often accomplished through ritual anointment,[65] which, as it is performed by a figure associated with YHWH, establishes the deity as the power behind the king. We see here the prophet not only predicting but also actively involved in regime change, a performative edge that destabilizes the account of the prophet as a preacher. Thus, when Elisha anoints Jehu through an intermediary (2 Kings 9:6) and informs Hazael that he is to be king (2 Kings 8:13), he knowingly sets in motion, indeed directs them, to their bloody coups.[66]

One of the ways in which the prophets' potency comes through most clearly can be seen in their involvement in military matters: "Whoever escapes the sword of Hazael shall be slain by Jehu, and whoever escapes the sword of Jehu shall be slain by Elisha. I will leave in Israel only seven thousand" (1 Kings 19:17–18). Is this a case of figurative speech? Perhaps, but Moses, Samuel, and Elijah all wield swords on behalf of YHWH. The prophets seem to be able to command at will the divine army, chariots and all (2 Kings 6:17). Their association with war receives further strengthening from their provision of oracles before a battle (whether asked or not) as to its outcome. These instances exist along a spectrum of immediacy—the prophet may directly cause destruction or only declare its imminence—but they all associate the prophet with military power, an assessment that, for instance, leads the king of Aram to hunt down Elisha (2 Kings 6:8–23).

The military activities of the prophets can serve as a broader rubric for comprehending their position vis-à-vis the state. At times, they appear to be a component of the state apparatus. At other times, they seem to be in hiding, at odds with the government, conducting a sort of guerilla warfare, popping in unexpectedly with grim news.[67] Even then, they are sometimes sought out by the leadership,[68] revealing that they must be seen as occupying a complex spectrum of varying degrees of proximity. However, the prophet comes into view most clearly in the Deuteronomistic History when he stands apart from the king, when the king has abandoned YHWH. It is no act of hyperbole to label the prophet the enemy of the king, as Ahab refers to Elijah (1 Kings 21:20). Elijah and Ahab are engaged in a power struggle, not unlike that of Moses and Pharaoh, in which the vanquishing, not the reformation, of Ahab is the aim.

Perhaps the foremost example of prophets acting is to be found in their penchant for producing "signs." The real question would seem to be whether such events are indeed signs—they represent some other reality—or whether they possess a causative element as well, that is, they are bound up in some fashion in the impending doom itself. In support of the latter, one might note the way in which prophetic oracles of doom seem to follow upon signs immediately as a consequence does upon its cause. Thus, Saul tears Samuel's cloak as he turns to leave, and then the prophet declares that YHWH has "torn" the kingdom away from Saul (1 Sam. 15:28). Or, when Elisha asks Joash to strike the ground with arrows and he only does so three times, Elisha concludes: "If only you had struck five or six times! Then you would have annihilated Aram; as it is, you shall defeat Aram only three times" (2 Kings 13:19). In part, the question is tied to our reading of oracles. Are the oracles themselves involved in the release of an evil decree or do they merely represent it? I suspect that both actions and words were seen as doing more than the term "sign" suggests. If so, we might do well to keep prophetic performance in mind when we interpret the oracles, seeing in both an effort to embody divine action in earthly instruments, an unleashing of disaster, rather than merely a representation of future action in order to induce fear and repentance.

Most telling are the narratives around Elijah. Into the wasteland that the land has become under Ahab's reign steps the prophet claiming, "As the LORD lives, the God of Israel whom I serve, there will be no dew or rain except at my bidding" (1 Kings 17:1). Not unlike Moses, Elijah acts as a kind of portable oasis bringing food and life against a backdrop of total barrenness wherever he travels (1 Kings 17). The story of Elijah's triumph over the prophets of Baal at Mount Carmel provides us with a climactic encapsulation of what such activity takes aim. Elijah, in front of all and in the name of the LORD, brings rain. When Elijah demands of the people: "How long will you keep hopping on the two boughs? If the LORD is God, follow him; and if Baal, follow him!" (1 Kings 18:21), this is not an invitation to introspection. As the narrative notes, the people do not answer Elijah; it is a rhetorical question that is answered by the successful descent of fire upon the altar, in response to which: "all the people flung themselves on their faces and cried out: 'YHWH alone is God, YHWH alone is God!'" (1 Kings 19:39). Prostration here is a physiological response to YHWH's overwhelming exhibition of power, a demonstration of what their accompanying words express. YHWH defeats Baal, not by educating the people, encouraging their reform, but by exercising his mastery, an event that is orchestrated and framed by his prophet.

In both their life-giving and life-taking capacities the prophets act as agents of YHWH, creating an earthly locus of action thoroughly associated with the deity. Such performance allows for an enactment and manifestation of divine power. It constitutes one of the two main foci of prophecy—the explanatory function being the other—as it figures in the various sources of the Deuteronomistic History.

In the standard scholarly account, the "deuteronomists" responsible for the editing of the Deuteronomistic History are the chief proponents of the view that the prophets preached repentance. This notion is derived largely from one key passage in the work, 2 Kings 17:7–23. The passage begins by describing how YHWH saved the nation from Egypt, but that Israel went on to worship other gods. At this point, the prophets enter the scene: "The LORD warned [*vayyaʿad*] Israel and Judah by every prophet [and] every seer, saying: 'Turn back from your wicked ways, and observe my commandments and my laws, according to all the teaching that I commanded your fathers and that I transmitted to you through my servants the prophets'" (2 Kings 17:13). It concludes that the people, nevertheless, "rejected all the commandments of the LORD their God" (17:16) and, therefore, were banished (17:18). The passage has been long recognized as a late editorial, exilic addition,[69] but one wonders straightaway how it is that an editor could characterize the work of the earlier prophets that lies before him, some of which we have just examined, in such seemingly divergent terms.

I would like to suggest that the reasoning behind this characterization may be clarified, in part, through the use of the term *he'id*, translated above as "warn." The verb usually introduces either a hortative statement—a command, as in the present case—or a declaration regarding the future. But, in either case, really it entails both. How so? The term *he'id* does not really mean "warn." It is not a rhetorical utterance designed to induce compliance through intimidation, part of a harsh pedagogy, as such a translation implies. Rather, it is an effective utterance; it sets something in motion and comes from the judicial realm. In fact, it is probably best understood closer to its etymological sense as "testify against." It establishes, before anticipated transgression, the punishment that will ensue.[70] Therefore, it participates in identifying the agent of violence and delineating its justification in a manner that resembles normal prophetic utterances. And so, in another passage in the Deuteronomistic History, Samuel is told to "testify against" the people regarding what their lives will be like living under a king in the new political system they seek to put into effect (1 Sam. 8:9). The point of this speech-act is not to dissuade the people—in the same verse, God tells Samuel to meet their request—but to rescind their right to cry out against the future harsh circumstances they are certain to encounter.

At the same time, in making manifest a certain future, an opportunity is opened up to take action that might mitigate its harshness, as we saw in the case of the letter from Mari. This is what our passage exploits in paraphrasing the prophets as telling the people to "turn back from your wicked ways." It offers an interpretation of prophecy, a paraphrase that, I would argue, does not seek to transform the significance of the basic unit of prophetic speech, the oracle, but rather to pull out, specify, and systematize—in the manner of the sort of rationalization that we saw *shuv* itself to undergo—another potential layer to prophecy, namely, the possibility of the people escaping the fate that has been pronounced upon them by removing sin from their midst.[71] In so doing, it combines with the oracular function other intermediary roles inherent to the prophet—intercessor on behalf of the people and conveyer of instructions, whether of a cultic, legal, or military nature.[72]

What purpose does this systematization—this elucidation of the possibilities for avoiding a negative fate—serve? Is this passage, as is generally assumed, really an exhortation to the present generation of exiles to reform their ways?[73] In fact, the exhortation found therein is entirely historical; there is no direct exhortation addressed to the exiles in the present, and the passage concludes with Israel's banishment "to this very day" (2 Kings 17:23). What the passage as a whole offers is not a program for redemption but an explanation for the people's current state.[74] It is an etiology of exile, and I would suggest that much of prophetic literature, transmitted as it was during the exile, must have operated within that framework, serving the needs of present understanding. Prophetic testimony established the people's punishment long ago; they had ample opportunity to avoid their fate but failed. The retroversion in this passage into the past of an exhortation to "turn back," supposedly a radical Deuteronomistic transformation of prophecy, folds back into the old prophetic discourse of delineating blame.[75]

INTERPRETING ISRAEL'S GEOPOLITICAL SITUATION: ISAIAH

How much changes when we move from narrative representations of the early prophets to the collections of oracles found among the so-called literary prophets? These are the prophets who are seen as the great theological innovators but, for our purposes, the dynamics of their speech seem strikingly similar to what we have already seen. We are left with the impression that this attribution of difference is largely enabled by the change of genre. I would like to explore these questions with regard to the Scroll of Isaiah, which, like the Deuteronomistic History, presents an amalgamation of sources from different time periods. Unique to Isaiah is the way in which, roughly speaking, these sources appear sequentially in the book, starting with pre-exilic material, moving to exilic and then postexilic material. We will focus on the first portion of the book, what is commonly called First Isaiah.[76]

First Isaiah lacks exhortative material.[77] There is little evidence that the prophet aimed to change the people's character. What does emerge clearly is that Isaiah offers an interpretation of the catastrophic events that are transpiring around the vulnerable and harassed kingdom of Judah. Nations are being uprooted, lands laid to waste. The known world is being destroyed at the hands of the approaching Assyrian imperial armies. How are these events to be treated? A modern historical reading might conclude that the military, economic, and political circumstances made Assyrian domination of the Levant all but inevitable. In the cultural-poetic terms of the ancient Near East, military success might be attributed to power residing inherently in the nation. The prophet places just such an interpretation into the mouth of the Assyrian nation: "By the might of my hand have I wrought it, by my skill, for I am clever: 'I have erased the borders of peoples; I have plundered their treasures, and exiled their vast populations. I was able to seize, like a nest, the wealth of peoples; as one gathers abandoned eggs, so I gathered all the earth: Nothing so much as flapped a wing or opened a mouth to peep'" (Isa. 10:13–14).

Isaiah's central mission could be seen as putting forward an alternative interpretation of these events. His less than obvious thesis is that it is YHWH who stands behind Assyrian power: "Does an ax boast over him who hews with it, or a saw magnify itself above him who wields it? As though the rod raised him who lifts it, as though the staff lifted that which is not wood!" (10:15). Assyria is simply YHWH's proxy designed to afflict the nations, especially his own, for their sins. And, he will someday afflict Assyria for its arrogance, what amounts to a failure to recognize YHWH's hand in events, thereby dispelling any doubt that it was he, not the foreign nation, who was responsible ultimately for the destruction of nations (10:16–19).

Isaiah's prophecies are part of the attempt of an oppressed nation subject to foreign control to envision a reversal of its fortunes that is at once realistic (it accounts for present circumstances) and utopian (it presumes radical future reversals). As part of its realism, the prophetic construction is exceptionally clear about, indeed perhaps accentuates, the humiliation and destruction that Judah, not to mention its neighbors, will endure. But, by claiming that Judah's deity lies behind its suffering, the prophet subverts this humiliation, using it to make an argument for the nation's continued vitality. The very power that destroyed Judah will destroy Assyria and redeem Zion.

What was the intended impact of Isaiah's words? Isaiah's oracles portray the states resulting from the unfolding divine action as those of terror: "Howl! For the day of YHWH is near; it shall come like havoc from Shaddai. Therefore all hands shall grow limp, and all men's hearts shall sink; and, overcome by terror, they shall be seized by pangs and throes, writhe like a woman in travail" (13:6–8), and humiliation: "Yea, man is bowed, and mortal brought low; brought low is the pride of the haughty" (5:15). Are such allusions to future human suffering meant as a threat to lead the people to repent? On the contrary, I would suggest that they are designed to perform, to induce, precisely the object upon which they most directly dwell: terror and humiliation. The prophet's extraordinarily vivid, relentless, and often downright brutal discourse compels the people to realize their own diminishment, as the gap between representation and reality blur in the emotional life of the prophet's audience. What these passages bring to the fore is the reduction of the self, the dismantlement of the prophet's audience, and they are, therefore, most frequently directed at those in power. The flipside of these circumscribed human states is, of course, the exaltation of the deity: "And the LORD of hosts has been exalted through judgment, the holy god sanctified through retribution" (5:16). In the end, the prophet's words are themselves a speech of conquest that constitute the power of YHWH, deploying events to generate an immediate presence for YHWH. Paradoxically, they end up undoing, in some measure, the trauma of powerlessness, by allowing the people to experience the power of the deity arrayed against them, thereby making palpable their only hope for eventual redemption.

The above analysis of Isaiah's interpretation of the geopolitical situation and its aim of enacting a YHWH-induced terror, not repentance, proceeds from an assessment of the pre-exilic, Isaianic material as a whole. But there is one passage that has provided a site for scholars to consider the nature of the prophetic "mission" in relation to repentance. It is here, in the presence of YHWH and his holy retinue, that Isaiah is given a special commission:

> I heard the voice of my Lord saying, "Whom shall I send? Who will go for us?" And I said, "Here am I; send me." And he said, "Go, say to that people: 'Hear, indeed, but do not understand; see, indeed, but do not grasp.' Dull that people's mind, stop its ears, and seal its eyes—lest seeing with its eyes, hearing with its ears, and grasping with its mind, it turns [*va-shav*] and is healed." (Isa.6:8–10)

Scholars take this command to the prophet to be exceptional. Generally, it is the mission of the prophet, so the argument goes, to encourage the people to "turn and be healed."[78] Perhaps Isaiah's vision arises from an unusual sense of frustration with his mission that the prophet has experienced, forcing him to reconceptualize his purpose or justify his failure.[79] Thus, in a moment of pessimism, Isaiah has turned away from the core aims of his office.

Does this passage truly configure a world that feels exceptional in the context of prophetic literature? I would like to argue that this passage is not a redirection of the prophetic mission but a commission of just one more prophetic act. In the heuristic model proposed earlier, we labeled as "stage one" a period in which a more or less functional relationship pertains between YHWH and Israel. They might suffer, perhaps even due to sin, but, in the words of our passage, they could still "turn and be healed." But, surely, these are not the conditions that pertain in most of prophetic literature, what I label as "stage two," when divine wrath reaches a tipping point—disaster seems inescapable—and appeal is no longer admissible.

How can appeal fail? How the barrier between YHWH and human beings is erected, how God avoids appeal, differs from one biblical account to the next. Is it a metaphorical cloud covering (Lam. 3:43) or Israel's innate stubbornness (Jer. 9:13)? But the basic fact of its existence remains. Like the case of Pharaoh, this passage maintains that the barrier is a construction of YHWH. Unlike the case of Pharaoh, the barrier is seen as a matter of ignorance rather than obstinance, lack of knowledge rather than power to refuse. Other passages in Isaiah portray the people's ignorance as a matter of a willful refusal to see the divine plan (Isa. 30:10) or their being too mired in earthly pleasures to recognize it (Isa. 5:11–12). In all of these cases, it is important to recognize that the knowledge the people lack is not of spiritual or moral goods but of the geopolitical situation, as interpreted by Isaiah, their impending doom at the hands of YHWH. If they knew, they would "turn." The failure of the people to react to Isaiah's rendering of events, if it is indeed compelling, requires explanation. This passage serves as an etiology of that failure; even the refusal to acknowledge YHWH's role derives from the deity himself. Accordingly, "turning" is not the first-order concern of prophecy but a potential outgrowth that must be cut back and controlled!

In this passage, Isaiah occupies the role of both prophet and avenging spirit. The duality of his role can be seen clearly through comparison with a remarkably similar passage found in the Deuteronomistic History that depicts the downfall of Ahab. Setting off to battle with Aram, the kings of Israel and Judah first consult with prophets of YHWH. All but one, Micaiah, assure them of victory. Micaiah goes on to explain his defiant stance: YHWH has sent a spirit from his divine council to confuse the other prophets, so that Israel's king, Ahab, would march out to battle and be destroyed. Oddly enough, Micaiah reveals this divine treachery to Ahab. He does not do so in an attempt to convince Ahab not to enter into battle; that would run against the divine plan. He is certain that Ahab will not alter his self-destructive course, and his speech accomplishes, therefore, another important aim. It establishes that the disaster that is to befall Ahab, including the very blindness of his prophets, is the work of YHWH. This ironic disclosure also justifies God's trickery. Ahab was warned, but chose to ignore YHWH's plot against him. By announcing YHWH's plot, Isaiah achieves the same aims as the prophet Micaiah, but he also functions in our passage as the "spirit" who volunteers to be the agent of YHWH and spread confusion. He is an enemy of the people, an actor in YHWH's plot.

But, what, precisely, does Isaiah *do* in this passage, how is he to effect the divine plot? In fact, we are told rather clearly. He must tell the people: "Hear, indeed, but do not understand; see, indeed, but do not grasp." We find a similar command in another Isaianic passage: "Act stupid and be stupefied! Act blind and be blinded! (They are drunk, but not from wine. They stagger, but not from liquor.) For the LORD has spread over you a spirit of deep sleep" (Isa. 29:9–10). The implication would seem to be that the prophet's words themselves are seen as efficacious, as having a certain power. Through their delivery, he unleashes the command of the divine council or, at least, acts in tandem with it, providing the explanatory verbal garb for the "spirit of deep sleep" that is brought by YHWH. Scholars have avoided this more obvious, less mediated reading, for it disrupts their basic structure for understanding prophetic speech as pedagogic and representative of reality, rather than bound up in its generation.

THE PLACE OF EXHORTATION: JEREMIAH AND EZEKIEL

Not withstanding a new, sometimes felicitous interest in integral wholes, much of the work of biblical scholarship continues to be the drawing of distinctions within source material and analysis of their causes. Such procedures have generated extensive discussion regarding the place of exhortation, specifically, calls for "repentance" in the scrolls attributed to the prophets, Jeremiah and Ezekiel. The finality and predominance of the oracles of doom found therein, combined with erstwhile commands to turn away from sin, has led to the formation of a scholarly crux. How are we to explain the presence of such divergence in a single prophetic work? Some locate the source of difference in the biography of the prophet, a movement from hope that the people would repent and avert disaster to despair (or the reverse);[80] others in redaction, a later editorial introduction of repentance as an address to exiles;[81] and yet others see a philosophical dialectic, a genuine tension between ideas of human freedom and determinism, within the prophet.[82] By accentuating difference, such readings, each in their own way, end up reifying "repentance" as an actual historical existent or, at least, a potentiality within the phenomenon of ancient Israelite prophecy.

Without denying the presence of genuine divergences internal to the prophetic works, I would like to shift the angle of inquiry to highlight another series of differences, those that lie between a dominant pedagogical image of the prophet and alternatives that, otherwise, might emerge. It is my contention that the failure to formulate consistently this broader comparison, to engage in a forthright manner the prejudgments of readers, can lead to an overdrawing of difference within the source material itself, as its commonalities appear in poor relief and contemporary dialectical categories are imputed to it. Indeed, it is the disparateness of ancient phenomena, the inherent impossibility of knowing them as such, that requires us to pursue, at times, the more minimalist forms of understanding allowed by such broad comparison.

In the case of the exhortations in Jeremiah and Ezekiel, we have already isolated a potential within the prophetic function for the prophet to issue cultic demands, often in the context of intercession on behalf of the people but also with respect to lawgiving.[83] Components of the material ascribed to Jeremiah and Ezekiel could be seen as fitting into this basic paradigm. Jeremiah stands at the gate of the "House of YHWH" and declares that only "if you execute justice between one another; if you do not oppress the stranger, the orphan, and the widow" will God let "you dwell in this place" (Jer. 7:1–7). In a slightly different vein, Ezekiel maintains that he has been appointed as a "watchman" for Israel to alert them to impending doom (Ezek. 33:7–9) and, in that role, exclaims: "turn back, turn back from your evil ways, that you may not die, O House of Israel!" (33:11).

The problem is that, while they seem to allude to a hypothetical social, institutional context of prophetic instruction, such passages can hardly be said to operate within it.[84] As they appear before us, each text radically reconfigures the significance of these prophetic utterances. For Jeremiah, the failure of the utterance is integrated into the very account of its delivery, as the prophet transitions to an explanation of the reasons for Judah's destruction (Jer. 7:8–11).[85] He goes on to declare that the "House of God" will be destroyed

(7:12–15) and his own intercessory capability shut down (7:16–20). The point is, perhaps, best developed in Ezekiel where the prophetic summons consistently and explicitly figure in the context of theodicy, as part of an attempt to counter the claim of "your fellow countrymen" that "the way of the LORD is unfair" (Ezek. 33:17). Israel should not imagine that they are being punished for their ancestor's sins, as it is put elsewhere, "parents eat sour grapes and their children's teeth are blunted" (18:3).[86] Rather, as the prophet insists throughout, YHWH only punishes for current iniquity; if the wicked "turn back," they live (33:12–16). But this turns out to be more of a theoretical possibility pertaining to the individual. Against the backdrop of the people's plaint and the fact of exile, it is clear that Israel as a nation has not opted in. Ezekiel's generation had a chance to "turn back" from their ancestors' transgressions but failed to do so.[87] In this context, the prophet's call to "turn back," indeed, the very rhetoric of "turning" as a possibility, ends up serving as nothing more than an extension of the prophetic function of blame.

Of course, the idea that such passages are to be read as intended to turn Israel back from its sins seems even less assured when weighed against a reading of the prophetic works as a whole, hence, the problem of divergence with which we began. From their very first chapters, both Jeremiah and Ezekiel present an unstoppable juggernaut descending upon Israel from the north: "From the north shall disaster break loose upon all the inhabitants of the land!" (Jer. 1:14). Likewise, Ezekiel suggests that the armies descending from the north are an earthly manifestation of an awe-inspiring divine chariot, which is on the move against Israel (Ezek. 1:4). And, over the course of both works, the inevitability and fact of exile is made clear. Indeed, for Jeremiah, the prophet even seems to be a part of the war machine set in motion against Israel, "a fortified city, and an iron pillar, and bronze walls against the whole land" (Jer. 1:18). And, indeed, to judge from King Jehoiakim's reaction to the written scrolls of Jeremiah's oracles (Jer. 36), the prophets' words may have been seen as having their own dreaded efficacy. But, by far, the most obvious reading of the prophetic scrolls and reason for their continued transmission, as already proposed in the discussion of 2 Kings 17, is that they explain Israel's exile. I do not see the exhortation passages in Jeremiah and Ezekiel as necessitating a radical departure from this overall assessment, even if, in a certain reading, they have provided a powerful basis for the pedagogical model of prophecy.

JONAH AND THE END OF PROPHECY

There are a few passages in postexilic works where an injunction to cease from sin seems to appear as a present possibility. Indeed, it is not hard to imagine that the grand explanation for the suffering of the exilic generation could be turned to the uses of the present. Thus, we find in Zechariah a call to "turn back" coupled with a plea to "not be like your fathers" (Zech. 1:4), who failed to heed their prophets (1:3–6).[88] Here, injunction is not conjoined, as in the earlier works, with an insistence that doom will follow. We also find in the postexilic Isaianic writings, in an explicitly liturgical context, a call for "the wicked to give up his ways" (Isa. 56:7). Again, such injunctions are not alien to a certain form of the prophetic function, even as the proto-apocalypticism of these works can hardly be said to accentuate its place in these books, as some have argued.[89] In fact, given the relatively minimal attestation of such injunctions, we might wonder whether we are encountering here a deliberate program of reform at all or, once again, merely a resource for imagining the source of the residual trouble that continues to plague the generations after the exile.

What I would like to focus on now is the book of Jonah, not because it can be seen as configuring the "turn away from sin" as a present possibility, which it may or may not do—as a narrative tale about non-Israelites, it does not explicitly address the question—but because of the way it reflects back on and seems to offer a criticism of the prophet as a figure. Indeed, Jonah has been read as a sort of parody, but of what, precisely? It begins by expanding dramatically upon the theme of the prophet's reticence to accept his office—Jonah runs away (Jon. 1:3)—and then transitions to the absurdity that the prophet, rather than being the one who identifies and orders the removal of the taboo, becomes the taboo that must be removed to save others (1:4–15). And, in the end, we find out that Jonah's avoidance of his office derives from an extreme form of misanthropy: he knows that YHWH is "a compassionate and gracious God, slow to anger, abounding in kindness, renouncing punishment" (4:2), and he does not want people to be saved. Is this not a critique that could be launched, fairly or not, at every Israelite prophet?[90] For, as has been noted repeatedly, the basic form of prophetic speech, judgment and accusation, hardly leaves open the hope or, even, expresses an interest in divine renouncement of punishment.

The question is what would be at stake in the author of this tract launching such a criticism. What I find unites Jonah and some of the late prophetic texts we have examined is a certain anxiety, an urgency, not to get their audience to change their ways but to assert something about the nature of YHWH— that he really does desire the protection and continuity of his people, that he prefers to renounce punishment whenever possible. As we find in the words Ezekiel attributes to YHWH: "Is it my desire that a wicked person shall die?. . . It is rather that he shall turn back from his ways and live" (Ezek. 18:24). This would appear to be, rather explicitly, the point of the last chapter of Jonah: God is all too happy to be given the opportunity to take the Ninevites within his care and protection. But, there is one significant difference. In Ezekiel, the prophet is presented as fulfilling what is framed as his obligation to warn the people (33:1–6); the office of the prophet, so closely associated with YHWH, also requires defense in light of the failure of the nation. In Jonah, however, the prophet is separated out from YHWH. The author turns on the figure of the prophet in service of the broader historic need to continue justifying a deity who, by all appearances, does not seem to be particularly bent on saving his people. It was the person of the prophet himself that accounts for the bitterness and helplessness of the oracles as an institution, even detected in the seeming finality of Jonah's utterance, "forty days more, and Nineveh shall be overthrown" (Jon. 3:4). As for the merciful deity, all along, he silently hoped for a change, not out of a primary pedagogical intent, concern to improve their moral lot but, as is made clear to Jonah, out of care for his creatures, which is only possible in the absence of sin (4:10–11).

SUMMARY

The chapter began with an exploration of the pedagogical image of Scripture, basic to so many practices of biblical interpretation. The reading of prophetic literature, in particular, remains within its thralls, often through the model of the sermon. Ancient Israelite prophets thus come to be configured as preachers of repentance or, in more nuanced accounts, as innovators and teachers of Israelite faith. The chapter was an attempt to reframe prophecy along alternative lines, largely in terms of its relation to power. In particular, it was suggested that we need to look again at the question of the efficacy of prophetic utterances and to recognize the ways in which the prophets are effective agents, interested parties, in the running conflict between a people and their deity. Part of the issue at stake has to do with the representation of the deity, taking seriously its anthropopathism. As portrayed by the prophets, divine anger, as a mode of rectification, aims at the destruction, not the edification, of its object. Rebellion against the deity requires a reactivation of divine power through acts of mastery. As a discourse, prophetic speech attaches the impotence imposed upon the nation by events to the power of their deity, affirming his potency and justifying his actions by developing an account of collective guilt.

These themes were traced through an example from ancient Near Eastern prophecy, Moses' confrontation as prophet with Pharaoh, the Deuteronomistic History, and the scrolls of Isaiah, Jeremiah, and Ezekiel. In particular, with the latter two, an effort was made to describe the place of exhortation in prophetic literature, with the conclusion being drawn that it is, once again, an effort to underline national culpability by maintaining that Israel, historically, had been given an opportunity to turn away from its sin but had failed to do so. The view of prophetic literature and its transmission as part of a reform movement in the exilic period and beyond is questioned. Instead, the reasons for the transmission of such literature would seem to belong to the sphere of etiology, to inform the people's present understanding of their position and explain their deity's apparent neglect. Finally, the chapter concludes with a discussion of the book of Jonah, which shows an awareness of the apparent finality of prophetic utterances, their lack of interest in reformation, but seeks to take the blame for their brutal message of abandonment off the deity and place it, instead, on the human figure of the prophet himself.

PART III

Religion

CHAPTER 6

cvo

Agency and Redemption

The LORD your God will circumcise your heart and the heart of your offspring.
Deuteronomy 30:6

"RELIGION," "REDEMPTION," AND "REPENTANCE"

We have considered how the interpretation of phenomena as penitential has been influenced by several overarching constructs: practices as "rites;" linguistic terms as part of a "language," a lexicon, of religious concepts; and public address as "pedagogy." These become not just ways of representing Scripture and its contents; they serve more broadly as components, as it will be recognized, of our very notion of religion. In its persistent conventional senses, "religion" often suggests the existence of a collective guided by particular beliefs and invested with a common purpose around certain forms of human virtue. This moralistic and, fundamentally, anthropological aim is thought to account for the appetitive quality of religions; they seek the acquisition of new souls through the conversion of those outside of the group and its parallel, the reformation of those within, in order to bring salvation to both. Alongside this teleological view of the aggregate, there exists an emphasis on the agency of the person. "Religion," though promoted in community, must be adopted, affirmed, and experienced by individuals. It ultimately exists on the level of the mind in the form of beliefs and other mental dispositions, even as it is instilled or receives expression through a variety of ritual performances. As a structure, it enables its adherents to improve themselves, to choose aright.

Even while this Enlightenment-inflected definition has been challenged on theoretical grounds, it continues to inform interpretation.[1] One way this manifests itself is in the place assigned to repentance in reigning scholarly accounts of redemptive expectations, those found in the Hebrew Bible and, in particular, early forms of Judaism and Christianity. A few biblical texts thought to allude to "repentance," such as Deuteronomy 4:29–31, are commonly singled out and understood as making programmatic statements, as setting an agenda for Israel in exile and beyond that is in line with a so-called Deuteronomistic school.[2] Israel will sin, be exiled, but will be redeemed if it repents. Accordingly, religious associations of the late Second Temple period, such as the Dead Sea sect and early Jesus movement, have been viewed as "penitential movements," motivated, at least in part, by a desire to induce Israel to repent.[3] Likewise, sectarian practices of initiation, baptism, prayer, and banishment come to be interpreted in keeping with a notion of repentance.

Such interpretations of early redemptive expectations serve a variety of readers as a way of grounding "religion," constructing a space for notions of morality and choice, in Judaism and Christianity by locating it already at their origins.[4] The claim that Israel believed redemption to await its repentance may be seen as a way of inserting a later form of individual, penitential piety into earlier biblical representations. Thus, Rabbi Eliezer, in the Babylonian Talmud, unambiguously declares, "If Israel repents, they will be redeemed" (b. Sanh. 97b), but the timing, stability, and totality of this formation cannot be assumed.[5] What is needed is a greater allowance for the subtleties and varieties of agency found in ancient texts.[6] In fact, we need to recognize that "agency" itself is "not a natural category," but rather that "the successive uses of this concept (their different grammars) have opened up or closed very different possibilities for acting and being."[7] Reconsidering redemptive expectations articulated in the Hebrew Bible and, subsequently, used as a basis for communal identity among Jews after the exile allows us to encounter forms of discourse that stand out from the dominant view of the relationship between the individual and the aggregate—that we are subject-agents that constitute ourselves, that make our own history, within a social structure that promotes such positive determinations. As such, this chapter follows in the mode of what has preceded in giving voice to an alternative, nonpenitential reading of a range of phenomena associated with the Bible, but it does so focusing on the period around the turn of the Common Era, in which a discourse around "repentance" and attendant notions of religion does, indeed, begin to emerge. These developments will be taken up at their point of origin in the next chapter.

In what follows, I will be looking, in particular, at articulations of redemptive expectations as modes of communal definition, rather than as sources for moral and religious demands enforced by the community and incumbent upon the individual, with the combination of teleology and agency such a structure presupposes. For these purposes, the Dead Sea Scrolls present us with an unprecedented resource and form the core of the present inquiry, moving us from the world of ancient Israel to postbiblical forms of Judaism. As a collection of texts, they represent a variety of genres, many of which directly treat communal formation or contain implications for it, allowing for a full treatment of the topic. They reflect explicitly or implicitly back on and, thereby, highlight otherwise dispersed biblical passages that treat notions of redemption and constitute, in most cases, the earliest interpretation of these verses. And they can be traced to the library of a single community, even if not all of the texts were authored within it. Furthermore, their chronological and geographic position allows us to reveal lines of continuity not only with the biblical material but with later forms of Judaism and Christianity and, especially, with the early Jesus movement. What emerges with clarity is a notion of divinely orchestrated "re-creation" that precedes repentance as a theory of human transformation and, like its biblical antecedents, differs from it significantly in not having recourse to normative understandings of moral agency. The question at stake throughout is not whether sectarians and others would have exercised what we would consider normal forms of human agency but whether they chose to conceive of their actions as such, to articulate this category, the position that has been assumed by modern scholarship.

Divine Re-creation and Apocalypticism

The book of Jubilees, a second-century B.C.E., protosectarian, pseudepigraphic work, a rewriting of the book of Genesis, was much beloved by the members of the Dead Sea sect, to judge from the number of (albeit incomplete) copies preserved among the scrolls and the direct references to it found therein.[8] It provides us with an initial focal point with which to begin working out this alternative notion of re-creation, as well as the place of agency as a category in interpretation.

Moses' Protest

The book of Jubilees begins with an evocative rendering of two key biblical formulations of redemption, Deuteronomy 4:29–31 and Deuteronomy 30:1–10. Like Deuteronomy 4:29–31, Deuteronomy 30:1–10 employs the language of *shuv*, "turning to YHWH," but it also speaks of a divinely initiated "circumcision of the heart" that is to occur in conjunction with an ingathering of exiles. Working within the existing paradigm of agency and redemption, the distinctions between the two passages have been ignored or overwritten by most modern scholars.[9] Both are seen as exemplary statements of a supposedly unified Deuteronomistic ideology, according to which Jubilees has also been read,[10] whereby sin leads to exile and repentance brings redemption. When divine intervention alone receives literary representation, "the LORD your God will circumcise your heart" (30:6), it is commonly assumed that some form of human initiative is also implied. This move constitutes as much a reading strategy for introducing agency as it does a particular modern, liberal form of theology, that human transformation necessarily arises from a complex combination of individual choice and divine guidance. One exception to this scholarly trend is a recent treatment that sees in the differences between the passages opposing notions of agency and, thus, evidence of multiple authorship. Deuteronomy 4:29–31 adheres to the Deuteronomistic notion of free will, while Deuteronomy 30:1–10 introduces a predestinarian idea more closely aligned with certain prophetic voices.[11] While this approach represents a critical advance in its attention to the differences between these passages, it too operates with the assumption that "agency," even in the form of its negation, is a natural category in ancient Israelite thought and, therefore, a basis for source-critical distinctions.

Returning to Jubilees, its first chapter purports to be a report of Moses' original interaction with God at Sinai. There, God reveals to Moses what awaits Israel upon its entrance into the Land. While this revelation includes some bad news, the eventuality of exile, it also contains promise of their redemption:[12]

> After this they will return to me from among the nations with all their minds, all their souls, and all their strength. Then I will gather them from among all the nations, and they will search for me so that I may be found by them when they have searched for me with all their minds and with all their souls. I will rightly disclose to them abundant peace. I will transform them into a righteous plant with all my mind and with all my soul. They will become a blessing, not a curse; they will become the head, not the tail. I will build my temple among them and will live with them; I will become their God and they will become my true and righteous people. I will neither abandon them nor become alienated from them, for I am the Lord their God. (1:15–18)

Rather remarkably, despite its seemingly favorable aspects, Moses, in the manner of a prophetic intercessor, protests this divine plan:

> Then Moses fell prostrate and prayed and said: "Lord my God, do not allow your people and your heritage to go along in the error of their minds, and do not deliver them into the control of the nations with the result that they rule over them lest they make them sin against you. May your mercy, Lord, be lifted over your people. Create for them a just spirit. May the spirit of Belial not rule them so as to bring charges against them before you and to trap them away from every proper path so that they may be destroyed from your presence. They are your people and your heritage whom you have rescued from Egyptian control by your great power. Create for them a pure mind and a holy spirit. May they not be trapped in their sins from now to eternity." (1:19–21)

The core of Moses' concern appears to be for Israel to avoid the religiously deleterious effects of exile, that they not be subjected to the "control of the nations" after having just been "rescued from Egyptian control." His proposal is that God change Israel's nature, now, as they stand at Sinai; free them from the power of sin, here personified as the "spirit of Belial"; and, thereby, prevent exile altogether.[13]

At this point, God responds to Moses with a second series of redemptive promises. It has not always been recognized that this second series actually constitutes a revision of the first, an adjustment in the terms of redemption. It adopts elements of Moses' preceding request without necessarily meeting all of his demands:[14]

> Then the Lord said to Moses: "I know their contrary nature, their way of thinking, and their stubbornness. They will not listen until they acknowledge their sins and the sins of their ancestors. After this they will return to me in a fully upright manner and with all [their] minds and all [their] souls. I will cut away the foreskins of their minds and the foreskins of their descendants' minds. I will create a holy spirit for them and will purify them in order that they may not turn away from me from that time forever. Their souls will adhere to me and to all my commandments. They will perform my commandments. I will become their father and they will become my children. All of them will be called children of the living God. Every angel and every spirit will know them. They will know that they are my children and that I am their father in a just and proper way and that I love them. (1:22–25)

God will not prevent Israel's initial exile but he will eventually change their nature, as Moses requested, to avoid additional ones. This second account of redemption incorporates language of re-creation and purification that was absent from God's initial account of redemption and clearly derives from Moses' own protest.

The tale of Moses' successful protest was not woven from whole cloth by Jubilees but constitutes a striking example of the creative biblical exegesis for which the author is known. Its main impetus appears to lie in the discrepancy between Deuteronomy 4:29–31 and Deuteronomy 30:1–10. How are we to explain, at once, the apparent redundancy, with both promising an eventual "turn back to YHWH," and, at the same time, account for their subtle differences, the addition in the latter of a promise of divine "circumcision of the heart?" Jubilees claims to provide the backstory behind these passages, with Deuteronomy 4:29–31 corresponding to the first series of redemptive promises and Deuteronomy 30:1–10 to the second.[15] Deuteronomy 30:1–10, Jubilees would argue, is, in fact, a revision of Deuteronomy 4:29–31, provoked by Moses' intercession. Between these two moments of revelation, he insisted that God carry out a permanent change in their nature, thus provoking a change in redemption's formulation.[16]

Unlike modern interpreters, the author of Jubilees shows no signs of need-ing to work out the place of agency in these passages, even as he sets forth a notion of human transformation that would seem to operate outside of its parameters.[17] Indeed, while the author reproduces Deuteronomy's language of *shuv*, there is no reason to assume that this term necessarily suggests an exercise of human free will, unless one presupposes its nominalization as the concept, "repentance." The interpretation of *shuv* and its significance, espe-cially among the sectarians, will be discussed later in this chapter. What is important to recognize now is that Jubilees rewrites the biblical material in such a way as to privilege the divine "circumcision of the heart," a notion that does not readily admit common, contemporary concerns for agency.

Becoming Cattle

What is this notion of "circumcision of the heart" and from where does it hail? We have already seen that it has a certain linguistic basis in the book of Deuteronomy. There are also passages in the books of Jeremiah and Ezekiel that formulate redemption as a matter of contending, in some fashion, with Israel's heart.[18] While the language of "circumcision," if we might be excused the modern analogy, suggests some sort of bypass surgery, Jeremiah's involves the implantation of a monitoring device, "I will put my teaching into their midst and inscribe it upon their hearts"[19] (Jer. 31:33), and Ezekiel a full heart transplant, "I will give you a new heart and put a new spirit into you; I will remove the heart of stone from your body and give you a heart of flesh"[20] (Ezek. 36:26). Jubilees would have found an important precedent in these passages. The passage from Ezekiel, like Jubilees, even integrates this language with that of a "purification" that goes beyond the ritual to entail a full transformation of the human being: "I will sprinkle clean water upon you, and you shall be clean; I will cleanse you from all your uncleanness and from all your fetishes" (Ezek. 36:25). For the biblical passages, the focus is quite consis-tently on the formation of what Jeremiah labels a "new covenant" (Jer. 31:31), coordinating arrival back in the land with the reascension of YHWH to the position of Israel's god, "I will be their God, and they shall be my people" (Jer. 31:33), achieved through an enactment of law, which requires a further act of creation to enable them to adhere to law. Covenant, in this view, is imposed upon the people.[21] None of this seems to have much to do with repentance, nor, for that matter, do passages in so-called Second and Third Isaiah that look at redemption as a cosmic event, as a "creation" of "a new heaven and a new earth" (65:17), language that Jubilees also adopts.[22]

Though "creation of a new heart," "purification," and "circumcision of the heart" have biblical bases, in their present formulation in Jubilees, which incorporates quite prominently as well the decidedly nonbiblical language of demonology,[23] they should be positioned in that broad series of social and ideological formations prevalent in the late Second Temple period known as apocalypticism. This impression is confirmed by the almost complete spiritualization of exile as a theme in Jubilees, in contradistinction to the above biblical passages,[24] and by other emphases found throughout Jubilees that will be explored below.[25] Indeed, this awaited divine re-creation of human beings should be seen as the anthropological dimension of a broader cosmic transformation at the end of days:

> The angel of the presence . . . took the tablets [which told] of the divisions of the years . . . from [the time of the creation until] the time of the new creation when the heavens, the earth, and all their creatures will be renewed like the powers of the sky and like all the creatures of the earth, until the time when the temple of the Lord will be created in Jerusalem on Mt. Zion. All the luminaries will be renewed for [the purposes of] healing, health, and blessing for all the elect ones of Israel and so that it may remain this way from that time throughout all the days of the earth. (Jub. 1:29)

Astrological renewal will ensure the permanence of the new creation and new temple that mark the ordained fulfillment of Israel's history.

Though it has not always been emphasized in the study of apocalypticism, such views of the future entailing a specifically anthropological re-creation in addition to a cosmic one are to be found throughout the literature. We find allusion to precisely such a process at the end of the second-century B.C.E. text known as the Animal Apocalypse.[26] The white sheep, representing Israel, find their way back to the house of their Lord and then:

> [T]he eyes of all were opened . . . and there was none among them that did not see . . . . And I saw how a white bull was born, and its horns were large. And all the wild beasts and all the birds of heaven were afraid of it and made petition to it continually. And I saw until all their species were changed, and they all became white cattle. (1 En. 90:35–38)[27]

All the animal species, representing the various nations, change species and turn into white cattle. While sheep tend to stray, a fact exploited throughout the Apocalypse's allegory, cattle are less likely to do so. At the end of days, in keeping with a grant of newfound knowledge, human nature will be transformed, not in the form of willed change but of re-creation. Likewise, in the third-century B.C.E. Book of the Watchers, also part of 1 Enoch's collected texts, we find a related formulation:

> Then wisdom will be given to all the chosen; and they will all live, and they will sin no more through godlessness or pride. In the enlightened man there will be light, and in the wise man, understanding. And they will transgress no more,

nor will they sin all the days of their life, nor will they die in the heat of [God's] wrath. (1 En. 5:8–9)

New understanding will render sin impossible at the end of days and ensure continual human well-being. It is the righteous who are to be transformed. Repentance of the wicked is not sounded as a theme here, elsewhere in the Enochic corpus, or in other apocalypses, such as those found in the book of Daniel. These passages all attest to a notion of divine re-creation as basic to apocalyptic discourse.[28]

Noah and the New Genesis

Typical of apocalyptic thought is a periodic view of history that sees in the past a precursor to the future.[29] We might expect, therefore, to find divine re-creation figuring in late Second Temple readings of the Flood story, which comes to be seen as a sort of "first end" (1 En. 93:4) in apocalyptic literature, a prototype of the final end of days.[30] And so it is that in 1 Enoch, at the time of the Flood, God commands his angels to bind the demons and instructs Michael:

> Cleanse the earth from all impurity and from all wrong and from all lawless-
> ness and from all sin; and godlessness and all impurities that have come upon
> the earth, remove. And all the sons of men will become righteous; and all the
> peoples will worship [me]; and all will bless me and prostrate themselves. And
> all the earth will be cleansed from all defilement and from all uncleanness; and
> I shall not again send upon them any wrath or scourge for all the generations of
> eternity. (10:20–22)

In this passage, God's promise never again to doom the world is linked to a new-found righteousness rather than to a grudging acceptance of its inhabitants' infirmity, as the Bible itself would seem to suggest in Genesis 8:21. Interestingly enough, the Enochic text addresses the same sequence of topics as the biblical text: (1) protection of the earth; (2) the righteousness, or lack thereof, of humankind; and (3) cessation of punishment against living beings. Rather than contradicting the biblical text, the passage from 1 Enoch may represent a particular interpretation of it. The phrase "for the devisings of man's mind are evil from his youth" (Gen. 8:21) does not come to explain why God will never *again* destroy the earth; indeed, human evil is what led to destruction in the first place (Gen. 6:5). Rather, it identifies the problem that God had to address in order to be able now to declare that he will "never again [or, perhaps: no longer] curse the earth on account of human beings" (Gen. 8:21). In 1 Enoch's account, the floodwaters were meant to effectuate this change in human nature, protecting the earth from pollution by cleansing it of human evil.[31]

Jubilees is even more explicit about a re-creation of human nature around the time of the Flood: "He made a new and righteous nature for all his creatures so that they would not sin with their whole nature until eternity. Everyone will be righteous—each according to his kind—for all time" (Jub. 5:12). It is noteworthy that this passage comes in Jubilees just after the book's account of the obliteration of the current evil generation, and not in connection with the promise never again to destroy the world. Its placement may be intended to highlight another part of the biblical narrative perceived to be relevant to the re-creation theme: "The LORD saw how great was the wickedness of man [*ha-'adam*] on the earth, and how every plan devised by the heart of man was nothing but evil all the time. And he repudiated having made man [*ha-'adam*] on the earth, and his heart troubled him. And the LORD said, 'I will blot out from the earth man [*ha-'adam*] whom I created'" (Gen. 6:6–7). In this passage, God realizes that there is something fundamentally wrong with humankind. However, the use here of the definite article (*ha-'adam*) before the term for man (*'adam*), along with the apparently superfluous qualifier "whom I created," could have suggested to the ancient biblical interpreter that the problem lay less with the overall possibilities of the human race—after all, God does allow humanity to continue—than with the way in which a *particular* batch of humans has turned out. "I will blot out from the earth *the* man-whom-I-have-created," God says, but he is not giving up on the idea of humanity altogether. In other words, the Bible's wording here could be read as suggesting the creation of a new, superior race. And so too, we find in Josephus: "He [God] condemned not them alone for their wickedness, but resolved to destroy *all humankind then existing* and to create another race pure of vice"[32] (*Ant.* 1:75).

Anthropological renewal was so basic to ancient readers' sense of the Flood as a "first end" that we find multiple, overlapping traditions, sometimes even in the same work or about the same verse, regarding its place in the Bible. Jubilees includes another striking story, this one said to transpire right after the Flood:

> During the third week of this jubilee impure demons began to mislead Noah's grandchildren, to make them act foolishly, and to destroy them . . . . He prayed before the Lord his God and said: "God of the spirits which are in all animate beings—you who have shown kindness to me . . . may your mercy be lifted over the children of your children; and may the wicked spirits not rule them in order to destroy them from the earth. Now you bless me and my children so that we may increase, become numerous, and fill the earth . . ." Then our God told us [i.e., the angels, one of whom is the purported narrator of Jubilees] to tie up each one. When Mastema, the leader of the spirits, came, he said: "Lord creator, leave some of them before me . . . because if none of them is left for me I shall not be able to exercise the authority of my will among mankind. For they are meant for

[the purposes of] destroying and misleading before my punishment *because the evil of mankind is great.*" Then he [God] said that a tenth of them should be left before him, while he would make nine parts descend to the place of judgment. (10:1–10)

Apparently, Jubilees views Noah's sacrifice in Genesis 8:20 as having included a plea for the removal of demons that provoked within the deity the following reflection: "[T]he LORD said to himself: 1) 'Never again will I doom the earth because of man, 2) for the devisings of man's mind are evil from his youth; 3) nor will I ever again destroy every living being, as I have done'" (Gen. 8:21). The three clauses in this verse are understood by Jubilees as the back-and-forth of an actual conversation that transpired in the divine realm. God commands the removal of the demons, who are responsible for misleading humanity and, hence, causing their destruction; Mastema protests; and God modifies his decree. Such an account explains the apparent redundancy of the last clause in the statement, "nor will I ever again destroy . . .," seeing it actually as a qualification of the first, "never again will I doom." God will allow the demons to continue to pursue humanity but not ". . . as I have done." It also explains why the second clause, that God will never again destroy humanity "for the devisings of man's mind are evil," sounds more like an argument against humanity than one in favor of it. In fact, Jubilees suggests, this was an accusation of Mastema as part of an argument to ensure his minions' survival.[33] Like the Sinai event, the Flood was understood to be the sort of cosmic upheaval that could have become the moment in which human nature was totally transformed. In each case, that final re-creation was pushed off, secured by Moses, in the end, at Sinai, but only for the distant future.

Apotropaic Prayer

Scholars have pointed to the formal affinities between the prayers of Noah and Moses in Jubilees, where requests are made for the removal of demons, and "apotropaic prayer," a genre of prayers for protection from demons common in the late Second Temple period.[34] Indeed, other prime examples may be found in Jubilees and related literature. According to Jubilees, Abraham's passage from idolatry to monotheism is marked by one such prayer: "Save me from the power of the evil spirits who rule the thoughts of people's minds. May they not mislead me from following you, my God. Do establish me and my posterity forever. May we not go astray from now until eternity" (12:20). Later on, he also utters a prayer specifically for Jacob and his descendants: "May the spirits of Mastema not rule over you and your descendants to remove you from following the Lord who is your God from now and forever" (19:28).[35] Likewise, in another text, the Prayer of Levi, a fragmentary Aramaic original of which was found among the Scrolls, Levi asks that his offspring be kept from evil.

Here is an excerpt from what appears to have been a later Greek translation of that text:[36]

> O Lord, you know all hearts, and you alone understand all the thoughts of minds. And now my children are with me, and grant me all the paths of truth. Make far from me, O Lord, the unrighteous spirit, and evil thought and fornication, and turn pride away from me. Let there be shown to me, O Lord, the holy spirit, and counsel, and wisdom and knowledge and grant me strength, in order to do that which is pleasing to you and find favor before you, and to praise your words with me, O Lord .... And that which is pleasant and good before you. And let not any satan have power over me, to make me stray from your path.

While the power of personified demons is less pronounced in this text, replaced in part by a more explicit concern for proper knowledge, it shares clear terminological similarities with the prayers in Jubilees and apotropaic prayer in general.

Nevertheless, the common designation of these texts as instances of a form of the critical category, "apotropaic prayer," should give us pause. Bound up in that identification lies the suggestion that such prayers are found because they correspond to a lived reality basic to their authors, an ongoing component of religious practice, whereby individuals used prayers such as these as part of an ongoing combat with their spiritual adversaries, the demons. Not surprisingly, there is a tendency to associate the themes found in them—knowledge, rectification of behavior, forgiveness—with a penitential piety.[37] But such an individual-oriented description of apotropaic prayer as a form misses the ways in which the specific literary representations before us are actually deployed, namely as part of an unfolding of the eschatological community. These prayers invariably go beyond requests for the petitioner's personal protection to encompass their offspring. They appear at key junctures in the gradual definition and refinement of God's people. Thus, Noah prays on behalf of his offspring, the world's new population after the Flood, Abraham on behalf of his offspring, the monotheists of the world, and again on behalf of Jacob, the progenitor of Israel. Moses, on the other hand, prays on behalf of a renewed Israel, the final reconception and hence re-creation of humanity. Likewise, in the Prayer of Levi, Levi prays for his descendants, the priests, yet another demarcation of humanity. With each progression, the hold of the demons slackens. As we find in the final chapter of Jubilees:

> The jubilees will pass by until Israel is pure of every sexual evil, impurity, contamination, sin, and error. Then they will live confidently in the entire land. They will no longer have any satan or any evil person. The land will be pure from that time until eternity. (50:5)

Jubilees thus uses apotropaic prayers as a literary form but, ultimately, positions them, not as part of an individual piety, but as discrete pivotal moments in a transgenerational epochal progression,[38] a revelation of specialized knowledge to members of an increasingly restricted in-group. Knowledge of the past, as well as of the cosmic renewal and divine re-creation that are to occur at the end of days, of the sort found in Jubilees, allows participants to see themselves as the end product of a long series of cosmic processes. It serves the purposes of identification, the formation of an eschatological community, rather than exhortation. In short, moral states seem to be tied to modes of identification and knowledge, an "opening of the eyes," not individual agency.

The Sense of Sin

One last component of apocalyptic knowing needs to be considered, and to do so we need to return to the first chapter of Jubilees and address an aspect of its overall context. God's revelation to Moses about the nature of redemption is part of a knowledge of all things past and future that is offered to him. Here, in a reconstruction that was made partially on the basis of a fragment found among the Scrolls (4Q216 I, 12–17) and partially on the Ethiopic text (1:4–6),[39] God explains the import of such knowledge:

> [He said to him: "Pay attention to all of the thi]ngs that I will reveal to you [on this mountain. Write them in a book so that] their descendants [will kn]ow that I have not abandoned them [on account of (less literally: despite) all the evil which they did in breaking the covenant which] I am making between me and you today [for their generations on Mt. Sinai. So it will be that when] all of [these] things [happ]en to th[em] [they will know that I was justified, not them,[40] in all] their [judgments] and [all] their curses. [They] will know [that I was steadfast with them."

Revelation, as contained in Moses' book, does not serve to warn the people, to prevent Israel's sin,[41] but to reassure them in exile, "that I have not abandoned them," and to vindicate God at the end of days by constituting an element of Israel's self-knowledge: "they will know that I was justified, not them."[42]

This theme is picked up later in the chapter in the exchange around Moses' protest. There is a historic opportunity at Sinai to end evil (as there had been during the Flood), but God allows it to persist. Why? By way of responding to Moses' challenge, God declares in his second series of redemptive promises: "I know their contrary nature, their way of thinking, and their stubbornness. They will not listen until they acknowledge their sins and the sins of their ancestors" (Jub. 1:22). God knows their depravity, but he will not transform their nature, enable them to "listen," until they too know it. Here, Jubilees calls upon the account of exile and return found in the book of Leviticus, in which Israel "shall acknowledge their sins and the sins of their ancestors" (Lev. 26:40). But, rather than seeing that acknowledgment as a culmination of the denigration that exile constitutes, as suggested in chapter 3, he construes it to be an existential realization, the very purpose of exile. Israel needs to suffer exile because it is only there that they can gain an understanding on an onto-logical level of their depravity, that a sense of sin can enter into their knowl-edge of themselves. This tension between human inadequacy and (eventual) divine intervention is basic to apocalypticism's organization of the world and religious communities as located on the borderline between past and future epochs, and it reveals important lines of connection with later formulations such as those found in the letters of Paul. The consciousness of sin does not seem to serve the purposes of activating human agency or setting a moral agenda for the community as much as defining its contours, its place in cosmic history and the transformative possibilities it offers. And so it is that "repen-tance" appears to figure not at all in Jubilees in contexts of national redemp-tion, but only in a few passages concerning individual liability, to be discussed in the chapter to follow.[43]

THE "PENITENTS OF ISRAEL"

Poised, as it is, at a critical juncture between the Hebrew Bible, on the one hand, and early Christianity and rabbinic Judaism, on the other, the Dead Sea Scrolls have become a major locus of interpretive activity in recent years. Their discovery provides us with an ideal case to consider for purposes of identify-ing ongoing interpretive tendencies. Scholarship on the Scrolls has been criti-cized for its Christian bias, for imagining the sect as protomonastic.[44] But the critique that is needed transcends denominational concerns and is basic to the presuppositions with which we, as moderns, read. With regard to repentance, the force of the penitential lens has made itself felt throughout all segments of the scholarly community and with regard to a variety of concerns. The sect has been viewed as a "penitential movement" in light of its apocalyptic expec-tation of an imminent end and "rigorous view of the law."[45] "Repentance" is thought to be at the center of the sect's concerns for both those outside of the community and those who sin within it. Initiation and purification rites, as well as the *hodayot*, a kind of poetic text peculiar to the sect, have been under-stood in this light. The sect's own forms of self-appellation, to be examined below, have fed into readings that would see the concern for repentance as an explicit component of sectarian identity.[46] Indeed, according to one scholar, "[i]n the Qumranic philosophy, repentance 'with faith and wholeness of heart' is regarded as the highest virtue a human being can attain."[47]

Actually, the alternative model developed above on the basis of Jubilees and other apocalyptic texts would seem to fit the Dead Sea sect much better.

We find related descriptions of end-time expectations throughout the Scrolls. The following passage from the Community Rule, a central statement of sectarian identity and practice, is typical of the sect:

> God . . . has determined an end to the existence of injustice and on the appointed
> time of the visitation he will obliterate it forever . . . . At that time, God will refine,
> with his truth, all man's deeds, and will purify for himself the structure of man,
> perfecting the spirit of injustice from the innermost part of his flesh, and cleans-
> ing him with the spirit of holiness from every wicked deed. He will sprinkle over
> him the spirit of truth like lustral water [in order to cleanse him] from all the
> abhorrences of deceit and [from] the defilement of the unclean spirit, instruct-
> ing the upright ones with knowledge of the Most High, and making understood
> the wisdom of the sons of heaven to those of perfect behavior. For those God
> has chosen for an everlasting covenant and to them shall belong all the glory of
> Adam. (IV, 18–23)

The divine being does not simply forgive past sin; his purification changes human nature, enabling the "upright ones" to attain "the glory of Adam." Mere mortals attain access to the secrets of the divine realm. This procedure seems to be represented as a single event at the end of time that also entails the for-mation of an eschatological community. As in Jubilees, a cultic metaphor of "purification" is employed, one that corresponds, we will see, to actual baptis-mal practices, as well as a suggestion of demonic possession, "the defilement of the unclean spirit." In the *Barkhi Nafshi* texts, also found among the Scrolls, the familiar imagery of "circumcision of the heart" is employed in a manner suggesting that the anticipated transformation has occurred already (4Q434ᵃ I, 4).⁴⁸ Most strikingly, the sectarians appear to have believed that they them-selves were in the midst of an anthropological re-creation, an eschatological sense that was grounded, as we shall see, in their forms of religious practice.

Initiation Rites

Initiation rites have been a focal point of those who would see a dominant role for repentance in sectarian religion. Further examination of these pro-cedures suggests that the common penitential associations may not neces-sarily emerge from the textual representations of the sect itself as much as from a mapping onto them of a more familiar ritual framework known from later forms of Judaism and Christianity. Let us consider this question through the sect's Community Rule, where depictions of such rituals are most densely clustered.

The scroll itself begins with a series of infinitive clauses. These include items such as "doing what is good and just" (1QS I, 3), welcoming "initiates"

(I, 7), and rejecting the "sons of darkness" (I, 10). Typically, scholars have understood these infinitives to be purpose clauses, as if they spell out the intention of the authors. The scroll exists "in order to" teach members how to serve God better. While such a reading is plausible, the infinitives here, actually, would seem to merely spell out the contents of the scroll, not its pedagogical intent. They delineate the basic categories of legal concern found in the scroll, which focuses, respectively, on matters pertaining to initiates and to those who refuse to join the sect. Indeed, the accepted reading of these infinitives accords with a common disciplinary view of the sect's operation as a whole: institutional practices, like the sect's literature, aim at training members, at improving their spiritual status.[49] This teleological view of the law proves quite problematic in the way it replaces a concern for the proper definition and fulfillment of the law itself, which would appear to be the major preoccupation of the sect, with concerns for individual progress better represented in later religious formations.

Next, we turn our attention to the main term used in the Rule to depict "initiates," *mitnaddevim*. Since the scroll was first discovered, the term, sometimes translated as "those who freely volunteer," has been used to impute a notion of free will, the presence of which is assumed to be essential to any "religion," to the sect.[50] However, such a nominalization of the term does not appear to hold up. Terms for indicating "will" in antiquity are notoriously difficult to unpack.[51] Our particular instance probably indicates a willingness and, correspondingly, the absence of any external compulsion to join the group in a usage quite similar to that of two late biblical passages (Ezra 7:13 and Neh. 11:2). New members are not conscripted from among the populace, but come forward on their own. However, rather than indicating a discursive concern around individual virtue and choice, this term, which is only ever applied to an aggregate in the Rule, functions to emphasize the sect's intrinsic desirability, indeed, one might say, the natural compulsion that a certain segment of the population experiences to join. This serves to underscore the legitimacy of the sect, even as it also contributes to a certain account of those who fail to join as inherent opponents. Thus, *mitnaddevim* are contrasted to those whose "soul loathes" sectarian ways (II, 26–III, 1). In the end, as sectarian ideology consistently states, there are "sons of light," who are destined to join the sect and recognize the validity of its claims about itself, and then there are the "sons of darkness."

We turn now to the first rite detailed in the Community Rule, an annual covenantal ceremony for new initiates and old. The ceremony follows a five-fold procedure: (1) the priests recount the righteous deeds of God; (2) the Levites recount the wicked deeds of Israel "during the dominion of Belial"; (3) the rest of the people, "those entering the covenant," acknowledge their sins and those of their ancestors and acknowledge God's good deeds; (4) the priests bless the "men of God's lot"; (5) the Levites curse the "men of Belial's lot"; and (6) the people respond "Amen" (I, 16–II, 10). In an earlier chapter, we discussed the nature of the interpretive framework whereby acknowledgment of sin is read as an external expression of inner contrition. But the common interpretation of this rite as a "ceremony of repentance"[52] proceeds from an additional point as well, the sense that entrance into a religious community must entail an existential choice. The priestly and levitical recitations are read as merely providing a conducive backdrop—perhaps, a hortatory framework, whereby sin is brought to the consciousness of the people—for the truly decisive moment in this passage, an inner act of conversion whereby "those entering the covenant" transform themselves.

An alternative would be to consider a structure that more evenly distributes meaning across the various recitations found in this rite. We encounter our initiates at a crossroads, a passage, between two identities but, also, two historical epochs. In the past, the people, including those present at the ceremony, were under "the dominion of Belial." God was righteous, but they erred and suffered. Now, two groups are being separated out, the "men of God's lot" and the "men of Belial's lot." Divine blessings are to be channeled to the former, and Israel's previously diffuse curse is to befall the latter, alone. A new group is formed, blessed with "life-giving discernment" and "eternal knowledge" (II, 3), but one that bases its formation on a knowledge of itself as otherwise depraved, a contrast we have seen in Jubilees. Confession is part of the articulation of this self-understanding, a history in brief, establishing the sect as previously part of the people and its tribulations but now separated out and the exclusive recipient of divine grace.

Ritual immersion comes under discussion as part of the privileges denied to any who do not join the sect and accept its precepts (III, 4–12).[53] Scholars have been quick to point out parallels between the Dead Sea sect's use of water for initiation and John the Baptist's desert activities, prompting them to designate the Rule's ritual too a "baptism of repentance."[54] But the relationship between baptism and repentance requires clarification. We may imagine, as Josephus does (*Ant.* 18:116–19), that its effective dimension is the individual's choice to cleanse him- or herself that precedes and merely receives symbolic expression through the actual immersion.[55] However, the inner experience of the initiate while immersing hardly comes into view in sectarian representations and only emerges for us because of the primacy of intent in our definition of "religion" and, hence, initiation. Rather, in conjunction with proper sectarian practice (1QS III, 8), the waters *produce an effect* upon the initiate; they "atone for his sin" (III, 6–7) "purify his flesh" (III, 8). It is true that only the committed sectarian may gain access to them, but that is precisely because of their peculiar power. The transformation enacted through the initiate's immersion draws its strength not from individual human consciousness but from the "holy spirit of the community" (III, 7), the power God has invested in the sect. Following the discussion of immersion, the Community

Rule presents an elaborate treatise about the secrets of creation (III, 13–IV, 26) to be taught to the "sons of light" (III, 13) by the Instructor. Why the juxtaposition? Rather than informing decision and pertaining to the domain of agency, knowledge is configured as a form of revelation, vouchsafed only to those who have already been remade. It is here that we find the Rule's formulation, quoted in full earlier, of immersion as an eschatological divine act of purification: "at that time . . . [God] will sprinkle over him the spirit of truth like lustral water " (III, 9). Apparently, the sort of metaphorical purification language found in the Ezekiel passage quoted earlier (Ezek. 36:25) has been concretized and understood as promising an efficacious baptism at the end of days. Overall, the logic and language used around this ritual would appear to fit better with a notion of divine re-creation, with its refusal to locate transformation in personal agency, than with the penitential framework that is often applied.

As scholars now recognize, the scroll of the Community Rule found in Cave 1 is likely to have been a composite document. No trace of the columns containing the rituals just discussed were found among the Cave 4 manuscript fragments of the Rule (columns one to four), and column five seems to mark the beginning of a new document.[56] Most prominent among the initiation procedures of this document is the oath. The initiate must commit himself to adopt sectarian law and eschew the company of nonsectarians: "Whoever enters the council of the Community . . . shall swear with a binding oath to return to the Law of Moses, according to all that he commanded, with whole heart and whole soul, in compliance with all that has been revealed of it to the sons of Zadok . . . . He should swear by the covenant to be segregated from all the men of injustice" (1QS V, 7–10). The temptation may be great to interpret this speech-act as an expression of inner conscience, especially since it employs *shuv* terminology to depict the *turn* to sectarian practice, a sectarian usage that will be discussed below. However, the functional, as opposed to expressive, aspects of the oath are clearly paramount: it marks a public embrace of sectarian identity, an official adoption of sectarian law. It effectuates the separation from nonsectarians. Now, the initiate can be expected to uphold the norms of his new group and can be punished accordingly. We find a similar treatment of the oath in the Damascus Document: "And on the day on which one has imposed upon himself to return to the law of Moses, the angel Mastema will turn aside from following him" (CD-A XVI, 4–5).[57] Verbal commitment to join the sect *results* in Mastema's retreat. He flees not because of the will of the initiate, but because the initiate's new status protects him.[58]

Also prominent in column five and elaborated further in column six is a process of testing, which members undergo yearly and to which initiates are subjected (V, 23–24; VI, 13–23). Analogous are the tests for readmission after a member has been banished for some infraction against sectarian law (e.g., IX, 2). Many have seen these tests as tests of compliance or even conscience.

Is the candidate/errant member truly following the community's standards; has he sincerely repented and reformed his ways?[59] But, even at the very beginning of his candidacy, before compliance would be an issue, the initiate is tested (better: measured) for "his mind and deeds" (VI, 14). It seems fairly clear that we are dealing rather with a test of *mettle*.[60] Is the individual of the quality necessary to be a member of the community? If so, at what level? The issue at stake is a sort of innate power, the degree of freedom from Belial's meddling, that has more to do with the sectarian's essential being than any mental processes he has undergone. Over time, one's status could alter, but there is no clear evidence for a presumption of growth on the part of the sectarians. The sectarians looked for something constant in human nature, what propelled the initiate to join the sect and the member to faithfully adhere to its dictates. For grave sins, the individual who strayed was given no chance to return, having revealed his true (lack of) worth; repentance is never presented as a possibility.

The "Genre" of the *Hodayot*

For those who successfully completed the initiation process and remained in the sect, a form of texts known as the *hodayot* must have played a prominent role. A complete scroll of the poetic compositions and many related fragments have been found among the Scrolls.[61] The *hodayot* provide us with an additional literary register with which to consider the matter of agency and sectarian identity. They also pose a particular interpretive challenge because of the extent to which the very image of poetry is bound up in a view of speech as an outward flow of the inner sentiment and as impacting the conscience of individual readers.

The *hodayot* seem to reflect on some of the sectarian initiation rites we have just examined, establishing a strong connection between initiation and re-creation:

> I give you thanks, Lord,
> for you rescued me from the abyss,
> and from the destructive pit lifted me out, to an infinite height,
> So that I might roam on an endless plain
> and know that there is assurance—
> for one whom you fashioned out of dust—of an eternal order
> The iniquitous spirit you purified from great depravity,
> to take a place among the array, the host of the holy;
> and enter the group, the congregation of the heavenly sons.
> You cast for a person an eternal lot with the enlightened ones;
> to praise your name in the glorifying community

and to tell of your wonders in front of all your creatures.
But I, a creature of clay, what am I? Mixed with water,
as whom shall I be considered?
What is my strength?
For I find myself at the boundary of wickedness
and share the lot of the scoundrels. (1QHᵃ XI, 20–25)

This passage, like others among the *hodayot*,[62] juxtaposes a divine act of human transformation with a continued sense of human worthlessness.[63] The effect is clear: it is only through God's intervention that humanity, forever susceptible to falling back on its true nature, can be purified. As stated, this transformation seems to be closely associated with initiation into the sect; indeed, the language of initiation—"purification," "taking a place," "entering," and "casting of lots"[64]—combines with numerous terms for the sect in its state of angelic perfection—"eternal order," "the array, the host of the holy," and "the group, the congregation of the heavenly sons."[65]

Also clear from this passage would seem to be an aspect of the setting of the *hodayot*: they are acts of praise that are to be recited among sectarians, subsequent to entrance into the group, to celebrate the described act of divine transformation, "to praise your name in the glorifying community." Re-creation, like physical salvation in the Psalms, is related verbally by its recipient, its human object, as an actual event, in order to attest before others to the power of God and cult—or, in this case, God and sect. As such, the practice of thanksgiving becomes an effective venue through which to rehearse the claims of the sect, that its formation and its members' initiation are the full manifestation of God's righteousness.[66] Most importantly, the *hodayot* serve as a mode of articulating sectarian identity as a re-created state of being; they establish the sectarian sense of self.[67]

What I would like to address at this point is the scope and nature of this sectarian self. Such a concern becomes particularly pressing in view of the oft-noted prominence of the first-person singular voice in the *hodayot*. This literary phenomenon has been comprehended within frameworks that end up rendering the "I" of the *hodayot* in line with contemporary notions of subjectivity. There is, to be sure, a disciplinary reading of the subject as a penitential "self." In this view, the *hodayot*, with their themes of redemption and sinfulness, become a way of striving for forgiveness and perfection by contending with guilt. Such a reading can lead to blatantly inaccurate interpretations, evident, for instance, in certain translations. Here's one example: "In my troubles you comfort me [*niḥamtani*], I delight in forgiveness, I regret [*'enaḥama*] my former offense. I know th[at] there is hope, thanks to your [ki]ndness, and trust, thanks to the abundance of your strength" (1QHᵃ XVII, 13–14).[68] Most problematic is the choice to render the second appearance of the root, *nḥm*, in a different sense, "regret," than the first, "comfort." Another translation might read: "I am comforted regarding my former sin . . ." The sectarian has "assurance" and "hope," has been "comforted," because he knows that he has received "forgiveness," that he has been released from his original state, "my former sin," through an act of divine intervention, "your [ki]ndness" and "abundance of your strength." What is at stake is the constitution of the sectarian, not the penitence of an individual.

Others have been inclined to see the *hodayot* as the "poetry of the individual," as expressive of their author's personal experience.[69] Another approach to the question moves away from this expressive model, but may be seen as adopting a teleological one instead. The *hodayot* play an "intentional and explicit" role in generating individual sectarian subjectivities;[70] they serve as a "model of the sentiments, values, insights, and diction expected of members."[71] In other words, they have a pedagogical purpose. This reading relocates agency from the individual to the community. Nevertheless, it sees the individual, his or her subjective experience and progress, as the final end of communal intervention.[72]

An alternative would be to see the "I" of the *hodayot* as a sectarian object that is used to establish a universal anthropology of inherent sin and to delineate the sectarian opportunities for redemption. The first-person singular voice, like that found in the Psalms, does not serve as a mode of expressing or generating individual subjectivity but as a way of framing an *event*, the repercussive moment of interaction between the deity and a known material entity, an individual being that can articulate and attest to what has transpired. Thus, the *hodayot* may constitute an important moment in the emergence of more familiar notions of the self, but we are still far from a situation in which individual experience is the primary matter of religious concern. Instead, discourse around the individual subject sets up a further possibility for the delineation of sectarian identity, for separating sectarians out from others.

Shuv Terminology in the Scrolls

The Dead Sea sect uses *shuv* terminology in a variety of phrases as a form of self-appellation. This designation is in large measure responsible for the view of "repentance as a way of life" among sectarians.[73] In a previous chapter, we discussed the ways in which this particular Hebrew root is singled out and identified as equivalent to "repentance." The same nominalization is in full effect in the common rendering of sectarian phrases, such as *shavey yisra'el*, as the "penitents of Israel," and *shavey pesha,'* as "those who convert from sin." Should we import such specific, developed content into this one verb? One notes straightaway that *shuv* in these phrases and others does not seem to represent a particular act in which the group is continuously engaged, nor one attributed to an individual agent. In short, it is not a quotidian element of sectarian practice.

Rather, it describes a specific group, one that has completed its turn away from transgression, that is, the sect, probably best translated, in the case of *shavey pesha*, as "those who *have* turned away from transgression." We see this, for instance, in the Hodayot Scroll, where the phrase appears opposite the terms "offenders" and "traitors" and parallel to the phrase "those on a straight path" (1QH³ X, 9–10). *Shavey pesha* are "those on a straight path."

The sect's use of *shuv* resembles that of the late biblical Hebrew usage, "cessation of sin," explored in chapter 4, in that it denotes a "turn" that entails an overall behavioral change. We find both positive and negative formulations with equivalent senses among the Scrolls, a "turn to the Law," as well as a "turn away from sin."[74] What is unique is that this terminology seems to be associated with entrance into the sect. Thus, the initiate must "swear with a binding oath to turn [*lashuv*] to the Law of Moses, according to all that he commanded, with whole heart and whole soul, in compliance with all that has been revealed of it to the sons of Zadok" (1QS V, 8–9). The positive "turn" is a life led steadfastly according to sectarian practice, the "Law of Moses," as interpreted by the sectarians. The negative "turn" is removal from nonsectarians and their ways: "This is the rule for the men of the Community who want to turn away from all evil and fulfill all that he commanded according to his will: to separate from the congregation of the men of injustice" (V, 1-2). Similarly, whereas Isaiah 59:20, "he shall come as redeemer to Zion, to those *in Jacob* who have turned back from sin [*shavey pesha be-ya'aqov*]," would seem to promise redemption for any among Jacob/Israel who have turned away from sin, the sectarians, applying the verse to themselves, understand it as promising redemption to "those who have turned away from the sin *of Jacob* [*shavey pesha' ya'aqov*]" (CD-B XX, 17). Indeed, the proper translation of the phrase *shavey yisra'el* is most likely "those who have turned away from Israel," that is, from the transgression of Israel. And so we find it defined in the Damascus Document as "[those] who have turned away from the path of the people" (CD-A VIII, 14–16).[75]

Why does the Dead Sea sect make such extensive use of *shuv* terminology? Aside from the above passage from Isaiah, the major source of this usage goes back to those key passages with which this chapter began, Deuteronomy 4:29–31 and 30:1–10. In line with the pedagogical model of Scripture, modern scholars have often read these passages as exhortations.[76] Actually, early instances of interpretation suggest that they were understood instead as prophecies, divine promises of redemption, that, in the end, after being exiled, Israel would "turn to YHWH" and receive his mercy.[77] For sectarians, the sect's formation was seen as the fulfillment of this promised "turn," when elements of Israel would turn away from their corrupted ways and observe the Law according to its proper (sectarian) interpretation. We see this quite clearly in the conclusion to the sectarian letter, 4QMMT. After reminding his audience of the sect's unique position on a variety of legal matters, its author states: "And *this* [i.e., now] is the end of days, when they, among Israel, will turn back to the L[aw]" (C 21). What the *shuv* prophecy predicts is nothing short of the emergence of the sect itself, the present elucidation and enactment of the Law of Moses by the discrete group represented in the letter. For their part, the letter's recipients are to recognize the moment for what it is and, accordingly, adopt the practices of the true Law of Moses. In this interaction, as in Jubilees, Scripture with its *shuv* terminology figures not as a scene for exhortation but as a source of apocalyptic knowledge, grounding for a "turn" to sectarian practice at the end of days.

Interpreted thus, this mandated moment of *shuv* lacks the agency that we have often come to associate with it. A similar perspective on *shuv* emerges in the "Words of the Luminaries," which like Jubilees is a protosectarian text found among the Scrolls:[78]

> You remembered your covenant . . . . You did not abandon us. You did favors to your people Israel among all [the] countries amongst whom you had exiled them, placing upon their heart to turn [*lashuv*] to you and to listen to your voice, [like] all that you commanded through the hand of Moses, your servant. [Fo]r you have poured your holy spirit upon us, [to be]stow your blessings to us . . . . [You have thrown awa]y f[r]om us all ou[r] failings and have [pu]rified us from our sin, for yourself. (1–2, 5:11–6:3)

This passage, drawing from the language of Deuteronomy, presents the sort of promise given to Moses at the beginning of Jubilees, combined here, as there, with the language of purification and the "holy spirit" found in Ezekiel, as having been already fulfilled. In this case, by making God, instead of Israel, the subject of the phrase, "and you will take to heart" found in Deuteronomy 30:1, no ambiguity really remains with regard to the source of agency in the passage. When sectarians use the *shuv* appellation, they do not imagine themselves to be taking on a moral/religious desideratum but to be assuming the mantle of the new, eschatological Israel, with its attendant practices and possibilities for transformation; such was the "covenant of turning" (*berit teshuva*) into which they entered (CD-B XIX, 16).

THE EARLY JESUS MOVEMENT

Until now, we have been reconsidering the role of repentance in apocalypticism and the formation of sectarian identity. The aim has been to call attention to the relationship that exists between our notion of the individual and that of "religion," whereby questions of agency, personal experience, and consciousness come to inform our interpretation of redemptive expectations. Without a doubt, much of the scholarly stake in the study of the Scrolls has been to provide "background" for early Christianity. The view of the Dead Sea sect and other apocalyptic groups as "penitential movements" thus originated with a parallel claim about the early Jesus movement.[79] Looking at the figures of John the Baptist, Jesus, and Paul, we will sketch out briefly the possibilities for the sorts of distinctions raised above to shed light on New Testament texts, as part of a study of the early Jesus movement as one among a multiplicity of late Second Temple apocalyptic sects, but one that quickly came to play a prime role in the formation of the notion of religion as it operates today.

"A Baptism of Repentance"

How might decentering the assumed place of agency in transformation and, specifically, the view of baptism adopted above relate to the figure of John the Baptist?[80] What we find is that the dominant account of John as a preacher of repentance, a preliminary to the ministry of Jesus, is bound up strongly in the representations of the Baptist found in Matthew and Luke. Each gospel has its own particular features. Whereas, in the Gospel of Mark, John appears in the wilderness "proclaiming a baptism of repentance for the forgiveness of sins" (1:4), in the Gospel of Matthew, we find what purport to be the actual words of this proclamation, an exhortation: "Repent, for the kingdom of heaven has come near" (3:2). In the hypothetical Sayings Gospel, Q, shared by Matthew and Luke, we find: "I baptize you [[in]] water, but the one to come after me is more powerful than I .... He will baptize you in [[holy]] Spirit and fire."[81] Matthew records this saying but inserts: "I baptize you in water *for repentance*" (3:11). Finally, the Sayings Gospel apparently had the following: "He said to the [[crowds coming to be]] bapti[[zed]]: Snakes' litter! Who warned you to run from the impending rage? So bear fruit worthy of repentance ... the ax already lies at the root of the trees. So every tree not bearing healthy fruit is to be chopped down and thrown on the fire."[82] The Gospel of Luke, however, attaches a further exchange to this speech: the crowds ask, "What then should we do?" and they receive the response that those with clothing and food must share with those who have none, tax collectors must not collect more than their due, and soldiers must not extort money (3:10–14).

   Are these differences meaningful? Many scholars assume a basic identity in this regard between the various sources, seeing John as a preacher of repentance,[83] but alternatives, based on our preceding account of the Scrolls, are available. John's proclamation of a "baptism of repentance," as found in Mark, could be understood in purely eschatological terms, as declaring the present to be the moment in which the cleansing promised in prophecies, such as that of Ezekiel,[84] has become available. In this reading, *metanoia*, which is translated here as "repentance," should be seen more as a consequence of baptism, a transformation in moral status of the sort described in the Dead Sea Scrolls, than as an independent act of agency, a prerequisite demanded of participants, which is what is suggested by the exhortative form proclamation assumes in Matthew. So too, in specifying "repentance" to be the purpose of John's baptism in water, Matthew may be redirecting the sense of the utterance in the Sayings Gospel, which, otherwise, could be seen as placing agency exclusively in the hands of John and the "one to come after me," who, as baptizers, are charged with carrying out acts of forgiveness and/or judgment in accord with recognized prophecies. Finally, without Luke, the second saying quoted from the Sayings Gospel seems to be suggesting that *metanoia*—translated as "repentance," but, perhaps, rendered better as "transformation" or, even, "forgiveness"—is a process that the people undergo, presumably, through baptism; the question at stake is whether it will be successful or not, whether they will "bear fruit worthy of repentance." Luke, however, seems to place "repentance" as a desideratum firmly in the hands of the crowds, as what is required of them now: "what then should we do?" They must choose themselves to abandon their current ways of life as sinners. In short, the discrepancies with regard to John the Baptist between the Synoptic Gospels and their hypothetical source materials could be seen as meaningful if questions of moral agency are made a criterion for differentiation.

Jesus as a Preacher of Repentance

There is generally presumed to be an identity between the proclamation (read: exhortation) of John the Baptist and that of Jesus. Indeed, the Gospel of Matthew places an almost identical formulation in the mouths of both: "Repent for the kingdom of heaven has come near!" (Matt 4:17; compare 3:2). Actually, "the relative paucity of explicit repentance-language in Jesus' teachings" has long been noted,[85] even leading one scholar to go as far as suggesting that the religious authorities rejected Jesus because he did not accept their common doctrine of repentance![86] In this view, the historical Jesus had an unnatural distaste for what is presumed (inaccurately, I would argue) to have been a naturalized concept at this period of time. More frequently, however, something like the following has been the oft-repeated conclusion: "the whole proclamation of Jesus, with its categorical demands for the sake of God's kingdom (the Sermon on the Mount, the sayings about discipleship), is a proclamation of μετάνοια [repentance] *even when the term is not used* [italics mine]."[87] What is bound up in this hermeneutical refusal to define certain discrepancies in formulation as actual difference? I would like to approach this question using several different kinds of source materials found in the Synoptic Gospels.

In recent years, the question of "repentance" has been most directly taken up by scholars with an interest in the quest for the historical Jesus. Scholars who generally oppose the eschatological or apocalyptic view of Jesus have supported the claim, mentioned above, that Jesus did not preach repentance.[88] Those in general sympathy with an apocalyptic interpretation of Jesus have been sharply critical, insisting that the Synoptics' representation of Jesus' proclamation as a preaching of repentance, as found, for instance, in the passage from Matthew quoted above, is accurate.[89] Both sides of the debate share a common assumption: eschatological expectations are inextricably linked to repentance.[90] But what precisely is the nature of this presumed relationship between eschatology and repentance? In one view, "repentance and moral renewal in prospect of the Kingdom of God are like a pressure which is exerted in order to compel its appearance."[91] Or, in a more straightforward formulation: "repentance … was what Israel must do if her exile is to come to an end."[92] Repentance is a precondition of redemption. Another perspective has been formulated as follows: "Most of us have heard street preachers (and others) whose message essentially is, 'The end is at hand, repent!'" Or, in another formulation, "'by the way, the last judgment is at hand, you better be ready, so repent!'"[93] Repentance follows naturally from the proclamation of a final judgment. Either way, discourse about the end receives its meaning, is understood to serve, a largely implicit concern for moral renewal that, if we follow our preceding discussions, constitutes a misunderstanding of apocalypticism.

The announcements of judgment that are found, in various forms, in Matthew and Luke and are thought to have been part of an original Sayings Gospel, Q, provide one place in which to test this association between apocalypticism and repentance. According to one scholar, "the call to repentance, the threat of apocalyptic judgment and the censure of 'this generation' for its recalcitrance are prominent in several clusters of Q sayings."[94] The judgment cluster that includes, according to one series of divisions, Q 7:1–10, 18–23, 24–26 (16:16), and 31–35 focuses on Israel's failure to accept the authority of Jesus.[95] The centurion's extraordinary belief in Jesus' power serves as a positive counterpoint to that failure (7:1–10).[96] Israel's intransigence is a failure to accept that he is "the one to come" on the basis of his exhibition of power, as Jesus assumes John the Baptist will do upon receiving reports of his miraculous actions (7:18–23). The cluster of sayings found in Q 11:14–26, 29–32, 33–36, 39–52 reflects a similar range of themes. The "Beelzebul Accusation" (11:14–15, 17–20) again depicts the refusal of the people to accept Jesus' miraculous power for what it is. Likewise, disappointment at the failure of "this generation" to recognize, through Jesus' exercise of miraculous power, his authority likely lies behind the "Double Saying" (Q 11:29–32). Solomon's wisdom was enough to attract the "queen of the South" to *learn* from him. Jonah's prophetic proclamation was enough to *turn* the Ninevites *away* from their evil deeds. Jesus' power should suffice to lead this generation to *acknowledge* him. The condemnation of "this generation" contained in these clusters of sayings has been construed as a warning that invites repentance. But it could be seen, perhaps more accurately, as a vehement expression of anger that, in spirit, aims at the destruction of those who have refrained from join-ing the sect—not their repentance!—and addresses concerns internal to it, namely, articulating Jesus' power against the backdrop of the failure of so many to enter into the movement's shared discourse.[97]

What is the relationship between the preaching of repentance and another important phenomenon in the Synoptic Gospels, Jesus' proclamation of good news? According to Matthew 4:17, quoted above, and its parallel, Mark 1:15, as well as Mark 6:12, the proclamation included an exhortation to repent in light of the coming kingdom. But these statements have been widely recog-nized as editorial.[98] They come at the beginning of Jesus' ministry or, as is the case in Mark 6:12, at the beginning of the disciples' ministry. They are not integrated literarily or thematically into the mass of narratives and say-ings found throughout. Furthermore, they seem to alter the very sense of *kērussō* (to "proclaim," not to "exhort") found in the Synoptics and the rest of the New Testament. Elsewhere, in Mark, for instance, proclamation invariably attends acts of exorcism or healing: "He went throughout Galilee, proclaiming in their synagogues and casting out demons" (Mark 1:39), or "he appointed twelve, whom he also named apostles, to be with him, and to be sent out to proclaim, and to have authority to cast out demons" (Mark 3:14). Sometimes acts of exorcism or healing lead the patient himself "to proclaim," evoking the disapproval of Jesus who prefers that his message be contained (Mark 1:45, 5:20, and 7:36). Surely this restricted proclamation is not the blanket call to repentance envisioned in Mark 1:14–15! It would seem to relate, rather, to the gradual unfolding of the eschaton. Proclamation constructs an association between healings and healer, between cure and the temporal context enabling it. It is the verbal garb of an anthropological renewal that hardly calls upon the agency of the redeemed patient; it allows for an understanding of extraor-dinary, present events in light of the coming of a new order, the kingdom of God. With the exception of Matthew 4:17, exhortation and any mention of repentance are similarly absent from representations of proclamation in the Gospels of Matthew and Luke, where it appears simply as an announcement of the good news. Nevertheless, despite these apparent discrepancies and the scholarly consensus that Matt 4:17, Mark 1:15, and Mark 6:12 are editorial, many have seen these three passages as an accurate summary of Jesus' preach-ing and the implied teaching of the Gospels.[99] Without entering into the his-torical question of whether Jesus *in fact* preached repentance, it is important to highlight the reading strategies whereby such a conclusion is reached, how a few statements are pulled out, and the language of "repentance" privileged as an account of the whole. Handled thus, these statements are seen to offer a teleological rendering of the early Jesus movement in line with contemporary views of the relationship that pertains between religion, moral agency, and human transformation.[100]

We ought to consider as well the traditions that point to a close associa-tion between Jesus and sinners. According to Luke, this relationship is to be explained by Jesus' concern for their repentance, a view that simultane-ously inputs a strong degree of moral purpose to the movement as a whole and agency to its participants. Thus, when the question is posed, in the Gospel of Mark, "Why does he eat with tax collectors and sinners?" (Mark 2:16), Jesus responds: "Those who are well have no need of a physician, but those who are sick; I have come to call not the righteous but sinners." Luke adds, "I have come to call not the righteous but sinners *to repen-tance*" (Luke 5:32). Likewise, Luke adds a moral to the parables of the lost sheep and the lost coin, which discuss the joy of finding a lost object and are thought to have been part of the hypothetical Sayings Gospel: "Just so, I tell you, there will be more joy in heaven over one sinner who repents than over ninety-nine righteous persons who need no repentance" (Luke 15:7, compare 15:10). Scholars generally assume that these editorial additions represent concerns more or less identical to those of their sources.[101] But alternatives are possible. In each of these cases, the source materials adopt imagery that addresses the actions of the redeemer, not the redeemed, the physician who heals, the shepherd who carries back the lost sheep, and the woman who finds her lost coin. Indeed, Jesus' call in Mark seems to *compel* response: "As he was walking along, he saw Levi son of Alphaeus sitting at the tax booth, and he said to him, 'Follow me.' And he got up and followed him" (Mark 2:14). This sense of immediacy in the narrative leaves little room for the sinner's own agency, no more than that of a lost sheep or coin. In addition, the locus of concern is not moral transformation, as it is, for instance, in Luke's account of the tax collector, Zacchaeus, who gives up his ill-gotten gains (Luke 19:1–10), but rather one of joining Jesus, attaching oneself to his body of followers.

As one finds in the so-called parables of the kingdom, some people get it, and some people don't.[102] The "it," the object of concern in these parables and in much of the material we have just seen, appears to be a recogni-tion of the momentousness of the present, the unfolding of an apocalyptic end bound up in the claims of a particular group. This cognitive dimension and its restriction to a few accord with what we have seen with regard to the Dead Sea sect. It limits the possibilities for an active program of moral change and takes attention away from the agency of participants to high-light, instead, an envisioned transformation of the broader world order. Thus, it is noteworthy that New Testament scholarship has resisted differ-entiation in this matter of "repentance" between early representations of Jesus and the work of the Synoptic editors, who will be discussed, along with the other authors of "repentance" as a discourse, in the chapter to follow.

Paul and Anthropological Renewal

It is fitting to end this discussion of the place of repentance in redemptive expectations and the attendant view of religion, with its teleological focus and concern for human agency, with mention of Paul. As in the above cases, interpreters are faced with apparent discrepancies between, on one hand, the representation of Paul's conversion in 1 Tim 1:13 as a turn from sin and the image of Paul in Acts 17:30 as preaching repentance and, on the other hand, the representations of his "conversion" and proclamation in his own letters. Though there has been, perhaps, some movement in the opposite direction in this matter,[103] scholars have tended to underscore difference in these cases.[104] As one writes, "Paul seldom speaks of repentance and never characterizes coming to faith as an act of repentance."[105] What are, perhaps, less well understood are the reasons for this absence,[106] which are sought in the realm of theology, based on the assumption that a doctrine of repentance would have been available to him through the Judaism of his day.[107] However, we have seen that repentance was not a part of apocalyptic discourse, of which Paul constitutes a varied and highly developed instance. Indeed, his writings attest quite clearly to a notion of divine re-creation of human beings[108] and, amid other influences, reveal multiple points of contact with the Scrolls.

What follows is a brief survey of a few of these points of connection. Like Jubilees, the Letter to the Romans focuses on how "our injustice serves to confirm the justice of God" (Rom. 3:5), a conclusion based on an apocalyptic rendering of Psalm 51 as describing end-time events.[109] As in Jubilees, it is this concern for the disclosure of God's righteousness that paradoxically necessitates delaying rectification of human nature: "What if God, desiring to show his wrath and to make known his power, has endured with much patience the objects of wrath that are made for destruction; and what if he has done so in order to make known the riches of his glory for the objects of mercy, which he has prepared beforehand for glory?" (Rom. 9:22–23). Such recognition of divine justice underscores the cognitive dimension of Paul's proclamation, what initiation entails, namely, identification with Christ as the moment and mechanism of God's disclosure of his righteousness (Rom. 3:21–26). It is this mechanism, embodied in the practice of baptism that allows initiates "who have been baptized into Christ Jesus" to be "baptized into his death" (6:3), "so that the body of sin might be destroyed, and we might no longer be enslaved to sin" (6:6). Once again, baptism transforms. In other letters, the result is described in positive terms: "So if anyone is in Christ, there is a new creation" (2 Cor. 5:17). As seen in the Dead Sea Scrolls, especially the *hodayot*, such transformation appears to entail the assumption of a new "spiritual body" (1 Cor. 15:44) that will allow the community of the faithful to enter "his [God's] presence" (2 Cor. 4:14), "so that grace, as it extends to more and more people, may increase thanksgiving, to the glory of God" (2 Cor. 4:15).

Though the image of Paul is often assimilated to later forms of Christian mission, we might still speak of Paul as inhabiting a moment before "religion," at least, if we recognize the ways in which that term ascribes to an ongoing communal entity a particular naturalized concern—the conversion of souls—and a degree of agency to those souls in its attainment.[110] Paul does not yet exhibit this degree of instrumental control—the view of bodies, simultaneously, as objects for pedagogy and as agents of choice and self-control—that is bound up in this common view. Thus, Paul speaks of "Christ God" as "reconciling the world to himself." What has been given to Paul is a ministry to *proclaim* this "message of reconciliation," to serve as "ambassador" for the new realm, not as a preacher of moral and religious doctrines (2 Cor. 5:18–20). In other words, the primacy of apocalyptic themes for Paul—cognitive recognition of the disclosure of God's righteousness, initiation through identification with that disclosure, and divinely orchestrated transformation of the self through that initiation—actually explains, rather than countermands, the relative lack of moral exhortation and repentance as a theme in his writings. Given the time frame within which Paul and other apocalyptic thinkers believed themselves to be operating—the imminence of an end—we need to allow for potential divergence between their concept of and concern for the person and the prioritization of moral formation and agency among readers who participate in what we now know as the stable, established entity, "religion."

Where we do find repentance in Paul will be important for understanding its history of development as a concept.[111] Paul's pedagogical concerns, which have been linked to themes in Hellenistic moral philosophy, are deployed in particular for those who have already accepted and, thereby, participated in the apocalyptic framework he proclaims. They do not appear to have direct bearing on that framework itself, but emerge as part of the problem of maintaining the status of the initiated as transformed in light of the delay in the arrival of the end. Repentance's place in securing this element of control will be taken up in the following chapter.

SUMMARY

In this chapter, the place of "agency" in interpretation rose to the fore of our discussion. One way in which scholars read repentance into biblical and, as it turns out, postbiblical texts is to impute various elements of agency to redemptive expectations, where, otherwise, it might not have been obvious. Indeed, the modern Western reader can hardly imagine a concept of redemption that does not rely, to some degree, on the initiative of the individual human subject. However, our review of various apocalyptic texts suggested the predominance of an alternative notion, that of a divine re-creation of human nature. This notion also appears to have been operative in a variety of sectarian practices as represented in the Dead Sea Scrolls. It is celebrated in the *hodayot* and informs the sectarian interpretation of *shuv* in Deuteronomy as a promised "turn" to sectarian practice at the end of days. Finally, we considered how New Testament scholarship has sometimes failed to differentiate with regard to questions of agency between the various strata of the Synoptics and conclude by noting connections between the apocalyptic notion of divine re-creation and Paul's own views regarding an imminent anthropological renewal.

CHAPTER 7

⌀⌀

The Genealogy of Repentance

Great is repentance for it reaches the Glorious Seat.
Babylonian Talmud, Yoma 86a

TOWARD A GENEALOGY OF THE CONCEPT

In the preceding chapters, I argued that we import certain categories—interiority, agency, moral transformation, pedagogy—appropriate to contemporary, dominant notions of the self and of the relations that obtain between selves when we use the concept, "repentance," to interpret various ancient Israelite practices. What I would like to explore in this chapter is how a certain discourse around repentance, one that is very much marked by the elevation of these categories to a matter of explicit concern, *can* be seen to emerge around the turn of the Common Era in early formations of Judaism and Christianity.[1] And so, the matter of how the sources themselves establish the definition of repentance and its contents will require our attention.

This running discussion of definition will be used as well to argue that, notwithstanding common scholarly attempts to impute uniqueness and innovation to specific participants in this discourse, it exhibits, in fact, a certain unity. That is to say, "repentance" is not the product of individual genius or even particular religious movements but, rather, constitutes a discourse, a shared cultural construction—a generation of language and related practices that exists prior to the individual subject.[2] This is not to deny the possibility of difference but to question its inherence, especially on the supposed theological level. As such, it offers an invitation to step back from supersessionist argumentation and rethink how we draw the lines of connection between early forms of Judaism and Christianity,[3] indeed, how we treat difference in religious and even secular identities in light of the common discursive formations that undergird them.[4] Furthermore, like any "discovery," its emergence can only be said to be sporadic and partial, with initial observation and usage moving gradually into more extensive forms of conceptualization and formulation.[5] Therefore, rather than putting forth a straightforward chronological narrative, which the difficulty of dating sources from this period otherwise resists, what follows is a broad-scale comparison of pertinent, extant corpora—proceeding from Hellenistic to late Second Temple, rabbinic Jewish, and early Christian sources—with the aim of testing, in its various configurations, the contours of "repentance."

The place of repentance within formative Judaism and Christianity goes a long way toward securing its naturalization, its promotion to the status of a universal, and, hence, its role in interpretation today. But, how did repentance come to take on the appearance of that which is obvious and original? How did it obtain its position as a necessary component of Judaism and Christianity, obscuring in the process its history, the contingency of its own becoming? Part of the answer lies in the grounding of repentance in Scripture, the penitential lens that it generated and which we have been examining, but more needs to be said in the context of its period of origination. We will see that the question of the origins of repentance was not alien to the sources to be examined.

Finally, and most importantly, we need to consider what a discourse around repentance brings into effect. By attributing to the human being an interior space, "repentance" grants an autonomy that, ultimately, can be used to bind the now readily transformable individual[6] to a broader project of adherence to communal discipline.[7] It corresponds to a period of governmentality in which the sect no longer rules the lives of its members through the prospect of inclusion and exclusion or the cultic site through that of access and royal power.[8] Now a "religion," with its stated series of beliefs and practices,[9] must seek to compete in a crowded marketplace by offering a relatively low barrier to entry and, at the same time, by ensuring compliance, a solidity of identity, through means that no longer readily include forms of external compulsion.[10] "Repentance" offers such an opportunity. Powered by a focused repudiation of past identities and deeds, the penitential self transforms and then monitors itself in accord with religious or communal affiliations.[11]

In the end, however, it should be noted that, even if the discourse of repentance is totalizing in its claims, there remains the fact of equivocation, as evident in its relative absence from the sources discussed in the preceding chapter. Judaism and Christianity are not merely taken over by repentance, but are vibrant movements with complex and often contradictory series of concerns. While this chapter forwards an account of the rise of repentance and attempts a representation of its logic, it cannot take up, but only serve as a basis for, the subsequent task of tracing the ebb and flow of repentance in the history of Judaism and Christianity—the history of its place in relationship to other competing demands, some of which can be traced back to those alternative notions of body, speech, agency, and power delineated in the preceding chapters.[12]

A NOTE ON TERMINOLOGY

Before we begin, it is important to gain some clarity about the relationship between "repentance" as a discourse and "repentance" as a term. What appears below is not meant as a word study, but as a broad analysis of a series of power relations that brought into effect a shared notion of the person rather like our own. Nevertheless, one of the means, and perhaps the most effective one, by which this development was secured had to do with language itself—the coining of new terms and their naturalization, their promotion as concepts, through inclusion in the emerging lexicon of what became dominant religious communities.[13]

To what in the ancient languages do we refer when using the term "repentance"? In his *Dictionary of the English Language*, Samuel Johnson defines "repentance" as "to have such sorrow for sin, as produces amendment of life."[14] This "definition" does not merely give the sense of a word but already presupposes a certain ontology of the act: that it is natural to have "sorrow for sin"; that such sorrow does, indeed, "produce" a transformation; and that there is a generally recognizable form that "amendment of life" could take. The point is that this sort of rendering corresponds quite closely in its major aspects to and, ultimately, derives from the use of certain terms that are already in evidence in early forms of Christianity and Judaism: *metanoia* in Greek, *paenitentia* in Latin (from which "repentance," as a Latinate form, most directly derives),[15] and *teshuva* in Mishnaic Hebrew.[16] My contention is that these words, despite their varied histories and the celebrated irreducibility of language in translation, become technical terms that, with allowance for some variation, signify something more or less like Johnson's "repentance." They are genetically related, even if they cross linguistic boundaries, not only because of their common historical origins but also because they participate in a shared discourse.

In order to take the full measure of repentance as a very specific sort of entity and begin detailing its particularities, it would be helpful to compare the postbiblical *metanoia-paenitentia-teshuva* complex to the use of the biblical Hebrew phrase, "turn away [*shuv*] from sin," that we examined in chapter 4. It is this relatively late biblical formulation, best rendered as a "cessation of sin," that ultimately opened up the possibility for a grounding of penitential terminology in the Hebrew Bible. Rabbinic *teshuva* presents itself as an etymological equivalent to biblical *shuv*,[17] while *metanoia* and its related verbal forms frequently figure as translations of *shuv*. But the postbiblical concept, repentance, presents sufficiently distinct features so as to be considered a separate entity, the product of a different time and place:

(1) Repentance is an *act*, a *discrete event*. Contrariwise, "cessation of sin" has no specific moment. It does not depict an actual process by which individuals cease sinning but a resulting state.

(2) Repentance is a *mental* act. "Cessation of sin" is a statement about the absence of proscribed material objects or actions.

(3) Repentance is a *retrospective* mental act. It cultivates sustained reflection on the past. "Cessation of sin" focuses on present states.

(4) Repentance utilizes an *emotion of sorrow*. "Cessation of sin" need not entail mourning and does not address the emotional state of the one who "turns away from sin."

(5) As an act, repentance indicates the existence of an *agent* and emphasizes *autonomy*. It is important that the individual chooses freely. For "cessation of sin," it matters little who initiates transformation.

(6) Repentance takes as its object a *specific* sin or series of sins. One can "repent of" something in particular. Such a formulation is impossible in biblical Hebrew. "Turning away" always signifies a more generalized reorientation.

(7) It follows therefore that the *righteous*, who live upright lives but occasionally err, can repent of their infractions. In the Hebrew Bible, only those who have attained the status of sinners are said to "turn away from sin."

(8) Repentance is an *efficacious* act. It exerts a power over future behavior and/or atones for sin. *Shuv* itself has no atoning power or influence over future behavior. It is effective insofar as, in the absence of clear and present transgression, the deity relents from announced punishment.

What emerges is repentance as a sort of "spiritual exercise" or "technology of the self."[18] It utilizes the resources of the self to operate upon the self, all the while developing what that very notion of "self" is. "Cessation of sin," on the other hand, is not an *act* of any such self. It operates in a different environment with a different set of presuppositions. One could label "cessation of sin" as a biblical conception of or precursor to repentance.[19] However, such an approach would have to be seen as participating in strategies of identification that arise, in ancient and, especially, modern times, from the ideological commitment to assert the normativity of Jewish and Christian concepts by aligning them with scriptural authority, naturalizing them as universal ideals present at all times, or privileging them as superseding incomplete but, nevertheless, related forms of earlier religion.

Finally, it is important to emphasize that this project, "to keep the words and change the meanings,"[20] leaves certain noticeable traces not only on the level of definition, the comparison of circumstances, and effect but on a formal linguistic level as well. Most obviously, the Mishnaic Hebrew term for "repentance," *teshuva*, is not attested in the Hebrew Bible in connection to "cessation of sin" but only as physical or temporal "return" or verbal "answer."[21] It must be seen, therefore, as a fresh nominalization of the biblical verb, *shuv*, based on this specific usage.[22] In turn, this neologism participates very differently in verbal phrases— ʿaśa teshuva, "to do/perform repentance"—than in such biblical phrases as "(re)turn to YHWH" or "turn away from sin."

We also find apparent evidence for semantic development in changing Greek translations of biblical *shuv*. As noted in chapter 4, the earliest and most authoritative Greek translation, the Septuagint, *not once* uses the Greek verb for "repent," *metanoeō*, in its translation of *shuv*.[23] It opts instead for prefixed forms of -*strefō*, which preserve the more literal sense of *shuv* as "turn." When *metanoeō* does appear in the Septuagint, it is used to translate a different Hebrew verb, *niham*, usually rendered as "to regret" or "change one's mind."[24] As an example, one might consider the following verse, where the two verbs are juxtaposed: "If that nation turns away [*shav*] from all its bad deeds, I will change my mind [*ve-niḥamti*] regarding the bad things that I planned to do to them" (Jer. 18:8). The distinction between these verbs is preserved in both the Hebrew and the Greek. But what we see happening in later Greek translations, such as Symmachus,[25] and in common usage in most Greek texts, from Philo to the New Testament,[26] is that the use of *metanoeō* spreads and comes to be used in place of forms of -*strefō*; "turning" elides into "regretting," even when a biblical passage with *shuv* is explicitly referenced, an especially striking development given the expected dominance of the Septuagintal tradition. So, in a sense, the story that needs to be told can be expressed in terms of language. How did biblical *shuv* become rabbinic *teshuva*, the Septuagint's use of -*strefō* replaced by the more popular *metanoeō*? The answer, in my view, has to do with the advent of a new concept of human transformation, "repentance."

THE MIND IN PAIN AND THE GREEKS

Is there a concept of repentance in Greek thought? Certainly, there is a term, *metanoia*, in its verbal form, *metanoeō*, that would appear to be a good candidate.[27] With the prefix *meta-* indicating a change of state and -*noeō* deriving from the noun for mind, *nous*, *metanoeō* may be taken to mean "to perceive afterward" (to have an afterthought), "to change one's mind," or simply, "to regret."[28] As such, it can depict the moment in which a subject reflects upon some specific prior act or thought with an attitude of rejection or emotion of regret. This may suggest a close semantic connection to repentance but, in truth, its normal usage moves us far away from the concept. It usually functions as a form of mental suffering, caused by making an improper decision,

which is ultimately fruitless and part of the pain suffered for acting in ignorance. This sense carries over into classical philosophy. In particular, the Stoics
are said to have adopted a negative stance toward *metanoia*. As Cicero puts it,
"the [Stoic] philosopher surmises nothing, repents of nothing, is never wrong,
never changes his opinion" (*Pro Murena* 61 [Lord, LCL]).[29] A broad scholarly
consensus has thus concluded that "Greek philosophy had little interest in
the feelings of regret or remorse that may at times lead an individual to a
complete reassessment of his former life path and his conversion to a fresh
course of existence."[30]

There are, however, a number of problems with this consensus. First of
all, it must be said that ancient philosophy shows considerable interest
in repentance as a psychological reality, if not as an actual technique for
self-improvement, then, by conjuring the pain it causes, as a way of highlighting the importance of proper prior assessment and decision-making.
Furthermore, this sort of representation of the place of repentance in classical thought simply fails to take into consideration the full range of evidence.
In favor of its own canon of early works, it neglects the diversity of such a
broad-scale movement as Platonism and its later formations, what is often
referred to as "Middle Platonism."[31] And, indeed, it is such later Hellenistic
thought that is most relevant to the early history of Judaism and Christianity.[32]
The vitality of repentance as a philosophical concept emerges with exceeding
clarity in the writings of Plutarch, one of the most important representatives
of this broader Platonic movement.

The Utility of Mental Pain: Plutarch

Plutarch develops a particularly clear account of the mechanism at work in
repentance.[33] According to him, a dreadful deed, "like an ulcer in the flesh,
leaves behind it in the soul regret, which ever continues to wound and prick
it. For the other pangs reason does away with, but regret is caused by reason
itself, since the soul, together with its feeling of shame, is stung and chas-
tised by itself" (*Moralia; On the Tranquility of Mind* 476, F [Helmbold, LCL]).[34]
Metanoia is a kind of extreme emotional pain, a *pathos*, that lasts beyond the
usual duration because it is generated by reason. Seeing *metanoia* as a product of the irrational part of the soul but ordered by reason places Plutarch
squarely in the Platonist school and at odds with what is usually presented as
the Stoic view.[35] Basic to Plutarch's analysis is a claim, comprehensible within
a philosophical framework that turns the soul into an object of reflection, that
repentance is a natural component of a unitary human experience, an innate
potentiality of our private lives. This existent in the soul stands in contrast to
material forms of distress, which, nevertheless, are employed by way of analogy to help lay claim to the reality of repentance. Indeed, repentance may be

said to outlast these forms, to have more reality than they, for it resides on what we might see as an *inner* or *spiritual* plane of being.[36]

What kind of being "repents?" For Plutarch, *metanoia* is part of a broad series of processes available to the sage committed to a life of progress in virtue.[37] Its reality and permanence, the storing of pain in memory, allow it to become an effective control on future behavior:

> Now the same remedy that helps to cure all disorders of the mind is especially indicated for those who yield easily to pressure: when forced by the disorder [of compliancy] to err against their judgment and succumb to embarrassment, they must keep it firmly in the memory and store up reminders of their remorse and regret and rehearse them and preserve them for a very long time. For as wayfarers who have stumbled over a stone, or skippers who have capsized off a headland, if they retain the circumstances in their memory, henceforth never fail to avoid with a shudder not only the occasion of their misadventure, but everything resembling it, so those who constantly hold up to their repentance and remorse the shame and loss involved in compliancy will in similar circumstances resist the feeling and not easily allow it to carry them away. (*On Compliancy* 536, 19 [De Lacy and Einarson, LCL)

Notwithstanding the pedestrian examples given by Plutarch, the wayfarer and the skipper, which lend an appearance of the natural to the proposed proceedings, we should not be dissuaded from recognizing the radical quality of the act proposed here. Those who would seek to attain the status of the virtuous must adopt a specific remedy for any imperfections; they must choose to place their errors before themselves and hold them there always. They thereby generate what we might call conscience, which, in turn, informs future decision-making. Through persistent mental exercise, the sage is said to attain a degree of self-control, a new constancy in action.

What is the relationship between this private experience and external events? When an individual's reason fails to materialize, it may be furnished—the necessary *pain* may be provided—through the sting of human rebuke[38] or through divinely wrought sufferings.[39] In both cases, the material is employed to generate the spiritual, to provoke a reaction in the essential core of a person. Actually, the founding positive image of *metanoia*, one that pervades both Plutarch and other Greek sources both early and late, may be the theme of a general *granting* his opponents *time* to rethink, to experience *metanoia* for their opposition in the face of defeat, as Plutarch writes, "offering an opportunity for the miscreants to repent and become better men" (*Sayings of Romans* 204, 7 [Babbitt, LCL]). In this scenario, initial pain provides an impetus for thought, while its temporary easing generates a break in the material world, an expanse of time that allows for and suggests the presence of an altogether different kind of nonmaterial operation. Applied to the divine realm, this amounts to an explanation as to why punishment of the wicked can be delayed. Thus, according to Plutarch, we ought to imitate God in showing forbearance and allowing an opportunity for others to repent ("On the Delays of the Divine Vengeance," 551, D). The same foundational theme is reproduced in *The Letter of Aristeas*, a Hellenistic Jewish work that actually predates Plutarch, in the form of advice to a king (188–89). This theme also appears in the Wisdom of Solomon, written by a Greek-speaking Jew around the turn of the Common Era, by way of explaining why God allowed non-Israelites to inhabit the Land as long as they did, "judging them little by little you gave them an opportunity to repent" (12:10).[40] For Plutarch and others, the military theme provides a way of naturalizing repentance, a powerful model for configuring material events—life's ebb and flow of suffering and relative tranquility—as pedagogical and, ultimately, generative of private, mental realities, the need to rethink.

The Source of Repentance: Philo

Writing slightly earlier than Plutarch around the turn of the Common Era, Philo of Alexandria also makes ample use of the term *metanoia*. On the basis of the consensus regarding the place of *metanoia* in classical philosophy, scholars have concluded that the importance accorded the concept by Philo must derive from his Jewish, rather than Greek, background.[41] This assessment has been influenced as well by a certain desire to see repentance as sui generis, as a particular, unique contribution of his Jewish heritage, and to configure Philo as a protoreligious philosopher, harmonizing two distinct essences, reason and religion, Greece and the Bible. In truth, both Plutarch and Philo seem to be serving as repositories for what are probably earlier philosophical positions.[42] What is at stake is not simply a matter of origins—from where the idea of repentance hails—but of a proper analysis of "conceptual personae"[43] and effect. What sort of person engages this concept of repentance, and what system does it, thereby, bring into being?

For Philo, as for Plutarch, repentance is the province of the sage: "To do no sin is peculiar to God; to repent, to the wise man" (*On Flight and Finding*, 157 [Colson and Whitaker, LCL]). Repentance is a constant necessity, because impulsive desires overwhelm the soul more rapidly than tardy reason can dispel them (*On Flight and Finding*, 157). Furthermore, in dedicating to it an entire discussion in his treatise, "On the Virtues," Philo enshrines *metanoia* as one of the philosophical virtues, a move that clearly indicates its arrival as a technical philosophical term.[44]

Philo's discussions of *metanoia* draw on the same concerns for pedagogy, interiority, agency, and moral transformation as Plutarch's. Thus, we see repentance as part of the gentle urging toward betterment that was considered to be proper pedagogy for a Hellenistic sage. According to Philo, the wise Joseph admonishes his fellow inmates with the teachings of philosophy and urges them through the example of his own virtue to repent of their earlier wrongs (*On Joseph* 8–87). Furthermore, the mechanism by which Philo seems to understand the workings of repentance, its efficacy as an act, fits a concern for care of the soul. The one who repents "becomes, convicted inwardly by his conscience, his own accuser" (*On the Special Laws* 1:235). *Metanoia* is thus experienced as a kind of inner "groaning," an emotional pain occasioned by one's sins (*Allegorical Interpretation* 3: 211–13), which serves as a "new counselor" who refuses to "flatter" and thereby prevents relapse into folly (*On Dreams* 2:292). The goods attained by *metanoia* are not scriptural but philosophical ideals: virtue and knowledge. But what begins to emerge in Philo and will be seen even more clearly in other Hellenistic treatments is the sense of *metanoia* as an actual existent—not just a natural aspect of human passion but a force, an entity of its own, a hypostatization of the mechanism at work in regret. Thus, for instance, Philo speaks of *metanoia* as a saving rock that one might grasp hold of to escape the stormy sea of the passions (*On the Posterity of Cain*, 178). In Philo's conception, *metanoia* is not merely an "ulcer" that reminds the sufferer not to err again; it is a cure for disease.

The most significant distinction with Plutarch is Philo's use of *metanoia* in contexts not only of the righteous who err but also of conversion—conversion from sinfulness to righteousness, from ignorance to knowledge, and from idolatry to Judaism. Philo, in fact, interprets much of Moses' discourses in Deuteronomy as "exhortations to repentance" (*On Repentance*, 183) and the process of *shuv* promised there as applying to converts to Judaism.[45] One who repents is said to not only leave behind the false worship of multiple gods but also attain a basic soundness of knowledge and uprightness of character. Clearly lurking in the background of Philo's presentation and informing his use of the term is the Hellenistic trope of conversion to philosophy, which sees implications for moral character in the acquisition of new knowledge and belief.[46] Indeed, there are excellent examples of this trope from outside of the world of Jewish literature that also have recourse to the language of repentance.[47] In the *Corpus Hermeticum*, a collection of syncretistic pagan writings from around the second century C.E., we find a call to conversion framed as an exhortation to repent: "You who have journeyed with error, who have partnered with ignorance, repent: escape the shadowy light; leave corruption behind and take a share in immortality."[48] Here, in an exhortation befitting Philo's Joseph, repentance is applied to a kind of conversion to new *gnosis*.[49] Similarly, in the *Tabula of Cebes*, a work of unknown origin that probably dates to the first century B.C.E. or C.E.,[50] we find *metanoia* as a hypostasis: a female figure, Repentance, who embodies the rejection of a prior way of life on the path to adopting new belief and releases individuals from their ills as she leads them on to proper Education.[51]

The Hypostatization of Repentance: *Joseph and Aseneth*

We encounter this same female figure, Repentance, in *Joseph and Aseneth*, the Hellenistic romance about how Aseneth, the idol-worshiping daughter of an Egyptian priest, converts and marries the biblical Joseph. The work is generally believed to have been written by a Greek-speaking Egyptian Jew in or before the first century C.E.[52] It can be seen in many ways as a dramatization of Philo's notion of *metanoia* as conversion. It too embraces its dual affective and intellectual elements. Realizing the error of her idolatrous ways, Aseneth destroys her idols and repeatedly sheds tears over her past (8:8ff), which she blames on ignorance. The quasi-divine figure, Repentance, intercedes on Aseneth's behalf (15:7), and she is able to go "from darkness to light, and from error to truth, and from death to life" (8:9) to convert and marry the Jew, Joseph. Both Philo and *Joseph and Aseneth* ascribe to *metanoia* the power to transform lives. In the case of the latter, this power is actually embodied as a transcendent existent. It is a component of a metaphysical reality.[53] What the hypostatization of repentance ultimately does, in this context, is to secure for various philosophically inclined groups, including Hellenistic Jews, a way of delineating identity. The mechanism at work for rejecting past error and ensuring a new constancy of action, whether in its naturalistic or supernaturalistic formulation, is what establishes the boundaries of the proposed community, marks its members off from others and their former lives. Representations of the power and reality of repentance, of the sort found in *Joseph and Aseneth*, thus attain the highest degree of priority.

REPENTANCE IN THE TIME OF THE LATE SECOND TEMPLE

Thus far, we have considered the role of *metanoia* in Greek works. Hebrew texts from this period share many of the same features. After all, whether writing in Hebrew, Aramaic, or Greek, Jews lived within the power structure of Hellenistic society with its attendant cultural norms.[54] The literature of late Second Temple Judaism, however, is notoriously difficult to work with. Its record is incomplete, with only a limited number of works preserved. The works that we do possess often no longer exist in their original Semitic language and are of uncertain provenance. At times, they are quite at odds with one another. Nevertheless, the period was extremely important and formative; it is from its soil that Christianity and rabbinic Judaism arose, and we can sometimes catch glimpses of their later trajectories through a careful analysis of the extant material. In this instance too, we may be able to detect intimations of repentance's emerging significance. In chapter 6, I challenged the consensus view that belief in the power of repentance to effect redemption was held in common by Jews, especially sectarians, living in the late Second Temple period. The literature of this period indeed does not reveal an over-whelming interest in the concept, but certain texts do assert its importance in the lives of individuals.

Repentance in the Life of Individual Righteousness: Ben Sira

First and foremost among those to emphasize the importance of repentance in the life of individuals is the Wisdom of Ben Sira. Composed at the begin-ning of the second century B.C.E.,[55] Ben Sira differs significantly from earlier Hebrew wisdom texts in the primacy it accords introspection: "Who will set whips over my thoughts, and the discipline of wisdom over my mind, so as not to spare me in my errors, and not overlook my sins?" (23:2). Ben Sira's sage internalizes disciplinary procedures; he seeks to inhabit a mental space generated by reason's own continual perception of errors. What does the sage then do with them? Though not yet formally bundled together as in later for-mulations,[56] a number of recurring methods of atonement are already alluded to in Ben Sira's work: fasting, prayer, almsgiving, and repentance.[57] Together they form a new kind of personal piety evidenced in the late Second Temple period.[58] Though it appears to share the priestly concern for expiating sin, this life of devotion was quite independent from the Temple. It takes the indi-vidual as its object of concern and uses "biblical" acts, such as fasting, as a way of securing (and demonstrating) his or her ongoing perfection.[59] While overtly absent from the Wisdom of Ben Sira, the political dimensions of this individual perfectionism emerge strongly in such narrative material from the period as Tobit and Judith, where the personal purity secured by pious deeds is set up as a bulwark against foreign imperialism. I would argue that it is against this backdrop, the life of individual piety, that repentance makes its first appearance as such in Hebrew literature.[60]

The work as a whole employs a variety of biblical phrases involving *shuv*, "turn to YHWH," "turn away from sin," and "turn" (without preposition).[61] Is Ben Sira's *shuv* a derivative of biblical *shuv*? The wide range of *shuv* formula-tions found in Ben Sira immediately makes it clear that he is reading Scripture, collecting phrases from here and there, rather than operating within a fixed, continuous tradition. However, his use of *shuv* without a preposition, unusual in biblical texts, in particular creates the suspicion that there is something new at work here, a move toward a nominalization of *shuv* as a particular sort of known religious performance.[62] In service of what does Ben Sira deploy the prestigious, biblical root?

"Do not be ashamed to turn back [*lashuv*] from sin" (4:26), reads the first use of *shuv* in the work. Why would anyone be ashamed to turn away from a life of wickedness? Perhaps because of this difficulty, the Greek translation of Ben Sira renders the phrase: "Do not be ashamed to confess your sins." But that does not appear to have been the language of Ben Sira himself, who is probably looking at the "turn back from sin" as a *mental* event and, hence, one susceptible to the inner pain, "shame," that ensues from consciousness of error. Likewise, Ben Sira, at times, seems to explicitly mark such a "turn" as internal: "Those who hate reproof walk in the sinner's steps, but those who fear the Lord will turn [back] *in their heart*" (21:6). This passage notes the interiority of such a "turn" but it may also be highlighting the agency behind it, suggesting that "those who fear the Lord" will turn back on their own cognizance, realizing error without reproof.

This heightened sense of "turning" as a discrete act and the individual as actor emerges particularly clearly in passages that treat the relationship between repentance and illness. As in Plutarch, where varieties of pain are deployed to generate a realm of private introspection, the righteous maintain their health by monitoring their mind. Here is one example that uses a verb of "turning" related to *shuv*: "My son, when sick, do not delay praying to God, for he will heal you. Turn away [here: *sur*] from iniquity and corruption; from all sins purify your heart" (38:9–10). Like prayer or consulting a doctor (38:12), "turning away from iniquity" is a discrete act that can be performed in a moment of trouble, one that entails an active mental process of identifying and repudiating error. This pedagogical structure is developed further in the following passage: "The compassion of human beings is for their neighbors, but the compassion of the Lord is for every living being. He rebukes, trains, teaches, and turns them back, as a shepherd his flock" (18:13). Suffering, brought on by the divine, must actually be seen as a form of instruction, *paideia*.

Ideally, mind substitutes altogether for the necessity of the material by generating its own consciousness of sin prior to suffering: "Before judgment comes, examine yourself; and at the time of scrutiny you will find forgiveness. Before falling ill, humble yourself; and, on the day you sin, turn back" (18:20–21). Continual, active self-monitoring produces an awareness of sin committed and allows for its repudiation. There is little room not to understand this "turning back" as a *discrete, retrospective, mental* act in connection to *specific* sins that is *efficacious* and proceeds without compunction from *human choice*. Here, we encounter in Ben Sira a most striking articulation of repentance as a technology of the self. Ben Sira seems to be operating within the Hellenistic model we have been exploring.[63] In fact, one notes that his formulation, "on the day you sin, turn back" (18:21),[64] is remarkably similar to an inscription attributed to a Delphic temple and thought to date to around 300 B.C.E., "repent upon erring [*metanoei hamartōn*]."[65]

Thus, Ben Sira seems to do the work of connecting biblical *shuv* to the contexts in which we have seen *metanoia* figure in Hellenistic literature. This identification of *shuv* with "repentance" is reinforced by a final terminological point. The Greek translator, Ben Sira's grandson, follows the tradition of the Septuagint in rendering instances of *shuv* with prefixed forms of -*strefō*, "turn." However, on two occasions, when the Hebrew original appears to lack a preposition (17:24, 48:15), making literal "turn" a difficult translation, he uses *metanoeō* in its stead.[66] Without a doubt, this choice shows that *shuv* has begun to be understood as "repent." This identification and the effacement of directionality it entails, probably already present, as noted earlier, in Ben Sira himself, is an essential early moment in the nominalization of repentance, the appropriation of *shuv* as a technical term indicating "repentance."

Demonstrable Repentance: The Book of Jubilees

We also find evidence of repentance playing a role with regard to individual culpability in certain legal contexts. The book of Jubilees, which we encountered in the previous chapter in connection to its apocalypticism, most likely was composed around or shortly after the Wisdom of Ben Sira. Among other things, it seeks to present the Genesis narratives as sources of law. In this regard, it runs into difficulty with the story of Judah and Tamar. Judah sleeps with his daughter-in-law, a serious transgression under any circumstances according to the Torah, but the narrative fails to acknowledge it as such. What Jubilees sets in motion is a rather complex reading of the biblical account that resolves this underlying tension by introducing a legal concept of repentance. First, he construes Judah's utterance exonerating Tamar, "she is in the right, as against me" (Gen. 38:26),[67] as an acknowledgment of sin. Then, he reads the narrative's conclusion, "And he was not intimate with her again" (Gen. 38:26), as part of a legal declaration that exonerates Judah and explains why his punishment has been commuted. As Jubilees writes in his imaginative reconstruction of this story: "We [i.e., the angels] told him in a dream that it would be forgiven for him because he had pleaded very much and because he had mourned *and did not do [it] again*" (Jub. 41:24).

The passage in Jubilees is significant as an instance of how early interpreters reinforce the obviousness of repentance as a naturalized component of Scripture by embedding it within biblical narrative, but it also provides us with particular insight into the concept's legal dimensions and definitional contours. The reason to exonerate Judah would seem to be clear: Tamar was disguised, and he did not know he was sleeping with his daughter-in-law. But, according to Jubilees, a misperception of circumstances is not sufficient to secure forgiveness. "He had forgiveness because he turned from his sin and from his ignorance" (Jub. 41:25). Jubilees spells out the sense of this "turning" in greater detail as follows: "In his own view he considered it [his sexual act with Tamar] evil, and he knew that he had done wrong and erred . . . he began to mourn and plead before the Lord because of his sin" (Jub. 41:23). Forgiveness depends on an act that must be performed within and by an autonomous individual, "in his own view," and, subsequently, receive expression in mourning and pleading. While biblical tradition has a category of errors done in ignorance,[68] the specified requirement of regret places Jubilees much closer to such an author as Aristotle:

> An act done through ignorance is in every case not voluntary, but it is involuntary only when it causes the agent pain and regret . . . . Acts done through ignorance therefore fall into two classes: if the agent regrets the act, we think that he has acted involuntarily; if he does not regret it, to mark the distinction we may call him a "non-voluntary" agent. (*Nicomachean Ethics* 1110b 18–24 [Rackham, LCL])

Judah would have to repent of his act, precisely what Jubilees writes into the biblical narrative, if he is to be considered an "involuntary agent." And, sure enough, to represent such an act, the repudiation of a specific sin committed in ignorance, Jubilees apparently uses the same biblical term as Ben Sira, *shuv*, "turn," a usage unattested in biblical Hebrew.

Furthermore, Judah's "turn" is parallel to and demonstrated by "mourning." Mourning fits the common view of *metanoia* and its philosophical depiction as a passion that spills forth into "disorderly movement,"[69] weeping and bodily contortions that give evidence of the distress bound up in repentance. What mourning does for Judah's repentance in Jubilees is to provide a visible, physical demonstration that he was an involuntary agent, direct insight into his conscience. It would also seem to be a way of integrating repentance with common biblical practices of mourning. Embedded in Jubilees' account of Judah's repentance, "he began to *mourn* and plead before the Lord *because of his sin*," is undoubtedly the biblical phrase, "mourning over sin." The *Testaments of the Twelve Patriarchs*, which shows a close connection to Jubilees and will be discussed further in the chapter, uses the same wording in representing Reuben as engaging in mourning practices on account of his sin with Bilhah: "I did not drink wine or strong drink, and meat did not enter into my mouth, nor did I taste any appetizing bread, *mourning over my sin*—for it was indeed great."[70] The phrase comes most immediately from Ezra 10:6, "he ate no bread and drank no water, for he was in *mourning over the trespass* of those who had returned from exile." In Ezra, the phrase figures as a component of the intercessor's response to the prospect of his people's doom.[71] In the case of Jubilees and the *Testaments*, who, incidentally, adds to Jubilees' depiction to specify that, like Ezra's, Judah's mourning includes fasting, the phrase appears in an entirely different context: the individual sinner's self-reflection over not the prospect of doom, but the impropriety of a prior act. This is not just a change in a phrase's usage; it reflects a full-scale appropriation of an ancient

Israelite practice. Mourning and, especially, fasting have become expressions of repentance.

Biblical practices of mourning provide fertile ground onto which to map the act of repentance and lay claim to its efficacy, for, as I suggested in chapter 1, they serve as a way of embodying forms of distress that are not yet manifest upon the body. In their new context, such practices still enact what would otherwise remain oblique, but the distress that they concretize is internal. As we saw above, this mode of embodiment takes on a special urgency in legal scenarios that depend upon mental events for their integrity. Its power of clarification renders mourning potentially significant in communal contexts as well, where there is a need, on one hand, to allow for a certain elasticity, in terms of the inevitable transgression of communal norms, and, on the other, to assert a solidity of identity through a powerful demonstration of the purity of participants' intention, their minds, and, hence, their essential being. We are now in a position to understand how repentance came to be written so prominently into the calendar of ancient Judaism, the earliest attestation of which is found in Jubilees: "Regarding the Israelites it has been written and ordained: 'If they turn to him in the right way, he will forgive all their wickedness and will pardon all their sins.' It has been written and ordained that he will have mercy on all who turn from their errors once each year" (5:17–18). Importing *shuv* terminology completely absent from the original depiction in Leviticus, this passage most likely makes the connection between the Day of Atonement and repentance through the idea that it is a day of "mourning over sin." Indeed, in another formulation found in Jubilees, we find: "this day is decreed so that they might mourn on it on account of their sins and on account of all their transgressions and on account of all their errors in order to purify themselves on this day, once a year" (34:19). For Jubilees and forms of Judaism that were to follow, the brute physicality of the day's events, the nationwide fast, is turned toward a demonstration of proper mental states.[72] It serves as an important reminder that discourses around interiority, even as they shift attention away from the material toward a new sort of mental space, need not lead to an abandonment of physical performance. If anything, they entail a further refinement and elaboration of its artistry—Aseneth's exaggerated acting out of repentance in *Joseph and Aseneth* comes to mind—as the need to make the non-manifest manifest heightens its urgency.[73]

The Construction of Penitent Sinners: *Testaments of the Twelve Patriarchs*

Thus far we have examined two (originally) Hebrew works from a century-and-a-half or so before the turn of the Common Era and noted a new element, albeit one dressed up in the old biblical language of *shuv*—the power of regret to effect atonement. The early date and language of Ben Sira and Jubilees are secure; actual fragments of their original Hebrew were preserved among the Dead Sea Scrolls. Similarly, possible fragments of a text mentioned above, *The Testaments of the Twelve Patriarchs*, or early versions of it were found among the Scrolls. To be sure, the Greek text in which the full work has been preserved includes a number of Christian pronouncements and, in its current form, must date to a later period. Whatever the status of the work in its final form,[74] the *Testaments* bring together a number of the themes we have been tracing and provide important elaborations regarding the character of repentance as a naturalized concept.

Most striking is the nature of its biblical interpretation. In its hands, Genesis becomes a book of exemplars, lessons in the life of individual piety, as each of Jacob's twelve sons report what they have learned over their lifetime in the form of an ethical testament. The *Testaments* portray at least four of the brothers, Reuben, Simeon, Judah, and Gad, as penitent sinners and include extensive discussions of repentance as a concept. There are exegetical bases for the *Testaments'* claims, but what matters at the present is the net effect of its readings.[75] In embedding such elaborate penitential accounts into Scripture, the *Testaments* represent an advanced stage in the naturalization of repentance, whereby biblical narrative, through the power of exemplification, is seen to vouchsafe the vitality of repentance in the lives of individuals.[76]

Much of what we find in the *Testaments*, regardless of its provenance, reinforces the claim regarding the unity of a discourse around "repentance." That is to say, despite the various contexts in which it figures, repentance helps bring into effect a shared notion of a being endowed with interiority, agency, and the potential for transformation.[77] Thus, according to the *Testament of Asher*, "if the soul chooses the good [impulse], everything it does will be [done] in righteousness, and [even] if it sins, it will repent right away"(1:6). As in Ben Sira, the being truly aligned with the good, who "chooses the good," can preserve that identification, since its true measure is inner intent, by repenting immediately upon erring. It is therefore not surprising to find a strong emphasis on an autonomous inner essence. Reuben presents his repentance as the "choice [*proairesis*] of my soul" (*T. Reuben* 1:9) and reveals that "to this day my conscience afflicts me concerning my sin" (4:3). In turn, the harassed conscience, the residual presence of pain, ensures the proper control of self. In the words of Reuben: "from that time until now, I have been on my guard and have not sinned" (4:4). As for the brothers, so too, we might imagine, for the community of the *Testaments'* author, repentance allows for the projection of an inner reality that enables the continued integrity of the family/community in the face of deviance.

For serious sins, Reuben's sleeping with Bilhah, Simeon's responsibility for the sale of Joseph, and Judah's sleeping with Tamar, the *Testaments* advocate an extreme form of mourning involving extended abstinence from alcohol and meat. This process is referred to in the *Testament of Judah* as "repentance of my flesh" (19:2), which probably should be understood as "repentance demonstrated in the flesh" and is to be juxtaposed to the internal repentance that suffices in cases of minor sin. Here, an extended, aggravated physical demonstration of regret is needed for maintaining the integration of the sinner. We find a related formulation in the *Testament of Reuben*: "for seven years I repented before the Lord" (1:9). Unlike anything found in Ben Sira or *Jubilees*, repentance in the *Testaments* can expand into a continuous state of being, defined like mourning in ancient Israel by a set period of time.[78] The formulation, though unusual, is found in various versions of the *Life of Adam and Eve*, where Adam and Eve are supposed to "repent for forty days."[79] It is also found in one early rabbinic work, *Seder Olam*, where Manasseh is said to "repent for thirty-three years" (24:6).[80] Indeed, it may suggest that *Seder Olam* has preserved, along with the other works, a genuinely early formulation, one that, at the very least, has important implications for later penitential practices within the Church, what Tertullian refers to as *exomologesis* ("confession"), in which extended physical performance establishes the sinner's identity as penitent, allowing for reintegration.[81] As Reuben comments: "For until my father's death I never had the courage to look him in the face or speak to any of my brothers because of my disgraceful act" (4:2). But, of course, it is that very shame, and its public demonstration, that allows him to remain in their presence.

Before leaving the *Testaments*, I would like to dwell on what is certainly its most striking and extensive discussion of repentance. In his testament, Gad produces a paeon to the concept:

> I finally learned these things myself, after I had repented for [what I did to] Joseph. For true repentance [that is done] in accord with God['s will] destroys ignorance and puts darkness to flight, brings light to the eyes and grants knowledge to the soul and turns the disposition [of the soul] in the direction of salvation. And what it has not learned from people, it will learn through repentance. (5:6–8)

The notion that new knowledge follows upon repentance figures in other testaments as well, albeit less explicitly, for the patriarchs tend to launch into discourses about the nature of morality and the power of demons immediately after alluding to their repentance.[82] The *gnosis* that Gad describes suggests that what begins as human regret ends up involving a quasi-divine hypostasis with independent power, like the figure of Repentance, that bestows knowledge and rids the penitent of disobedience. We have seen this conversionary sense in the *Tabula of Cebes* and Philo, but nowhere else than in the *Testaments* does the concept more clearly attain its own independent existence, becoming a power of its own.

Equivocation and the Semantics of Repentance: Josephus

The evidence gathered thus far suggests that a concept of repentance operated in the late Second Temple period within certain circles, but, overall, its
absence is still more striking than its presence. It is not found in such works
reflecting the piety of the period as Tobit or Judith, or 1 and 2 Maccabees
for that matter.[83] As discussed in the preceding chapter, it is not to be found
in the Enochic corpus or in the Dead Sea Scrolls.[84] To be sure, *shuv* terminology figures in the latter in prominent ways, and this may reflect a certain
interest common to the sect and Hellenistic movements at large in practices
of group initiation,[85] but this does not mean that the sect deploys the term
to signify "repentance," with its particular set of concerns around interiority and agency. Indeed, one suspects the first-century Latin geographer
and naturalist, Pliny the Elder, of turning the group into something of a
philosophical school, rather like Josephus famously does in a different context,[86] when he describes how their ranks are filled by those "wearied by the
fluctuations of fortune" and points out, with perhaps not a little irony, "so
fruitful for them is the repentance which others feel for their past lives."[87]
Repentance, here, constitutes the inner pain one has accumulated through
a life of vanity, and conversion to the group the fulfillment of a universalist
project of overcoming human limitation by rejecting materialist pursuits.
The contrast between Pliny's view and that of the sect's own representation
of initiation is instructive of the radical specificity of repentance, despite
Pliny's (and most contemporary scholars') assumption that it can carry over
to most contexts as a general interpretive tool. Indeed, some of the relative
absence of repentance may be due to accidents of literary genre and textual
preservation. But, on the whole, its distribution seems to be indicative of
a concept that has only partly penetrated a complex cultural milieu with
manifold layers of diversity.

In this regard, the first-century Jewish historian, Josephus, turns out to
be an important case in point. Though the term *metanoia* appears frequently
in his writings, Josephus has limited interest in repentance as a discourse.
He often uses the term in its standard sense of futile regret or, at best, reconsidering decisions before it is too late. We do find instances of rebuke, which
is what is needed in the Hellenistic model when one's own conscience fails,
such as when Joseph, in Josephus's retelling, exhorts his brothers in a rather
heightened rhetorical style to repent of their decision to murder him, for, if
they continue with their plan, their consciences will become their enemies
(*Ant.* 2.23–28). But the basic pattern—improper decision, opportunity and
exhortation to rethink—often fits the battlefield much more closely than the
philosophical school. It is good form to warn one's enemy and exhort them to
repent before destroying them. Thus Josephus records how he himself urged
one who was plotting against him to repent and turn loyal before it was too

late (*Vit.* 110). At the same time, Josephus has difficulty separating out *metanoia*, as a passion, from mourning practices when they appear in the Bible, as we have seen with others. Thus, he refers to David's tears in response to Nathan's accusing him of adultery as *metanoia* (*Ant.* 7.153), as well as to the *metanoia* of the people in the time of Ezra, "for in their repentance and sorrow over the sins which they had formerly committed, they would have a security and safeguard that the like would not happen again" (*Ant.* 11.156 [Marcus, LCL]). This formulation, of course, reflects the standard theory of repentance quite closely. All of this suggests to me that Josephus was aware of a certain rhetoric around "repentance" without having quite embraced it himself, at least not within any formal religious sphere.

A rather extraordinary indication of the concept's relative lack of penetration in Josephus's thought can be found in his reading of those pivotal *shuv* passages in the book of Deuteronomy that came to be closely associated with a supposedly biblical doctrine of repentance. Josephus understands Moses' words as warning Israel that, if they sin, they will come to experience *metanoia*, inner suffering brought on by a mistake one cannot undo (*Ant.* 4.191). Thus, in Josephus's account of the passages, *metanoia* is not a virtue, but part of the punishment of exile. This is precisely the futile feeling of regret that is most common among Greek writers.

Josephus's negative reading of *shuv* points to a semantic shift—from *shuv* as "turn away" to *shuv* as "regret"—that exists apart from but could have contributed to the positive ideological reading of *shuv* as "repentance" and that may figure in Ben Sira and Jubilees' use of the term as well. It is not, of course, hard to imagine such a change. What linguists label "grammaticalization," a variety of processes whereby concrete meanings tend to lose their material senses in favor of more abstract ones, could be seen as being at work here.[88] Consider the following: "For this the earth mourns, and skies are dark above—because I have spoken, I have planned, and I will not relent or turn back from it" (Jer. 4:28); or Moses' plea to God: "Turn back your blazing anger, and relent concerning the evil planned for your people" (Exod. 32:12). In both cases, "turn back" (*shuv*) appears with the verb "relent" (*niham*). The two work together to convey the sense of a change in plans, but they do so without *shuv*'s necessarily losing its specific sense of "turning back," whether from a plan or a state of anger. That said, it is easy to see how this embodied metaphor could slide into a more abstract sense of "regret," especially given its proximity in such instances to *niham*, which is, after all, translated in the Septuagint as *metanoeō*.

In this case, there also appears to be an additional sort of linguistic phenomenon at work, contact between languages, what is known as a "calque."[89] It is quite clear that, within postbiblical Hebrew, the Aramaic root, *ḥazar*, largely replaces *shuv* in conveying the sense of "return, turn back."[90] It is not that *shuv* ceases to appear altogether, but it is now used in a variety of specialized senses.[91] Now, *ḥazar* alone or, more commonly, combined with the preposition *b-*, can convey a sense of "regret," "change one's mind," or "repent."[92] The same range of meanings is also found for Aramaic *tuv*, which, ultimately, derives from the same Semitic root as *shuv*. Thus, for instance, the *targumim*, Aramaic translations of the Bible, will frequently translate *niham*, the Hebrew term considered above, with *tuv*, in the sense of "regret."[93] Given the dominance of Aramaic in Judea around the turn of the Common Era, it seems very likely that, for many readers of the Bible, including Josephus, *shuv* would have taken on the same range of meanings as *ḥazar* and *tuv*, a development that would also help explain the eventual, common non-Septuagintal practice of translating *shuv* into Greek as *metanoeō*. Though the semantic shift alone does not account for the valorization of repentance in the late Second Temple period, it did pave the way for the successful adoption of biblical *shuv* as a term that could be used to signify the emergent concept.

Naturalizing Repentance: The Prayer of Manasseh

I would like to conclude our discussion of repentance in the late Second Temple period with another idiosyncratic but extremely significant text, the Prayer of Manasseh. Its place within the Apocrypha in many modern bibles is already a matter of some interest, as it is only found appended to the Septuagint in a few manuscripts.[94] It is surely the centrality of the theme of repentance in the work that has secured its elevated status. This shortest of texts leaves us with little to no information about its provenance, but most believe that it comes from a Jewish milieu around the turn of the Common Era.[95] Most striking is the mode by which this text naturalizes repentance as a prediscursive practice. As we have seen, there is a common Hellenistic theme of military leaders (or God) granting a period of amnesty and hence a onetime opportunity to repent. Beginning with a discussion of God's ordering of heaven and earth, the Prayer of Manasseh suggests that God has permanently established this grant from the beginning of time, an act of mercy embedded in creation: "you have promised repentance and forgiveness to those who have sinned against you, and in the multitude of your mercies, you have constituted repentance for sinners, for salvation." (7) Repentance, it turns out, is hard-wired into the very order of things, a claim that reflects the hypostatization of repentance already seen in such texts as *Joseph and Aseneth*. Finally, one notes that the Prayer's focus is on repentance not as the self-monitoring of the righteous, as in Ben Sira, but as a mode of conversion: "Therefore you, O Lord, God of the righteous, have not constituted repentance for the righteous, for Abraham and Isaac and Jacob, who did not sin against you, but you have constituted repentance for me, who am a sinner" (8).[96] Manasseh's sin is, of course, idolatry, and it may very well be that, again, like *Joseph and Aseneth*, this text uses the concept of repentance, its being embedded in nature rather than in a specific covenant,[97] to develop a framework for conversion, one in which the very possibility of turning to the God of Israel, the "God of the righteous," and joining the descendants of "Abraham and Isaac and Jacob" has been decreed long ago.[98]

THE INSTITUTIONALIZATION OF REPENTANCE IN RABBINIC JUDAISM

Despite the chronological priority of New Testament literature, I continue now with a discussion of the place of repentance in rabbinic literature, in order to set up the possibility for questioning claims of Christian exceptionalism later in the chapter. Rabbinic literature spans a number of centuries, but its earliest texts date to the second century of the Common Era and may preserve some earlier traditions. The oldest, so-called tannaitic literature will be used when available, but we will have recourse to some later amoraic texts as well to elucidate a number of additional points. Rabbinic Judaism provides us with our first unambiguous instance of the widespread institutionalization of repentance within the framework of a known, defined religious community, a situation that serves as a precedent, with regard to its penetration and inevitability, for the position of repentance in contemporary lexicons. In particular, it gives us the opportunity to consider the nexus of language, interiority, and religion, how the generation of concepts proceeds from the development of normative contexts in which, to maintain communal identity, subjects must govern themselves from within themselves.[99]

The nominalization of repentance as a concept in rabbinic Judaism takes place in the form of the noun, *teshuva*. The frequency and uniformity of this term across the corpus of writings is remarkable.[100] Rabbinic literature declares repeatedly and unambiguously that *teshuva* atones for sin. *Teshuva* receives its own running discussion in the Babylonian Talmud, showing that it was indeed conceptualized as a distinct category in a work that rarely treats topics systematically (b. Yoma 85b–87a) and forms the subject of one of the blessings in the daily prayer, the *amidah*.[101] *Teshuva* also comes to be associated not only with the Day of Atonement, a view found already in Jubilees, but with the entire period of ten days between the New Year and the Day of Atonement, a whole season open to penitence.[102] Ultimately, *teshuva* finds itself front and center in the life of the righteous, which is said to revolve around "repentance and good deeds," a common refrain in the literature. But this life of the righteous, very close to what is found in Ben Sira,[103] becomes normative, incumbent, at least in the discourse maintained by rabbinic Judaism, upon all. Furthermore, it is no longer merely a question of fashioning one's life according to nature, as it was for Philo, but of living according to the Torah, an objectification of communal norms, of shaping one's identity around it, a process that requires, if anything, a more heightened form of interior activity, self-scrutiny, and introspection. Indeed, within rabbinic Judaism, concepts such as repentance carve out, amidst the physical behaviors ordained in the Torah, elements of an individual, interior self, an agent charged with the performance of the commandments.[104]

The Ascension of Repentance

I would like to introduce this discussion with a narrative rendering of Manasseh's prayer in 2 Chronicles 33:12–13, which should help us begin to appreciate how repentance takes its place in rabbinic Judaism, how it is instilled as a naturalized concept:

> A copper pot was prepared, he [Manasseh] was placed inside, and a fire was started beneath him. When he saw he was really in trouble, there was no idol to whom he did not appeal. When this didn't help him at all, he said to himself: "I recall that my father [Hezekiah] used to lead me in reciting the [following] verse in synagogue: 'When you are in distress because all these things have befallen you and, in the end, turn back to the LORD your God and obey him, for the LORD your God is a compassionate God, he will not fail you nor will he let you perish; he will not forget the covenant which he made on oath with your fathers' [Deut. 4:30–31]. I will recite the verse. If he answers me, great, and, if not, nothing is lost." The angels shut the windows [to the heavens] so that his prayer should not go up before the Holy One, blessed be he, and said to the Holy One, blessed be he: "Master of the Universe, a person who has worshiped idols and set up an idol in the Temple, you're going to accept in repentance?" He said to them: "If I do not accept him in repentance, I would be shutting the door before all penitents." What did he do? He dug a hole directly below his Glorious Throne and heard his plea. That is what is written: "In his distress . . . he prayed to him, he granted his prayer [*vayyeʿater*; read as the verb, *ḥtr*: dug a hole for him], heard his plea, and restored him" [2 Chron. 33:12–13]. (y. Sanhedrin 28:3)

Whereas the Prayer of Manasseh, just considered above, would seem to locate repentance already at the time of creation, this midrash embeds the concept in the Torah, in the verses from Deuteronomy 4:30–31 that Hezekiah taught Manasseh to recite. As in the writings of Philo, these verses are applied not to the nation, as they are in their original biblical context, but to the individual sinner; it is a statement of doctrine, a promise about the power of repentance in the life of the penitent. We find the same interpretation elsewhere in rabbinic literature, for instance, in an Aramaic translation, known as Targum Pseudo-Jonathan, to a similar verse from Deuteronomy 30:2: "The greatest among your righteous are the penitents, for, when they sin and repent, their repentance reaches the Glorious Seat of the Lord your God." The naturalization of repentance proceeds from the grounding of *teshuva* in a biblical verse, a verse that is recited and whose repetition, in turn, ensures the concept's reality.

However confidently this account sets forth repentance as a naturalized object, one that is embedded in the Torah, it still clearly reflects a certain anxiety around the status of the concept. The angels, after all, would seek to deny it. It takes special divine intervention, the digging of a hole in the firmament, for repentance to attain its place. The story of repentance's ascent, also suggested in Targum Pseudo-Jonathan, is based on a certain interpretation of the peculiar use of the preposition *ad*, which appears in the verses from Deuteronomy and suggests something like "up to." The connection is made explicit in a midrash on Hosea attributed to the same Rabbi Levi from whom the account of Manasseh is said to originate: "Great is repentance for it reaches the Glorious Seat, for it is written, 'Turn back, O Israel, to [*ad*] the LORD, your God'" (Hosea 14:2) (b. Yoma 86a). In other words, Hosea is understood to say: "the repentance of Israel [ascends] up to the Lord, your God." Here, "repentance," conceived in objective terms as a sort of ascending hypostasis, figures as the special provenance of God, a quasi-mystical doctrine undoubtedly drawn from the Hellenistic notion of Repentance as divine figure.

In my view, the Rabbis may pick up on and emphasize this theme precisely out of an anxiety that derives from the novelty of their coinage. "Repentance" cannot yet be fully naturalized; a special, separate reality must be carved out for it. Indeed, another excellent example can be found in the following midrash:

> Wisdom was asked, "What is the fate of sinners?" She responded: "Misfortune pursues sinners" (Prov. 14:21).
>
> When Prophecy was asked, she responded: "The one who sins shall surely die" (Ezek. 18:4).
>
> The Torah was asked, and she responded: "Let the sinner bring a guilt-offering and attain atonement."
>
> They then asked the Holy One, blessed be he, "what is the fate of sinners?" He responded: "The sinner should repent and be forgiven," as it is written: "Good and upright is the LORD; therefore *he* instructs sinners about the way [of repentance] [Ps. 25:8]. (Pesiqta de Rab Kahana 24:7; compare y. Makkot 31d)

Even while employing biblical verses, this fanciful personification of the Bible's tripartite canon suggests that "repentance" is not a known component of Scripture but a hidden doctrine of God himself. This view exists in a certain tension with the claim of Scripture as source, but it is a contradiction, a doubling back over the grounding of repentance, that is borne of the precariousness of the claims for "repentance" as a naturalized concept. Either way, what is noteworthy in these rabbinic passages and others is that the focus is not so much on enjoining others to repent as asserting the "greatness of repentance," forwarding *teshuva* as a special sort of existent (b. Yoma 86a–b).[105]

Defining *Teshuva*

I would like to return briefly to the midrashic reading seen above, wherein the phrase "turn back to [*'ad*] the Lord," found in Deuteronomy and the like, is understood as suggesting that "repentance" "reaches the Glorious Seat." What is striking about this reading is that it completely disrupts the normal syntactical relationship between verb and preposition. The preposition *'ad*, "to," no longer tells us something about the direction an agent must "turn." Rather, it affirms that a distinct entity, called *teshuva*, ascends to God. The nominalization of *shuv* has been completed; its directionality as a motion verb no longer matters. And, indeed, this point should be clear when we consider the Mishnaic Hebrew verbal phrase for "repenting," *'aśa teshuva*, which, likewise, eschews any interest in the directionality of the "turn."[106] However, scholars have generally resisted this view of *teshuva*, because it calls into question its status as unique to Judaism, based on its supposed roots in the Hebrew Bible. Consider a recent scholarly treatment of the term that defines it as "that immensely difficult psycho-social process designated in English (for lack of a better term) as 'repentance.' 'Returning' or 'turning around' might be more accurate."[107] This definition attempts to assess the meaning of the phrase through its etymology, on the basis of the biblical root *shuv*, but, as we must recognize, "the etymology of a word is not a statement about its meaning but about its history."[108] I would argue that one need not apologize, "for lack of a better term," for using the translation, "repentance." As we shall see, rabbinic *teshuva* adheres rather closely to the defining features of "repentance" laid out in the beginning of this chapter. Indeed, there appears to be a genealogical connection, a certain identity, between rabbinic *teshuva*, Greek *metanoia*, and Latin *paenitentia*.[109]

Teshuva does not merely mark a passage from sin to righteousness, like the biblical phrase "turn away from sin"; it is itself a discrete act, a mental performance. It is not incidental that the rabbinic phrase, *'aśa teshuva*, "to repent," employs the verb *'aśa*, "to do, make," with the sense of "performing" *teshuva*. Thus, we find that the term is frequently coupled with other kinds of performances: "repentance and good deeds are like a shield before retribution" (m. Avot 5:11). Likewise, "three things nullify a harsh decree: prayer, almsgiving, and repentance."[110] Such statements are extremely significant, for they organize, formulate as regimen, a series of performances that Ben Sira, for instance, had merely noted as valuable and effective over the course of the life of the righteous. Indeed, such regularized performances ultimately offer a way of conceptualizing life under the commandments. Pious worship and charitable deeds furnish a mode of identification within the community, but it is the practice of repentance that inexorably binds the individual to its norms, crafting a private, mental space for the exercise of self-governance.

The self that *teshuva* brings into effect differs considerably from that found in connection to *shuv* in the Hebrew Bible. This contrast becomes evident in the following passage from the Tosefta: "If an individual is evil all his days and repents in the end, God accepts him, as it is written: 'As for the evil of the wicked person, he will not stumble against it when he turns away [literally: on the day of his turning away] from the evil' [Ezek. 33:12]" (t. Qiddushin 1:16). Now, the verse quoted from Ezekiel—the use of which, incidentally, shows the absolute identification in rabbinic literature between *teshuva* and biblical *shuv*—does not really go as far as actually promoting the scenario envisioned in the rabbinic source, of the wicked individual who repents any "day," even on his last. For Ezekiel, the disaster from which "turning away from sin" saves is not to be found in the world-to-come but in the here and now. The wicked individual will be allowed to continue to live. On the contrary, what concerns the Tosefta is not the sinner's life but his soul, whether God will "accept" him in the end. This vision of repentance's end-of-life efficacy, also reflected in the rabbinic adage, "repent one day before your death" (m. Avot 2:10),[111] develops an image of a unified self receiving its final definition from a momentary act of repentance. How one thinks and feels—and it is clear here that we are dealing with a mental act, not a behavioral change, for how could such a change be measured at the end of one's life?—becomes all important.

The association between repentance and dying is quite strong throughout rabbinic literature,[112] but it receives somewhat clearer formulation in legal literature: "death and the Day of Atonement atone with [that is: when accompanied by] repentance" (m. Yoma 8:8). Here, we see a shift from the more homiletical passage quoted above; repentance alone does not atone for sin (at least not all sins), but rather must *attend* those activities that do atone. A passage in the Tosefta, for instance, further suggests that repentance must accompany sacrifice for its atoning powers to be felt (t. Yoma 4:9). Such passages show us one way rabbinic thought was able to integrate an emergent concern for interior states with the evident physicality of biblical performances. Sacrifice does not lose its independent identity as an atoning power; it is not merely an expression of repentance. But now it does require a certain penitential intention to exist alongside it. Sacrifice without proper intent would be infelicitous. In a certain circumstances, which one is subject to dispute, *teshuva* can even effect atonement by itself: "If he transgresses a positive commandment and repents, he does not move from that spot before being forgiven" (t. Yoma 4:6). Here we find confirmation that *teshuva* constitutes an instantaneous moment, addressing itself to specific, individual sins, that can only be seen as occurring within the mind.

The passages adduced above help affirm that the tannaitic or earliest layer of rabbinic Hebrew shared the late Second Temple view of *shuv* as a discrete process of regret. A few passages from later forms of rabbinic literature will help further clarify certain dimensions of this characterization. It is told of Nebuzaradan, the officer of Nebuchadnezzar, that he converted to Judaism. Here is part of the portrayal of this remarkable turning point in his life: "at that moment, he bestirred his mind with [a thought of] penitence: if this [has transpired] on account of [the death of] one person, how much more [punishment will ensue] for one who has killed all these people" (b. Gittin 57b). The process of *teshuva*, here, is modeled on what is seen as a logical operation of the mind, an a fortiori deduction. It is illuminating to consider how this account differs from earlier portrayals of bloody tyrants who convert. In the book of Daniel, Nebuchadnezzar is removed from his throne and forced into the position of an animal. Publicly acknowledging the superiority of God, blessing him, allows for reconciliation and restoration of his throne (4:25–34).[113] In 2 Maccabees' portrayal of Antiochus's conversion, the main interest of the author lies in portraying the terrible suffering of the despot and his eventual, albeit too late, verbal acknowledgment of God's role (9:5–18).[114] These passages all emphasize the physical force that God brings to bear upon the tyrant in the form of illness or otherwise. In the rabbinic version, most strikingly, God plays only an indirect role in creating the conditions by which Nebuzaradan recognizes his error; in the end, he does so through *his own cognition*.

The highlighting of agency as a category essential to the definition of "repentance" can be seen further in the following highly significant piece of biblical interpretation:

> R. Hami, son of R. Hanina, revealed a contradiction (between two parts of a verse): "It is written, 'Repent [in the rabbinic understanding, but literally: 'turn back'], O wayward children!' And it is written, 'I will heal your backslidings' [Jer. 3:22]. There is no contradiction; one case concerns (repentance) from love, the other from fear." R. Yehuda revealed a (further) contradiction: "It is written, 'Repent, O wayward children. I will heal your backslidings,' and it is written, 'I have taken possession of you and will take you, one from a city, two from a clan' [Jer. 3:14]. There is no contradiction, one case concerns (repentance) from love or fear, the other through suffering." (b. Yoma 86a)

In chapter 6, we discussed how representations of redemption in biblical and certain postbiblical apocalyptic writings fail to highlight agency as a category necessary to human transformation. In their interpretation of these passages from Jeremiah, however, the Rabbis create a taxonomy of repentance precisely around degrees of agency. Elements that would seem to negate agency are, instead, construed as describing the variety of motivations at work in repentance, with those allowing for greater degrees of freedom clearly privileged.

It is precisely the ease of identification and adherence afforded by repentance that makes it such a useful concept for rabbinic Judaism. But such a discourse of inner, individual control can be expected to generate a good deal of anxiety around the question of sincerity and motivation, as seen in the passage above. Thus, in rabbinic literature, we also find a concern for "deceptive repentance":[115]

> Let him [God] decree death for the wicked, not the righteous! But, [God does not do so] lest the wicked perform a *deceptive* repentance, thinking: "The righteous only live because they treasure up commandments and good deeds. Let us too treasure up commandments and good deeds." The result would be performance [of the commandments] *not for their own sake*. (Bereshit Rabba, 9:5)

The repentance portrayed in this passage is viewed as "deceptive," because it lacks the proper internal assent, even as it simulates adherence to communal norms. Throughout these passages, we find that the defining element of *teshuva* and, by extension, the performance of the commandments as a whole is an interior truth, as given voice in the expression, *teshuva sheleima*, literally, "complete repentance," indicating sincerity, fullness of intent.[116] It is such intent that is the final arbiter of communal and religious status.

We conclude our discussion of the meaning of *teshuva* in rabbinic literature with two more examples that establish its interiority and also explore the implications of that interiority for the assement of others. The Palestinian Talmud records an account of the death of the infamous heretic Elisha ben Abuya: "At that moment, Elisha wept and died. And Rabbi Meir rejoiced, saying: 'It seems as if (Elisha) died penitent'" (y. Hagiga 77:3). What this source points to is the fundamentally hermeneutical quality of repentance. That is to say, repentance is a way of monitoring oneself, but it is also just as significantly, if not more, a way of interpreting others. Rabbi Meir wants to see his former teacher as repenting, as achieving a reintegration into the community at the end of his days. Toward that aim, he chooses to interpret Elisha's weeping as an external sign of his "repentance." The very hermeneutic identified in earlier chapters, reading physical performances as manifestations of the internal, imputing interiority to the material, is born of a communal necessity for integration. It is a strategy that allows a community to construe the identity of its members as unified and singular. We find the same hermeneutical operation at work in the communal construction of the righteous: "If you see a scholar who has committed a transgression at night, don't think concerning him during the day: 'perhaps he has repented.' You think, 'perhaps?' It is certain that he has repented" (b. Berakhot 19a). Here, the requirement for an external manifestation of repentance is abandoned altogether. The status of the individual as righteous allows the observer/community to freely project the act of *teshuva* necessary for exoneration.

Contextualizing *Teshuva*

Thus far, we have considered the meaning of *teshuva*, its nature as an act, and have arrived at results that suggest a close relationship to *metanoia*, even as its modes of naturalization and what *teshuva* specifically brings into effect—a means of self-governance in relation to communal norms (i.e., the Law)—may show some divergence from other Hellenistic instances. Interestingly enough, rabbinic literature also preserves many of the same contexts as those already seen in the Greek sources. The similarities suggest, at least, in this regard, a vision of rabbinic Judaism as, in truth, a kind of Hellenistic movement, a religion born of a period of thorough Greek and Roman political and cultural control, not borrowing selectively from a supposed Greek background but simply prioritizing a concept that happens to originate in Hellenistic moral philosophy. Thus, we have already seen that the view of repentance as hypostasis, a divine entity, has its own iteration in rabbinic literature. It is also reflected in the rabbinic notion, based on a certain reading of Psalm 90:2–3, "Before the mountains came into being . . . you said, 'Return you mortals!'" that repentance "preceded the creation of the world."[117]

The view of the power of repentance to prevent relapse, articulated so clearly in Plutarch, fits precisely with the definition given the "penitent" (*ba'al teshuva*), one who literally "possesses repentance," in, at least, one rabbinic source: "Who constitutes a 'penitent'? [*ba'al teshuva*]. . . . It's like [one for whom] the sinful matter comes once, twice, but he is saved from it" (b. Yoma 86b). The stored-up memory of the pain caused by error allows the penitent to resist temptation. If that process is felicitous, if the repentance is real, future sin will be prevented.

The dispute within the Hellenistic world between the Stoics, who saw regret over a past act as a sign of moral deficiency, and what we saw as the Middle Platonist position, that repentance is an essential ingredient in the life of the righteous, seems to have a reflex within rabbinic literature.

> R. Yochanan said: "All the prophets only prophesied [regarding the reward] for penitents. As for [the reward of] the entirely righteous, 'no eye has seen, O God, except yours.'" (Isa. 64:3) [This statement] disagrees with that of R. Abahu, "Penitent sinners attain a position that even the perfectly righteous cannot, for it is written: 'There shall be peace for [those who are] far and [those who are] near.' (Isa. 57:19) 'For [those who are] far' is mentioned first and only then, 'for [those who are] near.'" (b. Berakhot 34b)

The difference between R. Yochanan and R. Abahu revolves around the relative merit of two identifiable groups of people, the entirely righteous and the "penitents." It may indicate the existence of a social differentiation between these groups within rabbinic Judaism, but the very terms of the debate are also suggestive of the philosophical conflict, reflecting the tension in the world of Hellenistic moral philosophy from which these two ideals derive. This tendency extends to the question of whether to claim certain biblical figures as penitents or as wholly righteous.[118]

Another indication of the proximity of rabbinic *teshuva* to Hellenistic *metanoia*, perhaps the most salient, is the oft-repeated theme of God granting a period of time during which sinners may secure amnesty through repentance. As discussed earlier, this practice most likely derives from military procedures, which call for giving adversaries, especially formerly loyal subjects, a chance to repent and change course. This theme is already found quite clearly in an early rabbinic interpretation of a verse from the Song at the Sea: "Your right hand, the LORD, is glorious in power/Your right hand, the LORD, shatters the enemy!" (Exod. 15:6). The Mekhilta breaks up the syntactic parallelism of the verse's two halves in order to read its components sequentially: (1) God is "glorious in power" because he shows forbearance to sinners, "extending for them [the time] to repent"; and only then (2) does he treat them as an "enemy." Likewise, the Tosefta maintains that an allowance of seven days was given after God decreed the Flood so as to grant the people an opportunity to repent (t. Sota 10:4). The same notion appears throughout Talmudic literature. A passage in the Palestinian Talmud conceives of the ten-day calendrical gap between the New Year and the Day of Atonement as such a period (y. Bikkurim 64:4). Finally, consider how the phrase for "forbearance" (*'erekh 'apayim*), found among the divine attributes of mercy, is interpreted in the following passage:

> R. Levi said: What is [the meaning of] *'erekh 'apayim*? (Exod. 34:6) Distancing anger [the root *'rk* is related to length]. [This can be compared] to a ruler who had two tough legions. The king said [to himself]: "If they are stationed here with me in the capital, then if the people of the city anger me, then they will get up and destroy them. Rather, I will send them far away. If the people of the city anger me, before I can send for them, the people will attempt to make peace with me, and I will accept their attempt." Likewise, the Holy One, blessed be He, [said to himself]: "Anger and wrath are destructive angels; I will send them far away. For if Israel anger me, before I can send for them and bring [them], Israel will repent, and I will accept their repentance." (y. Ta'anit 65:2)

The place of war in the imagery of repentance is made quite clear in this midrash. It attaches rabbinic *teshuva* directly to its Hellenistic context with "the Holy One" figuring as Israel's truest imperial ruler.

Finally, in chapter 5, we discussed the image of the prophet as a preacher, as one exhorting his audience to repent. This figures clearly in the following passage: "Ten came and sat before the prophet. He said to them: 'Repent'" (b. Sanhedrin 105a). In context, this scene, a fragment from a larger narrative, sums up what is seen to be the blanket sense of the prophetic message. It is followed by a dialogue, in which the people question the efficacy of repentance and the prophet provides further encouragement. This kind of gentle urging can also be said to be typical Hellenistic pedagogy.[119] Indeed, this whole passage sounds like it could transpire inside a philosophical school. It shows how the encounter with Scripture itself could be configured as an ongoing source of exhortation.

We have explored how the rabbinic movement had a particular interest in establishing "repentance" as an operative concept. Indeed, the literature often expends more rhetorical energy on asserting the existence of the concept and its efficacy than on actual demands for "repentance." Preceding discussions have stressed aspects of self-monitoring (i.e., when the righteous sin and repent), but we have also seen allusions to instances of inveterate "sinners," those who are portrayed as being outside of the community and seeking entrance into it. Rabbinic literature goes a long way not to identify as "sinners" any except those who are indelibly marked by broader society as such, those known for heresy,[120] bloodshed, sexual impropriety, or financial malfeasance. We saw above instances of "repentance" for those associated with heresy and bloodshed, Elisha ben Abuya and Nebuzaradan, respectively. The famous story of Elazar ben Durdaya tells of the repentance of one "who hadn't left a prostitute in the world with whom he hadn't had intercourse" (b. Avoda Zara 17a). Cases of financial malfeasance, however, are the most pervasive in rabbinic literature and run throughout its strata, in particular around the sins of robbery, lending on interest, and shepherding.[121] Thus, for instance, the famous rabbi, Resh Laqish, is said to have once been a highway robber.[122] Like the other transgressions, financial malfeasance marks the sinner as outside acceptable society, but what differentiates it and explains why it receives special treatment is the inherent difficulty and loss involved in repudiating such wrongdoing, for the sinner stands to lose substantial financial holdings. In the words of the Babylonian Talmud, "repentance for these things is difficult" (b. Bava Qama 94b). The Rabbis therefore insist that they be given a special dispensation, what comes to be known as the "penitents' edict" (b. Bava Qama 94b), that they not be even allowed to return stolen property lest it prevent others from repenting. They are concerned to ensure the availability of repentance as an existent for all. Here, the functionality ascribed to *teshuva* as a mechanism of change, its ability to process and transform those marked by society as miscreants, comes to the fore. Whether through a change in the status of actual individuals or as a hypothetical possibility, it is a way of envisioning all Israel as readily and eventually adhering to rabbinic ideology in the absence of such a reality.[123] What emerges in these cases is the appetitive quality of rabbinic Judaism itself, how an insistence on the reality of an interior process of change opens up the possibility for an acquisition of souls, whether actual missionizing is involved or not.[124] And so it is, in one last example, that Beruriah famously instructs her husband Rabbi Meir not to pray for the destruction of a local group of bandits but for their repentance (b. Berakhot 10a). Beruriah's proposed prayer may strike us a moral advance, but, first and foremost, it represents an improvement in technologies of control. The exercise of power now transpires within the soul itself.

"NEW TESTAMENT REPENTANCE"

Metanoia in the New Testament is said to have a meaning that goes beyond and, ultimately, supersedes that of its cultural background. To a certain extent, this matter of definition relates to an interpretive stance already examined in the preceding chapter, namely, a uniformitarian approach to the place of repentance in the Synoptic Gospels, one that would efface differences among source materials, especially those that operate within an apocalyptic framework, in favor of a view of repentance as the *telos* of the Jesus movement. As we saw, much of this has to do with the very way in which we think of, how we define, religion. But it is also enabled by an additional claim, a particular use of philology, to establish the unique status of *metanoia* in the New Testament and, by extension, that of Christianity itself,[125] a commitment to what has been referred to as the "language-molding power of Christianity."[126] Whereas the previous chapter focused on the problematic place of agency as a category in interpretation, including that of the New Testament, the following discussion focuses on the definition *metanoia* receives in New Testament scholarship and its place in emergent Christianity.

Supersessionism and the Philology of "Repentance"

The supersessionist interpretation of *metanoia* emerges with particular clarity in Kittel's *Theological Dictionary of the New Testament*,[127] whose remarks have become paradigmatic, echoed throughout subsequent generations of scholarship:

> Jesus transcends the OT proclamation of conversion ... and especially the conversion piety of Judaism ... God's definitive revelation demands final and unconditional decision on man's part. It demands radical conversion, a transformation of nature .... The whole proclamation of Jesus, with its categorical demands for the sake of God's kingdom (the Sermon on the Mount, the sayings about

discipleship), is a proclamation of μετάνοια even when the term is not used . . . .
In the preaching of Jesus faith grows out of conversion . . ., not as a second thing
which He requires, but as the development of the positive side of μετάνοια, the
turning to God. Conversion as Jesus understands it is not just negative . . . . For
all its pitiless severity the message of Jesus concerning μετάνοια does not drive
us to the torture of penitential works or to despair. It awakens joyous obedience
for a life according to God's will. This is because μετάνοια here is no longer Law,
as in Judaism, but Gospel.[128]

This approach to *metanoia* has several salient features: (1) though *metanoia*
is relatively rarely mentioned in the Synoptic Gospels, the concept is seen
as implicit in many other passages; (2) *metanoia* is understood, therefore, to
include a broad range of notions; and (3) *metanoia* in the teachings of Jesus is
seen as innovative, transcending its antecedents. The definition that emerges
views *metanoia* as having a "positive side" that relates strongly to "faith" and
"joyous obedience." It involves a "transformation of nature," hence the preference for the term "conversion" over the more conventional "repentance."
One senses already from its expansive, insistent tone that something is driving this account to push the definition of *metanoia* beyond its more obvious
boundaries.

Behind this broad conception of *metanoia*, there lurks (not so stealthily)
an etymological interpretation of the term that is directly responsible for its
common scholarly rendering as "change of mind" and that has a long, important history. It was actually first propounded by Martin Luther in his attack
on the traditional doctrine of *poenitentia* (a common medieval spelling for
paenitentia). Luther tells the story of its discovery and makes its components
explicit in the following passage from his 1518 letter to von Staupitz:

> After this it happened that I learned—thanks to the work and talent of the most
> learned men who teach us Greek and Hebrew with such great devotion—that
> the word *poenitentia* means *metanoia* in Greek; it is derived from *meta* and *noun*
> [sic, *nous*], that is, from "afterward" and "mind." . . . Then I progressed further
> and saw that *metanoia* could be understood as a composite not only of "after-
> ward" and "mind," but also of the [prefix] "trans" and "mind" . . ., so that *metanoia*
> could mean the transformation of one's mind and disposition. Yet it seemed to
> express not only the actual change of disposition but also the way by which this
> change is accomplished, that is, the grace of God.[129]

This etymological interpretation considers *transformation*, regardless of the
agent of change, to constitute the root meaning of *metanoia*. Luther thereby
attempts to bring *metanoia* closer to Pauline theology, with its emphasis on
the role of divine agency in human transformation, casting traditional penance aside.[130]

Luther's polemical etymology is not particularly surprising. What surprises is that more contemporary critical studies continue to put forth such exceptionalist views.[131] Here are some recent formulations: "Any conception of repenting . . . not wedded to faith in the gospel falls short of the full biblical message . . . . In a real sense, 'Repentance and faith are two sides of the same coin'";[132] "thus, repentance involves far more than intellectual change or remorse; it entails a new or renewed relationship with God that transforms all the dimensions of one's life, including conduct, and is akin to conversion";[133] and "the change is that of the soul, of the whole person (the new creature), who is purified of stains and whose life is transformed, metamorphosed."[134] But, as mentioned with regard to the meaning of *teshuva* in rabbinic literature, a word's etymology does not necessarily tell us about its meaning, only about its history.

The Meaning of *Metanoia*

What then, does *metanoia* mean in the New Testament? Contrary to the exceptionalist interpretation of *metanoia*, the term always appears to be structured around the repudiation of a negative source of past identity. Thus, it is to Mark's formulation, "I have come to call not the righteous but *sinners*" (2:16), that the Gospel of Luke adds "to repentance" (5:32). "Sinners" "repent," and works, such as Luke-Acts, that emphasize "repentance" consistently choose to construe the "repenting" subject as one in need of self-repudiation.[135] And, so, we find the same generic categories of sinners employed as in rabbinic literature. Instances of *financial malfeasance* come through with particular clarity in the Gospel of Luke, not only in the grouping of tax collectors and sinners as those in need of repentance (Luke 5:29–32), but also in the extended account of the tax collector Zacchaeus (19:1–10) and the rich man who refuses to share his food with the starving Lazarus (16:19–31). In the Acts of the Apostles, Peter demands repentance from the Jews for what is construed to be an instance of *bloodshed,* namely their responsibility for the death of Jesus (Acts 2:36–38, 3:17–19). Finally, in the representation of Paul's ministry to the Gentiles found in Acts, the call to repent figures as a charge to repudiate *idolatry* (Acts 17:30).[136] Outside of Luke-Acts, we find *sexual impropriety* thrown into the mix as well. Paul accuses his adversaries of "impurity, sexual immorality, and licentiousness" and demands that they repent (2 Cor. 12:21). The book of Revelation proves quite adept at using the language of repentance, with a focus on sexual impropriety and idolatry, to speak to what must have been, ultimately, matters of internal dispute.[137] It also includes a telling summary judgment on the sins of humanity and their failure to repent: "The rest of humankind . . . did not repent of the works of their hands or give up worshipping demons and idols . . . . And they did not repent of their murders or their sorceries or their fornication or their thefts" (Rev. 9:20–21). Here, we find a veritable catalogue of the generic categories of wrongdoing.

Now, one should hasten to add that in many of these cases, especially those found in Luke-Acts, repentance is associated with a broader transformation, the adoption of a new, positive identity, not just the repudiation of an old. But, in what way is that really out of keeping with the evidence for repentance in Hellenistic literature that we have already seen? The whole theory of repentance operates around the claim to the existence of a certain mechanism, one by which regret for a past deed or way of life produces a transformative effect within the penitent agent. Thus, we find John the Baptist's charge: "bear fruit worthy of repentance" (Matt. 3:8) and a similar one in Acts: "do deeds consistent with repentance" (Acts 26:20). Indeed, the necessary relationship between the negative and positive elements of "repentance" is well encapsulated in what might be referred to as the "dual formula."[138] It is evident in the passages quoted earlier from the *Corpus Hermeticum* and *Joseph and Aseneth*. Here is one from the Wisdom of Solomon: "Therefore you correct little by little those who trespass, and you remind and warn them of the things through which they sin, *so that they may be freed from wickedness and put their trust in you*, O Lord" (12:1). It is this phraseology that figures widely in the New Testament corpus: "repent and believe in the good news" (Mark 1:15); "repent and be baptized every one of you in the name of Jesus Christ" (Acts 2:38); "repent therefore and turn to God" (Acts 3:19; compare Acts 26:20); "repent therefore of this wickedness of yours and pray to the Lord" (Acts 8:22); "I testified to both Jews and Greeks regarding repentance with respect to God and faith with respect to our Lord Jesus" (Acts 20:21); "repent and come to know the truth" (2 Tim. 2:25); and "repentance from dead works and faith toward God" (Heb. 6:1). It would be a mistake to conclude that the first half of this formula is synonymous with the second half, that "repentance" too is a matter of "faith." The contexts of these passages, the usage of *metanoia* elsewhere, and, indeed, the very theory of "repentance" demand that we posit a negative act, the repudiation of a past identity, that generates the potential for a positive one, the adoption of a new form of identity.

The Systematicity of Repentance

What is most remarkable then about the deployment of repentance in New Testament texts is not its novelty but its systematicity in certain strata of the literature. Luke-Acts, in particular, consistently embeds its themes,[139] pointing to the pedagogical and ultimately Hellenistic framework within which Luke-Acts operates, how it calls on the conventions of *metanoia* as a philosophical trope to structure membership in the movement. Sinners are not merely opponents who have failed to recognize the power and place of Jesus;

they are universally acknowledged wrongdoers—Jews as murderers, Gentiles as idolaters—who must recognize the futility of their present lives. In this framework, Jesus in his work with sinners and Peter and Paul in their exhortations assume the role of pedagogues, preachers of repentance, who, in the words of the Wisdom of Solomon, "correct little by little."[140] And the result, of course, is not merely a movement away from falsehood but, by joining the group, one toward truth, *gnosis*.

In order to appreciate fully the systematization of repentance in the New Testament, we must return to a series of points addressed in the preceding chapter. Large portions of the early source material in the New Testament, like much of late Second Temple literature, seem to participate in an apocalyptic mode of thought that eschews repentance as a concern. The later editing of this material, especially evident in the Gospel of Luke but in Matthew as well, seems to introduce repentance into existing gospel traditions, and the same can be said for the representation of Paul in the Acts of the Apostles. These later sources make use of earlier eschatological language, such as that regarding the advent of a new divine kingdom, but they now configure it as part of a drive for conversion to a very particular sort of philosophy: "Repent, for the kingdom of heaven has come near" (Matt. 4:17). In a sense, this is no different from the parallel process at work with regard to the Hebrew Bible, whereby that collection of ancient texts is rewritten and interpreted in order to ground the idea of repentance. What drives this development, and what is its effect? I think that, as in rabbinic literature, we need to see the primacy of repentance as a move away from apocalypticism, as suiting the new institutional priorities of early Christianity.[141] A discourse of repentance puts into effect a theory of change, one that binds the individual to a religious community through the transformation in identity it sets in motion. It does not derive its strength from radical external events but from inner decision, the choice to abandon one's former life. It suits an emergent church, the need to acquire souls without manifest forms of power.

A Hellenistic "Repentance"

In any event, it is to *metanoia*, a concept available in Hellenistic culture, that certain early Christian communities turned to fashion a mode of initiation into the group. And, indeed, the Hellenistic aspects of *metanoia* remain recognizable throughout its use in the New Testament. To begin with, as seen elsewhere, the concept can be deployed not only in connection to conversion but for the maintenance of internal discipline as well: "If another disciple sins, you must rebuke the offender, and if there is repentance, you must forgive" (Luke 17:3).[142] And, indeed, we find precisely such an account of repentance for a specific trespass in Simon's offer of money to obtain the gifts of the

Holy Spirit (Acts 8:18–24). There is also an awareness of *metanoia* as a kind of grief: "Now I rejoice, not because you were grieved, but because your grief led to repentance; for you felt a godly grief, so that you were not harmed in any way by us. For godly grief produces a repentance that leads to salvation and brings no regret, but worldly grief produces death" (2 Cor. 7:9–10). Clearly familiar with the negative sense of *metanoia* as useless regret, Paul draws a careful distinction between that and its positive usage, regret that produces salvation. Another case in Hebrews associates repentance and mourning: "he [Esau] did not secure [i.e., was not granted] an opportunity to repent, even though he sought the blessing with tears" (12:17). Even though Esau repented earnestly (i.e., with tears), no "opportunity to repent" was given him. Indeed, the idea of repentance as a grant of time, so basic to its Hellenistic roots, is used by Paul, as it was in Plutarch, to explain why divine justice has been delayed: "Do you not realize that God's kindness [i.e., forbearance] is meant to lead you to repentance?" (Romans 2:4).[143] Finally, we also find an eschatological reworking of the Hellenistic notion of *metanoia* as a divine hypostasis. Here, Repentance has not been vouchsafed as part of creation, but has only just assumed its position: "God exalted him at his right hand as Leader and Savior that he might give repentance to Israel and forgiveness of sins" (Acts 5:31).[144] A grant of "repentance" has been made through Jesus; Jesus becomes the figure *Metanoia*.

Much work has been done on the history of penance in early Christianity. The present work does not aim to engage such an endeavor but to show the concept's becoming, how it takes hold as a discourse within early forms of Judaism and Christianity. Toward that aim, it is important to note that it would be a mistake to see the New Testament as the exclusive source for "repentance" in chronologically later Christian texts. They continue to draw on its Hellenistic framework in novel and productive ways.

By way of illustration, I would make brief mention of one second-century Christian work, the *Shepherd of Hermas*, that calls on repentance to do considerable work in developing an eschatology linked to human-driven transformation.[145] It is clear that, by this time, unlike in the New Testament, but rather like in rabbinic literature,[146] repentance has become an uncontested, normative component of, at least, the form of Christianity represented in the *Shepherd*, which includes explicit reflections on the concept as part of a technical religious terminology. The work also signifies a certain crisis in the naturalization of repentance and its application to communal life. Individuals who performed repentance as part of their initiation into Christianity have since sinned. As a mechanism that is meant to effectuate change, the very status of repentance as an existent is called into question by such failure. The *Shepherd* offers a solution. An "angel of repentance" has been authorized to offer lapsed Christians a "second penitence," a final onetime opportunity to repent and be included in the building of the "tower" that represents the church. Once the tower has been built, it will be too late to rejoin. The notion of a limited time grant for repentance comes through with clarity here, as does the theme of repentance as a hypostasis.[147] Here, too, we find the theme of *metanoia* as producing "great understanding" (Mandate 4.2.2); as a form of grief that induces weeping (Vision 1); and as a repudiation of discrete sins, such as that of anger (Mandate 5.1.7). Most significantly, the offer of the angel is narrated from the perspective of an individual seeking, through repentance, to realign himself with the church. Here, the basis of repentance as a doctrine that helps conceptualize the individual self in institutional life becomes fully manifest.[148] Hermas's identification with the church does not rest on its earthly power, but is ensured by a hypostasized existent that is both above and within him.

SUMMARY

From where we inherit "repentance" and how we came to be subject to it is the story this chapter has attempted to tell. It is found within Hellenistic moral philosophy and is embedded in the works of Philo. It also figures in certain texts focused on individual culpability and piety in late Second Temple literature, but it is in the writings of rabbinic Judaism and early Christianity that it attains the status of a technical term, a basic item of an emerging religious lexicon. As a discourse, it is marked by concerns for agency, interiority, and moral amendment. What it seems to bring into effect, what "repentance" does, is to instill a mode of internal discipline and initiation that allows for identification with growing religious communities without reliance on the presence of external force. Practitioners govern themselves from within themselves.

In the preceding chapters, we encountered a view of repentance as an essence, a specter ever present in interpretation. But, here, we have uncovered the other side of that specter. There is a relationship between positing a universal, present in all times and places, and assigning particulars the power to express unique, subjective meanings. Repentance may be an essence, but it is said to receive a particular, higher form of expression within the "language-molding power of Christianity." Concepts must be universals if they are to be overcome; that is, in many ways, the dominant narrative of Christianity as a universal religion.[149] To configure ideas otherwise, to recognize their basis in discourse, in power relations, is to expose the non-inevitability, the contingency of current religious formations, while simultaneously undermining their claim to uniqueness. And, indeed, we have found that the discourse is privileged in certain texts but not others. When it does figure in significant ways, "repentance" seems to exhibit a fairly stable sense. At least in this respect, Judaism and Christianity appear to have been constituted as religions by related discursive concerns.

POSTSCRIPT

This book presents us with a choice. We are free to continue reading with the "penitential lens," a series of reading practices whereby a wide range of biblical texts and the phenomena described therein are understood as reflecting and, indeed, grounding a concept of repentance. As I have attempted to show, it is internally consistent and compelling, especially for those, most of us really, who operate within a framework that would configure Scripture as some sort of basis for contemporary values. Such an approach necessitates psychological forms of understanding, attempts to discern certain universals, inner realities, behind the actions and words contained within the biblical texts that readers, supposedly, can access because of their shared convictions and experiences of life. Thus, one can maintain that a figure such as Ahab surely felt some regret in the face of his actions or that we must see in the biblical "cessation of sin" an early form of repentance. Neither of these claims find a place in the paradigm pursued here, but they do have a certain logic to them, one that we cannot or, perhaps, do not wholly wish to escape. I have attempted, however, to introduce an alternative mode of reading that focuses on the material representations of the texts themselves, Ahab's manifestation of physical diminishment, and that sees in the quest for "repentance's" historicity the playing out of a discourse dedicated to the grounding of institutional priorities in biblical language. The concern throughout has been to identify common reading patterns, to present evidence for the existence of other (more material) possibilities, and to highlight the religious formations by which repentance was put into effect. As noted in the introduction, the book, therefore, participates in a broader paradigm shift, increasingly evident within biblical studies, of historicizing not just the Bible but also its readers.

A number of advantages accrue from this approach. There is, first of all, the explanatory power of the model presented here, and this may be of the greatest significance to scholars of the Bible. It resolves difficulties present in the current paradigm, such as the multiplicity of the contexts in which fasting figures in the Hebrew Bible, the seeming finality of prophetic utterances, or the differences among the Synoptic Gospels over why Jesus associated with sinners. It also restores sense to many biblical elements present in contemporary practice—for example, the sheer wordiness of prayer not as an expression of personal anguish but as an attempt to grab the attention of the deity and configure the petitioner as one in need. Furthermore, it presents us with a wealth of alternative perspectives on such matters as the body, speech, and power. So, for instance, we might want to reflect seriously on the resources available in the Bible, as seen in the example of confession, for developing a notion of speech as not a description of inner states but the realization of a certain state of affairs. There is also no small advantage to revealing the historical contingencies behind certain purported essences, the role repentance plays in the emerging institutional needs of Judaism and Christianity, in view of the sheer power the construction of such ideals exerts over our lives.

However, having lived with the material presented in this book for a number of years now, I must say that my greatest abiding concern lies not with its textual insights, its potential theoretical applications, or any freedom it might provide from dominant forms of institutional power. This work does not put me in a position to offer definitive insights into the contest between the interior notion of self that is responsible for the penitential lens and the possibilities present in contemporary culture for alternative configurations. What I do think I can say, however, as a student of interpretation, is that there is something very concerning about the hermeneutical mode such dominant notions of the self have spawned and by which, in turn, they have been generated. It seems large-hearted, moral, and charitable to read more deeply, to discern the human depths that are beyond the mere words of the Bible, and thus to read morality rather than power, inwardness rather than performance. We are dealing not just with an interpretive framework but with the sense of piety attached to it, a sense of ourselves and our status as spiritual creatures being at stake. But we need to recognize that there are very real hazards present for our understanding of others in a mode of reading that trains us to look beyond, within, or under, at everything except that which is immediately before us.

One area in which such a concern has been identified is in gender studies. Judith Butler, in her seminal *Gender Trouble*, points to how gender and, indeed, other aspects of the "interior soul" are produced through the "play of signifying absences," inscriptions upon the body that configure the body as a lack that gestures at that which cannot be shown but only signified, namely, the soul. As she writes, "words, acts and gestures, articulated and enacted desires create the illusion of an interior and organizing gender core, an illusion discursively maintained for the purposes of the regulation of sexuality within the obligatory frame of reproductive heterosexuality . . . the displacement of a political and discursive origin of gender identity onto a psychological 'core' precludes an analysis of the political constitution of the gendered subject and its fabricated notions about the ineffable interiority of its sex or of its true identity" (136). The implications of such suppression of performance for understanding gender are immense, but so are their implications for other forms of interpretation, as we have seen in the present study. The privileging of interiority commits us to a hermeneutic of absence, to looking at all material representations as merely surface phenomena expressing some more essential reality. Such a hermeneutic allows manifestations of difference to be subsumed, colonized, you might say, by our existing, universal categories. Whether in the study of biblical texts, the analysis of foreign peoples, or other forms of interpersonal interaction, such a mode of interpretation seems misguided at best and, indeed, likely to be hazardous. The interpretations presented here, alone, do not offer a coherent, new hermeneutic. Rather they represent a pastiche, a variety of reading moments that together point to a sort of underlying collective nonsense, albeit one that is basic to our sense of ourselves and that we still might choose, now somewhat more knowingly, to engage in, the attempt to order as a value what cannot really be considered a universal essence, the inner, in this case, penitential self.

NOTES

INTRODUCTION

1. Tiger Woods' recent apology for marital infidelity is an excellent, highly meticulous example. For a full transcript of his public remarks, see "Full Transcript of Tiger Woods's Statement," *New York Times*, February 19, 2010.
2. For one proposal regarding the range of repentance's possible applications in modern society, see Schimmel, *Wounds Not Healed by Time.*
3. See Derrida, "On Forgiveness." Derrida sees a "process of Christianisation which has no more need for the Christian church" (31), a "globalisation" or "globalatinization" of the notion of "forgiveness," because of its basis in the heritage of Latin Christendom. "No alleged disenchantment, no secularisation comes to interrupt it" (32). The same may be said for "repentance."
4. For a similar series of problematizations around "confession," see Brooks, *Troubling Confessions*, 1–7.
5. For one instance of equivocation, the tension between "unconditional" forgiveness and a conditional forgiveness based on repentance, see Derrida, "On Forgiveness," 34–35.
6. A representative and influential example can be found in Cohen, *Reason and Hope*, 201–2.
7. For the sake of brevity, I often refer to this composition as the "Bible" and, in its canonical function, as "Scripture," and to the component of the Christian Bible known as the "New Testament" separately as such. That said, many observations hold for both, as the two testaments have been read together for centuries within a multitude of communities. This usage has the added benefit of not conforming to any canonical assumptions of my own but rather of addressing the state of the canon for early Jews and Christians alike around the turn of the Common Era and the fact that many did not encounter the "Hebrew Bible" as a Hebrew text. There is, of course, no "Bible" as such within most of the ancient Israelite texts that will be discussed. As a concept, it is chiefly useful for denoting the textual phenomenon to which later readers address themselves.
8. For the general phenomenon, see Eagleton, *Literary Theory*, 47–78.
9. For representative and highly influential instances of each, see, respectively, Fishbane, *Biblical Interpretation in Ancient Israel*; Childs, *Introduction to the Old Testament as Scripture*; and Collins, *Apocalyptic Imagination.*
10. See Kugel, *In Potiphar's House* and *Traditions of the Bible.*
11. For this hermeneutical perspective, see Gadamer, *Truth and Method*, 268–306.
12. Stanley Fish, *Is There a Text in This Class?*, 164–73.

13. For a similar sense of the cultural hegemony of the modern West as inescapable and, therefore, for our purposes, constitutive of ourselves as interpreters, see Asad, *Genealogies of Religion*, 1–24. Another opportunity for observing the workings of the "penitential lens," albeit of a more confined nature, can be found in a variety of early colonial interactions. See, for instance, the discussion of the Franciscan interpretation of Nahua rites of purification as a form of contrition in Pardo, *Origins of Mexican Catholicism*, 89–99.

14. See, further, the beginning of chapter 5 and throughout chapter 7. Indeed, it would be possible to put together a massive compendium, spanning from the beginning of the Common Era to the present day, of instances in which interpreters of the Bible introduce repentance in their readings. The emphasis of the present volume will be on identifying the main channels by which such readings are forwarded in contemporary research.

15. Bibliographies are introduced in chapters dedicated to the respective topics. The only available overall treatments of the topic, of which I am aware, are Dietrich, *Die Umkehr*; and Boda and Smith, *Repentance in Christian Theology*. Konstan, *Before Forgiveness*, has addressed a related topic, but largely from the perspective of classical literature.

16. See Tentler, *Sin and Confession*, for an overview. For further recent, stimulating treatments, see Mansfield, *Humiliation of Sinners*; and Rittgers, *Reformation of the Keys*.

17. See Gadamer's discussion of "The Concept of Expression" in *Truth and Method*, 503–4; and, in particular, Butler's discussion, "From Interiority to Gender Performatives," in *Gender Trouble*, 134–41.

18. Gadamer, "Reply to My Critics," 276.

19. They are closely aligned with the hermeneutics of Friedrich Schleiermacher. See Gadamer's critique, *Truth and Method*, 184–95; and the discussion of Schleiermacher and also Wilhelm Dilthey in Schmidt, *Understanding Hermeneutics*, 10–48.

20. Indeed, this evangelism may be basic to the endeavor of translation and, more broadly, hermeneutics or, at least, certain versions of them: "the traditional figure of the Jew is often and conventionally situated on the side of the body and the letter . . . whereas after St. Paul the Christian is on the side of the spirit or sense, of *interiority* [italics mine], of spiritual circumcision. This relation of the letter to the spirit, of the body of literalness to the ideal *interiority* of sense is also the site of the passage of translation, of this conversion that is called translation" (Derrida, "What Is a 'Relevant' Translation?," 431). See, further, the discussion in Seidman, *Faithful Renderings*, 17–19; and Boyarin, *Carnal Israel*. As Boyarin states, "hermeneutics becomes anthropology" (ibid., 9).

21. Altieri, *Canons and Consequences*, 24.

22. Altieri, *Canons and Consequences*, 24.

23. Geertz, *Interpretation of Cultures*, 36.

24. This point is particularly clearly developed, on the basis of the work of Gilles Deleuze and Pierre-Félix Guattari, in Mackenzie, *Idea of Pure Critique*.

25. Some overview of these developments is provided in Collins, *Bible after Babel*.

26. George Lindbeck draws a helpful distinction between "experiential-expressive" approaches, which assume the universality of human experience and attribute difference largely to variations in expression, and "cultural-linguistic" ones, which recognize the power of language, broadly conceived, to generate intrinsically different religious systems for comprehending and acting in the world. See his *Nature of Doctrine*, 1–31.

27. Potential models within the field of biblical studies for such an approach may be found in Moran, "Ancient Near Eastern Background," 77–87; Greenfield, "Adi baltu," 912–19; Muffs, *Love & Joy*, 121–93; and Anderson, *A Time to Mourn, A Time to Dance*. For an example from contemporary ethnographic work, note the avoidance of the term "spirit" in discussions of the dead because of its "Christian and Western philosophical influences" in Ochoa, *Society of the Dead*, 45–46. Such a form of translation has a certain affinity with the literal but does not, I would argue, dissolve into it. On the relationship between "literal" translation and the "anthropological" concern to respect difference, see Greenstein, "Theories of Modern Bible Translation," 13–14. Naomi Seidman configures the "literal" slightly differently as a "resistance to translation," which she sees as one important strand within the history of Jews and Judaism (*Faithful Renderings*, 1–36). In philosophical terms, one may note a certain affinity with the view of Ludwig Wittgenstein that "the meaning is the use," a statement that is made in opposition to psychological forms of understanding that would see mental processes, the "mind," as the locus of meaning, as giving life to, otherwise, "dead" signs. (See Stroud, "Mind, Meaning, and Practice," 296–319.)
28. Geertz, "Thick Description: Toward an Interpretive Theory of Culture," in his *Interpretation of Cultures*, 3–30.
29. On comparison and, especially, the scholar's role in defining what differences are of interest, see Smith, *Drudgery Divine*, 36–53.
30. Kristeva, *Powers of Horror*, 113, and 113–32, throughout.
31. For this problem, see, in general, Smith, *Drudgery Divine*.
32. Klawans, *Impurity and Sin in Ancient Judaism*; and Anderson, *Sin: A History*. For their diachronic approach, see also the work of Levenson, including *Creation and the Persistence of Evil* and *Resurrection and the Restoration of Israel*; Hayes, *Gentile Impurities and Jewish Identities*; and Rosen-Zvi, *Demonic Desires*. Note as well the methodological comments in the latter (8–10).
33. Work on the genealogy of sexuality provides a useful parallel. See Foucault, *History of Sexuality, Volume 1*; and Butler, *Gender Trouble*, 1–34.
34. On "discourse," see Foucault, *Archeology of Knowledge*.
35. This book, therefore, stands in a certain degree of tension with the recent work of Konstan, *Before Forgiveness*, who would see a true notion of "forgiveness" and its correlate, "repentance," at once, as biblical and, at the same time, as only truly emerging in the modern period. Part of this apparently contradictory stance emerges from the evolutionary framework, "the representation of forgiveness in the Hebrew Bible falls short of the full modern conception" (105), which is adopted at times in the book, even if unintentionally.
36. The phrase, of course, comes from Nietzsche, *Untimely Meditations*. See, in particular, "On the Uses and Disadvantages of History for Life," 57–124.
37. Foucault, *History of Sexuality, Volume 2*, 7.
38. Ibid., 9.
39. Taylor, *Sources of the Self*, 111–207, remains a helpful guide.
40. Compare the approach of Konstan, *Before Forgiveness*.

CHAPTER 1

1. See Asad, *Genealogies of Religion*, 55–79, for the place of symbolism in the interpretation of ritual.

2. See, here, the comments of Handelman, "Conceptual Alternatives to 'Ritual.'"
3. MacCulloch, "Fasting," 5:759. Later treatments, e.g., Rader, "Fasting," 5:286–90, draw heavily on MacCulloch's article.
4. Brongers, "Fasting in Israel in Biblical and Post-Biblical Times," 1–21; Muddiman, "Fasting," 2:773–74; Milgrom, "Fasting and Fast Days," 6:1190; Guthrie, "Fast, Fasting," 2:241–43; Podella, *Ṣôm-Fasten,* 117–223; and Olyan, *Biblical Mourning.*
5. On ways to move beyond a focus on the intention of the individual actor in ritual performance, see Sax, "Agency."
6. "The claim of many radical critics that hegemonic power necessarily suppresses difference in favor of unity is quite mistaken. To secure its unity—to make its own history—dominant power has worked best through differentiating and classifying practices" (Asad, *Genealogies of Religion,* 17).
7. Olyan, *Biblical Mourning,* 75. Extended self-imposed affliction is also readily read as a sign of "penitent shame." Consider the comments of the noted anthropologist, Victor Turner, on the Ndembu rituals of afflictions:

> In the idiom of the rituals of affliction it is *as though* [italics mine] the Ndembu said: "It is only when a person is reduced to misery by misfortune, and repents of the acts that caused him to be afflicted, that ritual expressing an underlying unity in diverse things may fittingly be enacted for him." For the patient in rituals of affliction must sit, clad only in a waistcloth, in an attitude of penitent shame .... This is not to imply that Ndembu paganism is on an ethical or epistemological parity with the great world religions, but there is some satisfaction from a humanistic standpoint in finding similarities between men's modes of worship the world over. (*Drums of Affliction,* 22)

Here too we find a clear sense of the universality of ritual expression.
8. For a critique of the tendency in modern biblical scholarship to view "emotional experience" as "prior to any behavioral expression," see Anderson, "Introduction: The Expression of Emotion in Cross-Cultural Perspective," 1–18.
9. E.g., Aquinas, *Summa Theologiae,* "Supplement to the Third Part," articles 12–15.
10. In this respect and others, the phenomenon fits into what Philip Fisher in *The Vehement Passions* sees as the workings of *passion,* as opposed to merely the expressions of *emotion.* The passions absorb concentration around "one monopolizing fact," focusing exclusively on an object of dread (57–58) and displaying what Fisher refers to as "thoroughness," by which all else, including the prudential self, is pushed out (44). It also bears similarities to the way in which the standard subject-object distinction does not hold in Kristeva's notion of "abjection," whereby that which is rejected comes to define the subject (*Powers of Horror,* esp. 1–8).
11. On mourning in general, see Anderson, *A Time to Mourn, A Time to Dance;* Wright, *Ritual in Narrative,* 139–97; and Olyan, *Biblical Mourning.*
12. For the translation, see Coogan and Smith, *Stories from Ancient Canaan,* 143–44.
13. Scarry, *The Body in Pain,* 3–11. See the critique of Scarry in Asad, *Formations of the Secular,* 80–81. On pain as being subject to varied forms of cultural construction, see DeVecchio et al., *Pain as Human Experience: An Anthropological Perspective,* 1–28, and the literature cited there.
14. In addition to the cases that appear below, see Isa. 32:11–12 and Jer. 6:26. Upon hearing the Torah read, the people weep in Neh. 8:9 on account of the doom pronounced within it for those who have transgressed its stipulations. The refusal

to mourn is particularly problematic; see Jer. 36:24, as it calls into question the deity's power.

15. The practice of fasting in ancient Israel therefore fits well with premodern disciplinary procedures as described by Foucault in *Discipline and Punish*.

16. For this text and pertinent bibliography, see Nissinen, *Prophets and Prophecy in the Ancient Near East*, 207–11. The quoted text is from Combination 1, line 4.

17. Miller (*They Cried to the Lord*, 52–54) takes an important step in recognizing the connection between fasting and prayer, though he associates these rites with "contrition and humility."

18. Miller (ibid., 55–134) stresses the centrality of affliction in the biblical experience of prayer. See also Kugel, "The Cry of the Victim," 109–36. Compare the position of Moshe Greenberg, who stresses the importance of the moral status of the speaker and his or her sincerity as the major determinants in the effectiveness of prayer (*Biblical Prose Prayer*, 48–51).

19. See Sontag, *Regarding the Pain of Others*. Photographs of anonymous victims of war cause those who regard them to condemn *all* war. The justice of the victim's cause becomes irrelevant in the face of this immediate human response to suffering (3–17).

20. There may be a connection of sorts between one biblical term for an afflicted person, ʿanî, and one of the terms used to denote fasting. The phrase, ʿinâ nefesh, generally understood as constituting or at least including fasting (see Isa. 58:3, 5; Ps. 35:13; Ezra 8:21; and Dan. 10:12), was probably understood as "to afflict oneself," as suggested by the use of the reflexive form in Ezra 8:21 and Dan. 10:12. (The possible, original etymological sense of the phrase, "afflicting the throat," does not appear to be in play.) Some have viewed this term as inherently penitential, suggesting the translation, "to afflict one's soul" (Muddiman, *Anchor Bible Dictionary*, 2:773). It is probably best to understand it (rather loosely) as "to engage in certain acts of ritual affliction that render oneself afflicted"—that is, functionally equivalent to a ʿanî. Fasting is precisely one of those kinds of acts.

21. Indeed, it is the responsibility of the deity *in his capacity as king* to protect the disempowered. See Fensham, "Widow, Orphan, and the Poor," 129–39. Translations of Hebrew Bible passages are a modified form of the New Jewish Publication Society translation (hereafter NJPS).

22. What Judith Butler writes concerning the relationship between the body and gender (*Gender Trouble*, 128–41) holds with regard to the body and grief as well. In fasting, the body does not express some inner essence, i.e., suffering. Rather, it performs that suffering and brings into effect the actor's identity as afflicted.

23. Turner, "Humility and Hierarchy," 166–203, discusses the need for the privileged to engage in "status reversal," i.e., humiliation, at key religious junctures.

24. See introductory comments of Muffs, *Love and Joy*, 4–5.

25. Anderson, *A Time to Mourn, A Time to Dance*, throughout emphasizes the way in which rituals of grief do not simply give way to normalcy but rather transition into positive expression of joy. The same can be said for the shift from lament to praise that is frequently found in the Psalms. See Westermann, *Praise and Lament*, 79–81. This point also undergirds Levenson, *Resurrection and the Restoration of Israel*.

26. Walter Brueggemann emphasizes the protest element of the lament ("A Shape for Old Testament Theology, I," 28–46; and "A Shape for Old Testament Theology, II," 395–415).

27. Patrick D. Miller applies this term to the lament ("Trouble and Woe," 34).

28. For an account of one modern hunger strike that, like the biblical version, involved other bodily performances, see Aretxage, "Dirty Protest," 123–48.
29. For the connection between pain and power in the lament psalms, see Cottrill, "Articulate Body," 103–12.
30. See Greenfield, "Zakir Inscription and the Danklied," 178–80, for a discussion of the place of *'ani* as a technical term in these and other prayers.
31. See, for instance, F. Stolz, "צוּם," *Theological Lexicon of the Old Testament*, 2:1066. David in the preceding passage had confessed his sin and already had it commuted (12:13). The problem is that, as the fruit of an illicit union, the infant continues to constitute an affront to God and must be eradicated (12:14), hence David's *subsequent* appeal.
32. See Kristeva, *Powers of Horror*, 2–4.
33. See also Esther's response to Mordecai in Esther 4:4.
34. Ps. 35:13, like the David narrative, also connects fasting to prayer for the sick.
35. Reflecting a common spiritualizing tendency in reading the psalms, Gunkel and Begrich, *Introduction to Psalms*, 149, suggest that the afflicted would have been reviled in ancient Israel because it would have been assumed he had sinned. The proposed reading of these passages suggests that the source of repulsion is material, not spiritual.
36. Indeed, the lament psalms are marked by a focus on what enemies say (Westermann, *Praise and Lament*, 189–90).
37. Miller, *They Cried to the Lord*, 80. See, further, Cottrill, *Language, Power, and Identity*, 29–57.
38. Gunkel, *Introduction to Psalms*, 135.
39. See, e.g., Cogan, *1 Kings*, 483; and Gray, *I & II Kings*, 443.
40. Note, also, the response of Josiah to the reading of the scroll discovered in the temple of YHWH (2 Kings 22:11–14); and Huldah's assessment of his activities as a form of submission (2 Kings 22:19).
41. For this phrase, see Fisher, *Vehement Passions*, 181–84.
42. Considering the possibility of fasting attending the many communal laments attested in the Hebrew Bible may help us fulfill the mandate of Gunkel and Begrich to "visualize the prominently portrayed practices of the lament festival if one wants to understand this poetry" (*Introduction to Psalms*, 85).
43. See, for instance, Mowinckel, *Psalms in Israel's Worship*, 193.
44. Prayer is seen as the key moment of the fast day in rabbinic law, as well. (See *m. Ta'an* 2:2.)
45. Compare Jon. 4:11.
46. Many scholars consider fasting here to be penitential. See, e.g., Wolff, *Joel and Amos*, 29, 33; and Crenshaw, *Joel*, 98, 101, 105. Their impetus, in part, is from the call to "turn" in Joel 2:12–14. In its position and form, however, this call to "turn" is quite separate from the initial call to lament, as well as from the call to lament that appears in 2:15–17.
47. Note also the juxtaposition of fasting and lamenting in Zech. 7:5.
48. See n. 25.
49. This pattern is basic to the form justice assumes in the Deuteronomic Code. See, e.g., Deut. 13:2–6. On human justice as "spot remover," see Halpern, "Jerusalem and the Lineages," 12.
50. For the "logic of appeal" apart from penitence, see the beginning of the next chapter. Continued discussion of the mercy and justice tracks appears throughout chapter 2 and at the end of chapter 4, as well as later in this chapter.

51. For mourning in response to military defeat, see also Judg. 20:26.

52. Olyan, *Biblical Mourning,* 50–59. For other instances of mourning out of a solidarity of concern, see Esther 4:13–16 and Judg. 11:37.

53. A recent reformulation and reassertion of the standard scholarly view can be found in Barton, "Prophets and the Cult," 111–22.

54. It seems to be the prerogative of the leadership to declare a fast. See the above passages from Chronicles and Joel, as well as that from Jonah below.

55. See Milgrom, "Fasting and Fast Days"; and Guthrie, *Interpreter's Dictionary of the Bible,* 2:243.

56. See Andersen, "Socio-Juridicial Background," 56.

57. See Gray, *I & II Kings,* 441; and Cogan, *1 Kings,* 479.

58. Podella (*Ṣôm-Fasten,* 265–89) focuses on fast days and maintains that there is a fundamental evolution from fasting as lament to fasting as penitence.

59. Westermann, *Isaiah 40–66,* 335–36.

60. Simon, *Jonah,* 30; Limburg, *Jonah,* 80; Sasson, *Jonah,* 244–45, 255, 257; Brongers, "Fasting in Israel in Biblical and Post-Biblical Times," 12; and Guthrie, *Interpreter's Dictionary of the Bible,* 2:243.

61. See Joel 1:18 for the role of groaning beasts on fast days. The "possessions" mentioned in Ezra 8:21 may very well refer to livestock. See also Judg. 4:10. The practice of *ḥerem,* the total annihilation of one's enemy in accord with a divine mandate, included the destruction of cattle as well (1 Sam. 15:3).

62. Thus, for instance, he (and his angels) must descend to Sodom to witness present wrongdoing for themselves and only then to punish (Gen. 18:21).

63. Further instances are Jer. 36:6–7 and Joel 2:12–13.

64. Knohl, *Sanctuary of Silence,* 27–34.

65. Milgrom, *Leviticus 1–16,* 1066. Gane, *Cult and Character,* 380, also sees self-affliction as an expression of repentance. Likewise, the Babylonian *akitu* festival has been interpreted as penitential; see, e.g., Frankfort, *Kingship and the Gods,* 320; and Milgrom, *Leviticus,* 1068.

CHAPTER 2

1. See Gunkel and Begrich, *Introduction to Psalms*; and Westermann, *Praise and Lament.*

2. See Werline, *Penitential Prayers in Second Temple Judaism;* Boda, *Praying the Tradition*; Bautch, *Developments in Genre;* and the three volumes that resulted from the "Penitential Prayer" consultation at the Annual Meetings of the Society of Biblical Literature from 2003 to 2005: Boda and Werline, *Seeking the Favor of God,* vol. 1; *Seeking the Favor of God,* vol. 2; and *Seeking the Favor of God,* vol. 3.

3. It is also often associated with the trumpeted rise of individual prayer in the ancient Near East. See Hallo, "Individual Prayer in Sumerian," 71–89; and Jacobsen, *Treasures of Darkness,* 147–64. The category of penitential prayer has come to be widely applied to Near Eastern texts. See Hallo, "Lamentations and Prayers in Sumer and Akkad," 1875; and, most recently, Jaques, " 'To Talk to One's God,' " 114–23.

4. Boda, "Confession as Theological Expression," 27–34.

5. Werline, "Defining Penitential Prayer," xvii.

6. See Greenberg, *Biblical Prose Prayer,* 48–57, who sees "sincerity" and moral status as the essential qualities of prayer.

7. See Nasuti, *Defining the Sacred Songs,* 30–56, for an insightful discussion of the history of "penitential prayer" as a form critical category.

8. See, further, Asad, *Genealogies of Religion*, 36.

9. For other examples, see Tigay, "On Some Aspects of Prayer in the Bible," 363–72; Greenberg, *Biblical Prose Prayer*, 19–22; and Holtz, "Prayer as a Plaintiff," 258–79.

10. In this account, I have found the "The Cry of the Victim" in Kugel, *God of Old*, 109–36, and Muffs, *Love & Joy*, 9–48, to be of particular use. For other treatments of prayer, see Greenberg, "On the Refinement," 57–92; Miller, *They Cried to the Lord*; and Balentine, *Prayer in the Hebrew Bible*.

11. The diffuse aspect of divine wrath is sometimes understood as indicative of a notion of "corporate responsibility" in ancient Israel, which generates a responsibility to "actively prevent others from sinning" (Kaminsky, *Corporate Responsibility*, 11). This presupposes an intrinsic standard of justice for all divine actions, which need not be the case.

12. Carasik, "Limits of Omniscience," 221–32.

13. As found throughout the world, the deity and its cult seek to "grow" in material terms. It is mostly in Western forms of religious discourse that such self-interest is denied. For a striking instance, see Ochoa, *Society of the Dead*, esp. 114.

14. For a collection of prayer texts from outside of Israel, see Pritchard, *Ancient Near Eastern Texts*, 365–400.

15. Miller, *Interpreting the Psalms*, 49–52.

16. Elsewhere in Genesis, for instance, we also find forms of appeal for water (21:17), healing (20:17), and assurance of safety prior to travel (28:20, 46:1–3).

17. Gunkel remarks, in the Psalms, "it is often impossible to coordinate the individual references of the complaint in the graphic descriptions created by the images" and, therefore, concludes that the psalmist "appropriates an image as an expression of his feeling to the extent that it appropriately suggests the mood of his spiritual condition" (*Introduction to Psalms*, 134). Variation, alone, is not a reason to see the Psalms as moving beyond material conditions; they too are subject to construction and multiple forms of portrayal, thus allowing a single fixed prayer text to suit a variety of circumstances.

18. See Creach, *Yahweh as Refuge*; as well as Holtz, "God as Refuge," 17–26.

19. See, as well, Cottrill's discussion of patronage as a model for comprehending the divine-human relationship in the Psalms in *Language, Power, and Identity*, 100–137.

20. Anderson, *Sin*, 15–26; and Schwartz, "Bearing of Sin," 3–21.

21. Dalglish, *Psalm Fifty-One*, 108.

22. Likewise, in 2 Sam. 24:10, though David's objective is clearly the protection of his subjects, he formulates his request in terms of his sin. Other aspects of Psalm 51 will be discussed in the next chapter.

23. For a survey, see Boyce, *Cry to God*.

24. E.g., Exod. 16:1–12. Note, also, the use of the term, "cry out," in Num. 11:2.

25. Compare Judg. 8:22.

26. The same logic underlies the problematic quality of crying out in the wilderness narratives. Complaint becomes sedition.

27. See Weitzman, *Song and Story in Biblical Narrative*, 15–36.

28. See also Ps. 9:13.

29. See Wolff, "Kerygma," 83–100, esp. 86–90; McCarthy, "II Sam. 7," 131–38; and Cross, *Canaanite Myth and Hebrew Epic*, 278.

30. Greenspahn, "Theology of the Framework of Judges," 385–96.

31. For the centrality of the plea in the broader ancient Near Eastern lament tradition, see Gwaltney, "Biblical Book of Lamentations," 242–65.

32. Compare Berlin, *Lamentations,* 95–96.
33. Brettler, "Interpretation and Prayer," 16–35.
34. See, in particular, Muffs, "Who Will Stand in the Breach?" 9–48. The centrality of this institution may also be reflected in the Hebrew term for "prophet" if we are to accept the position of Fleming, "Etymological Origins of the Hebrew *nābî,*" 217–24. But, compare Huehnergard, "On the Etymology and Meaning of Hebrew *nābî,*" 88–93. See also Widmer, *Moses, God, and the Dynamics of Intercessory Prayer.*
35. See, in particular, the collection of texts, Nissinen, *Prophets and Prophecy in the Ancient Near East.*
36. The passage appears in the story of *Aqhat.* See Coogan and Smith, *Stories from Ancient Canaan,* 35.
37. Sweeney, "Intercessory Prayer," 213–30, sees this feature as unique to ancient Israel, not found in ancient Egypt.
38. See, also, Jer. 11:11 and Zech. 7:13.
39. This may explain why intercession is absent from most prophetic scrolls. Thus, for instance, Amos appeals successfully on behalf of the people two times but presumably ceases to intercede when his third attempt ends in failure (Amos 7:1–9). Compare Balentine, "Prophet as Intercessor: A Reassessment," 161–73. Note, also, Ezek. 20:3 as a possible instance of rejected prophetic intercession.
40. See, e.g., Isa. 65:24 and Zech. 10:6.

CHAPTER 3

1. Thus, even the work of Brooks, *Troubling Confessions,* which usually recognizes heterogeneity in the practice—for instance, the distinctly Romanticist sense of confession as a form of self-expression (9) and Enlightenment sense of confession as the product of a "free and rational will" (63)—still runs into trouble in seeing in the *religious* tradition of confession a homogeneous "quintessential form of confession, the form that is closely linked to our understanding of the self, its private sphere, its inwardness, and the needs both to express this self, and to maintain the privileged status of the expression" (90). See, further, his discussion, "Confession, Selfhood, and the Religious Tradition," 88–112. Within biblical studies, one notes that there is no attempt to analyze the nature of confessional speech in the three volumes recently dedicated to penitential prayer (Boda, *Seeking the Favor of God,* vols. 1–3). The exception that proves the rule is the attempt at analysis of confession as a speech-act by Hogewood, "Speech Act of Confession," 1:69–82, which ends up only affirming the common association of confession with moral amendment: "Acknowledging sin commits the community to rid itself of sin, iniquity and transgression, while it also shapes the behavior of the community" (72).
2. For a treatment of this work, see Twersky, *Introduction to the Code of Maimonides (Mishneh Torah).*
3. This model is the main one adopted within medieval treatments of the Christian sacrament of penance, which divide the sacrament into contrition, confession, and satisfaction, with confession and satisfaction dependent on the intent to atone found in contrition but still operating with their own integral logic. See Aquinas, *Summa Theologiae,* Part Three, Question 90, Articles 1–3. See, further, Tentler, *Sin and Confession.*
4. These last two models bear some resemblance to what Michel Foucault refers to as two early forms of Christian confession, *exomologesis* as a "dramatic expression by

the penitent of his status of sinner" and *exagoreusis* as a "way of renouncing self" ("About the Beginning," 169).

5. See, e.g., Greenberg, *Biblical Prose Prayer*, 24–30.

6. Such is the view of speech and confession, for instance, taken by Kristeva (*Powers of Horror*, 113–32, esp. 129–30). As she writes, "Communication brings my most intimate subjectivity into being for the other" (129).

7. A point that, in the study of *Egyptian* literature, is allowed to emerge: "What is not required here is an internal process of turning, of repentance, or 'contrition'" (Assmann, "Confession in Ancient Egypt," 236).

8. Indeed, it is not that ancient Israelites lacked the language necessary to express something like this sentiment. In fact, it is from biblical Hebrew that Maimonides draws the term he uses to signify regret (*niḥam*): "The LORD regretted that he made humankind on earth" (Gen. 6:6).

9. What Austin calls a "performative" rather than a "constative" utterance. Austin notes "performative" utterances are commonly misidentified (*How to Do Things with Words*, 3), a tendency that is very much at work in the view that is taken of confession as a form of expression.

10. This term will be discussed later in the chapter.

11. Speiser, *Genesis*, 324. See also Sternberg, *Poetics of Biblical Narrative*, 291.

12. See chap. 2n20.

13. Not surprisingly, this is the conclusion drawn by, at least, one psychoanalytic approach to confession. See Reik, *Compulsion to Confess*, 175–356.

14. See Alter, "Narration and Knowledge," chap. 8 in his *Art of Biblical Narrative*, 155–77, esp. 174–75.

15. Alter, *Art of Biblical Narrative*, 11. Alter also sees the brothers' confessional utterance as an "expression of remorse" (167). Like Alter, Menn views Judah's utterance as an indication of his "personal progress" (*Judah and Tamar*, 45).

16. The earliest instance of this interpretation may be that found in Jubilees 41:23. See the discussion of that text in chapter 7.

17. For this understanding of the phrase, see Gesenius, Cowley, and Kautzsch, *Gesenius' Hebrew Grammar*, 430n2. Waltke and O'Conner understand the phrase as employing a "comparison of exclusion" and would translate, also in opposition to the standard rendering, "She is in the right, *not* I" (*Introduction to Biblical Hebrew Syntax*, 265).

18. The question of whether "acknowledgment," *todâ*, means "praise" or "confession" seems misplaced. It suggests, on a basic level, bringing out into the open certain information that is only known to a privileged few. Compare Boda, "Words and Meanings," 277–97.

19. This would also seem to be close to the reading in the Old Latin and the Vulgate. The Masoretic Text, the meaning of which appears to be garbled, most likely suffers here from haplography, for which see Tov, *Textual Criticism*, 237–38. On the meaning of the term *pll*, here translated as "appeal," see Speiser, "Stem PLL in Hebrew," 304–5; compare Berlin, "On the Meaning of *pll* in the Bible." On 1 Sam. 2:25, see, further, de Ward, "Eli's Rhetorical Question: 1 Sam 2:25."

20. See Foucault, *Discipline and Punish*, 32–69.

21. Since the classic essay of von Rad, "The Joseph Narrative and Ancient Wisdom," in *The Problem of the Hexateuch and Other Essays*, esp. 292, scholars have read the Joseph narratives as more or less a unity. See, more recently, Rendsburg, "Redactional Structuring in the Joseph Story: Genesis 37–50"; and Ska, "Judah, Joseph, and the Reader."

22. Sternberg, *Poetics*, 286.
23. Ibid., 285–308, emphasizes all three motivations, but especially the pedagogic, character formation, which he refers to as a "process of crystallization" (295–96).
24. Ibid., 307–8; and Alter, *Art*, 175.
25. For the connection between the Joseph narratives and proverbial wisdom, see von Rad, "Joseph Narrative," 292–300.
26. Contra Richard J. Clifford, who sees this verse as "the only verse in Proverbs that refers to God's forgiveness of the penitent sinner" (*Proverbs*, 245). Fox extends this observation to "the entirety of didactic Wisdom" (*Proverbs 10–31*, 826). The anachronism of such a reading, given the absence of repentance from the rest of wisdom literature, should be clear. In this verse, "confession" serves as identification, not expression; "abandonment" entails the transfer of real property or cessation of a heinous act, not the matter of intention; and "mercy" need not refer to divine forgiveness. For the preferred rendering of "mercy" as a term of familial integration, see the NJPS translation to Hosea 1:6, 2:3, 6, 25. Hosea 14:4 is another clear example.
27. In modern scholarship, this view is most clearly articulated by Milgrom, "Priestly Doctrine of Repentance," 186–205; this appears as well in I: Migrom, *Cult and Conscience*, esp. 104–28. See also Milgrom, *Leviticus 1–16*, 373–78.
28. Strikingly, to explain his position, Milgrom quotes the Hellenistic Jewish philosopher Philo, who obviously lived in quite a different world than that of the priestly writer:

> [I]f then after having apparently escaped conviction by his accusers, he becomes, convicted inwardly by his conscience, his own accuser, reproaches himself for his disavowals and perjuries, makes a plain confession of the wrong he has committed and asks for pardon—then the lawgiver orders that forgiveness be extended to such a person on condition that he verifies his repentance . . . and when he has thus propitiated the injured person, he must follow it up, says the lawgiver, by proceeding to the temple to ask for remission of his sins, taking with him as his irreproachable advocate, the soul-felt conviction which has saved him from a fatal disaster. ("Priestly Doctrine," 197)

Roy Gane, likewise, sees sacrifice as a way of "showing repentance" (*Cult and Character*, 318).
29. Gane, *Cult and Character*, 317: "[T]he Israelite system . . . simultaneously recognizes the frailty of human nature, with its penchant for fleeting repentance, provides assurance that the moral equilibrium is restored, and encourages long-term moral rehabilitation."
30. See, further, Levine, *Leviticus*, 22.
31. See, further, ibid., 106.
32. See also Ps. 38:16–19, 51:3–6.
33. See the references in chap. 2n2.
34. As found in Jacobsen, *Treasures of Darkness*, 154. Other examples are produced in 147–55.
35. A parallel narrative of confession with regard to David appears in 2 Sam. 24.
36. Halberstam, *Law and Truth*, 163. Polzin speaks of the "pedagogical impact—or moment of recognition provided David and the story's readers [the nation as a whole] by Nathan's oracle" (*David and the Deuteronomist*, 127).
37. Simon, "Poor Man's Ewe-Lamb," 232; Keys, *Wages of Sin*, 148.

38. For a juridical reading of this story, see Simon, "Poor Man's Ewe-Lamb," 220–25.
39. Psalm 82 is an important exposition of judgment as an assertion of power.
40. Indeed, the cases of both David and Ahab concern the question of the king's right to "take" what does not belong to him. See Janzen, "Condemnation of David's Taking," 209–20.
41. Following the King James Version, many modern translations, e.g., the NRSV, without any apparent indication from the text to support their syntactic claim, pull out this phrase as the protasis of a conditional sentence, thus establishing confession as the efficacious ritual that brings about redemption: "But if they confess . . . ."
42. Milgrom, *Leviticus 23–27*, 2329–43; and Levine, *Leviticus*, 190–91.
43. The term used here, *yimmaqqu* ("rot away"), is furnished with the interiorizing sense, "be heartsick," in the NJPS translation, for little apparent reason other than to allow a penitential interpretation.
44. The same holds true for related passages in Ezekiel, e.g., Ezek. 36:22–32, where acknowledgment of sin too (36:31) is not the effective instrument of redemption but the culmination of the punishment and humiliation of exile. See Schwartz, "Ezekiel's Dim View," 43–67. On the connections between this passage in Leviticus and Ezekiel, see Milgrom, "Leviticus 26 and Ezekiel," in 57–62.
45. See chap. 2n2.

CHAPTER 4

1. See, e.g., Japhet, *Ideology of the Book of Chronicles*, 170, 260, where "humility" is said to indicate repentance as its precondition. In the cases Japhet adduces, appeal, rather than penitence, once again seems to be the operative concern. For the eventual derivation of the penitential term, important in later developments, as "compunction" from translations of the Hebrew Bible, see Harl, "Les Origines Grecques," 3–21. Also commonly assumed to refer to "repentance" are terms for seeking (*drš* and *bqš*). See *Theological Lexicon of the Old Testament*, 1:253.
2. Thus, for instance, Milgrom argues that "P [the priestly source] devised its terminology at a time when *šwb* had not become the standard idiom for repentance. However, under the influence of the prophets, especially Jeremiah and Ezekiel, the root *šwb* overwhelmed all of its competitors, including *ʾšm*" ("Priestly Doctrine," 203). Most noteworthy is the assumption of total identification, for all intents and purposes, between *ʾšm* (*ʾashem*) and *šwb* (*shuv*) around "repentance," that it was just a matter of finding the right word to express what is deemed to be a universal concept.
3. Thus, William Lee Holladay concludes his magisterial study of the term as follows: "it is to the merit of Jeremiah that he saw this clearly and explored the potentialities of the idea to its limit, using a word, deepening the word, and carving out an idea with the word, an idea which left Jewish thinking enriched in all the years thereafter" (*ŠÛBH*, 157).
4. Holladay, *ŠÛBH*, 120.
5. Ibid., 116–57. In various places, Holladay indicates, in turn, that he takes this "return to obedience" to be synonymous with "repentance," e.g., ibid., 146, 157.
6. Wolff, "Kerygma," 98, refers to it as "less a human deed and more a psychological event."
7. Vološinov, *Marxism and the Philosophy of Language*, 23.

8. This is the view that Lindbeck labels as "experiential-expressivism." See *Nature of Doctrine*, 1–31.

9. Vološinov, *Philosophy of Language*, 21–24.

10. In this chapter, I generally make use of the NRSV as an example of the traditional translation of *shuv*.

11. See, also, Fabry, *Theological Dictionary of the Old Testament*, 14:464. For its distinctions from other verbs of turning, see Holladay, *ŠÛBH*, 54–55.

12. Thus, definition I.1.a in the Oxford English Dictionary is "to come or go back to a place or person." See *Oxford English Dictionary*, 3rd ed., s.v. "return, v.1," http://www.oed.com/view/Entry/164596?result=2&rskey=ZqKqgl&. Accessed July 3, 2015.

13. It may have been natural for *shuv* to come to be understood as "return" as most of its attestations involve completion, even if completion is not part of its verbal semantics.

14. See Holladay, *ŠÛBH*, 1–2.

15. For other studies contravening the multiplication of meanings, see Steiner, "Does the Biblical Hebrew Conjunction ־ו Have Many Meanings"; and Schwartz, "Bearing of Sin."

16. The misunderstanding of *shuv* in this passage has led to various speculative proposals. See Pope, *Song of Songs*, 595–96.

17. This translation is found in the NJPS.

18. Compare NJPS.

19. A related phenomenon is discussed, though from a different angle, in Polak, "Verbs of Motion," 161–97.

20. Thus, one also finds examples of an interrupted *shuv*, where one heads back in a certain direction but does not attain the intended destination, e.g., Josh. 22:9–10, as well as *shuv* to a place that was not one's previous point of departure, e.g., Esther 2:14.

21. For a survey of relevant literature, recent and old, see Hahn, "Covenant in the Old and New Testaments," 263–92.

22. This is especially evident in its ready adaption for use in recent postbiblical research. Note, for instance, its role in Sanders, *Paul and Palestinian Judaism*.

23. See Ps. 9:11, 22:27, 24:6, 34:11. See, also, *Theological Lexicon of the Old Testament*, I:346–51.

24. See also Num. 23:15, the pertinence of which is noted already in Propp, *Exodus 1–18*, 258. Deut. 1:45 may provide another example. The people are crushed in battle and then *shuv* and "weep before YHWH." Here, *shuv* is commonly translated as "again," but there is no mention in the narrative of their having wept before YHWH previously. This proposal would solve the problems aptly noted in Tigay, *JPS Torah Commentary*, 22.

25. For the political dimensions of exclusivity in oracle seeking, see Huffmon, "Exclusivity of Divine Communication," 67–81.

26. This passage, like several other early attestations of the phrase (e.g., Isa. 9:12), uses the preposition *'ad* ("to, up to") rather than *'el* ("to, unto"). While their meanings partially overlap, *'ad* usually emphases travel "up to" a particular object and, thus, may reinforce the sense of motion, as opposed to attainment of a prior point of departure, for which I argue here. For a similar use of *'ad* in the context of consultation, see Exod. 22:8. On the sense of *'ad* with verbs of motion, see Waltke and O'Connor, *Introduction to Biblical Hebrew Syntax*, 215.

27. One common way this separation is effectuated and repentance, thereby, read into the passage is by positing a prophetic injunction that is off the text's plane of representation as what this movement of *shuv* is meant to respond to. See Andersen and Freedman, *Amos*, 445–47. See also Jacobs, "YHWH's Call," 18. Barstad, *Religious Polemics of Amos*, 37–75, goes as far as declaring *shuv* to be a form of "conversion," a reading that originates in New Testament scholarship and will be addressed in the concluding chapter.

28. On the phenomenon of peripheral intermediation, see Wilson, *Prophecy and Society*, 69–86.

29. See also Hosea 3:5, 5:4–6, 5:15–16:1, and the use of related terminology in 12:7.

30. See, also, Hosea 5:13, 11:5, and 14:4.

31. The term, here, is *'ashem*, discussed in the previous chapter.

32. See, for instance, Unterman, "Repentance and Redemption in Hosea," who maintains that *shuv*'s failure is because God "demands sincere repentance to avoid divine punishment" (543).

33. See also Hosea 5:4–6. Note, further, there the parallelism between *shuv* and "seeking" and that "seeking YHWH" involves bringing gifts as part of the material exchange that is at the heart of oracular inquiry as an institution.

34. It is this narrative of "return to a prior relationship" that people may allow to inform their understanding of prophetic *shuv* in general, despite its overall absence from other passages. But, even here, the language of "turning" corresponds most specifically to the seeking out of material support, not the renewal of some abstract prior relational entity, what we call "marriage."

35. For an extended economic reading of the Hosea passage, see Yee, "'She Is Not My Wife,'" 345–83. On hierarchy in ancient Israel, see also the comments of Meyers, "Contesting the Notion of Patriarchy," 84–105.

36. Note, also, the use of *shuv* in a similar political context in Judg. 11:8.

37. For the immediacy of the connection between appeal and healing, see also Gen. 20:17, Num. 12:13, Ps. 30:3, and Ps. 107:20.

38. Note the discussion of *bṭḥ* in chapter 2.

39. See the use of this term for petition in Isa. 17:7, as well as 2 Sam. 22:42. Compare Psalm 18, where the same Psalm as that in 2 Samuel appears but with the variant, *yeshavv 'u*, "they cried out" (Ps. 18:42).

40. See Isa. 10:24.

41. See the NJPS translation. This tradition has persisted since the time of the Vulgate, which, otherwise, usually uses forms of the verb, *-verto*. See, for instance, the Vulgate (and the NJPS) to 1 Kings 8:47.

42. For the application of the theme of *shuv* to other nations, see Ps. 22:28 as well.

43. Candidates include 1 Kings 8:33, 47; Lam. 3:40; and Joel 2:12–13. In the case of 1 Kings 8:33, 47, *shuv* appears in a context of petition with other verbs of petition, but compare 1 Kings 8:35, which unambiguously uses a different sense of *shuv*. Likewise, Lam. 3:40 appears to use *shuv* in a context of petition (even if it fails, as we see in 3:41), but a number of ambiguities pertain to the language used in this passage. It begins with the cohortative, "Let us search and examine our ways." Is this examination a practice of self-examination, as it might sound to modern Western ears, a preliminary to a cessation of sin, or a call to recognize the state of Israel's sin-induced affliction (compare Hag. 1:5, 7), a message in keeping with Lamentations in general as we saw in a preceding chapter, a preliminary to appeal? Also at stake here is the significance of "heart" as an image, "let us lift up our hearts to our hands" (Lam. 3:41); and, "turn back to me with all your heart . . .

rend your heart and not [just] your garments" (Joel 2:12–13). It could signify an end to a certain hardness of "heart," or disobedience; compare Lev. 26:41. But "heart" also figures in contexts of appeal as an image for a totality of desperation; compare Lam. 2:18 and Ps. 62:9. Certainly the rest of the phraseology in the Joel passage suggests appeal, but the precise sense of *shuv* in the passage remains, in my view, like the others, hard to determine. This very ambiguity may suggest that the sense of *shuv*, indeed, has begun to shift away from appeal, but that its old forms are preserved and continue to be presented in contexts of appeal.

44. For a recent overview of scholarship on the issue of Jeremiah and its sources, see Holladay, "Elusive Deuteronomists," 56–58.

45. Even when differences of phraseology are acknowledged, their sense is taken to be, more or less, identical. See Holladay, *ŠÛBH*, 138–39; and Jeremiah Unterman, *From Repentance to Redemption*, 11.

46. For a review of all instances of the term in Jeremiah, see Holladay, *ŠÛBH*, 128–39.

47. Lam. 5:21 and Isa. 44:22 would seem to follow this usage.

48. Likewise, we find "turning to God" clearly delineated as a rectification in behavior in other passages considered late. See Deut. 30:1–2, Isa. 56:7, Ps. 51:15, and Neh. 1:9.

49. Examples of other late texts that employ the negative formulation include Isa. 59:20, Zech. 1:4, Mal. 2:6, Jon. 3:8, Job 36:10, Neh. 9:35, 2 Chron. 7:14, and Dan. 9:13. The latter is particularly instructive, for it is dependent on the passages from Deuteronomy (4:30, 30:1–2) and reformulates them in negative terms.

50. See, e.g., Zech 1:3–5.

51. The same strategy figures at Qumran, where we find the phrase "to turn to the Law of Moses," e.g., 1 QS V 8–9. Note also Targum Neophyti to Deut. 4:30: "And you shall turn back to the Teaching of the Torah of the Lord and heed his voice." There is also a parallel movement from "inquiry" of YHWH to "inquiry" of Torah. See Mandel, "Origins of Midrash," 12–13.

52. Aspects of this view are to be found in the discussion of Ezekiel in Levinson, *Legal Revision and Religious Renewal*, 60–71.

53. This juxtaposition of seemingly unrelated concerns is a common if underrecognized phenomenon. See, further, Psalms 34 and 95.

54. In a sense, this juxtaposition is at work in the prophetic exhortations found, for instance, in 1 Sam. 7:3 and Jer. 7:1–11, both of which occur, necessarily, against the backdrop of cultic worship.

55. See, also, the use of the attributes in Deut. 4:30–31, Joel 2:13, Jon. 4:2, and, perhaps, Isa. 55:6. For studies of the attributes, see Dentan, "Literary Affinities," 34–51; and Dozeman, "Inner-Biblical Interpretation," 207–23.

56. For the use of this term, see Newman, *Praying by the Book*.

57. This process is particularly evident in the range and regularity of terms for appeal amassed in the Chronicler. See, e.g., 2 Chron. 12:6, 16:12, 32:26, 33:12.

CHAPTER 5

1. See Hadot, *Philosophy as a Way of Life*, esp. 81–125; and Foucault, "Technologies of the Self," 16–49.

2. See, in particular, Barton, *Oracles of God*, 154–78. I would differ from Barton in his viewing the pedagogical reading of Scripture as inevitable; it is the project of a particular time and place and emerges for particular reasons, as explored in the last chapter of this book.

3. Of course, as Roland Barthes writes, "We know now that a text is not a line of words releasing a single 'theological' meaning (the 'message' of the Author-God) but a multi-dimensional space in which a variety of writings, none of them original, blend and clash" ("Death of the Author," 146).

4. On literature as a particular sort of cultural formation, see Eagleton, *Literary Theory: An Introduction*, 1–14; and on the pedagogical dimensions of literature, see ibid., 15–46.

5. Kugel, *Traditions of the Bible*, 15–17. For more on the use of exemplarity in the period, see Najman, *Past Renewals*, esp. 243–56.

6. Kugel, *Traditions of the Bible*, 17–18.

7. For the place of repentance in the interpreted lives of these Pentateuchal figures and others, see Kugel, *Traditions of the Bible*, 142–43, 155, 178–79, 193–94, see, further, Anderson, "Penitence Narrative in *The Life of Adam and Eve*," 1–38.

8. For an example from rabbinic literature, see *Pesiqta de-Rav Kahanah* 24:11.

9. Kugel, "Reuben's Sin with Bilhah," 545–47.

10. "[F]or it is only during the course of an eventful life that men are differentiated into full individuality; and it is this history of a personality which the Old Testament presents to us as the formation undergone by those whom God has chosen to be examples" (Auerbach, *Mimesis*, 18).

11. As Alter writes in *The Art of Biblical Narrative*: "The biblical tale might usefully be regarded as a narrative experiment in the possibilities of moral, spiritual, and historical knowledge, undertaken through a process of studied contrasts between the variously limited knowledge of the human characters and the divine omniscience quietly but firmly represented by the narrator" (157).

12. Kugel, *Traditions of the Bible*, 185–86.

13. See, e.g., Thayer, *Penitence, Preaching, and the Coming of the Reformation*.

14. Note, for instance, the anachronism evident in Maimonides' reference to prophecy as a biblical grounding for the practice of preaching: "all of the prophets rebuked Israel such that they would repent. Therefore, it is necessary to appoint in every congregation of Israel a great, elderly sage . . . who can rebuke the masses and bring them around in repentance" (Mishneh Torah, "Laws of Repentance," 4:2).

15. These terms are commonplace throughout the literature. They appear, for instance, throughout the work of Blenkinsopp, *History of Prophecy in Israel*, even if he otherwise sees the preaching of repentance as a later "Deuteronomic" response (161–65).

16. See, e.g., how O'Brien, *Challenging Prophetic Metaphor*, configures prophecy as a "persuasive literature" that aims to change readers' "thinking, feeling, and, ultimately, their behavior" through the "rhetorical device" of metaphor (xvi–xvii).

17. See, in particular, the argument formulated against the image of the prophet as a preacher of repentance in Westermann, *Basic Forms of Prophetic Speech*, esp. 19. Westermann also designates "messenger" as the basic role of the prophet (98–128), a role not in keeping with preacher, and the "judicial verdict" as his basic unit of speech (129–98), a form that does not admit the possibility of repentance.

18. This model is found, for instance, in Maimonides' notion of prophecy as rebuke. As he explains in the same passage noted above (n. 14), "rebuke *leads to* repentance. For when a person is informed of his sin and thereby humiliated, he repents" (Mishneh Torah, "Laws of Repentance," 4:2). Again, one finds a medieval compulsion to explain what moderns now take for granted.

19. Heschel, *Prophets*, 12.

20. For a critique of the language of "reproach" and "threat," see Westermann, *Basic Forms*, 28–30.

21. Hunter, *Seek the Lord!*
22. Westermann, *Basic Forms*, 205–9; O'Brien, *Deuteronomistic History Hypothesis*, 283–87. This view is also said to be found in Chronicles (Japhet, *Ideology*, 176–91).
23. Mason, *Preaching the Tradition*; and Barton, *Oracles of God*, 158. Historical chronicles, especially the so-called Deuteronomistic History, were also supposedly turned into sources for exemplification, demonstrating what would happen to the people if they continued to sin (Barton, *Oracles of God*, 157).
24. A similar critique emerges in Rösel, "Why 2 Kings 17," 85–90. For some initial critique of this phenomenon of Deuteronomism, see the collection *Those Elusive Deuteronomists* (ed. Shearing and McKenzie).
25. This is the view implicit, for instance, in Boda, "Penitential Innovations," 391–407.
26. As he himself notes (273), despite their different starting points, Barton's project dovetails in the end with that of Julius Wellhausen: "In reality, we should have to say, they were not what the ancient world called prophets; they were individuals without a status, lone geniuses whom any generic title belittles" (*Oracles of God*, 272). Blenkinsopp, *History of Prophecy*, refers to the prophet as a "dissident intellectual" (96), a stance obviously derived from the contemporary position of scholars. Likewise, the stated goal of "peripheral intermediation" throughout Wilson, *Prophecy and Society*, is "bringing about social change" (71).
27. For a critique of the view of religion as a "transhistorical essence" that is separate from concerns of power and politics, see Asad, *Genealogies of Religion*, 27–54, esp. 28–29.
28. For a review of those positions that emphasize discontinuity and argument for a degree of continuity, see Wilson, "Early Israelite Prophecy," 3–16.
29. Note, in particular, Heschel's discussion of prophetic "sympathy" for the divine (*Prophets*, 393–413).
30. Again, Austin, *How to Do Things with Words*, provides an important corrective. See the application of Austin's work to prophecy in Houston, "What Did the Prophets Think They Were Doing?" 167–88.
31. For a study of oracles against the nations, see Christensen, *Transformations of the War Oracle*.
32. E.g., Isa. 1:24–26.
33. The classic statement is to be found in Heschel's *The Prophets*, 285–382. The theme of anthropopathism is picked up on and developed in Muffs, *Love & Joy*, esp. 9–48. Here, I am particularly indebted to the view of Muffs's model as elucidated to me in private communication by Baruch Schwartz. More broadly on representations of the deity as possessed of a body, see Sommer, *Bodies of God and the World of Ancient Israel*.
34. Muffs, *Love & Joy*, 4–5.
35. Fisher, *Vehement Passions*.
36. Ibid., 45.
37. Ibid., 43.
38. Ibid., 44.
39. Ibid., 157–70, 181–87.
40. Ibid., 168.
41. Foucault, *Discipline and Punish*, 44.
42. Ibid., 40.
43. Ibid., 49.
44. Ibid., 48.
45. Ibid., 49.
46. I owe the turn of phrase to Baruch Schwartz, private communication.

47. Fisher, *Vehement Passions*, 99.
48. Note the earlier discussion of Ahab and Josiah, in chapter 1, including n. 40.
49. See Psalm 82.
50. See the excellent discussion in Barton, "Prophecy and Theodicy," 73–86.
51. Westermann, *Basic Forms*.
52. See Barstad, "*Sic dicit dominus*," 21–52.
53. For this text, see Nissinen, *Prophets and Prophecy in the Ancient Near East*, 38–39. See bibliography there for further discussion.
54. Compare Deut. 18:14–22.
55. Interestingly, even this episode is read by some as involving a prophetic call to repentance. See the critique of this position in Hayes, "Golden Calf Stories," 63–64.
56. See Shatz, "Freedom," 478–509.
57. Note the parallels drawn in chapter 4 between the plague narratives and Amos 4:6–10.
58. For an analysis of the sources in these narratives, see Propp, *Exodus 1–18*, 310–17.
59. For a related reading of the Exodus narratives, see Dozeman, *God at War*.
60. For the connection of the theme of "hardening of the heart" to holy war, see Wilson, "Hardening of Pharaoh's Heart," 33–35. Wilson also sees the narrative as performing a pedagogical function, linking Israel's actions to Pharaoh's and, therefore, warning future generations.
61. For a recent review of scholarship and introduction to the work, see Römer, *So-Called Deuteronomistic History*.
62. See, e.g., 2 Kings 21:12–15.
63. For this view of the History, see Noth, *Deuteronomistic History*, 134–45.
64. Consider, for instance, 1 Sam. 15:26–28 and 1 Kings 21:20–24.
65. See, further, 1 Sam. 16:13. On the anointment of kings, see Halpern, *Constitution of the Monarchy in Israel*, 13–19.
66. See, further, 1 Kings 11:29–39.
67. See 1 Kings 19 and 1 Kings 21:20–24.
68. E.g., 2 Kings 1.
69. For a recent survey, see Rösel, "Why 2 Kings 17," 85–90.
70. The framework to the Deuteronomic Law puts the Law into effect as covenant in a similar fashion and also therefore, should be seen as employing *he ʿid* in a sense of "testify against," not "warn." See Deut. 4:26. Japhet, *Ideology*, also sees a legal principle of "warning" at work in Chronicles (183–90).
71. The contrasting portrayals of the kings, Jeroboam and Josiah, provide clear instances of how an opportunity for "turning back" from evil can be introduced against the backdrop of a straightforward oracle of doom that does not aim, in principle, at the rectification or even redemption of its recipients. See 1 Kings 13:1–6, 33; and 2 Kings 22:11–20, 23:25. It is noteworthy that, despite Josiah's "turn," punishment is still brought upon Israel, as prophesied; its arrival is only delayed.
72. The combination of intercession and cultic instruction can be seen in 1 Sam. 7:3 as well.
73. This assumption is clearly at work in Wolff, "Kerygma," 83–100.
74. For this view of the Deuteronomistic History in general, see Haran, *Biblical Collection*, 287–91.
75. It is not clear to me how a real, present phenomenon of prophets preaching repentance in the time of the Chronicler, as is often assumed, is indicated by the literary phenomenon of prophecy in the book. What we seem to find there is a continued interest in the capacity of prophecy to establish blame. But, as Japhet has

demonstrated in *Ideology*, in the case of the Chronicler, that concern has shifted from the nation to a question of theodicy in the context of the individual.

76. For an introduction to the work, see Blenkinsopp, *History of Prophecy*, 97–110.

77. Isa. 1:16–17 is the one exception, though it is uncertain, in my view, whether this belongs to the pre-exilic Isaianic material or whether it should be seen as a later summary of the work as a whole. In any event, like the passage from Jeremiah examined below, the exhortation in this passage figures in an overall context of destruction and seems to provide the reason for the failure of Israel's appeal rather than constituting a genuine possibility in the present.

78. Tsevat, "Throne Vision of Isaiah," in his *Meaning of the Book of Job*, 155–76.

79. Blenkinsopp, *Isaiah 1–39*, 224. On the supposed transformation in Isaiah's mission, see, further, the comments by Sommer in Berlin et al., *Jewish Study Bible*, 796–97.

80. See, e.g., Greenberg, *Ezekiel 21–37*, 680; and Unterman, *From Repentance to Redemption*.

81. This view is commonplace in scholarship of Jeremiah, though it is harder to maintain in the case of Ezekiel. See, e.g., Nicholson, *Preaching to the Exiles*.

82. Lapsley, *Can These Bones Live?*

83. An attempt to reconstruct such a hypothetical demand can be seen in Raitt, "Prophetic Summons to Repentance," 30–49.

84. See, further, Schwartz, "Repentance and Determinism in Ezekiel," 123–30. For a standard view of Ezekiel as a prophet of repentance, see Strine, "Role of Repentance," 467–91.

85. Similarly, Jer. 11:1–14 incorporates exhortation and then makes plain its failure—see also Jer. 21:11–13—as do the narrative passages, Jer. 26 and 36.

86. A similar argument appears in Jer. 16:10–13.

87. See, further, Paul Joyce, *Divine Initiative*, which recognizes the stress Ezekiel places on Israel's responsibility for exile.

88. Note that the suggestion of Zech. 1:4 is not that the old prophetic words are designed to lead the present generation to "turn back." They explain, rather, why the past generation suffered. It is the current prophet who issues the injunction to "turn" in present time.

89. See Boda, "Penitential Innovation"; and Mason, *Preaching the Tradition*, 145–262.

90. See, further, Hallo, "Jonah and the Uses of Parody," 285–91.

CHAPTER 6

1. See, further, Smith, "Bible and Religion," in his *Relating Religion*, 197–214; and Asad, *Genealogies of Religion*, 27–54.

2. See, in particular, Steck, *Israel und das gewaltsame Geschick der Propheten*; and, more recently, Schmid, "Deuteronomistic Image of History," 369–88.

3. This oft-repeated view can be traced to Hengel, *Judaism and Hellenism*, I:179–80. It is assumed by New Testament scholars, from Sanders in *Paul and Palestinian Judaism* to N. T. Wright, "repentance . . . was what Israel must do if her exile is to come to an end" (*Christian Origins*, 2: 248). It is also found among Jewish scholars. Urbach, "Redemption and Repentance," 194, for instance, presents Bar Kokhba and his supporters as "penitents."

4. See, for rabbinic Judaism, Soloveitchik, "Redemption and the Power of Man," 51–77, as well as the way in which a similar claim fits the Enlightenment agenda of Reimarus: "This demand [to repent] was not only reasonable in all ages, but

also was considered necessary among the Jews for the advent of the Messiah, just as they indeed believe *to this present day* [italics mine] that it is particularly the lack of repentance and betterment that delays the Messiah's advent, so that if they once were to do the proper penance the Messiah would come immediately" (*Reimarus: Fragments*, 66–67). This admitted anachronism suits more than just Reimarus's Deism. To posit a Jewish nation in need of repentance fits well, of course, with the agenda of certain forms of Christian historiography.

5. See, further, Urbach, "Redemption and Repentance," 190–206. Urbach draws a helpful distinction there between "repentance" and "redemption."

6. Vernant, "Intimations of the Will in Greek Tragedy," in his *Myth and Tragedy*, 49–84. Compare Williams, *Shame and Necessity*, 21–49.

7. Asad, *Formations*, 73. See, further, his chapter "Thinking about Agency and Pain," in Asad, *Formations*, 67–99, esp. 73–79.

8. For more on this work, see VanderKam, "Recent Scholarship on the Book of Jubilees," 405–31; and, now, Kugel, *Walk through Jubilees*.

9. See, e.g., Wolff, "Kerygma," 83–100; Weinfeld, *Deuteronomy 1–11*, 215–16; and Tigay, *Deuteronomy*, 283–84.

10. See Davenport, *Eschatology*, 26–27; VanderKam, "Studies on the Prologue and Jubilees," 1, 267; Hubbard, *New Creation*, 45; Jacobson, "Literary Unity of Q," 384n93; Nickelsburg, "Nature and Function," 104–5; and Werline, *Penitential Prayers*, 135–38.

11. Brettler, "Predestination in Deuteronomy 30.1–10," in Shearing et al., *Those Elusive Deuteronomists*, 171–88. A similar distinction is drawn, in non-source-critical terms, in the commentary of the medieval exegete Nachmanides on Deut. 30:6.

12. Translations of Jubilees, unless otherwise noted, are based on VanderKam, *Book of Jubilees*.

13. Compare 4 Ezra 3:17–20.

14. Likewise, in its biblical representations, prophetic intercession often appears in the context of oracles of redemption and serves as a catalyst for divine promises of eventual favor, e.g., Jer. 32:16–44 and Ezek. 11:13–21, without necessarily succeeding in obviating the need for short-term suffering.

15. See, also, Kister, "Studies in 4QMiqṣat Maʿaśe Ha-Torah," 349–50. Additionally, a term for "searching" appears in the first divine plan and in Deut. 4:29–31, but is absent from the second plan and from Deut. 30:1–10.

16. A hint for the existence of this intervention might be found, for Jubilees, in Deut. 9:19: "and the LORD heeded me, *that time too*," situated, as it is, between the two Deuteronomy passages. That would seem to locate the events described in the opening chapter of Jubilees as transpiring after the sin of the Golden Calf or, perhaps, in immediate anticipation of them. Accordingly, Jubilees would interpret Moses' plea that God *disregard* Israel's stubbornness and forgive them (Exod. 34:9) as a general plea that God permanently *transform* them and remove sin from their midst.

17. My conclusions here differ subtly in this regard from my position in an earlier article, "Did Israel Believe," 631–50.

18. See, further, Weinfeld, "Jeremiah and the Spiritual Metamorphosis of Israel," 2–56.

19. See, also, Jer. 32:40.

20. See, also, Ezek. 11:19.

21. These passages have been juxtaposed with others from the same prophetic books (Jer. 4:4, Ezek. 18:31, Ezek. 14:6) that seem to suggest that responsibility for such a transformation rests with Israel. As with the twin passages in

Deuteronomy, scholars have concluded that there is little difference between them (Weinfeld, "Jeremiah," 35n63). In other words, one must understand the prophets as adopting a blend of grace and human initiative, even when no role is explicitly attributed to human agency. See, also, Zimmerli, *Ezekiel 1*, 386. Such an analysis refrains from taking seriously the actual language of the different passages, but it also fails to recognize their very different contexts. As explored in the previous chapter, the summons to "turn," as part of which the passages stressing Israel's responsibility figure, comes to explain why Israel currently suffers in exile, not to exhort them in the present to secure their own redemption. Most significantly, references to an "ingathering of exiles," that is to say, passages about redemption, are found only in those passages that stress divine responsibility for Israel's transformation. (See Deut. 30:3–5, Jer. 32:37, Ezek. 11:17, and Ezek. 36:24.)

22. There have been, of course, attempts to see repentance at work even in these contexts. See, for instance, Scheuer, *Return of YHWH*.

23. Most recently, on demonology in the period, see Bland, *Evil Within and Without*, 149–253.

24. See Knibb, "Exile," 253–72.

25. The unity of Jubilees has become an important question in recent scholarship. See Segal, *Book of Jubilees*. In any event, we would expect some correspondence in this matter between both source and redactional material, as what is being described here is basic to the apocalypticism prevalent in the time of Jubilees.

26. See Tiller, *Commentary on the Animal Apocalypse*, 61–79, for the dating of this text; and Nicklesburg, *1 Enoch 1*, 8.

27. Translations of 1 Enoch are from Nicklesburg, *1 Enoch 1*.

28. See also 1 Enoch 91:14 and 10:21. See Nicklesburg, *1 Enoch 1*, 449, for 91:14, and Loren T. Stuckenbruck, *1 Enoch 91–108*, 139–45. Nicklesburg ignores the importance of these passages in seeing forgiveness of sins and conversion as incidental in 1 Enoch (*1 Enoch 1*, 54).

29. See, for instance, Licht, "Time and Eschatology," 177–82.

30. See Dimant, "Noah in Early Jewish Literature," 123–50, esp. 135; VanderKam, "Righteousness of Noah," 25–26; and Nicklesburg, *1 Enoch 1*, 224. Most recently and extensively, see Segal, *Book of Jubilees*, 103–44. See also Werman, "The Story of the Flood," 183–202. For the significance of Noah in the Dead Sea Scrolls, see Bernstein, "Noah and the Flood," 199–231. The typological reading of the Flood story is, of course, developed in the New Testament as well. See Matt. 24:37–39 (and Luke 17:26), 1 Pet. 3:20–21, and 2 Pet. 3:5–7.

31. On the image of the Flood as not just destruction but purification in early biblical interpretation, see Kugel, *Traditions*, 188–90 and 199–200.

32. For parallels with Greco-Roman literature, see Feldman, "Josephus' Portrait of Noah," 42–43; but Josephus does seem to reflect an awareness of the same interpretive tradition with which Jubilees is working.

33. Further connections between the Jubilees account and Gen. 8:20–9:5 are adduced in Lambert, "Topics," 107–12.

34. For the phenomenon of apotropaic prayer in Second Temple Judaism, see Flusser, "Qumran and Jewish 'Apotropaic' Prayers," in his *Judaism and the Origins of Christianity*, 214–25; Stone and Greenfield, "Prayer of Levi," 247–66; Eshel, "Apotropaic Prayers in the Second Temple Period," 69–88; and Kister, "Studies in 4QMMT," 352–54.

35. See also Jub. 22:14–15, 19–20.

36. For discussion of this text and translation, see Greenfield, Stone, and Eshel, *Aramaic Levi Document,* 123–34.
37. See, e.g., Weinfeld, "Prayers for Knowledge," 186–200.
38. In a similar vein, like Ezekiel in 36:25–26, Jubilees recasts purification language, here, taken from Psalm 51, as a request for a onetime act of divine re-creation at the end of days.
39. The text and reconstruction come from VanderKam, *Qumran Cave 4.VIII,* 5. The translation provided is based on VanderKam but differs in a few places.
40. See chapter 3n17, for the question of how to translate this syntactic structure.
41. VanderKam, "Studies on the Prologue and *Jubilees* 1," 272, developing a suggestion made by James Kugel concerning the meaning of *te ʿuda* as "solemn warning" (see "The Jubilees Apocalypse," 328–31), interprets Jub. 1:5–25 as a "solemn warning about violation of covenantal stipulations" and, later on, as a "powerful exhortation" (279). But Kugel intended something more technical, "warning" as a legal mode of establishing guilt. In that sense, Jub. 1:5–25 is closer to prediction than exhortation. For other understandings of the term *te ʿuda,* see Werman, "*Te ʿuda*"; Kister, "Two Formulae," 294–300; and Segal, *Book of Jubilees,* 282–91.
42. In this respect, Jubilees comes quite close to Ezekiel, who finds a place for the people's utter self-deprecation without framing it as a virtue and redeems only to save his name among the nations (e.g., Ezek. 36:32). See Schwartz, "Ultimate Aim," 305–19.
43. It is noteworthy that the "repentance" passages in Jubilees (5:13–19 and 41:23–26), for distinct reasons, are considered to be later interpolations in Kugel, *Outside the Bible,* 278–81. See, also, Kugel, *Walk through Jubilees,* 56 and 183–85. Though his analysis differs in several respects, Segal also sees these passages as the work of a later redactor (*Book of Jubilees,* 137–42 and 65–71, respectively).
44. Schiffman, *Reclaiming the Dead Sea Scrolls.*
45. Hengel, 1:179–80.
46. For its broad application to the Dead Sea sect, see Schiffman, *Reclaiming,* 103, 148, 156, 299, and 330; and Nitzan, "Repentance in the Dead Sea Scrolls," 145–70.
47. Nitzan, "Repentance," 167.
48. For a discussion of this fragment, see Seely, "The 'Circumcised Heart,'" 527–35.
49. See, e.g., Newsom, *Self as Symbolic Space,* 109.
50. Licht, "Concept of Free Will," 77–84.
51. See n. 6.
52. Nitzan, "Repentance," 156. See the initial qualifications of this view in Arnold, "Repentance and the Qumran Covenant Ceremony," in Boda et al., *Seeking the Favor of God,* 2:159–75.
53. For a discussion of immersion among sectarians and, especially, its archeological remains, see Magness, *Archeology of Qumran,* 134–62.
54. See Pfann, "Essene Yearly Renewal Ceremony," 337–52.
55. See, e.g., Fredricksen, *Jesus of Nazareth,* 189.
56. Metso, *Textual Development of the Qumran Community Rule,* 113.
57. The passage continues: "if he upholds/effectuates/affirms his words." I take that clause to refer back to the beginning of the sentence and to allude to the process of verbal commitment.
58. Compare Kister, "Demons, Theology and Abraham's Covenant," 173–74.
59. Shemesh, "Expulsion and Exclusion," 59.
60. See, further, Anderson, "Two Notes," 141–47; and Kister, "Physical and Metaphysical Measurements," 153–76.
61. For an introduction to these texts, see Schuller and Newsom, *Hodayot.*

62. E.g., 1QH^a XII: 29–38.
63. Newsom has labeled this juxtaposition the "masochistic sublime" (*Self as Symbolic Space*, 229).
64. See, also, 1QH^a VI: 16–19.
65. See, also, 1QH^a XV and 1QH^a XIX:7–14.
66. Thus, Eileen Schuller emphasizes the relative dominance of praise over petition in the sectarian writings. See "Petitionary Prayer," 29–45.
67. The whole series of questions around the nature of the self and its formulation in the context of the *hodayot* and other scrolls is aptly raised in Newsom, *Self as Symbolic Space*.
68. Martinez and Tigchelaar, *Dead Sea Scrolls,* 1:185.
69. See, for instance, Nitzan, *Qumran Prayer,* 325.
70. Newsom, *Self as Symbolic Space*, 193.
71. Newsom, *Self as Symbolic Space*, 275–76.
72. See, in general, the discussion, "What Do Hodayot Do? Language and the Construction of the Self in Sectarian Prayer," in Newsom, *Self as Symbolic Space*, 191–286.
73. Nitzan, "Repentance," 146.
74. The two, for instance, appear in parallel in 4QPsalms Pesher II, 2–3. In the Temple Scroll, one finds the older positive *shuv* phrase preserved but with its later emphasis on law (11Q19 LIX, 9–10).
75. Compare Kister, "Studies in 4QMiqṣat Maʿaśe Ha-Torah," 349–50.
76. An earlier rejection of this view can be found in von Rad, *Deuteronomy,* 183–84.
77. This pivotal point emerges clearly, as well, in Brettler, "Predestination," 171–88. Part of what is at stake is a matter of syntax, and, specifically, the rather arbitrary practice of translating certain components of the vav-consecutive forms found in Deuteronomy as the protasis of a conditional sentence, "if you return." *Shuv* as divine promise appears in Dan 9:13 and Baruch 2:27–35. The difference is that in Daniel the promised "turn" has not transpired, whereas, in Baruch, it has transpired but redemption has not yet arrived. See, further, Bar 3:7–8.
78. For discussion of this work, see Chazon, "Is *Divrei Ha-Meʾorot* a Sectarian Prayer?" 3–17.
79. See, for instance, Theissen and Merz, *Historical Jesus,* 373.
80. In general, on John the Baptist in his historical context, see Taylor, *Immerser.*
81. Q 3:16b–17. The numbering of Q is based on Luke. The reconstruction used here comes from Robinson, Hoffmann, and Kloppenborg, *Sayings Gospel Q.*
82. Q 3:7–9.
83. See, e.g., Meier, *Marginal Jew,* 2:7.
84. See, further, Mal. 3:1–5, 3:23.
85. Lunde, "Repentance," in Green et al., *Dictionary of Jesus and the Gospels,* 669.
86. Sanders, *Jesus and Judaism,* 106–13. Sanders's position provoked a tidal wave of criticism: Allison, "Jesus and the Covenant," 57–78; Young, "'Jesus and the Sinners,'" 73–75; Chilton, "Jesus and the Repentance of E. P. Sanders," 1–18; Räisänen, "Jesus in Context," 14–16; Crossan, *Birth of Christianity,* 337–42; Fredriksen, *Jesus of Nazareth,* 191–97 and 289 (top); Lunde, "Repentance," 669; the book-length response of Choi, *Jesus' Teaching on Repentance*; and, most recently, Hägerland, "Jesus and the Rites of Repentance," 166–87.
87. Behm, "μετανοέω, μετάνοια," *Theological Dictionary of the New Testament,* 4:1002–3. This same position is repeated without much alteration in formulation in modern New Testament scholarship. See, for instance, Allison, *Jesus of Nazareth,* 104.
88. Borg, *Jesus in Contemporary Scholarship,* 87; and Crossan, *Birth of Christianity,* 339.

89. Fredriksen, *Jesus of Nazareth*, 193–97; Wright, *Jesus and the Victory of God*, 246-258; and Allison, *Jesus of Nazareth*, throughout. See, also, before them, Schweitzer, *Mystery of the Kingdom of God*, 106–12.

90. Note, for instance, how Borg, *Jesus*, 87, views Mark 1:15, 9:1, and the little apocalypse (Mark 13) as "all of a piece."

91. Schweitzer, *Mystery*, 65.

92. Wright, *Jesus*, 248.

93. Borg, *Jesus*, 83.

94. Kloppenborg, *Formation of Q*, 102; see also 101. Jacobsen, "Literary Unity of Q," 383–88, also sees the so-called Deuteronomistic paradigm as defining the theology of Q.

95. See Kloppenborg, *Formation of Q*, 100–101, for the division of Q into clusters.

96. As discussed by Kloppenborg, *Formation of Q*, 117–18.

97. Thus, in "The Kingdom That Didn't Come," Mack argues that the apocalyptic speeches in Q should not be seen as "scripts appropriate to public proclamation" (621) and, as such, are not part of a "call to repentance in preparation for the judgment" (635). They are rather for the instruction of the community and are part of a "myth of origin."

98. See, for instance, Bultmann, *History of the Synoptic Tradition*, 341–42; and Hedrick, "Role of 'Summary Statements,'" 129.

99. Borg, *Jesus*, 87, makes a similar point. Charlesworth, "Historical Jesus," 451–76, is but one example of a portrayal of Jesus' teachings that proceeds from Mark 1:15.

100. Thus, it is telling that one foundational moment in this interpretation is found in the the Wolfenbüttel Fragments: "Jesus' discourses in the four evangelists can not only be read through quickly, but we also immediately find the entire content and intention of his teaching expressed and summarized in his own words: "Repent, and believe in the gospel" (*Reimarus: Fragments*, 65).

101. For an exception, see Bovon, *Luke the Theologian*, 285–86.

102. E.g., Mark 4:1–34.

103. Usually, this comes in the form of emphasizing the Hellenistic, philosophical, and, hence, pedagogical aspect of Paul's work. See, in particular, "Turning: Moral Consequences of Conversion," in Meeks, *Origins of Christian Morality*, 18–36; and Malherbe, *Paul and the Thessalonians*, 21–33.

104. In this regard, see the classic essay of Stendahl, "Paul and the Introspective Consciousness of the West," in Stendahl, *Paul among Jews and Gentiles*, 78–96. See, further, Sanders, *Paul*, 499–501; and Dunn, *New Perspective on Paul*, 367. On the difficulty of taking Acts 17 as characteristic of Paul's "preaching," see Stowers, "Social Status, Public Speaking and Private Teaching," 59–82.

105. Gaventa, *From Darkness to Light*, 42.

106. Note the puzzlement of Segal on the absence of "repentance" terminology in light of Paul's conversion (*Paul the Convert*, 18–21).

107. Sanders, *Paul*, 499–501.

108. For further consideration of this question in Paul, see Martyn, "Epilogue: An Essay in Pauline Meta-Ethics," in his *Divine and Human Agency*, 173–83; and Hubbard, *New Creation in Paul's Letters and Thought*.

109. Also, note the connections between Moses' protest in the book of Jubilees, as discussed above, and Psalm 51. He too seems to have placed its requests for purification into an eschatological framework.

110. Influential, here, are the definitions of conversion in Nock, *Conversion,* 7; and James, *Varieties of Religious Experience,* 165, both of which are careful to incorporate an element of agency into conversion.
111. Rom. 2:4, 2 Cor. 7:9, and 2 Cor. 12:21.

CHAPTER 7

1. This study, therefore, runs counter to many recent studies of "conversion," which tend to take their object as a universal, as existing outside of particular religious traditions and merely subject to differing forms of expression. See Rambo, *Understanding Religious Conversion*; and Rambo and Farhadian, *Oxford Handbook of Religious Conversion.* Of course, long ago, such a scholar as Arthur Darby Nock in his classic work *Conversion* already showed the advent of "conversion" to be a matter of historical contingency.
2. See Foucault, *Archeology of Knowledge,* esp. 21–30.
3. Important examples of how that work has begun to transpire include Sanders, *Paul and Palestinian Judaism*; Levenson,*The Death and Resurrection of the Beloved Son*; Boyarin, *Border Lines;* and, from a different angle, Kugel, *Traditions of the Bible*, who shows the common basis for Jewish and Christian readings of the Bible in shared interpretive traditions.
4. Asad, *Formations of the Secular.*
5. Kuhn, *Structure of Scientific Revolutions*, 52–65.
6. On how "dominant power realizes itself through the very discourse of mobility," in this case of a spiritual or moral sort, see the discussion of Hannah Arendt in Asad, *Genealogies of Religion*, 10–11.
7. Note the comments of Michel Foucault: "One has to take into account the points where the technologies of domination of individuals over one another have recourse to processes by which the individual acts upon himself . . . in the broad meaning of the word, governing people is not a way to force people to do what the governor wants; it is always a versatile equilibrium, with complementarity and conflicts between techniques which assure coercion and processes through which the self is constructed or modified by oneself" ("About the Beginning," 162). See, further, Boyarin and Castelli, "Foucault's *The History of Sexuality.*"
8. On the end of Jewish sectarianism and the plurality of the Rabbis, see Cohen, "Significance of Yavneh: Pharisees, Rabbis, and the End of Jewish Sectarianism." As he writes, "the dominant ethic here is not exclusivity but elasticity" (29). See Wilson, *Magic and the Millennium*, 35–41, for the conditions under which newly formed religious sects become "conversionist."
9. The genealogy of "religion" is exceedingly complex and not susceptible to singular histories, with various scholars pointing to different moments in the emergence of what we call "religion." See, further, Asad, *Genealogies of Religion*; Masuzawa, *Invention of World Religions;* and Nongbri, *Before Religion.* My sense is that we do have a vital moment of emergence already at this point in late antiquity. See, further, Stroumsa, *End of Sacrifice,* esp. 84–109.
10. Meeks's *First Urban Christians* remains a model discussion of such processes of identification.
11. On the social effects of conversion accounts, see Meeks, *Origins of Christian Morality,* 33–36.

12. For an overview of the history of penance, see Tentler, *Sin and Confession*. Aspects of this history could be more sharply delineated with a critical awareness of its early origins. For instance, the medieval dispute between "attrition" and "contrition" (250–63) could be better elucidated, perhaps, with an appreciation for the divergent notions of divine re-creation, discussed in the preceding chapter, and repentance, the subject of the present chapter. As Kevin Uhalde notes, "it would be enough to know whether it was Christianity that changed what penance meant to ancient people, or the other way around—that is, whether ancient ideas and forms of repentance shaped Christianity" ("Sinful Subject," 414). For recent work on the topic, see Firey, *New History of Penance*.

13. For a classic article on the phenomenon, see Nock, "Vocabulary of the New Testament."

14. London, 1799, 2:456.

15. *Oxford English Dictionary*, 3rd ed., s.v. "repent, v.," http://www.oed.com/view/Entr y/162742?result=4&rskey=u4yPKk&. Accessed September 14, 2014.

16. Note the similarities, for instance, with the definition of *teshuva* given in Maimonides' Mishneh Torah: "What is repentance? That the sinner abandon his sin and remove it from his designs, making the mental determination not to do it again . . . he must also regret what happened . . . and make the Knower of Secrets bear witness to his intention never to repeat this sin" (2:2).

17. Thus, for instance, note Targum Pseudo-Jonathan to Deut. 30:2.

18. See chap. 5n1.

19. See, for instance, the general approach in Konstan, *Before Forgiveness*, 99–107.

20. Smith, *Drudgery Divine*, 18.

21. See, respectively, 1 Sam. 7:17, 2 Sam. 11:1, and Job 21:34.

22. On Mishnaic Hebrew and its relationship to Biblical Hebrew, see Bar-Asher, "Mishnaic Hebrew."

23. See Würthwein, "μετανοέω, μετάνοια," 989–91.

24. There are also problems pertaining to the translation of *niḥam*. As a term, *niḥam*, unlike *shuv*, rarely has a positive valence and, then, only with God as agent. This has been a source of misunderstanding, at times, for interpreters most familiar with the positive usage of its translation equivalent, *metanoeō*.

25. See Symmachus to Isa. 31:6, 55:7; Jer. 18:8; Ezek. 33:12; Hosea 11:5; and Job 36:10. See, further, Würthwein, "μετανοέω, μετάνοια," 990. For more on Symmachus, see Marcos, *Septuagint in Context*, 123–41.

26. For examples, see Philo, *On Repentance*, 175; and Luke 11:32.

27. Another verb, *metamelei*, would also be a close match, but it never becomes a technical term in the same way as *metanoeō*. A noteworthy attempt to suggest otherwise in connection to Matt. 27:3 can be found in Daube, "Judas." But, the term in this passage seems to me to suggest the typical Greek trope of regret that comes too late and only leads to the suffering brought on by futility, which, in this case, results in Judas's suicide.

28. See the entries "μετανοέω" and "μετάνοια, ή," Liddell and Scott, *Greek-English Lexicon*, 2:1115.

29. See, further, the collection of sources in Winston, "Philo's Doctrine of Repentance"; and Wolfson, *Philo*, 2:252–53. See, also, C. H. Dodd, *Bible and the Greeks*, 180.

30. Winston, "Philo's Doctrine of Repentance," 29. This view is broadly shared by classicists, such as David Konstan in his recent book, *Before Forgiveness*, who, therefore, concludes: "Now, the sources of the attitude toward repentance and redemption . . . have their origin, clearly, in the Jewish Bible" (99).

31. See, e.g., Dillon, *Middle Platonists.*
32. See, e.g., the corpus of writings on the topic produced by Abraham Malherbe, collected in *Light from the Gentiles*; and the recent collection, *Stoicism in Early Christianity*. For a thought-provoking example from rabbinic literature, see Tropper, *Wisdom, Politics, and Historiography,* 136–56.
33. For a discussion of Plutarch and other pertinent sources, see Pleše, *Poetics of the Gnostic Universe,* 247–56. A good overview also appears in Sterling, "Turning to God," 71–74.
34. Translation from Plutarch, *Moralia* 4:235–37.
35. Pleše, *Poetics of the Gnostic Universe,* 252.
36. See Taylor, *Sources of the Self,* 119, for a discussion of the Platonic basis for a notion of "inwardness."
37. See Wright, "Plutarch on Moral Progress," 136–50.
38. See *How to Tell a Flatterer* 74, C and *On Moral Virtue* 452, C.
39. *How to Tell a Flatterer* 68, F.
40. Translations of the Apocrypha are from the NRSV unless noted otherwise.
41. See, in particular, Winston, "Philo's Doctrine of Repentance"; and Wolfson, *Philo,* 2:252–59.
42. See Pleše, *Poetics of the Gnostic Universe,* 251, for Philo and Plutarch as "epitomizers of earlier philosophical and exegetical traditions."
43. Deleuze and Guattari, *What Is Philosophy?* 2.
44. An excellent discussion of the treatise and its connections to Hellenistic moral philosophy can be found in Wilson, *Philo of Alexandria,* 359–64, though the author cannot help but hear in Philo "the sort of change familiar from the all too frequent appeals in scripture for the people to 'turn' or 'return' to God" (359), to which Philo, in fact, hardly alludes.
45. On the place of conversion in Philo's thought, see Birnbaum, *Place of Judaism in Philo's Thought,* 193–219, esp. 203; and Niehoff, *Philo on Jewish Identity and Culture,* 29–31. On conversion to Judaism in general, see Cohen, *Beginnings of Jewishness;* and Schwartz, "Conversion to Judaism in the Second Temple Period," 195–206.
46. See Nock, *Conversion,* 164–86.
47. Malherbe, *Paul and the Thessalonians,* 26n89.
48. *Corpus Hermeticum* I:28. The translation with slight emendation comes from Copenhaver, *Hermetica.* For an introduction to the work, see Copenhaver, *Hermetica,* xiii–lxi. For a similar exhortation in an Egyptian context, see *Sibylline Oracles,* 1:153–56.
49. It is also worth mentioning that this sort of exhortation fits rhetorical patterns very common in Hellenistic moral philosophy even when it decidedly does not use the term "repentance." See, e.g., Long, *Epictetus,* 52–64.
50. See Fitzgerald and White, *Tabula of Cebes.*
51. 10.4 B–11.
52. See, most recently, Ahearne-Kroll, "*Joseph and Aseneth* and Jewish Identity in Greco-Roman Egypt." Compare Kraemer, *When Aseneth Met Joseph.* On conversion in *Joseph and Aseneth,* see Chesnutt, *From Death to Life.* For a recent translation and commentary, see Ahearne-Kroll, "Joseph and Aseneth."
53. See, further, Sterling, "Turning to God," 80–81.
54. On rabbinic Judaism as a provincial Roman phenomenon, see, most recently, Lapin, *Rabbis as Romans.* See, also, Schwartz, *Were the Jews a Mediterranean Society?*
55. For an extensive introduction to the work, see Skehan and Di Lella, *Wisdom of Ben Sira,* 3–127.

56. They appear, for instance, in Matt. 6:2–18 and the liturgical piece for Yom Kippur, "*u-netanneh toqef.*"

57. Prayer, almsgiving, and repentance appear together in 17:22–24. Fasting appears in 34:30–31.

58. The first three appear together, for instance, in Tobit 12:8. Judith incorporates the first two and, perhaps, by implication of being a righteous wealthy woman, the third as well (8:1–9:14). For more on the history of almsgiving, see Anderson, *Charity*. For more on the history of fasting, see Lambert, "Fasting as a Penitential Rite," 509–12.

59. On perfectionism in ancient Judaism, see Najman, "La Recherche de la Perfection dans le Judaïsme Ancien," 99–116.

60. For general discussions of its role in Ben Sira, see Gilbert, "God, Sin and Mercy," esp. 129–32; and Murphy, "Sin, Repentance, and Forgiveness in Sirach."

61. For a positive "turn" to God, see 17:25–26. For the other cases see the discussion that follows. Much of the Hebrew of Ben Sira must be reconstructed from the Greek. But the very variety of the phraseology suggests similar underlying divergences in the original. For a Hebrew reconstruction, see Segal, *Complete Book of Ben Sira* (Hebrew). For the existing Hebrew manuscripts, see Beentjes, *Book of Ben Sira in Hebrew.*

62. For linguistic innovation in Ben Sira, see Hurvitz, "The Linguistic Status of Ben Sira," 72–86.

63. For overviews of the question of Hellenistic influence on Ben Sira, see Sanders, "Concerning Ben Sira"; Goff, "Hellenistic Instruction in Palestine and Egypt"; Mattila, "Ben Sira and the Stoics"; and Wicke-Reuter, *Göttliche Providenz und menschliche Verantwortung bei Ben Sira und in der Frühen Stoa.*

64. For a similar sentiment, see Ben Sira 5:7. Also, for this reconstruction, compare there the Greek to the original Hebrew.

65. For a discussion of this inscription, see Pleše, *Poetics of the Gnostic Universe,* 256n117.

66. A similar practice appears in Jerome and other translators. See, further, chapter 4n40.

67. See the earlier discussion of this verse in chapter 3. For more on the history of the interpretation of this verse, see Hayes, "Midrashic Career of the Confession of Judah [Pt. I]," 67–70, and "Midrashic Career of the Confession of Judah [Pt. II]," 174–87; Kugel, *Traditions of the Bible,* 453–55; and Menn, *Judah and Tamar,* 242–56.

68. See Anderson, "Intentional and Unintentional Sin in the Dead Sea Scrolls."

69. Pleše, *Poetics of the Gnostic Universe,* 249. This motion also helps explain the unusual interpretation of Gen. 3:19 in Genesis Rabba 20:10 where "sweat" (*z 'h*), understood as the word for "shake" (*zy '*), is said to signify "repentance."

70. Translations of the *Testaments* are from Kugel, "*Testaments of the Twelve Patriarchs,*" 2:1697–1855. See, also, *T. Simeon* 4:2.

71. See also Deut. 9:18–20 and Dan. 10:2

72. For other studies of the Day of Atonement and its early history, see Schiffman, "Case of the Day of Atonement Ritual"; Baumgarten, "Yom Kippur in the Qumran Scrolls and Second Temple Sources"; and Hieke and Nicklas, *Day of Atonement.*

73. Foucault, *Discipline and Punish,* 28–31. See, further, the discussion of a positive role for the body in Hellenistic Jewish discourse, otherwise known for its emphasis

on the soul, in Mirguet, "Introductory Reflections on Embodiment in Hellenistic Judaism."

74. On this question, see Kugel, *Ladder of Jacob,* 152–65; and Kugel, "Some Translation and Copying Mistakes." See, also, the further suggestion in Marcus, "*Testaments of the Twelve Patriarchs* and the *Didascalia Apostolorum*."

75. See, further, Lambert, "Topics in the History of Repentance," 157–93.

76. See further the discussion of *exempla* in chapter 5.

77. On the interiorization of sexuality as "desire" in the *Testaments,* see Rosen-Zvi, "Bilhah the Temptress."

78. See, also, *T. Simeon* 3:4.

79. 4:3–6:2, following the text published in Anderson, "Life of Adam and Eve," *Outside the Bible,* 2:1331–58.

80. A parallel appears in b. Sanhedrin 103a. For further discussion of the theme of Manasseh as a penitent sinner, see Milikowsky, *Seder Olam,* 386 and n. 12.

81. *On Penitence,* 9. On repentance in Tertullian, see Stroumsa, "From Repentance to Penance in Early Christianity." It also bears some similarity to the medieval penitential practices of Jewish pietists in German lands. See Marcus, *Piety and Society.*

82. E.g., *T. Reuben* 2:1.

83. For the case of 2 Mac. 9:11–17, Antiochus's supposed repentance, see later in this chapter.

84. On occasion, this ambivalence around "repentance" has been noted by historians. See Cohen, *From the Maccabees to the Mishnah,* 88–92. But there is still a tendency to end up asserting its normativity on account of its supposed basis in scriptural sources.

85. See, e.g., the lines of connection explored in Weinfeld, *Organizational Pattern and the Penal Code of the Qumran Sect.*

86. *War* 2:119–161. For a recent treatment of this important passage and other related texts, see Klawans, *Josephus and the Theologies of Ancient Judaism,* esp. 1–43.

87. Pliny, *Natural History* 5, 17, 4 (73). Translation from Vermes and Goodman, *The Essenes according to the Classical Sources,* 33. For the connection between the Essene group described above and the Qumran sect, see Taylor, "On Pliny, the Essene Location and Kh. Qumran."

88. "Grammaticalization" is a widely discussed phenomenon. See, e.g., Fortson, "Approach to Semantic Change," esp. 656.

89. For another example involving Hebrew and Aramaic, see Bar-Asher, "Mishnaic Hebrew," 391.

90. See Kutscher, *Words and Their History,* 76–77.

91. See, the entry, "שוב," in Jastrow, *Dictionary of the Targumim,* 1528.

92. See Sokoloff, "חזר,"*Dictionary of Jewish Palestinian Aramaic of the Byzantine Period,* 195; "הדר,"*Dictionary of Jewish Babylonian Aramaic of the Talmudic and Geonic Periods,* 367. See, also, "חזר" and "תוב,"Tal, *Dictionary of Samaritan Aramaic,* 1:261–62 and 2:943, respectively. For the term in Syriac, see Smith, *Syriac Dictionary,* 606.

93. See, e.g., Targum Onkelos to Gen. 6:6.

94. For a study of this work, see van der Horst and Newman, *Early Jewish Prayers in Greek,* 147–64. See, further, Newman, "Form and Settings of the Prayer of Manasseh," 2:105–25.

95. Compare Davila, "Is the Prayer of Manasseh a Jewish Work?"

96. Van der Horst and Newman, *Early Jewish Prayers in Greek,* 174, also note the unusual quality of this pronouncement.

97. Compare the comments of van der Horst and Newman, *Early Jewish Prayers in Greek*, 171.

98. For the potential of repentance as a universalist theme, see Sterling, "Turning to God," 69–95.

99. On processes of internalization related to demonology in rabbinic texts, see Rosen-Zvi, *Demonic Desires*. Rosen-Zvi offers an important complication of the internalization theory, one that I accept: we are, by no means, dealing with a full-fledged notion of an "inner self" at this stage (esp. 127–34). At the same time, it complicates the thesis proposed by Boyarin in *Carnal Israel* that dualism within Judaism really only arrives in the Middle Ages with the renewed contact between Greek philosophy and the Jews (esp. 29).

100. There are many studies that identify as a topic and, generally, celebrate the place of repentance in rabbinic literature. See Schechter, *Some Aspects of Rabbinic Theology*, 313–43; Moore, *Judaism*, 507–34; and Urbach, *Sages*, 462–71. These studies invariably see the rabbis as heightening what is already present in the Bible and, therefore, miss the ways in which such a discourse brings into effect a new form of the subject. Also, see the collection of texts available in Bialik and Ravnitzky, *Book of Legends*, 556–61. See, further, for a recent overview, Morgan, "Mercy, Repentance, and Forgiveness in Ancient Judaism."

101. See Weinfeld, "Prayers for Knowledge," 186–200; and Reuven Kimelman, "Penitential Part of the Amidah and Personal Redemption," in Boda and Werline, *Seeking the Favor of God*, 3:71–84.

102. Note, for instance, the collection of homilies for the Sabbath occurring in that period in Pesiqta de-Rav Kahana, Pisqa 24. See, esp., 24:3.

103. On the place of Ben Sira among the Rabbis, see, most recently, Labendz, "Book of Ben Sira in Rabbinic Literature."

104. Another example, aside from *teshuva*, would be the concept of *kavvana*, "intention." See Eilberg-Schwartz, *Human Will in Judaism*; and Zahavy, "*Kavvanah* for Prayer in the Mishnah and Talmud." For studies on individuality in rabbinic literature, see Fonrobert, "'Humanity Was Created as an Individual;'" and Balberg, "Pricing Persons."

105. See further Adam's "discovery" of *teshuva* as an existent in Genesis Rabba 22:13, "so great is the power of repentance, and I didn't know!" Similarly, in the homilies on repentance found in Pesiqta de-Rav Kahana, Anisfeld notes an emphasis on "indulgence" rather than "rebuke" (*Sustain Me with Raisin-Cakes*, 87–90).

106. The history of another rabbinic phrase, *ḥazar bi-tshuva*, commonly used in Amoraic texts, requires further thought. On the one hand, it poses a difficulty in that it is essentially a double rendering of the original, biblical *shuv*, as verb and noun. On the other hand, the term *ḥazar*, "return" but also "regret," as discussed earlier, more clearly conveys a sense of "repentance" and fits common Aramaic usage well. *Ḥazar bi-tshuva* could be a later attempt to restore greater semantic sense to the somewhat stilted *ʿaśa teshuva*, while maintaining the traditional nominalization, *teshuva*.

107. Levenson, "Did God Forgive Adam?" 165. An extended similar argument can be found in Bowman, "Significance of Teshubah." Compare the definition in Urbach, *Sages*, 464.

108. Barr, *Semantics*, 109 and, further, 107–60.

109. One notes further even the similarities of the rabbinic verbal phrase and the Latin, *agere paenitentiam*.

110. Y. Taʿan 65b, Gen. Rab. 44:12, and Pesiq. Rab Kah. 28:3.

111. Here we encounter the older verbal form of *shuv*, without a preposition, in the same usage as that found in Ben Sira, which does appear occasionally in the Mishna.
112. See, further, Ruzer, "Death Motif."
113. For more on the story of Nebuchadnezzar in the book of Daniel and especially its history of interpretation, see Henze, *Madness of King Nebuchadnezzar.*
114. Of course, scholars have tended to elide this form of transformation into the later idea of repentance. See, for instance, the comments to 2 Macc. 9:11–17 in Schwartz, *2 Maccabees,* 350 and 361.
115. Its opposite is probably found in another common phrase, "whole [i.e., sincere] repentance" (*teshuva sheleima*), e.g., y. Berakhot 7:4. See Muffs, *Love & Joy,* 176, for the root, *šlm,* as indicating "proper intent."
116. Note the usage, for instance, in the sixth blessing of the daily ʿamida prayer.
117. See Midrash Tehillim 90:12; and b. Pesahim 54a.
118. See, e.g., b. Shabbat 56b.
119. See Abraham J. Malherbe, "Gentle as a Nurse."
120. The identity of "heretics" in rabbinic Judaism has received extensive treatment. See, most recently, Schremer, "Wayward Jews."
121. See, e.g., m. Nedarim 9:3, t. Sheviʿit 8:11, t. Bava Qamma 8:15, 10:39, t. Bava Metziʿa 5:25, and b. Bava Qamma 80a.
122. B. Bava Metziʿa 84a.
123. See the perceptive discussion of the "Sinners of Israel" in Stern, *Jewish Identity in Early Rabbinic Writings,* 120–35.
124. On missionizing in general and its relative absence in ancient forms of Judaism, see Goodman, *Mission and Conversion.*
125. See, further, Smith, *Drudgery Divine,* 54–84.
126. Barr, *Semantics of Biblical Language,* 257.
127. On the fundamentally antisemitic leanings of this great work of German scholarship, see Meeks, "Nazi New Testament Professor Reads His Bible," esp. 534–43.
128. Behm, "μετανοέω, μετάνοια," *TDNT,* 4:1002–3.
129. Luther, *Luther's Works,* 48:66–67. A helpful discussion of these sources is found in Dirksen, "New Testament Concept of Metanoia," 73.
130. In this regard, note the comment of Bovon, *Luke,* 279, about the tendency of Protestant scholars to overemphasize the role of grace in Luke's notion of *metanoia.*
131. See, e.g., the argument about penitential ritual in Hägerland, "Jesus and the Rites of Repentance," which is really based on an exceptionalist reading of the meaning of *metanoia* in the Synoptic Gospels (170–71). The same holds for the definition of *metanoia* in the study of other early Christian works. See, for instance, the discussion of its meaning in Osiek, *Shepherd of Hermas,* 29–30.
132. Luter, "Repentance," *Anchor Bible Dictionary,* 5:673.
133. Gench, "Repentance in the NT," *New Interpreter's Dictionary of the Bible,* 4:763.
134. Spicq, "μετανοέω, μετάνοια," *TLNT,* 2:475.
135. See, further, Luke 13:1–5.
136. Consider, also, e.g., Luke 24:47 and Acts 11:18.
137. E.g., Rev 2:16. Note, also, for instance, 1 Clement 57:1.
138. For further examples, see Ben Sira 17:25–26; and *Letter of Aristeas* 188–89.
139. See, further, Bovon, *Luke the Theologian,* 279; and Nave, *Role and Function of Repentance in Luke-Acts,* 1–6.

140. Note the close connections between the *Wisdom of Solomon* passage and 2 Tim 2:24–26.

141. One model for such an approach can be found in Achtemeier, "Apocalyptic Shift in Early Christian Tradition."

142. On reproof in the late Second Temple period, see Kugel, "On Hidden Hatred and Open Reproach"; and Kister, "Divorce, Reproof, and Other Sayings in the Synoptic Gospels." It is noteworthy that repentance, an inner assent of the sinner, is not required in Lev. 19:17 or, significantly, in Matt. 18:15–17, 21–22, but does appear in the Lukan version, 17:3–4, as well as *T. Gad* 6:3–4. This would appear to be a later addition to a traditional practice of rebuke. See, also, the rebuke formula in Rev. 3:19.

143. See also 2 Peter 3:9.

144. See also Luke 24:47.

145. For a translation and introduction to the work, see Osiek, *Shepherd of Hermas*.

146. On connections between the *Shepherd of Hermas* and rabbinic texts concerning the internalization of demons, see Rosen-Zvi, *Demonic Desires*, 55–58.

147. For the subsequent significance of this theme in monastic circles, see Torrance, "Angel and the Spirit of Repentance."

148. See, further, Rüpke, "Fighting for Differences," esp. 329.

149. This point emerges with particular clarity in the Christian basis of the comparative study of religion. See Masuzawa, *Invention of World Religions*.

BIBLIOGRAPHY

Achtemeier, Paul J. "An Apocalyptic Shift in Early Christian Tradition: Reflections on Some Canonical Evidence." *Catholic Biblical Quarterly* 45 (1983): 231–48.

Ahearne-Kroll, Patricia. "Joseph and Aseneth." In *Outside the Bible: Ancient Jewish Writings Related to Scripture*, ed. L. H. Feldman, J. L. Kugel, and L. H. Schiffman, 2525–89. Philadelphia: Jewish Publication Society, 2013.

———. "Joseph and Aseneth and Jewish Identity in Greco-Roman Egypt." Ph.D. dissertation, University of Chicago Divinity School, 2005.

Allison, Dale C. "Jesus and the Covenant: A Response to E. P. Sanders." *Journal for the Study of the New Testament* 29 (1987): 57–78.

———. *Jesus of Nazareth: Millenarian Prophet*. Minneapolis: Fortress Press, 1998.

Alter, Robert. *The Art of Biblical Narrative*. New York: Basic Books, 1981.

Altieri, Charles. *Canons and Consequences: Reflections on the Ethical Force of Imaginative Ideals*. Evanston, IL: Northwestern University Press, 1990.

Andersen, Francis I. "The Socio-Juridicial Background of the Naboth Incident." *Journal of Biblical Literature* 85 (1966): 46–57.

Andersen, Francis I., and David Noel Freedman. *Amos: A New Translation with Introduction and Commentary*. New York: Doubleday, 1989.

Anderson, Gary. *A Time to Mourn, A Time to Dance: The Expression of Grief and Joy in Israelite Religion*. University Park: Pennsylvania State University Press, 1991.

———. *Charity: The Place of the Poor in the Biblical Tradition*. New Haven, CT: Yale University Press, 2013.

———. "Intentional and Unintentional Sin in the Dead Sea Scrolls." In *Pomegranates and Golden Bells: Studies in Biblical, Jewish, and Near Eastern Ritual, Law, and Literature in Honor of Jacob Milgrom*, ed. David P. Wright, David Noel Freedman, and Avi Hurvitz, 49–64. Winona Lake, IN: Eisenbrauns, 1995.

———. *Sin: A History*. New Haven, CT: Yale University Press, 2009.

———. "The Penitence Narrative in *The Life of Adam and Eve*." *Hebrew Union College Annual* 63 (1992): 1–38.

———. "Two Notes on Measuring Character and Sin at Qumran." In *Things Revealed: Studies in Early Jewish and Christian Literature in Honor of Michael E. Stone*, ed. Ester G. Chazon, David Satran, and Ruth A. Clements, 141–47. Leiden: Brill, 2004.

Anisfeld, Rachel A. *Sustain Me with Raisin-Cakes: Pesikta deRav Kahana and the Popularization of Rabbinic Judaism*. Leiden: Brill, 2009.

Aretxage, Begoña. "Dirty Protest: Symbolic Overdetermination and Gender in Northern Ireland Ethnic Violence." *Ethos* 23 (1995): 123–48.

Aristotle. *Nicomachean Ethics*. Trans. H. Rackham. Loeb Classical Library. Cambridge, MA: Harvard University Press, 1982 [1934].

Asad, Talal. *Formations of the Secular: Christianity, Islam, Modernity*. Stanford, CA: Stanford University Press, 2003.

———. *Genealogies of Religion: Discipline and Reasons of Power in Christianity and Islam*. Baltimore: Johns Hopkins University Press, 1993.

Assmann, Jan. "Confession in Ancient Egypt." In *Transformations of the Inner Self in Ancient Religions*, ed. Jan Assmann and G. G. Stroumsa, 231–44. Leiden: Brill, 1999.

Auerbach, Erich. *Mimesis: The Representation of Reality in Western Literature*. Trans. W. R. Trask. Princeton, NJ: Princeton University Press, 2003.

Austin, J. L. *How to Do Things with Words*. Cambridge, MA: Harvard University Press, 1962.

Balberg, Mira. "Pricing Persons: Consecration, Compensation, and Individuality in the Mishnah." *Jewish Quarterly Review* 103, no. 2 (2013): 169–95.

Balentine, Samuel E. *Prayer in the Hebrew Bible: The Drama of Divine-Human Encounter*. Minneapolis: Fortress Press, 1993.

———. "The Prophet as Intercessor: A Reassessment." *Journal of Biblical Literature* 103 (1984): 161–73.

Bar-Asher, Moshe. "Mishnaic Hebrew: An Introductory Survey. "In *Cambridge History of Judaism IV: The Late Roman-Rabbinic Period*, ed. Steven T. Katz, 369–403. Cambridge: Cambridge University Press, 2006.

Barr, James. *The Semantics of Biblical Language*. Oxford: Oxford University Press, 1961.

Barstad, Hans M. "*Sic dicit dominus:* Mari Prophetic Texts and the Hebrew Bible." In *Essays on Ancient Israel in Its Near Eastern Context: A Tribute to Nadav Na'aman*, ed. Yairah Amit, Ehud Ben Zvi, Israel Finkelstein, and Oded Lipschits, 21–52. Winona Lake, IN: Eisenbrauns, 2006.

———. *The Religious Polemics of Amos*. Leiden: Brill, 1984.

Barton, John. *Oracles of God: Perceptions of Ancient Prophecy in Israel after the Exile*. London: Darton, Longman and Todd, 1986.

———. "Prophecy and Theodicy." In *Thus Says the Lord: Essays on the Former and Latter Prophets in Honor of Robert R. Wilson*, ed. J. J. Ahn and S. L. Cook, 73–86. New York: T & T Clark, 2009.

———. "The Prophets and the Cult." In *Temple and Worship in Biblical Israel*, ed. John Day, 111–22. New York: T & T Clark, 2005.

Barthes, Roland. "The Death of the Author." In *Image-Music-Text*, ed. and trans. Stephen Heath, 142–48. New York: Hill & Wang, 1977.

Baumgarten, Joseph. "Yom Kippur in the Qumran Scrolls and Second Temple Sources." *Dead Sea Discoveries* 6, no. 2 (1999): 184–91.

Bautch, Richard J. *Developments in Genre between Post-Exilic Penitential Prayers and the Psalms of Communal Lament*. Atlanta: Society of Biblical Literature, 2003.

Beentjes, Pancratius. *The Book of Ben Sira in Hebrew: A Text Edition of All Extant Hebrew Manuscripts and a Synopsis of all Parallel Hebrew Ben Sira Texts*. Leiden: Brill, 1997.

Berlin, Adele. *Lamentations: A Commentary*. Louisville: Westminster John Knox Press, 2002.

———. "On the Meaning of *pll* in the Bible." *Revue Biblique* 96 (1989): 345–51.

Berlin, Adele, Marc Zvi Brettler, and Michael Fishbane, eds. *The Jewish Study Bible*. Oxford: Oxford University Press, 2004.

Bernstein, Moshe J. "Noah and the Flood at Qumran." In *The Provo International Conference on the Dead Sea Scrolls: Technological Innovations, New Texts, and Reformulated Issues*, ed. D. W. Parry and E. Ulrich, 199–231. Leiden: Brill, 1999.

Bialik, H. N., and Y. H. Ravnitzky, eds. *The Book of Legends: Sefer ha-Aggadah: Legends from the Talmud and Midrash.* Trans. W. G. Braude. New York: Schocken, 1992.

Birnbaum, Ellen. *The Place of Judaism in Philo's Thought: Israel, Jews, and Proselytes.* Atlanta: Scholars Press, 1996.

Bland, Miryam. *Evil Within and Without: The Source of Sin and Its Nature as Portrayed in Late Second Temple Literature.* Göttingen: Vandenhoeck & Ruprecht, 2013.

Blenkinsopp, Joseph. *A History of Prophecy in Israel.* Louisville: Westminster John Knox Press, 1996.

———. *Isaiah 1–39: A New Translation with Introduction and Commentary.* New York: Doubleday, 2000.

Boda, Mark J. "Confession as Theological Expression: Ideological Origins of Penitential Prayer." In *Seeking the Favor of God, Vol. 1: The Origins of Penitential Prayer in Second Temple Judaism*, ed. Mark J. Boda and Rodney A. Werline, 27–34. Atlanta: Society of Biblical Literature, 2006.

———. "Penitential Innovations within the Twelve." In *On Stone and Scroll: Essays in Honour of Graham Ivor Davies*, ed. J. K. Aiken, Katharine J. Dell, and Brian A. Mastin, 391–407. Berlin: De Gruyter, 2011.

———. *Praying the Tradition: The Origin and Use of Tradition in Nehemiah 9.* Berlin: De Gruyter, 1999.

———. "Words and Meanings: ידה in Hebzrew Research." *Westminster Theological Journal* 57 (1995): 277–97.

Boda, Mark J., and G. T. Smith, eds. *Repentance in Christian Theology.* Collegeville, MN: Liturgical Press, 2006.

Boda, Mark J., and Rodney A. Werline, eds. *Seeking the Favor of God.* Vol. 1, *The Origins of Penitential Prayer in Second Temple Judaism.* Atlanta: Society of Biblical Literature, 2006.

———. *Seeking the Favor of God.* Vol. 2, *The Development of Penitential Prayer in Second Temple Judaism.* Atlanta: Society of Biblical Literature, 2007.

———. *Seeking the Favor of God.* Vol. 3, *The Impact of Penitential Prayer beyond Second Temple Judaism.* Atlanta: Society of Biblical Literature, 2009.

Borg, Marcus J. *Jesus in Contemporary Scholarship.* Valley Forge, PA: Trinity Press International, 1994.

Bovan, François. *Luke The Theologian: Thirty-Three Years of Research (1950–1983).* Trans. Ken McKinney. Allison Park, PA: Pickwick, 1987.

Bowman, John. "The Significance of Teshubah." *Abr-Nahrain* 15 (1974–1975): 27–34.

Boyarin, Daniel. *Border Lines: The Partition of Judaeo-Christianity.* Philadelphia: University of Pennsylvania Press, 2004.

———. *Carnal Israel: Reading Sex in Talmudic Culture.* Berkeley: University of California Press, 1993.

Boyarin, Daniel, and Elizabeth Castelli. "Foucault's *The History of Sexuality*: The Fourth Volume, or a Field Left Fallow for Others to Till." *Journal of the History of Sexuality* 10 (2001): 357–64.

Boyce, R. N. *The Cry to God in the Old Testament.* Atlanta: Scholars Press, 1988.

Brettler, Marc. "Interpretation and Prayer: Notes on the Composition of 1 Kings 8:15–53." In *Minḥah le-Naḥum: Biblical and Other Studies Presented to Nahum M. Sarna in Honour of His 70th Birthday*, ed. Marc Brettler and Michael Fishbane, 16–35. Sheffield, UK: JSOT Press, 1993.

———. "Predestination in Deuteronomy 30.1–10." *Journal for the Study of the Old Testament Supplement Series* (1999): 171–88.

Brongers, Hendrik A. "Fasting in Israel in Biblical and Post-Biblical Times." In *Instruction and Interpretation: Studies in Hebrew Language, Palestinian Archaeology and Biblical*

Exegesis: Papers Read at the Joint British-Dutch Old Testament Conference Held at Louvain, 1976, from 30 August to 2 September, ed. Hendrick A. Brongers, 1–21. Leiden: E. J. Brill, 1977.

Brooks, Peter. *Troubling Confessions: Speaking Guilt in Law and Literature*. Chicago: University of Chicago Press, 2000.

Brueggemann, Walter. "A Shape for Old Testament Theology, I: Structure Legitimation." *Catholic Biblical Quarterly* 47 (1985): 28–46.

———. "A Shape for Old Testament Theology, II: Embrace of Pain." *Catholic Biblical Quarterly* 47 (1985): 395–415.

Bultmann, Rudolf. *The History of the Synoptic Tradition*. Trans. J. Marsh. Oxford: Basil Blackwell, 1963.

Butler, Judith. *Gender Trouble: Feminism and the Subversion of Identity*. New York: Routledge, 1990.

Buttrick, G. A. *The Interpreter's Dictionary of the Bible*. 4 vols. Nashville: Abingdon, 1962.

Carasik, Michael. "The Limits of Omniscience." *Journal of Biblical Literature* 119 (2000): 221–32.

Charlesworth, James H. "The Historical Jesus in Light of Writings Contemporaneous with Him." *Aufstieg und Niedergang der römischen Welt* 25 (1982): 451–76.

Chazon, Esther G. "Is *Divrei Ha-Me'orot* a Sectarian Prayer?" In *The Dead Sea Scrolls: Forty Years of Research*, ed. D. Dimant and U. Rappaport, 3–17. Leiden: Brill, 1992.

Chesnutt, Randall D. *From Death to Life: Conversion in "Joseph and Aseneth."* Sheffield, UK: Sheffield Academic Press, 1995.

Childs, Brevard S. *Introduction to the Old Testament as Scripture*. Philadelphia: Fortress Press, 1979.

Chilton, Bruce D. "Jesus and the Repentance of E. P. Sanders." *Tyndale Bulletin* 39 (1988): 1–18.

Choi, J. D. *Jesus' Teaching on Repentance*. Binghamton, NY: Global Publications, 2000.

Christensen, Duane L. *Transformations of the War Oracle in the Old Testament Prophecy*. Ann Arbor, MI: Scholars Press, 1975.

Cicero. Trans. Louis E. Lord et al. Loeb Classical Library. 28 vols. Cambridge, MA: Harvard University Press, 1967.

Clifford, Richard J. *Proverbs: A Commentary*. Louisville: Westminster John Knox Press, 1999.

Cogan, Mordechai. *1 Kings: A New Translation with Introduction and Commentary*. New York: Doubleday, 2001.

Cohen, Hermann. *Reason and Hope: Selections from the Jewish Writings of Hermann Cohen*. Trans. Eva Jospe. New York: Norton, 1971.

Cohen, Shaye D. *From the Maccabees to the Mishnah*. 2nd ed. Louisville: Westminster John Knox Press, 2006.

———. *The Beginnings of Jewishness: Boundaries, Varieties, Uncertainties*. Berkeley: University of California Press, 1999.

———. "The Significance of Yavneh: Pharisees, Rabbis, and the End of Jewish Sectarianism." *Hebrew Union College Annual* 55 (1984): 27–53.

Collins, John J. *The Apocalyptic Imagination: An Introduction to the Jewish Matrix of Christianity*. New York: Crossroad, 1984.

———. *The Bible after Babel: Historical Criticism in a Postmodern Age*. Grand Rapids, MI: W. B. Eerdmans, 2005.

Coogan, Michael David, and Mark S. Smith. *Stories from Ancient Canaan*. Louisville: Westminster Press, 2012.

Copenhaver, Brian P. *Hermetica: The Greek* Corpus Hermeticum *and the Latin* Asclepius *in a New English Translation, with Notes and Introduction*. Cambridge: Cambridge University Press, 1992.

Cottrill, Amy C. *Language, Power, and Identity in the Lament Psalms of the Individual*. New York: T & T Clark, 2008.

———. "The Articulate Body: The Language of Suffering in the Laments of the Individual." In *Lamentations in Ancient and Contemporary Cultural Contexts*, ed. Nancy C. Lee and Carleen Mandolfo, 103–22. Leiden: Brill, 2008.

Creach, Jerome F. D. *Yahweh as Refuge and the Editing of the Hebrew Psalter*. Sheffield, UK: Sheffield Academic Press, 1996.

Crenshaw, James L. *Joel*. New York: Doubleday, 1995

Cross, Frank Moore. *Canaanite Myth and Hebrew Epic: Essays in the History of the Religion of Israel*. Cambridge, MA: Harvard University Press, 1973.

Crossan, John Dominic. *The Birth of Christianity: Discovering What Happened in the Years Immediately after the Execution of Jesus*. New York: HarperSanFranciso, 1998.

Dalglish, Edward R. *Psalm Fifty-One in the Light of Ancient Near Eastern Patternism*. Leiden: Brill, 1962.

Daube, David. "Judas." *California Law Review* 82, no. 1 (1994): 95–108.

Davenport, Gene L. *The Eschatology of the Book of Jubilees*. Leiden: Brill, 1971.

Davila, James R. "Is the Prayer of Manasseh a Jewish Work?" In *Heavenly Tablets: Interpretation, Identity and Tradition in Ancient Judaism*, ed. Lynn LiDonnici and Andrea Lieber, 75–86. Leiden: Brill, 2007.

Dentan, Robert C. "The Literary Affinities of Exodus XXXIV 6f." *Vetus Testamentum* 13 (1963): 34–51.

Derrida, Jacques. "On Forgiveness." In *Cosmopolitanism and Forgiveness*, 27–60. London: Routledge, 2001.

———. "What Is a 'Relevant' Translation?" In *The Translation Studies Reader*, ed. Lawrence Venuti, 423–46. New York: Routledge, 2004.

de Ward, Eileen F. "Eli's Rhetorical Question: 1 Sam. 2:25." *Journal of Jewish Studies* 27, no. 2 (1976): 117–37.

Dietrich, Erich. *Die Umkehr (Bekehrung und Busse) im Alten Testament und im Judentum*. Stuttgart: W. Kohlhammer, 1936.

Dillon, John. *The Middle Platonists: A Study of Platonism, 80* B.C. *to* A.D. *220*. London: Duckworth, 1977.

Dimant, Devorah. "Noah in Early Jewish Literature." In *Biblical Figures Outside the Bible*, ed. M. E. Stone and T. A. Bergren, 123–50. Harrisburg, PA: Trinity, 1998.

Dirksen, Aloys H. "The New Testament Concept of Metanoia." Ph.D. dissertation, Catholic University of America, 1932.

Dodd, C. H. *The Bible and the Greeks*. London: Hodder & Stoughton, 1935.

Dozeman, Thomas B. *God at War: Power in the Exodus Tradition*. Oxford: Oxford University Press, 1996.

———. "Inner-Biblical Interpretation of Yahweh's Gracious and Compassionate Character." *Journal of Biblical Literature* 108, no. 2 (1989): 207–23.

Dunn, James D. G. *The New Perspective on Paul*. Grand Rapids, MI: Eerdmans, 2008.

Eagleton, Terry. *Literary Theory: An Introduction*. Minneapolis: University of Minnesota Press, 2008.

Eilberg-Schwartz, Howard. *The Human Will in Judaism: The Mishnah's Philosophy of Intention*. Atlanta: Scholars Press, 1986.

Eliade, Mercea, ed. *Encyclopedia of Religion*. 16 vols. New York: Macmillan, 1987.

Eshel, Esther. "Apotropaic Prayers in the Second Temple Period." In *Liturgical Perspectives: Prayer and Poetry in Light of the Dead Sea Scrolls*, ed. Esther G. Chazon, 69–88. Supplements to the Journal for the Study of Judaism 48. Leiden: Brill, 2003.

Feldman, Louis H. "Josephus' Portrait of Noah and Its Parallels in Philo, Pseudo-Philo's *Biblical Antiquities*, and Rabbinic Midrashim." *Proceedings of the American Academy for Jewish Research* 55 (1988): 31–57.

Fensham, F. Charles. "Widow, Orphan, and the Poor in Ancient Near Eastern Legal and Wisdom Literature." *Journal of Near Eastern Studies* 21 (1962): 129–39.

Firey, Abigail, ed. *A New History of Penance*. Leiden: Brill, 2008

Fish, Stanley. *Is There a Text in This Class? The Authority of Interpretive Communities*. Cambridge, MA: Harvard University Press, 1980.

Fishbane, Michael A. *Biblical Interpretation in Ancient Israel*. Oxford: Clarendon, 1985.

Fisher, Philip. *The Vehement Passions*. Princeton, NJ: Princeton University Press, 2002.

Fitzgerald, John T., and L. Michael White. *The Tabula of Cebes*. Chico, CA: Scholars Press, 1983.

Fleming, Daniel E. "The Etymological Origins of the Hebrew *nābî'*: The One Who Invokes God." *Catholic Biblical Quarterly* 55 (1993): 217–24.

Flusser, David. *Judaism and the Origins of Christianity*. Jerusalem: Magnes, 1988.

Fonrobert, Charlotte Elisheva. "'Humanity Was Created as an Individual': Synechdocal Individuality in the Mishnah as a Jewish Response to Romanization." In *The Individual in the Religions of the Ancient Mediterranean*, ed. Jörge Rüpke, 489–521. Oxford: Oxford University Press, 2013.

Fortson, Benjamin W., IV. "An Approach to Semantic Change." In *The Handbook of Historical Linguistics*, ed. B. D. Joseph and R. D. Janda, 648–66. Malden, MA: Blackwell, 2003.

Foucault, Michel. "About the Beginning of the Hermeneutics of the Self." In *Religion and Culture*, ed. J. R. Carrette, 158–81. New York: Routledge, 1999.

———. *Discipline and Punish*. Trans. Alan Sheridan. New York: Vintage, 1979.

———. "Technologies of the Self." In *Technologies of the Self: A Seminar with Michel Foucault*, ed. Luther H. Martin, Huck Gutman, and Patrick H. Hutton, 16–49 Amherst: University of Massachusetts Press, 1988.

———. *The Archaeology of Knowledge*. Trans. A. M. Sheridan Smith. London: Tavistock, 1972.

———. *The History of Sexuality, Volume 1: An Introduction*. Trans. R. Hurley. New York: Vintage, 1988.

———. *The History of Sexuality, Volume 2: The Use of Pleasure*. Trans. R. Hurley. New York: Vintage, 1990.

Fox, Michael V. *Proverbs 10–31*. New Haven, CT: Yale University Press, 2009.

Frankfort, Henri. *Kingship and the Gods*. Chicago: University of Chicago Press, 1948.

Fredricksen, Paula. *Jesus of Nazareth. King of the Jews: A Jewish Life and the Emergence of Christianity*. New York: Knopf, 2000.

Freedman, David Noel, ed. *Anchor Bible Dictionary*. 6 vols. New York: Doubleday, 1992.

Gadamer, Hans-Georg. "Reply to My Critics." In *The Hermeneutic Tradition: From Ast to Ricoeur*, ed. Gayle L. Ormiston and Aland D. Schrift, 273–97. Albany: State University of New York Press, 1990.

———. *Truth and Method*. New York: Continuum, 1975.

Gane, Roy. *Cult and Character: Purification Offerings, Day of Atonement, and Theodicy*. Winona Lake, IN: Eisenbrauns, 2005.

Gaventa, Beverly Roberts. *From Darkness to Light: Aspects of Conversion in the New Testament*. Philadelphia: Fortress, 1986.

Geertz, Clifford. *The Interpretation of Cultures*. New York: Basic Books, 1973.

Gesenius, Friedrich H. W., A. E. Cowley, and Emil F. Kautzsch. *Gesenius' Hebrew Grammar: As Edited and Enlarged by E. Kautzsch*. Oxford: Clarendon, 1982 [1910].

Gilbert, Maurice. "God, Sin, and Mercy: Sirach 15:11–18:14." In *Ben Sira's God Proceedings of the International Ben Sira Conference: Durham—Ushaw College 2001*, ed. R. Egger-Wenzel, 118–35. Berlin: de Gruyter, 2002.

Goff, Matthew J. "Hellenistic Instruction in Palestine and Egypt: Ben Sira and Papyrus Insinger." *Journal for the Study of Judaism* 36 (2005): 147–72.

Good, Mary-Jo DelVecchio, Paul E. Brodwin, Byron J. Good, and Arthur Kleinman, eds. *Pain as Human Experience: An Anthropological Perspective*. Berkeley: University of California Press, 1992.

Goodman, Martin. *Mission and Conversion: Proselytizing in the Religious History of the Roman Empire*. Oxford: Clarendon, 1994.

Gray, John. *I & II Kings: A Commentary*. London: SCM, 1970.

Green, Joel B., and Scot McKnight, eds. *Dictionary of Jesus and the Gospels*. Downers Grove, IL: Intervarsity, 1992.

Greenberg, Moshe. *Biblical Prose Prayer: As a Window to the Popular Religion of Ancient Israel*. Berkeley: University of California Press, 1983.

———. *Ezekiel 21–37: A New Translation with Introduction and Commentary*. New York: Doubleday, 1997.

———. "On the Refinement of the Conception of Prayer in Hebrew Scriptures." *Association of Jewish Studies Review* 1 (1976): 57–92.

Greenfield, Jonas C. "Adi balṭu: Care for the Elderly and Its Rewards." In *'Al Kanfei Yonah: Collected Studies of Jonas C. Greenfield on Semitic Philology*, ed. Šālôm M. Paul, Michael E. Stone, and Jonas C. Greenfield, 912–19, Boston: Brill, 2001

———. "The Zakir Inscription and the Danklied." In *'Al Kanfei Yonah: Collected Studies of Jones C. Greenfield on Semitic Philology*, ed. Shalom M. Paul, Michael E. Stone, and Jonas C. Greenfield, 75–92. Boston: Brill, 2001.

Greenfield, Jonas C., Michael E. Stone, and Esther Eshel, eds. *The Aramaic Levi Document: Edition, Translation, Commentary*. Leiden: Brill, 2004.

Greenspahn, Frederick E. "The Theology of the Framework of Judges." *Vetus Testamentum* 36, no. 4 (1986): 385–96.

Greenstein, Edward L. "Theories of Modern Bible Translation." *Prooftexts* 3, no. 1 (1983): 9–39.

Gunkel, Hermann, and Joachim Begrich. *Introduction to Psalms: The Genres of the Religious Lyric of Israel*. Trans. J. D. Nogalski. Macon, GA: Mercer University Press, 1998.

Gwaltney, W. C., Jr. "The Biblical Book of Lamentations in the Context of Near Eastern Lament Literature." In *Essential Papers on Israel and the Ancient Near East*, ed. Frederick E. Greenspahn, 242–65. New York: New York University Press, 1991.

Hadot, Pierre. *Philosophy as a Way of Life: Spiritual Exercises from Socrates to Foucault*. Oxford: Blackwell, 1995.

Hägerland, Tobias. "Jesus and the Rites of Repentance." *New Testament Studies* 52 (2006): 166–87.

Hahn, Scott. "Covenant in the Old and New Testaments: Some Recent Research (1994–2004)." *Currents in Biblical Research* 3, no. 2 (2005): 263–92.

Halberstam, Chaya. *Law and Truth in Biblical and Rabbinic Literature*. Bloomington: Indiana University Press, 2010.

Hallo, William H. "Individual Prayer in Sumerian: The Continuity of a Tradition." *Journal of the American Oriental Society* 88, no. 1 (1968): 71–89.

———. "Jonah and the Uses of Parody." In *Thus Says the Lord: Essays on the Former and Latter Prophets in Honor of Robert R. Wilson*, ed. J. J. Ahn and S. L. Cook, 285–91. New York: T & T Clark, 2009.

———. "Lamentations and Prayers in Sumer and Akkad." In *Civilizations of the Ancient Near East: Volume III*, ed. Jack M. Sasson, 1871–81. New York: Charles Scribner's Sons, 1995.

Halpern, Baruch. "Jerusalem and the Lineages in the Seventh Century BCE: Kinship and the Rise of Individual Moral Liability." In *Law and Ideology in Monarchic Israel*, ed. Baruch Halpern and Deborah W. Hobson, 11–107. Journal for the Study of the Old Testament Supplement Series 124. Sheffield, UK: JSOT Press, 1991.

———. *The Constitution of the Monarchy in Israel*. Ann Arbor, MI: Scholars Press, 1981.

Handelman, Dan. "Conceptual Alternatives to 'Ritual.'" In *Theorizing Rituals: Issues, Topics, Approaches, Concepts*, ed. J. Kreinath, Jan Snoek, and Michael Stausberg, 37–49. Leiden: Brill, 2006.

Haran, Menahem. *The Biblical Collection: Its Consolidation to the End of the Second Temple Times and Changes of Form to the End of the Middle Ages, Volume 2* (Hebrew). Jerusalem: Magness Press, 2003.

Harl, Marguerite. "Les origines grecques du most et de la notion de 'componction' dans la Septante et chez ses commentateurs (KATANUSSESTHAI)." *Revue des Études Augustiniennes* 32 (1986): 3–21.

Hastings, J., ed. *Encyclopedia of Religion and Ethics*. 13 vols. New York: Charles Scribner's Sons, 1908–1927.

Hayes, Christine. *Gentile Impurities and Jewish Identities: Intermarriage and Conversion from the Bible to the Talmud*. Oxford: Oxford University Press, 2002.

———. "Golden Calf Stories: The Relationship of Exodus 32 and Deuteronomy 9–10." In *The Idea of Biblical Interpretation: Essays in Honor of James L. Kugel*, ed. Hindy Najman and Judith H. Newman, 45–94. Supplements to the Journal for the Study of Judaism 83. Leiden: Brill, 2004.

———. "The Midrashic Career of the Confession of Judah [Pt. I]." *VT* 45, no. 1 (1995): 62–81.

———. "The Midrashic Career of the Confession of Judah [Pt. II]." *VT* 45, no. 2 (1995): 174–87.

Hedrick, C. W. "The Role of 'Summary Statements' in the Composition of the Gospel of Mark: A Dialogue with Karl Schmidt and Norman Perrin." *Novum Testamentum* 26, no. 4 (1984): 289–311.

Hengel, Martin. *Judaism and Hellenism: Studies in Their Encounter in Palestine during the Early Hellenistic Period*. Vol. 1. Philadelphia: Fortress, 1974.

Henze, Matthias. *The Madness of King Nebuchadnezzar: The Ancient Near Eastern Origins and Early History of Interpretation of Daniel 4*. Leiden: Brill, 1999.

Heschel, Abraham Joshua. *The Prophets*. New York: Harper & Row, 1969.

Hieke, Thomas, and Tobias Nicklas, eds. *The Day of Atonement: Its Interpretations in Early Jewish and Christian Traditions*. Leiden: Brill, 2012.

Hogewood, Jay C. "The Speech Act of Confession: Priestly Performative Utterance in Leviticus 16 and Ezra 9–10." In *Seeking the Favor of God. Vol 1, The Origins of Penitential Prayer in Second Temple Judaism*, ed. Mark J. Boda and Rodney A. Werline, 69–82. Atlanta: Society of Biblical Literature, 2006.

Holladay, William Lee. "Elusive Deuteronomists, Jeremiah, and Proto-Deuteronomy." *Catholic Biblical Quarterly* 66, no. 1 (2004): 55–77.

———. *The Root ŠÛBH in the Old Testament: With Particular Reference to Its Usages in Covenantal Context*. Leiden: Brill, 1958.

Holtz, Shalom E. "God as Refuge and the Temple as Refuge in the Psalms." In *In the Temple of Jerusalem: From Moses to the Messiah, In Honor of Professor Louis H. Feldman*, ed. Steven Fine, 17–26. Leiden: Brill, 2011.

———. "Prayer as a Plaintiff." *Vetus Testamentum* 61 (2011): 258–79.

Houston, Walter. "What Did the Prophets Think They Were Doing? Speech Acts and Prophetic Discourse in the Old Testament." *Biblical Interpretation* 1, no. 2 (1993): 167–88.

Hubbard, Moyer V. *New Creation in Paul's Letters and Thought*. Cambridge: Cambridge University Press, 2002.

Huehnergard, John. "On the Etymology and Meaning of Hebrew *nābî'*." *Eretz Israel* 26 (1999): 88–93.

Huffmon, Herbert B. "The Exclusivity of Divine Communication in Ancient Israel: False Prophecy in the Hebrew Bible and the Ancient Near East." In *Mediating between Heaven and Earth: Communication with the Divine in the Ancient Near East*, ed. C. L. Crouch, Jonathan Stökl, and Anna Elise Zernecke, 67–81. New York: T & T Clark, 2012.

Hunter, A. Vanlier. *Seek the Lord! A Study of the Meaning and Function of the Exhortations in Amos, Hosea, Isaiah, Micah, and Zephaniah*. Baltimore: St. Mary's Seminary and University, 1982.

Hurvitz, Avi. "The Linguistic Status of Ben Sira as a Link between Biblical and Mishnaic Hebrew: Lexicographical Aspects." In *The Hebrew of the Dead Sea Scrolls and Ben Sira: Proceedings of a Symposium Held at Leiden University, 11–14 December 1995*, ed. T. Muraoka and J. F. Elwold, 72–86. Leiden: Brill, 1997.

Jacobs, Mignon R. "YHWH's Call for Israel's 'Return': Command, Invitation, or Threat." *Horizons in Biblical Theology* 32 (2010): 17–32.

Jacobsen, Thorkild. *The Treasures of Darkness: A History of Mesopotamian Religion*. New Haven, CT: Yale University Press, 1976.

Jacobson, Arland. "The Literary Unity of Q." *Journal of Biblical Literature* 101 (1982): 365–89.

James, William. *Varieties of Religious Experience: A Study in Human Nature*. London: Routledge, 2002.

Janzen, David. "The Condemnation of David's Taking in 2 Sam 12:1–14." *Journal of Biblical Literature* 131, no. 2 (2012): 209–20.

Japhet, Sara. *The Ideology of the Book of Chronicles and Its Place in Biblical Thought*. New York: P. Lang, 1989.

Jaques, Margaret. " 'To Talk to One's God': Penitential Prayers in Mesopotamia." In *Mediating between Heaven and Earth; Communication with the Divine in the Ancient Near East*, ed. C. L. Crouch, Jonathan Stökl, and Anna Elise Zernecke, 114–23. New York: T & T Clark, 2012.

Jastrow, Marcus. *A Dictionary of the Targumim, the Talmud Babli and Yerushalmi, and the Midrashic Literature*. London: Luzac, 1903.

Jenni, Ernst, and Claus Westermann, eds. *Theological Lexicon of the Old Testament*. Trans. M. E. Biddle. 3 vols. Peabody, MA: Hendrickson, 1997.

Josephus. *Jewish Antiquities*. Trans. Ralph Marcus et al. Loeb Classical Library. Cambridge, MA: Harvard University Press, 1927–1965.

Joyce, Paul. *Divine Initiative and Human Response in Ezekiel*. Sheffield, UK: Sheffield Academic Press, 1989.

Kaminsky, Joel S. *Corporate Responsibility in the Hebrew Bible*. Sheffield, UK: Sheffield Academic Press, 1995.

Keys, Gillian. *The Wages of Sin: A Reappraisal of the "Succession Narrative."* Sheffield, UK: Sheffield Academic Press, 1996.

Kister, Menahem. "Demons, Theology and Abraham's Covenant (CD 16:4–6 and Related Texts)." In *The Dead Sea Scrolls at Fifty: Proceedings of the 1997 Society of Biblical Literature Qumran Section Meetings*, ed. R. A. Kugler and E. M. Schuller, 167–84. Atlanta: Scholars Press, 1997.

———. "Divorce, Reproof, and Other Sayings in the Synoptic Gospels: Jesus Traditions in the Context of 'Qumranic' and Other Texts." In *Text, Thought, and Practice in Qumran and Early Christianity*, ed. R. A. Clements and D. R. Schwartz, 212–29. Leiden: Brill, 2009.

———. "Physical and Metaphysical Measurements Ordained by God in the Second Temple Period." In *Reworking the Bible: Apocryphal and Related Texts at Qumran*, ed. E. G. Chazon, Devorah Dimant, and Ruth A. Clements, 153–76. Leiden: Brill, 2005.

———. "Studies in 4QMiqṣat Maʿaśe Ha-Torah and Related Texts: Law, Theology, Language and Calendar Hebrew" (Hebrew). *Tarbiz* 68 (1999): 317–71.

___. "Two Formulae in the Book of Jubilees" (Hebrew). *Tarbiz* 70 (2001): 294–300.

Kittel, Gerhard, Geoffrey William Bromiley, and Gerhard Friedrich, eds. *Theological Dictionary of the New Testament*. Vols. 1–9. Grand Rapids, MI: Wm. B. Eerdmans, 1973.

Klawans, Jonathan. *Impurity and Sin in Ancient Judaism*. Oxford: Oxford University Press, 2000.

———. *Josephus and the Theologies of Ancient Judaism*. Oxford: Oxford University Press, 2013.

Kloppenborg, John S. *The Formation of Q: Trajectories in Ancient Wisdom Collections*. Philadelphia: Fortress, 1987.

Knibb, Michael. "The Exile in the Literature of the Intertestamental Period." *Heythrop Journal* 17 (1976): 253–72.

Knohl, Israel. *The Sanctuary of Silence: The Priestly Torah and the Holiness School*. Minneapolis: Fortress, 1995.

Konstan, David. *Before Forgiveness: The Origins of a Moral Idea*. Cambridge: Cambridge University Press, 2010.

Kraemer, Ross Shepard. *When Aseneth Met Joseph: A Late Antique Tale of the Biblical Patriarch and His Egyptian Wife, Reconsidered*. New York: Oxford University Press, 1998.

Kristeva, Julia. *Powers of Horror: An Essay on Abjection*. Trans. Leon Roudiez. New York: Columbia University Press, 1982.

Kugel, James L. *A Walk through Jubilees: Studies in the Book of Jubilees and the World of Its Creation*. Leiden: Brill, 2012.

———. *In Potiphar's House: The Interpretive Life of Biblical Texts*. San Francisco: Harper SanFrancisco, 1990.

———. "On Hidden Hatred and Open Reproach: Early Exegesis of Leviticus 19:17." *Harvard Theological Review* 80, no. 1 (1987): 43–61.

———. "Reuben's Sin with Bilhah in the Testament of Reuben." In *Pomegranates and Golden Bells: Studies in Biblical, Jewish, and Near Eastern Ritual, Law, and Literature in Honor of Jacob Milgrom*, ed. David P. Wright, David Noel Freedman, and Avi Hurvitz, 525–54. Winona Lake, IN: Eisenbrauns, 1995.

———. "Some Translation and Copying Mistakes from the Original Hebrew of the Testaments of the Twelve Patriarchs." In *The Dead Sea Scrolls: Transmission of*

Traditions and Production of Texts, ed. Sarianna Metso, Hindy Najman, and Eileen Schuller, 45–56. Leiden: Brill, 2010.

———. *The God of Old.* New York: Free Press, 2003.

———. "The Jubilees Apocalypse." *Dead Sea Discoveries* 1, no. 3 (1994): 322–37.

———. *The Ladder of Jacob: Ancient Interpretations of the Biblical Story of Jacob and His Children.* Princeton, NJ: Princeton University Press, 2006.

———. *Traditions of the Bible: A Guide to the Bible as It Was at the Start of the Common Era.* Cambridge, MA: Harvard University Press, 1998.

———. "Wisdom and the Anthological Temper." *Prooftexts* 17 (1997): 9–32.

Kugel, James L., Louis H. Feldman, and Lawrence Schiffman, eds. *Outside the Bible: Ancient Jewish Writings Related to Scripture.* Philadelphia: Jewish Publication Society, 2013.

Kuhn, Thomas S. *The Structure of Scientific Revolutions.* Chicago: University of Chicago Press, 1962.

Kutscher, E. Y. *Words and Their History* (Hebrew). Jerusalem: Kiryath-Sepher, 1974.

Labendz, Jenny R. "The Book of Ben Sira in Rabbinic Literature." *Association for Jewish Studies Review* 30, no. 2 (2006): 347–92.

Lambert, David A. "Did Israel Believe That Redemption Awaited Its Repentance? The Case of Jubilees 1." *Catholic Biblical Quarterly* 68, no. 4 (2006): 631–50.

———. "Fasting as a Penitential Rite: A Biblical Phenomenon?" *Harvard Theological Review* 96, no.4 (2003): 477–512.

———. "Topics in the History of Repentance: From the Hebrew Bible to Early Judaism and Christianity." Ph.D. dissertation, Harvard University, 2004.

———. "Was the Dead Sea Sect a Penitential Movement?" In *Oxford Handbook of the Dead Sea Scrolls*, ed. Timothy H. Lim and John J. Collins, 501–13. Oxford: Oxford University Press, 2010.

Lapin, Hayim. *Rabbis as Romans: The Rabbinic Movement in Palestine, 100–400 C.E.* New York: Oxford University Press, 2012.

Lapsley, Jacqueline E. *Can These Bones Live? The Problem of the Moral Self in the Book of Ezekiel.* Berlin: Walter de Gruyter, 2000.

Levenson, Jon D. *Creation and the Persistence of Evil: The Jewish Drama of Divine Omnipotence.* 2nd ed. Princeton, NJ: Princeton University Press, 1994.

———. "Did God Forgive Adam? An Exercise in Comparative Midrash." In *Jews and Christians: People of God*, ed. Carl E. Braaten and Robert W. Jenson, 148–70. Grand Rapids, MI: Eerdmans, 2003.

———. *Resurrection and the Restoration of Israel: The Ultimate Victory of the God of Life.* New Haven, CT: Yale University Press, 2006.

———. *The Death and Resurrection of the Beloved Son: The Transformation of Child Sacrifice in Judaism and Christianity.* New Haven, CT: Yale University Press, 1993.

Levine, Baruch. *The JPS Torah Commentary: Leviticus.* Philadelphia: Jewish Publication Society, 1989.

Levinson, Bernard M. *Legal Revision and Religious Renewal in Ancient Israel.* Cambridge: Cambridge University Press, 2008.

Licht, Jacob. "The Concept of Free Will in the Writings of the Sect of the Judean Desert" (Hebrew). In *Studies in the Dead Sea Scrolls: Lectures Delivered at the Third Annual Conference (1957) in Memory of E. L. Sukenik*, ed. Jacob Liver, 77–84. Jerusalem: Kiryat Sepher, 1957.

———. "Time and Eschatology in Apocalyptic Literature and in Qumran." *Journal of Jewish Studies* 16 (1965): 177–82.

Liddell, Henry George, and Robert Scott. *Greek-English Lexicon*. 9th ed. Oxford: Oxford University Press, 1948.

Limburg, James. *Jonah: A Commentary*. London: SCM Press, 1993.

Lindbeck, George. *The Nature of Doctrine: Religion and Theology in a Postliberal Age*. Philadelphia: Westminster, 1984.

Long, A. A. *Epictetus: A Stoic and Socratic Guide to Life*. Oxford: Oxford University Press, 2002.

Luther, Martin. *Luther's Works*. Vol. 48. Ed, Gottfried G. Krodel and Helmut T. Lehmann. Trans. Gottfried G. Krodel. Philadelphia: Fortress, 1963.

MacCulloch, John A. "Fasting." In *Encyclopedia of Religion and Ethics*, ed. J. Hastings, 759. Vol. 5. New York: Charles Scribner's Sons, 1912.

Mack, Burton L. "The Kingdom That Didn't Come: A Social History of the Q Tradents." *Society of Biblical Literature 1988 Seminar Papers* (1988): 608–35.

Mackenzie, Iain M. *The Idea of Pure Critique*. New York: Continuum, 2004.

Magness, Jodi. *The Archaeology of Qumran and the Dead Sea Scrolls*. Grand Rapids, MI: Eerdmans, 2002.

Malherbe, Abraham J. "Gentle as a Nurse: The Cynic Background to 1 Thess 2." *Novum Testamentum* 12, no. 2 (1970): 203–17.

———. *Light from the Gentiles: Hellenistic Philosophy and Early Christianity: Collected Essays, 1959–2012*. Vol. 1. Ed. C. R. Holladay, John T. Fitzgerald, Gregory E. Sterling, and James W. Thompson. Leiden: Brill, 2014.

———. *Paul and the Thessalonians: The Philosophic Tradition of Pastoral Care*. Philadelphia: Fortress, 1987.

Mandel, Paul. "The Origins of *Midrash* in the Second Temple Period." In *Current Trends in the Study of Midrash*, ed. Carol Bakhos, 9–34. Supplements to the Journal for the Study of Judaism 106. Leiden: Brill, 2006.

Mansfield, Mary C. *The Humiliation of Sinners: Public Penance in Thirteenth-Century France*. Ithaca: Cornell University Press, 1995.

Marcos, Natalio Fernández. *The Septuagint in Context: Introduction to the Greek Versions of the Bible*. Leiden: Brill, 2000.

Marcus, Ivan G. *Piety and Society: The Jewish Pietists of Medieval Germany*. Leiden: Brill, 1981.

Marcus, Joel. "*The Testaments of the Twelve Patriarchs* and the *Didascalia Apostolorum*: a Common Jewish Christian Milieu?" *Journal of Theological Studies* 61, no. 2 (2010): 596–626.

Martinez, Florentino Garcia, and Eibert J. C. Tigchelaar. *The Dead Scrolls: Study Edition*. Vol. 1. Leiden: Brill, 1997.

Martyn, J. Louis. *Divine and Human Agency in Paul and His Cultural Environment*. New York: T & T Clark, 2006.

Mason, Rex. *Preaching the Tradition: Homily and Hermeneutics after the Exile*. Cambridge: Cambridge University Press, 1990.

Masuzawa, Tomoko. *The Invention of World Religions; or, How European Universalism Was Preserved in the Language of Pluralism*. Chicago: University of Chicago Press, 2005.

Mattila, Sharon Lea. "Ben Sira and the Stoics: A Reexamination of the Evidence." *Journal of Biblical Literature* 119, no. 3 (2000): 473–501.

McCarthy, D. J. "II Sam. 7 and the structure of the Deuteronomic History." *Journal of Biblical Literature* 84 (1965): 131–38.

Meeks, Wayne A. "A Nazi New Testament Professor Reads His Bible: The Strange Case of Gerhard Kittel." In *The Idea of Biblical Interpretation: Essays in Honor of James L. Kugel*, ed. H. Najman and J. H. Newman, 513–44. Leiden: Brill, 2004.

———. *The First Urban Christians: The Social World of the Apostle Paul.* New Haven, CT: Yale University Press, 1983.

———. *The Origins of Christian Morality: The First Two Centuries.* New Haven, CT: Yale University Press, 1993.

Meier, John P. *A Marginal Jew.* Vol. 2, *Rethinking the Historical Jesus.* New York: Doubleday, 1994.

Menn, Esther. *Judah and Tamar (Genesis 38) in Ancient Jewish Exegesis: Studies in Literary Form and Hermeneutics.* Leiden: Brill, 1997.

Metso, Sarianna. *The Textual Development of the Qumran Community Rule.* Leiden: Brill, 1997.

Meyers, Carol. "Contesting the Notion of Patriarchy: Anthropology and the Theorizing of Gender in Ancient Israel." In *A Question of Sex? Gender and Difference in the Hebrew Bible and Beyond,* ed. Deborah W. Rooke. Sheffield, UK: Sheffield University Press, 2007.

Milgrom, Jacob. *Cult and Conscience: The* Asham *and the Priestly Doctrine of Repentance.* Leiden: Brill, 1976.

———. "Fasting and Fast Days." In *Encyclopedia Judaica,* 1190. Vol. 6. Jerusalem: Keter, 1974.

———. *Leviticus 1–16: A New Translation with Introduction and Commentary.* New York: Doubleday, 1991.

———. *Leviticus 23–27: A New Translation with Introduction and Commentary.* New York: Doubleday, 2001.

———. "Levitics 26 and Ezekiel." In *Quest for Context and Meaning: Studies in Biblical Intertextuality in Honor of James A. Sanders,* ed. Craig A. Evans and Shemaryahu Talmon, 57–62. Leiden: Brill, 1997.

———. "The Priestly Doctrine of Repentance." *Revue Biblique* 82:2 (1975): 186–205.

Milikowski, Chaim. *Seder Olam: Critical Edition, Commentary, and Introduction.* Jerusalem: Yad Ben-Zvi Press, 2013.

Miller, Patrick D. *Interpreting the Psalms.* Philadelphia: Fortress, 1986.

———. *They Cried to the Lord: The Form and Theology of Biblical Prayer.* Minneapolis: Fortress, 1994.

———. "Trouble and Woe: Interpreting the Biblical Laments." *Interpretation* 37 (1983): 32–45.

Mirguet, François. "Introductory Reflections on Embodiment in Hellenistic Judaism." *Journal for the Study of Pseudepigrapha* 21, no. 1 (2011): 5–19.

Moore, George Foot. *Judaism In the First Centuries of the Christian Era: The Age of the Tannaim.* Cambridge, MA: Harvard University Press, 1946.

Moran, William L. "Ancient Near Eastern Background of the Love of God in Deuteronomy." *Catholic Biblical Quarterly* 25, no. 1 (1963): 77–87.

Morgan, Michael L. "Mercy, Repentance, and Forgiveness in Ancient Judaism." In *Ancient Forgiveness: Classical, Judaic, and Christian,* ed. C. L. Griswold and D. Konstan, 144–56. Cambridge: Cambridge University Press, 2012.

Mowinckel, Sigmund. *The Psalms in Israel's Worship.* Oxford: Basil Blackwell, 1962.

Muffs, Yochanan. *Love & Joy: Law, Language, and Religion in Ancient Israel.* New York: Jewish Theological Seminary of America, 1992.

Murphy, Roland E. "Sin, Repentance, and Forgiveness in Sirach." In *Der Einzelne und seine Gemeinschaft bei Ben Sira,* ed. R. Egger-Wenzel and I. Krammer, 260–70. Berlin: de Gruyter, 1998.

Najman, Hindy. "La Recherche de la Perfection dans le Judaïsme Ancien." In *Élites Dans le Monde Biblique,* ed. Jean Riaud, 99–116. Paris: Honoré Champion, 2008.

Najman, Hindy. *Past Renewals: Interpretative Authority, Renewed Revelation, and the Quest for Perfection in Jewish Antiquity*. Leiden: Brill, 2010.

Nasuti, Harry P. *Defining the Sacred Songs: Genre, Tradition and the Post-Critical Interpretation of the Psalms*. Sheffield, UK: Sheffield Academic Press, 1999.

Nave, Guy D., Jr. *The Role and Function of Repentance in Luke-Acts*. Atlanta: Society of Biblical Literature, 2002.

Newman, Judith H. *Praying by the Book: The Scripturalization of Prayer in Second Temple Judaism*. Atlanta: Scholars Press, 1999.

Newsom, Carol. *The Self as Symbolic Space: Constructing Identity and Community at Qumran*. Leiden: Brill, 2004.

Nicholson, Ernest Wilson. *Preaching to the Exiles: A Study of the Prose Tradition in the Book of Jeremiah*. New York: Schocken, 1971.

Nickelsburg, George W. E. *1 Enoch 1*. Minneapolis: Fortress, 2001.

———. "The Nature and Function of Revelation in 1 Enoch, Jubilees, and Some Qumranic Documents." In *Pseudepigraphic Perspectives: The Apocrypha and Pseudepigrapha in Light of the Dead Sea Scrolls*, ed. Esther G. Chazon and Michael Stone, 91–120. Leiden: Brill, 1999.

Niehoff, Maren. *Philo on Jewish Identity and Culture*. Tübingen: Mohr Siebeck, 2001.

Nietzsche, Friedrich Wilhelm. *Untimely Meditations*. Cambridge: Cambridge University Press, 1997.

Nissinen, Martti. *Prophets and Prophecy in the Ancient Near East*. Writings from the Ancient World 12. Leiden: Brill, 2003.

Nitzan, Bilhah. *Qumran Prayer and Religious Poetry*. Leiden: Brill, 1994.

———. "Repentance in the Dead Sea Scrolls." In *The Dead Sea Scrolls after Fifty Years: A Comprehensive Assessment*, ed. P. W. Flint and J. C. VanderKam, 145–70. Vol. 2. Leiden: Brill, 1999.

Nock, Arthur Darby. *Conversion: The Old and the New in Religion from Alexander the Great to Augustine of Hippo*. Oxford: Oxford University Press, 1933; reprint ed., Baltimore, MD: Johns Hopkins University Press, 1998.

———. "The Vocabulary of the New Testament." *Journal of Biblical Literature* 52 (1933): 131–39.

Nongbri, Brent. *Before Religion: A History of a Modern Concept*. New Haven, CT: Yale University Press, 2013.

Noth, Martin. *The Deuteronomistic History*. Sheffield, UK: Sheffield Academic Press, 1991.

O'Brien, Julia M. *Challenging Prophetic Metaphor: Theology and Ideology in the Prophets*. Louisville: Westminster John Knox, 2008.

O'Brien, Mark A. *The Deuteronomistic History Hypothesis: A Reassessment*. Freiburg: Universitaetsverlag, 1989.

Ochoa, Todd. *Society of the Dead: Quita Manaquita and Palo Praise in Cuba*. Berkeley: University of California Press, 2010.

Olyan, Saul. *Biblical Mourning: Ritual and Social Dimensions*. Oxford: Oxford University Press, 2004.

Osiek, Caroline. *The Shepherd of Hermas: A Commentary*. Hermeneia Vol. 83. Ed. Helmut Koester. Minneapolis: Fortress, 1999.

Pardo, Osvaldo F. *The Origins of Mexican Catholicism: Nahua Rituals and Christian Sacraments in Sixteenth-Century Mexico*. Ann Arbor: University of Michigan Press, 2004.

Pfann, Stephen J. "The Essene Yearly Renewal Ceremony and the Baptism of Repentance." In *The Provo International Conference on the Dead Sea Scrolls: Technological*

Innovations, New Texts, and Reformulated Issues, ed. D. W. Parry and E. Ulrich, 337–52. Leiden: Brill, 1999.

Philo. Trans. F. H. Colson and G. H. Whitaker et al. 10 vols. Cambridge, MA: Harvard University Press, 1929–1962.

Pleše, Zlatko. *Poetics of the Gnostic Universe: Narrative and Cosmology in Apocryphon of John*. Leiden: Brill, 2006.

Plutarch. *Moralia*. Trans. W. C. Helmbold et al. 15 vols. Loeb Classical Library. Cambridge, MA: Harvard University Press, 1927–1969.

Podella, Thomas. *Ṣôm-Fasten: Kollektive Trauer um den verborgenen Gott im Alten Testament*. Neukirchen-Vluyn: Neukirchener Verlag, 1989.

Polak, Frank H. "Verbs of Motion in Biblical Hebrew: Lexical Shifts and Syntactic Structure." In *A Palimpsest: Rhetoric, Ideology, Stylistics, and Language Relating to Persian Israel*, ed. Ehud Ben Zvi, Diana Edelman, and Frank H. Polak, 161–97. Piscataway, NJ: Gorgias Press, 2009.

Polzin, Robert. *David and the Deuteronomist: A Literary Study of the Deuteronomistic History: Part Three, 2 Samuel*. Bloomington: Indiana University Press, 1993.

Pope, Marvin. *Song of Songs: A New Translation with Introduction and Commentary*. New York: Doubleday, 1977.

Pritchard, James B., ed. *Ancient Near Eastern Texts Relating to the Old Testament; Third Edition with Supplement*. Princeton, NJ: Princeton University Press, 1969.

Propp, William H. C. *Exodus 1–18*. New York: Doubleday, 1998.

Räisänen, Heikki. "Jesus in Context." *Reviews in Religion and Theology* 2 (1994): 14–16.

Raitt, Thomas M. "The Prophetic Summons to Repentance." *Zeitschrift für die alttestamentliche Wissenschaft* 83 (1971): 30–49.

Rambo, Lewis R. *Understanding Religious Conversion*. New Haven, CT: Yale University Press, 1993.

Rambo, Lewis R., and Charles E. Farhadian, eds. *The Oxford Handbook of Religious Conversion*. New York: Oxford University Press, 2014.

Rasimus, Tuomas, Troels Engberg-Pedersen, and Ismo Dunderberg, eds. *Stoicism in Early Christianity*. Grand Rapids, MI: Baker Academic, 2010.

Reik, Theodor. *The Compulsion to Confess: On the Psychoanalysis of Crime and Punishment*. New York: Farrar, Straus & Cudahy, 1959.

Reimarus, Hermann Samuel. *Reimarus: Fragments*. Ed. C. H. Talbert. Trans. R. S. Fraser. Philadephia: Fortress, 1970.

Rendsburg, Gary A. "Redactional Structuring in the Joseph Story: Genesis 37–50." In *Mappings of the Biblical Terrain: The Bible as Text*, ed. John R. Maier and Vincent L. Tollers, 215–32. London: Bucknell University Press, 1990.

Rittgers, Ronald. *The Reformation of the Keys: Confession, Conscience, and Authority in Sixteenth-Century Germany*. Cambridge, MA: Harvard University Press, 2004.

Robinson, James M., Paul Hoffmann, and John S. Kloppenborg, eds. *The Sayings Gospel Q in Greek and English*. Minneapolis: Fortress, 2002.

Römer, Thomas C. *The So-Called Deuteronomistic History: A Sociological, Historical and Literary Introduction*. New York: T & T Clark, 2005.

Rösel, Hartmut N. "Why 2 Kings 17 Does Not Constitute a Chapter of Reflection in the 'Deuteronomistic History.'" *Journal of Biblical Literature* 128, no. 1 (2009): 85–90.

Rosen-Zvi, Ishay. "Bilhah the Temptress: The 'Testament of Reuben' and 'The Birth of Sexuality.'" *Jewish Quarterly Review* 96 (2006): 65–94.

———. *Demonic Desires: Yetzer Hara and the Problem of Evil in Late Antiquity*. Philadelphia: University of Pennsylvania Press, 2011.

Roth, Cecil, and Geoffrey Wigoder, eds. *Encyclopedia Judaica*. Jerusalem: Encyclopedia Judaica, 1972.

Rüpke, Jörg. "Fighting for Differences: Forms and Limits of Religious Individuality in the 'Shepherd of Hermas.'" In *The Individual in the Religions of the Ancient Mediterranean*, ed. Jörge Rüpke, 315–41. Oxford: Oxford University Press, 2013.

Ruzer, Serge. "The Death Motif in Late Antique *Teshuva* Narrative Patterns. With a Note on Romans 5–8." In *Transformations of the Inner Self in Ancient Religions*, ed. Jan Assmann and Guy G. Stroumsa, 151–65. Leiden: Brill, 1999.

Sanders, E. P. *Jesus and Judaism*. Philadelphia: Fortress, 1985.

———. *Paul and Palestinian Judaism: A Comparison of Patterns of Religion*. London: SCM, 1977.

Sanders, Jack T. "Concerning Ben Sira and Demotic Wisdom: A Response to Matthew J. Goff." *Journal for the Study of Judaism* 38 (2007): 297–306.

Sasson, J. M. *Jonah*. New York: Doubleday, 1990.

Sax, William S. "Agency." In *Theorizing Rituals. Issues, Topics, Approaches, Concepts*, ed. J. Kreinath, Jan Snoek, and Michael Stausberg, 473–81. Leiden: Brill, 2006.

Scarry, Elaine. *The Body in Pain: The Making and Unmaking of the World*. New York: Oxford University Press, 1985.

Schearing, L. S., and S. L. McKenzie, eds. *Those Elusive Deuteronomists: The Phenomenon of Pan-Deuteronomism*. Sheffield, UK: Sheffield Academic Press, 1999.

Schechter, Solomon. *Some Aspects of Rabbinic Theology*. London: Adam and Charles Black, 1909.

Scheuer, Blaženka. *The Return of YHWH: The Tension between Deliverance and Repentance in Isaiah 40–55*. Berlin: Walter de Gruyter, 2008.

Schiffman, Lawrence. *Reclaiming the Dead Sea Scrolls: The History of Judaism, the Background of Christianity, the Lost Library of Qumran*. Philadelphia: Jewish Publication Society, 1994.

———. "The Case of the Day of Atonement Ritual." In *Biblical Perspectives: Early Use and Interpretation of the Bible in Light of the Dead Sea Scrolls: Proceedings of the First International Symposium of the Orion Center for the Study of the Dead Sea Scrolls and Associated Literature, 12–14 May, 1996*, ed. M. E. Stone and E. G. Chazon, 181–88. Leiden: Brill, 1998.

Schimmel, Solomon. *Wounds Not Healed by Time: The Power of Repentance and Forgiveness*. Oxford: Oxford University Press, 2002.

Schmid, Konrad. "The Deuteronomistic Image of History as Interpretive Device in the Second Temple Period: Towards a Long Term Interpretation of 'Deuteronomism.'" In *Congress Volume Helsinki 2010*, ed. Martti Nissinen, 369–88. Leiden: Brill, 2012.

Schmidt, Lawrence K. *Understanding Hermeneutics*. Stocksfield, U.K: Acumen, 2006.

Schremer, Adiel. "Wayward Jews: *Minim* in Early Rabbinic Literature." *Journal of Jewish Studies* 64, no. 2 (2013): 242–63.

Schuller, Eileen M. "Petitionary Prayer and the Religion of Qumran." In *Religion in the Dead Sea Scrolls*, ed. J. J. Collins and R. A. Kugler, 29–45. Grand Rapids, MI: Eerdmans, 2000.

Schuller, Eileen M., and Carol A. Newsom. *The Hodayot (The Thanksgiving Psalms): A Study Edition of 1QHa*. Atlanta: Society of Biblical Literature, 2012.

Schwartz, Baruch J. "Ezekiel's Dim View of Israel's Restoration." In *The Book of Ezekiel: Theological and Anthropological Perspectives*, ed. M. S. Odell and J. T. Strong, 43–67. Atlanta: Society of Biblical Literature, 2000.

———. "Repentance and Determinism in Ezekiel." In *Proceedings of the Eleventh World Congress of Jewish Studies*, ed. David Assaf, 123–30. Jerusalem: Magness Press, 1994.

———. "The Bearing of Sin in Priestly Literature." In *Pomegranates and Golden Bells: Studies in Biblical, Jewish and Near Eastern Ritual, Law and Literature in Honor of Jacob Milgrom*, ed. David Pearson Wright, David Noel Freedman, and Avi Hurvitz, 3–21. Winona Lake, IN: Eisenbrauns, 1995.

———. "The Ultimate Aim of Israel's Restoration in Ezekiel." In *Birkat Shalom: Studies in the Bible, Ancient Near Eastern Literature, and Postbiblical Judaism Presented to Shalom M. Paul on the Occasion of His Seventieth Birthday*, vol. 1, ed. Chaim Cohen and Shalom M. Paul, 305–19. Winona Lake, IN: Eisenbrauns, 2008.

Schwartz, Daniel R. *2 Maccabees*. Berlin: de Gruyter, 2008.

Schwartz, Seth. "Conversion to Judaism in the Second Temple Period: A Functionalist Approach." In *Studies in Josephus and the Varieties of Ancient Judaism: Louis H. Feldman Jubilee Volume*, ed. S. J. D. Cohen and J. J. Schwartz, 195–206 Leiden: Brill, 2007.

———. *Were the Jews a Mediterranean Society? Reciprocity and Solidarity in Ancient Judaism*. Princeton, NJ: Princeton University Press, 2010.

Schweitzer, Albert. *The Mystery of the Kingdom of God: The Secret of Jesus' Messiahship and Passion*. Trans. W. Lowrie. New York: Macmillan, 1950.

Seely, David Rolph. "The 'Circumcised Heart' in 4Q434 Barkhi Nafshi." *Revue de Qumran* 17, no. 4 (1996): 527–35.

Segal, Alan. *Paul the Convert: The Apostolate and the Apostasy of Saul the Pharisee*. New Haven, CT: Yale University Press, 1990.

Segal, Michael. *The Book of Jubilees: Rewritten Bible, Redaction, Ideology, and Theology*. Leiden: Brill, 2007.

Segal, Moshe Tzvi. *The Complete Book of Ben Sira* (Hebrew). Jerusalem: Bialik Foundation, 1971.

Seidman, Naomi. *Faithful Renderings: Jewish-Christian Difference and the Politics of Translation*. Chicago: University of Chicago Press, 2006.

Shatz, David. "Freedom, Repentance, and Hardening of the Hearts: Albo vs. Maimonides." *Faith and Philosophy* 14, no. 4 (1997): 478–509.

Shemesh, Aharon. "Expulsion and Exclusion in the Community Rule and the Damascus Document." *Dead Sea Discoveries* 9 (2002): 44–74.

Simon Uriel. *Jonah*. Philadelphia: Jewish Publication Society, 1999.

———. "The Poor Man's Ewe-Lamb: An Example of a Juridical Parable." *Biblica* 48, no. 2 (1967): 207–42.

Ska, Jean Louis. "Judah, Joseph, and the Reader (Gen. 42:6–9 and 44:18–34)." In *Das Alte Testament—ein Geschichtsbuch*, ed. Erhard Blum, William Johnstone, and Christoph Markschies, 27–39. Altes Testament und Moderne 10. Münster: Lit, 2005.

Skehan, Patrick W., and Alexander A. Di Lella, eds. *The Wisdom of Ben Sira*. New York: Doubleday, 1987.

Smith, J. Payne. *A Compendious Syriac Dictionary*. Winona Lake, IN: Eisenbrauns, 1998.

Smith, Jonathan Z. *Drudgery Divine: On the Comparison of Early Christianities and the Religions of Late Antiquity*. Chicago: University of Chicago Press, 1990.

———. *Relating Religion: Essays in the Study of Religion*. Chicago: University of Chicago Press, 2004.

Sokoloff, Michael. *A Dictionary of Jewish Babylonian Aramaic of the Talmudic and Geonic Periods*. Baltimore: Johns Hopkins University Press, 2002.

Sokoloff, Michael. *A Dictionary of Jewish Palestinian Aramaic of the Byzantine Period.* Baltimore: Johns Hopkins University Press, 2002.

Soloveitchik, Meir. "Redemption and the Power of Man." *Azure* 16 (2004): 51–77.

Sommer, Benjamin D. *The Bodies of God and the World of Ancient Israel.* Cambridge: Cambridge University Press, 2009.

Sontag, Susan. *Regarding the Pain of Others.* New York: Farrar, Straus & Giroux, 2003.

Speiser, E. A. *Genesis: Introduction, Translation, and Notes.* Garden City, NY: Doubleday, 1964.

———. "Stem PLL in Hebrew." *Journal of Biblical Literature* 82 (1963): 301–6.

Steck, Odil Hannes. *Israel und das gewaltsame Geschick der Propheten.* Neukirchen-Vluyn: Neukirchener Verlag, 1967.

Steiner, Richard C. "Does the Biblical Hebrew Conjunction ־ו Have Many Meanings, One Meaning, or No Meaning at All?" *Journal of Biblical Literature* 119 (2000): 249–67.

Stendahl, Krister. *Paul among Jews and Gentiles and Other Essays.* Philadelphia: Fortress, 1976.

Sterling, Gregory. "Turning to God: Conversion in Greek-Speaking Judaism and Early Christianity." In *Scripture and Traditions: Essays on Early Judaism and Christianity in Honor of Carl R. Holladay,* ed. Patrick Gray and Gail R. O'Day, 69–95. Leiden: Brill, 2008.

Stern, Sacha. *Jewish Identity in Early Rabbinic Writings.* Leiden: Brill, 1994.

Sternberg, Meir. *The Poetics of Biblical Narrative: Ideological Literature and the Drama of Reading.* Bloomington: Indiana University Press, 1987.

Stone, Michael E., and Jonas C. Greenfield. "The Prayer of Levi." *Journal of Biblical Literature* 112, no. 2 (1993): 247–66.

Stowers, Stanley K. "Social Status, Public Speaking and Private Teaching: The Circumstances of Paul's Preaching Activity." *Novum Testamentum* 26, no. 1 (1984): 59–82.

Strine, Casey A. "The Role of Repentance in the Book of Ezekiel: A Second Chance for the Second Generation." *Journal of Theological Studies* 63, no. 2 (2012): 467–91.

Stroud, Barry. "Mind, Meaning, and Practice." In *The Cambridge Companion to Wittgenstein,* ed. Hans Sluga and David G. Stern, 296–319. New York: Cambridge University Press, 1996.

Stroumsa, Guy G. "From Repentance to Penance in Early Christianity: Tertullian's *De Paenitentia* in Context." In *Transformations of the Inner Self in Ancient Religions,* ed. Jan Assmann and Guy G. Stroumsa, 167–78. Leiden: Brill, 1999.

———. *The End of Sacrifice: Religious Transformations in Late Antiquity.* Trans. Susan Emanuel. Chicago: University of Chicago Press, 2009.

Stuckenbruck, Loren T. *1 Enoch 91–108.* Berlin: de Gruyter, 2007.

Sweeney, Deborah. "Intercessory Prayer in Ancient Egypt and the Bible." In *Pharaonic Egypt: The Bible and Christianity,* ed. Sarah Israelit-Groll, 213–30. Jerusalem: Magness Press, 1985.

Tal, Abraham. *A Dictionary of Samaritan Aramaic.* 2 vols. Leiden: Brill, 2000.

Taylor, Charles. *Sources of the Self: The Making of the Modern Identity.* Cambridge: Cambridge University Press, 1989.

Taylor, Joan E. "On Pliny, the Essene Location and Kh. Qumran." *Dead Sea Discoveries* 16, no. 1 (2009): 1–21

———. *The Immerser: John the Baptist within Second Temple Judaism.* Grand Rapids, MI: Eerdmans, 1997.

Tentler, Thomas N. *Sin and Confession on the Eve of the Reformation.* Princeton, NJ: Princeton University Press, 1977.

Thayer, Anne T. *Penitence, Preaching, and the Coming of the Reformation.* Burlington, VT: Ashgate, 2002.

Theissen, Gerd and Annette Merz. *The Historical Jesus: A Comprehensive Guide.* Trans. J. Bowden. Minneapolis: Fortress, 1998.

Tigay, Jeffrey H. "On Some Aspects of Prayer in the Bible." *Association of Jewish Studies Review* 1 (1976): 363–72.

———. *The JPS Torah Commentary: Deuteronomy.* Philadelphia: Jewish Publication Society, 1996.

Tiller, Patrick A. *A Commentary on the Animal Apocalypse of 1 Enoch.* Society of Biblical Literature Early Judaism and Its Literature 4. Atlanta: Scholars Press, 1993.

Torrance, Alexis. "The Angel and the Spirit of Repentance: Hermas and the Early Monastic Concept of Metanoia." *Studia Patristica* 64 (2013): 15–20.

Tov, Emanuel. *Textual Criticism of the Hebrew Bible.* 2nd rev. ed. Minneapolis: Fortress, 1992.

Tropper, Amram. *Wisdom, Politics, and Historiography: Tractate Avot in the Context of the Graeco-Roman Near East.* Oxford: Oxford University Press, 2004.

Tsevat, Matitiahu. *The Meaning of the Book of Job and Other Biblical Studies: Essays on the Literature and Religion of the Hebrew Bible.* New York: Ktav, 1980.

Turner, Victor. *The Drums of Affliction: A Study of Religious Processes among the Ndembu of Zambia.* Oxford: Clarendon Press, 1968.

———. *The Ritual Process: Structure and Anti-Structure.* Chicago: Aldine, 1969.

Twersky, Isadore. *Introduction to the Code of Maimonides (Mishneh Torah).* New Haven, CT: Yale University Press, 1980.

Uhalde, Kevin. "The Sinful Subject: Doing Penance in Rome." *Studia Patristica* 44 (2010): 405–14.

Unterman, Jeremiah. *From Repentance to Redemption: Jeremiah's Thought in Transition.* Sheffield, UK: Sheffield University Press, 1987.

———. "Repentance and Redemption in Hosea." *SBL Seminar Papers* 21 (1982): 541–50.

Urbach, Ephraim E. "Redemption and Repentance in Talmudic Judaism." In *Types of Redemption,* ed. R. J. Z. Werblowsky and C. Jouco Bleeker, 190–206. Studies in the History of Religion 18. Leiden: Brill, 1970.

———. *The Sages: Their Concepts and Beliefs.* Trans. I. Abrahams. Jerusalem: Magness Press, 1975.

van der Horst, Pieter W., and Judith H. Newman. *Early Jewish Prayers in Greek.* Berlin: de Gruyter, 2008.

VanderKam, James C. *Qumran Cave 4.VIII: Parabiblical Texts, Part 1.* Discoveries in the Judaean Desert 13. Oxford: Clarendon, 1994.

———. "Recent Scholarship on the Book of Jubilees." *Currents in Biblical Research* 6, no. 3 (2008): 405–31.

———. "Studies on the Prologue and *Jubilees* 1." In *For a Later Generation: The Transformation of Tradition in Israel, Early Judaism, and Early Christianity,* ed. R. A. Argall, Beverly Bow, Rodney Alan Werline, and George W. E. Nickelsburg, 266–79. Harrisburg, PA: Trinity Press International, 2000.

———. *The Book of Jubilees, Volume 2.* Louvain: Peeters, 1989.

———. "The Righteousness of Noah." In *Ideal Figures in Ancient Judaism,* ed. John J. Collins and George W. E. Nickelsburg, 13–32. Ann Arbor, MI: Scholars Press, 1980.

Vermes, Geza, and Martin D. Goodman, eds. *The Essenes according to the Classical Sources.* Sheffield, UK: JSOT Press, 1989.

Vernant, Jean-Pierre. *Myth and Tragedy in Ancient Greece.* New York: Zone, 1988.

Vološinov, V. N. *Marxism and the Philosophy of Language.* Trans. L. Matejka and I. R. Titunik. Cambridge, MA: Harvard University Press, 1986.

von Rad, Gerhard. *Deuteronomy: A Commentary.* London: SCM Press, 1966.

———. *The Problem of the Hexateuch and Other Essays.* New York: McGraw-Hill, 1966.

Waltke, Bruce K., and M. O'Connor. *An Introduction to Biblical Hebrew Syntax.* Winona Lake, IN: Eisenbrauns, 1990.

Weinfeld, Moshe. *Deuteronomy 1–11.* New York: Doubleday, 1991.

———. "Jeremiah and the Spiritual Metamorphosis of Israel." *Zeitschrift für die alttestamentliche Wissenschaft* 88 (1976): 2–56.

———. "Prayers for Knowledge, Repentance, and Forgiveness in the Eighteen-Benediction Prayer: Nature of the Prayers, Their Parallels at Qumran, and Their Roots in the Bible" (Hebrew). *Tarbiz* 48 (1979): 186–200.

———. *The Organizational Pattern and the Penal Code of the Qumran Sect. A Comparison with Guilds and Religious Associations of the Hellenistic-Roman Period.* Göttingen: Vandenhoeck and Ruprecht, 1986.

Weitzman, Steven. *Song and Story in Biblical Narrative: The History of a Literary Convention in Ancient Israel.* Bloomington, IN: Indiana University Press, 1997.

Werline, Rodney A. "Defining Penitential Prayer." In *Seeking the Favor of God; Vol 1, The Origins of Penitential Prayer in Second Temple Judaism,* ed. Mark J. Boda and Rodney A. Werline, xiii–xvii. Atlanta: Society of Biblical Literature, 2006

———. *Penitential Prayers in Second Temple Judaism: The Development of a Religious Institution.* Atlanta: Scholars Press, 1998.

Werman, Cana. "*Te'uda*: Toward an Explanation of the Term" (Hebrew). In *Fifty Years of Dead Sea Scrolls Research: Studies in Memory of Jacob Licht,* ed. G. Brin and B. Nitzan, 231–43. Jerusalem: Yad Yitshak ben-Tsevi, 2001.

———. "The Story of the Flood in the Book of Jubilees" (Hebrew). *Tarbiz* 64 (1995): 183–202.

Westermann, Claus. *Basic Forms of Prophetic Speech.* Philadelphia: Westminster Press, 1967.

———. *Isaiah 40–66.* Philadelphia: Westminster, 1969.

———. *Praise and Lament in the Psalms.* Atlanta: Westminster John Knox, 1981.

Wicke-Reuter, Ursel. *Göttliche Providenz und menschliche Verantwortung bei Ben Sira und in der Frühen Stoa.* Berlin: de Gruyter, 2000.

Widmer, Michael. *Moses, God, and the Dynamics of Intercessory Prayer: A Study of Exodus 32–34 and Numbers 13–14.* Tübingen: Mohr Siebeck, 2004.

Williams, Bernard. *Shame and Necessity.* Berkeley: University of California Press, 1993.

Wilson, Bryan R. *Magic and the Millenium: A Sociological Study of Religious Movements of Protest among Tribal and Third-World Peoples.* London: Heinemann, 1973.

Wilson, Robert R. "Early Israelite Prophecy." *Interpretation* 32, no. 3 (1978): 3–16.

———. "The Hardening of Pharaoh's Heart." *Catholic Biblical Quarterly* 41 (1979): 18–36.

———. *Prophecy and Society in Ancient Israel.* Philadelphia: Fortress, 1980.

Wilson, Walter T. *Philo of Alexandria: On Virtues: Introduction, Translation, and Commentary.* Vol. 3. Philo of Alexandria Commentary Series. Leiden: Brill, 2011.

Winston, David. "Philo's Doctrine of Repentance." In *The School of Moses: Studies in Philo and Hellenistic Religion: In Memory of Horst R. Moehring,* ed. J. P. Kennedy, 29–40. Atlanta: Scholars Press, 1995.

Wolff, Hans Walter. *Joel and Amos.* Ed. S. Dean McBride Jr. Trans. Waldemar Janzen, S. Dean McBride Jr., and Charles A. Muenchow. Philadelphia: Fortress, 1977.

———. "The Kerygma of the Deuteronomistic Historical Work." In *The Vitality of Old Testament Traditions,* ed. Walter Brueggemann and Hans Walter Wolff, 83–100. Trans. F. C. Prussner. 2nd ed. Atlanta: John Knox, 1982.

Wolfson, Harry A. *Philo: Foundations of Religious Philosophy in Judaism, Christianity, and Islam.* Cambridge, MA: Harvard University Press, 1947.

Wright, David P. *Ritual In Narrative: The Dynamics of Feasting, Mourning, and Retaliation Rites in the Ugaritic Tale of Aqhat.* Winona Lake, IN: Eisenbrauns, 2001.

Wright, N. T. *Christians Origins and the Question of God.* Vol. 2. Minneapolis: Fortress, 1997.

———. *Jesus and the Victory of God.* Minneapolis: Fortress, 1996.

Wright, Richard A. "Plutarch on Moral Progress." In *Passions and Moral Progress in Greco-Roman Thought,* ed. J. T. Fitzgerald, 136–50. New York: Routledge, 2008.

Würthwein, Ernst. "μετανοέω, μετάνοια." In *The Theological Dictionary of the New Testament,* vol. 4, ed. Gerhard Kittel and Gerhard Friedrich, trans. Geoffrey W. Bromiley, 989–91. Grand Rapids, MI: Wm. B. Eerdmans, 1995 [1974].

Yee, Gale A. "'She Is Not My Wife and I Am Not Her Husband:' A Materialist Analysis of Hosea 1–2." *Biblical Interpretation* 9, no. 4 (2001): 345–83.

Young, Norman H. "'Jesus and the Sinners': Some Queries." *Journal for the Study of the New Testament* 24 (1985): 73–75.

Zahavy, Tzvee. "*Kavvanah* for Prayer in the Mishnah and Talmud." In *New Perspectives on Ancient Judaism: Vol. 1: Religion, Literature, and Society in Ancient Israel, Formative Christianity and Judaism,* ed. Jacob Neusner, Peder Borgen, Ernest S. Frerichs, and Richard A. Horsley, 35–48. Atlanta: Scholars, 1990.

Zimmerli, Walther. *Ezekiel 1.* Philadelphia: Fortress, 1979.

PRIMARY SOURCES

II. New Testament

III. Septuagint, Other Greek Translations, and Deuterocanonical Works
Septuagint

Symmachus

SUBJECT INDEX

Abraham, 36, 47, 48, 130, 131
Abraham ibn Ezra, 42
Absalom, 25, 40, 41, 42
Achan, 54, 55, 65
Adam and Eve, 92, 167
Affliction: centrality to prayer,
     197n18; confession's affect on,
     58; fasting as, 197n20; rituals of,
     196n7; self-affliction, 199n65;
     self-imposed, 196n7; unseemliness
     of, 19–21
Agency, 14, 86, 95, 121–150; and
     anthropological renewal, 148–149;
     and apocalypticism, 123–133;
     and apotropaic prayer, 130–132;
     and autonomy, 154; and baptism,
     143–144; and circumcision of the
     heart, 123, 126–128; and Dead
     Sea Scrolls, 133–142; and divine
     re-creation, 123–133; and fasting,
     14; and *hodayot*, 138–140; and
     initiation rites, 134–138; and
     prayer, 35; and prophecy, 95;
     and Rabbinic Judaism, 176; and
     religion, 121–133; and self, 151;
     and *shuv* terminology, 140–142;
     and sin, 132–133; of YHWH, 82
Ahab, 21, 64, 106, 107, 108, 113, 189
Almsgiving, 161
Alter, Robert, 202n15, 208n11
Altieri, Charles 194n21, 194n22
Amnon, 15, 41, 42
Anderson, Gary, 195n32, 196n8, 197n25
Anger, 98, 100. *see also* Wrath
'*anî*, 18–19, 197n20, 198n30
Anthropological renewal, 129, 148–149.
     See also Re-creation (divine)
Anthropomorphism, 72, 86

Anthropopathism, 97–100, 117, 209n33
Appeal, 19, 23–28, 34–41, 87–89, 96–97;
     and confession, 58, 62; efficacy of,
     47–48; and prophecy, 46–48; and
     shuv, 75, 79–80, 81–83. *See also*
     Prayer
Apocalypticism, 123–50; and the Dead
     Sea community, 133–42; and
     the Jesus movement, 142–47;
     and Jubilees, 123–33; and Paul,
     148–49. *See also* Re-creation
     (divine)
Aristotle, 164
Asad, Talal, 194n13, 195n1, 196n6,
     196n13, 200n8, 209n27, 211n1,
     212n7, 217n4, 217n6, 217n9
'*ashem*, 53, 59, 60, 61, 71
Assmann, Jan, 202n7
Atonement, 60, 136, 154, 161, 166, 171.
     See also Day of Atonement (*yom
     ha-kippurim*)
Auerbach, Erich, 208n10
Austin, J. L., 202n9, 209n30
Autonomy (Autonomous), 5, 9, 14, 33,
     93, 152, 154, 164, 166

Baal, 14, 46, 48, 108
Baptism, 122, 136, 143–144, 148
Barr, James, 222n108, 223n126
Barthes, Roland, 208n3
Barton, John, 199n53, 207n2, 209n23,
     209n26, 210n50
Bathsheba, 18, 39
Begrich, Joachim, 198n35,
     198n42, 199n1
Ben Sira, 161–163, 166, 169, 171
Beruriah, 181
Bloodshed, 180, 183

Kristeva, Julia, 195n30, 196n10,
    198n32, 202n6
Kugel, James, 193n10, 197n18, 200n10,
    208n5, 208n6, 208n7, 208n9,
    208n12, 212n8, 213n31, 214n41,
    214n43, 217n3, 220n67, 221n74,
    224n142
Kuhn, Thomas S., 217n5

Lamentations: 44, 49
Lament literature, 17, 20
Levenson, Jon D., 195n32, 197n25,
    217n3, 222n107
Liminality, 14, 95–97
Lindbeck, George, 194n26, 205n8
Luther, Martin, 182, 183

Maimonides, 51, 52, 53, 66, 202n8,
    208n14, 208n18, 218n16
Malherbe, Abraham, 216n103, 219n32,
    219n47, 223n119
Mari letters, 102–103, 109
Material (Materiality), 5, 7–8, 34, 36, 55,
    57–58, 66–67, 75, 91, 96
Meeks, Wayne A., 216n103, 217n10,
    217n11, 223n127
Mercy track, 24–27, 48–49, 87, 198n50.
    See also Justice track
metanoia: and agency, 143, 144; Ben
    Sira on, 163; as divine hypostasis,
    186; and Hellenistic thought,
    185; Josephus on, 168, 169,
    170; and mourning, 164; in New
    Testament, 183–184; Philo on,
    158, 159, 160; Plutarch on, 157;
    and Christian supersessionism,
    181–182; in teachings of Jesus,
    182; terminology of, 72, 153, 155;
    and *teshuva*, 174, 179
Middle Platonism, 156, 178
Milgrom, Jacob, 199n65, 203n27, 204n2
Miller, Patrick D., 197n27
Mishneh Torah, 51
Models of repentance, 92–94
Moses: exhortations to repentance of,
    159, 169; as intercessor, 46–48, 56,
    131; and prayer, 34, 41; as prophet,
    95, 103–105, 107, 117
Mourning: as communal activity, 30; and
    confession, 61; as demonstrable

repentance, 164, 165; fasting as act
    of, 13, 15–17, 164, 165; and mercy,
    25; and *metanoia*, 169; in New
    Testament, 186
Muffs, Yochanan, 195n27, 197n24,
    200n10, 201n34, 209n33, 209n34

Naboth, 21, 26
Nathan, 63, 64, 169
Naturalized (Naturalization, Natural),
    xi, 1–2, 4, 9, 73, 91, 144, 149, 163,
    166, 172–74
Nebuchadnezzar, 176
Nebuzaradan, 176, 180
Newsom, Carol, 215n63
Nietzsche, Friedrich Wilhelm, 195n36
niham, 155, 170, 202n8
nikhna', 21, 71
Nineveh, 27, 103, 117
Noah, 93, 130, 131
Nock, Arthur Darby, 217n1
Nominalization, 5, 88, 171

Obedience, 72, 75, 81, 83–84,
    182, 204n5
Ontology of the self, 2–3, 7, 15–16,
    57–58, 154, 162, 190–91
Oracles, 76, 83–84, 93–103, 107–117
Oracular inquiry, 75–77; Oracles of
    doom, 16, 100, 105, 107, 114;
    Oracles of redemption, 93, 212n14

paenitentia, 153, 174, 182
Pain, 16, 34–36, 42, 47, 49, 53–59, 79,
    81–82; mental, 155–68
Parables of the kingdom, 147
Passions, theory of, 98, 99
Paul, 143, 183, 185, 186
Pedagogy (Pedagogue), 5, 37, 49, 57, 80,
    91–95, 109, 113–18, 135, 140–1,
    149, 158, 162; and Luke-Acts,
    184–85; and scripture, 91–98, 141,
    and Philo, 157–58
Penance: in early Christianity, 186,
    201n3, 218n12; medieval practices
    of, 201n3, 218n12, 221n81;
    sacrament of, 14
Penitential discipline, 1, 4, 13, 93
Penitential lens, 3, 4, 10, 133,
    189, 194n13